THE NATURALIST IN BRITAIN

THE NATURALIST IN BRITAIN

A SOCIAL HISTORY

David Elliston Allen

PRINCETON UNIVERSITY PRESS   PRINCETON, NEW JERSEY

Published by Princeton University Press, 41 William Street,
Princeton, New Jersey 08540
In the United Kingdom by Princeton University Press,
Chichester, West Sussex
Copyright © 1976 by David Elliston Allen
All Rights Reserved
Originally published in the United Kingdom by Penguin Books;
second edition, with corrections and new preface, published by
Princeton University Press, 1994

Library of Congress Cataloging-in-Publication Data
Allen, David Elliston.
The naturalist in Britain : a social history / David Elliston Allen.
p.   cm.
Originally published: London : A. Lane. 1976.
Includes bibliographical references and index.
ISBN 0-691-03628-4 (CL) ISBN 0-691-03632-2 (PA)
1. Natural history—Great Britain—History.   2. Naturalists—Great
Britain—History.   I. Title.
QH137.A57   1994
508.41'09—dc20   93-43900

Princeton University Press books are printed
on acid-free paper and meet the guidelines
for permanence and durability of the Committee
on Production Guidelines for Book Longevity
of the Council on Library Resources

First Princeton Paperback printing, 1994

Printed in the United States of America

1   3   5   7   9   10   8   6   4   2

To Clare

ALL THE FACTS IN NATURAL HISTORY,

TAKEN BY THEMSELVES, HAVE NO VALUE,

BUT ARE BARREN LIKE A SINGLE SEX.

BUT MARRY IT TO HUMAN HISTORY,

AND IT IS FULL OF LIFE.

Emerson, Address on 'Nature', 1836

Contents

List of Plates   xi

List of Illustrations   xiii

Preface (1994)   xv

Preface to the First Edition   xvii

Chapter One
Organization Begins   3

Chapter Two
The Rise to Fashion   22

Chapter Three
Wonders of the Past   45

Chapter Four
The Victorian Setting   64

Chapter Five
The Fruits of Efficiency   83

Chapter Six
Exploring the Fringes   108

Chapter Seven
Deadlier Weapons   126

Chapter Eight
The Field Club   142

Chapter Nine
The Parting of the Ways   158

Chapter Ten
Dispersed Efforts   175

Chapter Eleven
Recovery on the Coasts   186

Chapter Twelve
An Infusion of Mobility   202

Chapter Thirteen
A Break for Play   220

Chapter Fourteen
The Eventual Combining   227

Notes on Sources   245

Index   257

List of Plates

1. Insect-collecting in the 1760s. Hand-painted frontispiece to Moses Harris, *The Aurelian,* 1765

2. William Buckland equipped as a glacialist, from Sir Archibald Geikie, *Life of Sir R. I. Murchison,* 1875

3. The rapaciousness of Fashion, from *Punch,* May 1892

4. Children's playing cards, c. 1843 (*The London Museum*)

5. 'Seaside Sirens' (*Radio Times Hulton Picture Library*)

6. 'Collecting Ferns', from the *Illustrated London News,* July 1871 (*Radio Times Hulton Picture Library*)

7. An excursion of the Liverpool Naturalists' Field Club, 1860

8. First admission of lady Fellows to the Linnean Society of London, 1905. Painting by James Sant, R.A. (*Linnean Soczety of London*)

9. Members of the British Pteridological Society on their annual excursion, 1900. (*British Pteridological Society*)

10. The photographic gun, from *Le Nature,* 1882

11. Bird photography under difficulties, from R. Kearton, *Wild Life at Home,* 1899

12. G. C. Druce (standing), with members of the Ashmolean Natural History Society, 1904 (*Ashmolean Natural History Society*)

13. Nature Study class, 1923 (*Radio Times Hulton Picture Library*)

List of Illustrations

Capturing insects, 1839, from *History of Insects,* 1839 (Anon.) (*Linnean Society of London*) ii

Geological field-work in the 1840s, from *Memoirs of the Geological Survey,* 1846 (*Institute of Geological Sciences*) vi

The dandelion. Engraving by Thomas Bewick, from Thomas Hugo, *Bewick's Woodcuts,* 1870 (*Linnean Society of London*) 3

Part of the Linnaean sexual system of plants, from James Lee, *An Introduction to Botany,* 1776 (*Linnean Society of London*) 22

Geological tools (*Mary Evans Picture Library*) 45

Victorian urn, from Philip Henry Gosse, *An Introduction to Zoology,* vol. II (*Linnean Society of London*) 64

Magpie moth, from *The Royal Natural History,* vol. VI, 1896 (*Linnean Society of London*) 83

Herring gull, from *The Royal Natural History,* vol. IV, 1895 (*Linnean Society of London*) 108

Equipment for trapping and laying out butterflies and insects (*Mary Evans Picture Library*) 126

Leicester in the 1870s, from F. S. Williams, *The Midland Railway,* 1877 (*Science Museum Library*) 142

A four-man microscope, from Dionysius Lardner, *The Microscope,* 1856 (*Linnean Society of London*) 158

Field glasses, from an advertisement from 1917 5(*Science Museum Library*) 175

Naturalists dredging off Whitenose, from Philip Henry Gosse, *The Aquarium,* 1854 (*Linnean Society of London*) 186

A country club run, from Viscount Bury and G. Lacy Hillier, *Cycling,* 1887 (*Science Museum Library*) 202

A weekend in the country, from *The Motor,* March 1927 (*Science Museum Library*) 220

The birdwatcher's field equipment, from C. F. Tunnicliffe, *Bird Portraiture,* 1945 (*Linnean Society of London*) 227

Preface (1994)

WHEN this book was first published, almost twenty years ago, I expected it to find its readership mainly among fellow naturalists—for whom I had primarily intended the book all along. It had not occurred to me that it filled what at that time was a rather gaping hole in the literature of the history of science, and that it would consequently receive a welcome from that academic quarter too. It came as a particular surprise, however, that many of those academic readers proved to be across the Atlantic, for I had supposed the subject matter likely to be of interest only to inhabitants of Britain and Ireland.

By a double piece of good fortune, historians of science had not only largely failed to penentrate to this farther part of their field until then, they were also deep in a debate about how much attention should rightly be given to the social context in which scientific ideas have developed. Unwittingly, I had produced a work which was modish, even provocative, in identifying itself wholeheartedly with the "externalist" point of view.

In the years since, history of science has increasingly shifted its gaze to biology and natural history, particularly to their more recent periods. Journals devoted to this area of the subject have made their appearance, and numerous hitherto-neglected corners—the birth of plant ecology is but one outstanding example—have at last come in for scholarly study. As a result, our knowledge of some of the matters treated in this book has been considerably widened and deepened, though it is probably fair to claim that the broad outline of the story has not been modified in any very significant respect. Certain chapters, indeed, can still stand essentially as they were written; however, the most unsatisfactory is undoubtedly Chapter Three, which even when it appeared did less than justice, I have long been conscious, to the work of the especially numerous and prolific historians of geology.

Unfortunately, for a long time now copies of the book have been unobtainable (in English-speaking countries, that is; a Japanese edition came out in 1990). In the U.S. they were almost impossible to come by from the very first. Yet to judge from the number of inquiries, especially from outside Britain, there apparently continue to be many who would like to have a copy for their personal shelves. In view of this I trust it will not be thought presumptuously early for the work to be brought before the public again.

THIS BOOK arose out of a small exhibit that I prepared for a conference of the Botanical Society of the British Isles in the spring of 1952. In this I attempted an analysis of how the Society's membership had altered in its social composition down the years, and was at once struck by the faithfulness with which broad national trends had evidently been reflected in this miniature world.

Some of these trends were clearly social ones, in the narrow meaning of that word. But others seemed to be the product of no more than changes in Taste—suggesting that the elusive entity that we term 'the spirit of the age' is capable of leaving its imprint even on subjects conventionally thought of as purely objective. The implication was that even quite transitory shifts within society at large might have a far greater influence than anyone appeared to have suggested on the development of areas of science more especially exposed to them. Social forces and fashion, in other words, might exert a gravitational pull, deflecting energies and helping to abort or delay a particular science's advance. For this reason the study of the past development of subjects like botany and zoology appeared to demand a very much wider perspective than it is customarily accorded. Indeed, only by such an approach did it seem that the true character of 'natural history' could be captured and encompassed. Finding nothing in the literature along these lines, I decided to take up the challenge.

The task proved formidable. Little or nothing, it emerged, had been published on great areas of the field, and much primary research was unavoidable. However, as anyone will know who has browsed through the writings of earlier naturalists and, in particular, turned the pages of those delightful, now largely forgotten periodicals, this has been more of a pleasure than a labour—even if, at times, it seemed to have no end. For the amount of written matter apparently worth sifting is infinite and the nuggets worthy of extraction are few. Natural history literature is of a kind from which it is peculiarly difficult to quarry 'social' detail. The main mass, devoted to field observations or long lists of species, is ever on its guard against just those more mundane remarks of value to the social historian. It is usually only where it has been allowed to 'leak'—in the more chatty periodicals, the more sharply etched obituaries, the more graphic accounts of meetings and excursions, in certain inaugural lectures and presidential addresses, above all in the far too rare published collections of letters and private journals and volumes of reminiscences—that one can pick up clues to how naturalists of former times worked and walked and ate, whom they mixed with, and why they noted some things and missed a great deal else altogether. In truth, this might be dubbed more aptly the *archaeology* of natural history: the piecing together of the living reality of the past from the merest unintended fragments.

Concentrating on the purely social also brings its own distortion. Not all naturalists are or ever have been sociable; and an account focused on collective endeavour cannot but understate the often very important contribution made by those working right away from the highroads of the subject. At times the role of these lone individuals has even been crucial, as they pioneered new fields or methods which later became general. If too little is said about such people in these pages, it is not that their achievements are unappreciated: it is merely that they lie outside the intrinsic scope of the book.

The 'Britain' of the title is in effect the whole of the British Isles, for Ireland's natural history cannot justifiably be treated as an independent entity. 'Naturalist' and 'natural history', similarly, I have preferred to use in their convenient vagueness. To have attempted to define them more precisely would have required another chapter to the book. The terms, in any case, have shifted in their meaning over time and even today are applied in more than a single sense. I have been content to take them as covering roughly what we today understand by ecology and systematics ('the diversity and inter-relationships of organisms', in the words of the Aims of the Linnean Society of London—but extending this to the geological aspects of scenery) and as made up of the range of sciences still embraced by the British Museum (Natural History). But, as will be evident from the pages that follow, I do not think natural history can be truly interpreted by a simplistic equation with one or more aspects of scientific inquiry in particular; moreover, the very act of observing natural objects involves a strong aesthetic element which interpenetrates the scientific. It is this dual character, surely, which accounts for so much of the subject's special fascination—and which in this age of the Two Cultures gives it an especial importance.

A book so long in generation inevitably accumulates down the years a sizeable moraine of indebtedness, far too large to be picked through in all its individual terms. There are one or two, even so, who must be singled out for thanking in particular: Dr W. S. Bristowe, Mr R. S. R. Fitter and Mr J. E. Lousley, for undertaking the onerous task of reading through the entire manuscript and giving me the benefit of their comments; Professor and Mrs Joseph Ewan and Professor G. S. Rousseau, for taking time off during all-too-brief visits to this country to bring their unrivalled expertise to bear on the early chapters; Miss Margaret Deacon, for similarly scrutinizing Chapters Six and Eleven in the light of her extensive knowledge of the history of oceanography; Dr Averil Lysaght and Dr W. E. Swinton, for reading through an early draft of Chapter Eight—and, even more, for their words of encouragement at a time when the project was flagging; Mr G. D. R. Bridson, Professor E. L. Jones, Miss Sandra Raphael, Dr R. S. Wilkinson and other fellow historians of the subject too numerous to mention, for the stimulating discussions I have enjoyed with them and for the fresh insights and leads to additional material that they have invariably provided. I also owe a very special debt of gratitude to Mr J. S. L. Gilmour, for the loan long ago of his manuscript notes on the history of local floras—and thereby, quite unwittingly, for the first opening of my eyes to the possibilities that have eventually found their embodiment in this book. I would not want to omit from this list, too, those libraries in which it has been my privilege principally to work: the London Library, Birmingham City Reference Library, the library of the Linnean Society of London and, above all, the various libraries of the British Museum (Natural History), for access to whose inexhaustible riches, like many another outsider before me, I shall always be profoundly grateful. Finally, I thank my wife for her help and patience during the closing stages.

D.E.A.

THE NATURALIST IN BRITAIN

CHAPTER ONE

Organization Begins

THERE comes a point in the history of every pursuit at which its following becomes sufficient to entitle it to be termed a social activity. At this stage it begins to acquire some substance. It takes on a life over and above that of its individual adherents and through the pattern of its own development starts to influence, and sometimes even govern, the way in which they think and act.

For natural history in Britain this point was reached some time in the course of the seventeenth century. For long before then, to be sure, naturalists had existed; but they had been few and scattered and had necessarily

worked in isolation. They had seldom had others near by whose help could
be invoked and who could be counted on to share their keenness, and
there had not ordinarily been any means of knowing what was being discovered elsewhere except by continual and often importunate correspondence or by the regular acquisition of large numbers of extremely expensive books. After 1600 the first decisive steps began to be taken towards a
more formalized coming-together. By the end of that century the earliest
society that we know of exclusively devoted to the subject had been
born—a legacy in part of that great new surge of disinterested inquiry that
characterized what we now know as the Enlightenment—and the key
items of field equipment of the principal constituent studies were also beginning to appear. The first known mention of the geologist's hammer
is in 1696; botanists were carrying collecting-tins (or 'vascula') by 1704;
the butterfly-net was in use by 1711. Called into being by the elementary
requirements of their respective pursuits, all three doubtless fulfilled as
well from the first their time-honoured role as group-emblems, providing for their users both a means of mutual recognition and a sense of
collective identity. Only just preceding them had come the first standard
works of identification on the more conspicuous of the country's animals
and plants: Francis Willoughby's—or, more accurately, John Ray's—
Ornithologia (brought out, significantly, in an English translation in 1678,
two years after its original publication), Ray's own *Catalogus Plantarum
Angliae* and its long-copied successor, the *Synopsis Methodica Stirpium Britannicarum,* and Martin Lister's *Historiae Animalium Angliae.* For the local
worker there were already Robert Plot's *Natural History of Oxfordshire* and
Natural History of Staffordshire to serve as a stimulating model of what
could be accomplished merely close at hand, and in James Petiver's little
pamphlets, *Memoirs for the Curious,* the first sign is even recognizable of the
emergence of a deliberately more popular literature. The launching by the
Royal Society in 1665 of its *Philosophical Transactions*—and almost simultaneously of the *Journal des Savants* on the Continent—had also proved the
value of the specialist journal as a means of scientific communication and
accustomed the leaders of learning to its use.

It was in botany that the first and greatest strides in these directions had
been achieved. The study of plants had obvious practical applications for
the infant science of medicine, and as a result of this, alone of the various
branches of natural history, could count at this time on organized support
from a professional quarter. It lent itself the most readily, moreover, to
pursuit in the field in groups and could be carried out without incurring
excessive embarrassment or attracting much suspicion. Not surprisingly,
therefore, of the earliest specialist societies of which a mention has come
down to us all but one were botanical—and most of these were brought
into being from motives that were more vocational, or even monetary,

than purely scientific. We owe it to the needs of the trade, in fact, that the first substantial numbers of persons were brought together from amongst whom, more or less by accident, the first permanent social nexus of naturalists was enabled to emerge. And it was ostensibly for profit to the pocket, rather than to the senses or the head, that most of them were first introduced to the delights of exploring and investigating.

The agency that we have to thank for this is the Society of Apothecaries, one of the old-established livery companies of the City of London. The primary purpose of this body was to exercise control over the practice there of what we should nowadays recognize as the greater part of the twin professions of medicine and pharmacy. In theory—though, especially latterly, by no means always in practice—only a Freeman of this Society was permitted to trade as an apothecary in the City and within a radius of seven miles; and in order to become a Freeman, it was normally necessary to have served a seven- or eight-year apprenticeship. Apprentices were usually bound at about thirteen or fourteen and learned on the job, accompanying their masters on their rounds and performing a great deal of routine drudgery. Only when they had gained their Freedom were they permitted to marry. Compared with the general run of livery companies, the Society was small and fairly intimate: its members, who functioned essentially as the general practitioners of those days (leaving the physicians to cater for the upper reaches of society, after the manner of consultants), were jealous of their skills and rightly demanded high standards of all would-be entrants. Accordingly, as the culmination of their training, the apprentices were required to undergo stiff tests in order to satisfy the Society of their general proficiency. One of these, not unexpectedly, was in the correct recognition of the 'simples', or drug plants, that formed the raw material of their trade; and as these needed to be known in the fresh state, the Society had to take it upon itself to maintain a botanic garden—latterly the famous Physic Garden at Chelsea, established in 1673 and still flourishing today—and to organize special 'herbarizings', or field excursions into the countryside, on which the apprentices could be duly instructed in locating in the wild the commoner species then in use in medicine.

The earliest of these excursions that can be traced in the Society's records was in May 1620—the year in which the *Mayflower* set sail for America. The Simpling Day that month was fixed to start at five o'clock in the morning—a quite normal time for apprentices to be up and about—and the rendezvous was to be at St Paul's. After some time the number of these excursions was increased to six a year, one in each month from April to September. The first in each season was always led by the Master of the Society, who personally bore the cost of providing the evening's dinner; while the one in July, known as the 'General Herbarizing', was traditionally much more elaborate, being attended by large numbers of the

Freemen and rounded off with an impressive banquet, at which the star turn was always a haunch of venison (and from which, it is presumed, the apprentices were debarred, if only by the high contribution towards their cost levied on those attending). For this grand occasion the Society's cere-monial barge was also regularly brought into use, at least in the eighteenth century, and in one year, 1749, even a band of musicians was hired— though not without recriminations afterwards over the absurd extrava-gance of such a gesture.

The excursions were conducted at first by a senior member of the Soci-ety with a personal enthusiasm for botany; but in later years, as the supply of willing volunteers for the task no doubt became unreliable, a special paid official came to be appointed for the purpose, at an annual salary of £10, with the title of Demonstrator of Plants. In addition to this duty he was required to take up his stand in the Garden every last Wednesday in each summer month and, in the manner long customary in physic gardens designed for teaching, to expound the names and uses of the more impor-tant plants. He needed, clearly, to be someone with a reasonable knowl-edge. At the same time it was almost more essential that he should be capable of exercising firmness of discipline. For the apprentices, it seems, accustomed to being worked very hard, found these breaks from routine rather dangerously heady, and the excursions, unless strictly supervised, tended to become unruly. In 1724, for example, the committee responsible for organizing them noted in its minute-book that 'severall complaints have of late been made of disorders frequently happening on the day ap-pointed for the private herbarizing' and laid down that in future any ap-prentice wishing to attend must bring with him a permit from his master, while non-members of the Society would only be allowed on them if known to and approved by the Leader. For a time this tightening-up doubtless had the desired effect. By 1767, however, after the scholarly but over-mild William Hudson had been appointed Demonstrator, a fresh de-terioration appears to have taken place. For in that year certain Freemen of the Society complained that they had been deterred from sending their apprentices 'to the Lectures and Botannick Walks, so often as they would have done, by the Irregularity and indecent Behaviour of some Persons who have frequented those Walks, fearing their own apprentices might be corrupted by such Examples'.

Subsequent holders of the office fortunately coped better. William Curtis, like Hudson a botanist of national reputation, was a person of drive and evidently infectious enthusiasm. His comparatively brief stay of four years must have done much to repair the tradition. On his departure in 1777, his place was taken by the redoubtable Thomas Wheeler, a born teacher, who succeeded over a very long period of years in building up the 'Herbarizings' to such a pitch of popularity that they came to take on the character almost of a sacred ritual. Some rather picturesque accounts of his later years have happily come down to us: they depict Wheeler turning up, ever predictably, in an old hat, very threadbare suit and a pair of long leather gaiters; and, even though by then well into his seventies, putting everyone to shame by his inexhaustible good spirits and agility. But even this was not sufficient to save the excursions indefinitely. In 1834 it was reluctantly decided that London's fast-growing sprawl rendered them no longer practicable, and except for the single, never primarily instructional Grand Herbarizing (which lingered on for some years further) they were finally abandoned.

These excursions, without any doubt, were the major seminal influence in the establishment of the great field tradition that forms the core of modern natural history. Apart from the many field botanists who owed to them their first introduction to the subject, they were important for a wide variety of institutions and usages to which in one way or another they gave rise by their example. For the Apothecaries, by dint of many years of trial and error, had succeeded in evolving a sort of magic formula: a near-perfect blend of helpful 'live' instruction, healthy, purposeful exercise and large-scale, unstrained good companionship.

Their first fruitful by-product had come into being almost at the outset. This was the band of keen young workers, almost all of them, apparently, one-time apprentices in the Society, who in the years 1629–39 made the earliest collective sweeps across Southern England and Wales in search of plants under the leadership of an energetic Yorkshireman, Thomas Johnson, an apothecary in Snow Hill. Best known for his able revision of Gerard's *Herball* and for the delightful, detailed accounts of some of these excursions—the earliest local lists—that he fortunately preserved for us in print, Johnson was a friend of the country's other foremost botanists, such as John Goodyer and John Parkinson, and was just the kind of man, of obvious organizing ability and abundant drive, who might well have created the first permanent formal body exclusively devoted to the study of our native flora and fauna. In the event his tragic death in the Civil War, at the early age of forty or thereabouts, put paid to any such likelihood.

The founding of the Royal Society of London, within twenty years of Johnson's death, was no real substitute. For all the brilliance of its members, the great breadth of its concerns allowed little room for specialized interests of this nature. It was, besides, chair-bound on the whole, and favoured lofty speculation rather than grubbing in the field for data. For isolated workers, of whom John Ray is the outstanding example, it did provide an intellectual communications centre of the greatest comfort and assistance. Certainly, too, it fostered a most impressive outburst of scientific effort; it lent its prestige to secure the publication of many much-needed books; it gave the study of subjects such as botany and zoology a social standing and an air of respectability that before then they had scarcely known. But for all this its influence on the course of organized natural history was little more than marginal—except in one respect: it served at last to bring together most of the leading botanists in the country and then, by reason of its very catholicity, pushed them into taking intellectual refuge in the more specialized company of one another. Thus was born in or about 1698, as an unofficial outgrowth, a 'Temple Coffee House Botanic Club', the earliest natural history society in Britain and probably in the world.

This was no ordinary club. For a start it had, apparently, no formal organization, such as officers and rules: it functioned, it seems, as little more than a loose coterie of friends. Perhaps because of this unofficial character no mention of it appears to have found its way into print; and it was only when the correspondence of its members came to be thoroughly scrutinized within the last few years that its existence was revealed. To have been invited along to the Coffee House for one of the Club's regular Friday evening meetings must have been a singularly stimulating experience —and a good deal more rewarding, in view of the intellectual climate of the time, than attending a session of some latter-day natural history dining-club. It was more than a dining-club, in any case; for it also made excursions to places of interest in and around London.

Several members of the Club, including Petiver, Buddle and Doody, who made many plant-hunting expeditions together round London in the early years of the new century, also attended the Herbarizings of the Apothecaries as often as they could. A notebook of Doody's has survived in which he has jotted down as a reminder the dates of the 'herberizing dayes' for 1687–8; and in one of the many references to them in the letters of the period Petiver can be found writing in September 1712 of the last one of that season having ended up, as usual, at Chelsea, 'where we dined at the Swan'. The excursions of the Botanic Club, which must have alternated with those of the Apothecaries and ranged on occasion a good way into Kent, could thus hardly have helped but be influenced by their example.

A close parallel to the Apothecaries' field tradition, in the meantime, had appeared in Scotland (then still an independent country). Not long after 1670 the city of Edinburgh had been prevailed upon by two of its leading physicians to set aside a piece of ground as a public botanic garden, freely consultable by all local medical men, and to vote funds for its support out of the revenues of the University. James Sutherland, a keen young botanist in his thirties, was appointed Intendant and, as he relates in his catalogue of the garden published in 1683, his duties extended to making numerous field excursions for the purpose of building up its stock of medicinal plants. It is possible that on some of these he was accompanied by numbers of pupils, after the Chelsea pattern. There is no record of anything of this kind, however, before 1695, when a special act was passed authorizing Sutherland to instruct the apprentices of the College of Surgeons at 'a solemn publick herborizing in the fields four severall times every year'. This sounds suspiciously like a straightforward borrowing from the London Apothecaries. We know that the two Gardens were frequently in touch, and it is hard to believe that no reports had filtered north of the London Herbarizings and their continuing value and vitality.

How long the tradition persisted, once established by Sutherland, is uncertain. For the whole of the period from 1695 to 1800 there is no clear evidence that teaching excursions were still being undertaken by either the University or the Garden, but until the contemporary correspondence has been more exhaustively examined it is unsafe to assume that this mere lack of trace necessarily implies their nonexistence. But if it was the case that the tradition here proved abortive, it is not hard to find one very likely reason: the sudden break in direction that occurred in the time of Sutherland's successor, the ill-fated William Arthur. Deeply implicated—unlikely though it seemed—in the Jacobite rising of 1715, this hapless man had no alternative but to flee both the Garden and Scotland when it collapsed, never to succeed in returning.

Another victim, apparently, of the Jacobite débâcle was Patrick Blair, a local apothecary of wide scientific interests and manifest ability, who early created a considerable stir by dissecting an elephant and then reconstructing and mounting the skeleton from its bones. By 1712 he had gained a doctorate from Aberdeen and was corresponding with several of the leading figures of the day; including Boerhaave, the great teacher of medicine and botany at Leyden. What was clearly destined to be a useful and influential career was at that point utterly shattered by the fateful events of 1715. Impressed—as he maintained, against his will—into the Jacobite army and later convicted of complicity when the rising was crushed, he found himself torn away from his home and background and sentenced to a term in Newgate Prison. He emerged a ruined man, and lived for a time in London in great poverty. Some years later, in 1720, he was appointed Physician to the Port of Boston, in Lincolnshire, and contrived in some degree to put his fortunes in repair. Here he resumed his natural history interests and, for all we know, may well have finished his career as he began it: as a member of a local botanic club for one had been founded in that town, by a coincidence, some years earlier by William Stukeley, the famous antiquary. 'The apothecarys and I', Stukeley later recalled in his memoirs, 'went out a simpling once a week. We bought Ray's 3 folios of a joint stock'. But, as usual, we are not told how long this club succeeded in surviving.

One of the people to befriend the exiled Blair in his hardest days in

London was the young son of a wealthy City merchant, named John Martyn. Martyn had developed a passion for natural history—and more particularly for botany—in the course of his teens, and by the age of twenty had already made the acquaintance of many of the experts in the subject at the time living in the Metropolis. This led to his being invited to join in the excursions of the Apothecaries and this, in turn, to his making friends with the keener of the apprentices. The idea then arose of forming a separate botanical society (conceivably suggested by Blair, in the light of his one-time efforts at Dundee), to cater for the apprentices and others who wanted to pursue the subject somewhat more thoroughly; and this was duly brought into being, with all the necessary formalities, late in 1721. Thanks to the printed collections of Martyn's son, published in 1770, and to the lucky preservation of one of its minute-books, this is a body about which we know a considerable amount. We know that it held together till the end of 1726. We know it had a president—to begin with the German botanist, J. J. Dillenius, who had just been brought over by James Sherard to work on his *Pinax* (and who was thus, apparently, the first person in history to enjoy full-time paid employment as a taxonomist)—a secretary, in the person of Martyn, and also a full-scale set of rules. We know the meetings were held every Saturday at six in the evening, at first in the Rainbow Coffee House in Watling Street and later in the home of one of the members. And we know that at these, in accordance with the rules, every member in turn had to exhibit a specified number of plants, give their names and make observations on their uses: in other words, every member his own Demonstrator of Plants. The names of twenty-three of these members (probably the full total) have come down to us and, because of their known connection with botany or medicine, it has recently proved possible to identify all but two of them with reasonable certainty. They turn out to have been, as one might well have expected, mostly very young: of those whose age can be established all but six were under twenty-five in the year of the Society's founding. The only two verging on middle age—apart from the president—evidently preferred to keep in the background. It was thus a typical students' association. It also had a strongly vocational impetus: one third were destined to be apothecaries, one third physicians, most of the rest surgeons or surgeon-apothecaries. And if their subsequent careers are anything to go by, they were well above average in intelligence—though few in actual fact made any very useful contributions to botanical knowledge in later years. Perhaps most interesting of all, they originated for the most part from what Coleridge was later to term the 'clerisy', that segment of society that lives by its intellectual skills and predominantly guides it by its thinking. Three, possibly five, were sons of clergymen—significantly Dissenters as often as Anglican parsons, presaging the vital role about to be played in English higher education by the dissenting academies—five followed fathers who were medical men already, two had uncles at the Bar, and two exemplified the growing tradition for the landed gentry to place their younger sons in a learned profession. Only the teaching profession was under-represented.

Apart from Philip Miller, who was in charge of the Chelsea Garden and thus straddled the worlds of both medicine and horticulture, Martyn's Botanical Society shared no members with another small contemporary body, the Society of Gardeners, which was composed exclusively of London nurserymen and met at Newhall's Coffee House in Chelsea. Nor was there any overlap, perhaps more surprisingly (for naturalists in those days were so frequently all-rounders), with the handful of individuals named—amongst others—in the preface to Benjamin Wilkes's *The English Moths and Butterflies* (1748–9), who probably constituted the nucleus of the earliest-known specialist body in the field of zoology, the Society of Aurelians.

The Aurelians—as the lepidopterists of those days liked to call themselves (from the golden chrysalis, or *aureolus,* of a certain kind of butterfly)—were clearly less numerous than the botanists and lagged a good way behind in the race to band together in formal organizations. We do not know when or how the Society of Aurelians was founded. All that is certain, thanks to a fragment of autobiography let slip by Wilkes in the preface to the work already mentioned, is that it was already flourishing by 1740. It could well have been much older still; for its leading spirit at that time and its most likely founder, Joseph Dandridge, had been a noted London collector ever since the 1690s (when he had contributed many records and specimens to Ray).

Dandridge is the great forgotten figure of English entomology. Due to the fact that he left no printed works, his existence has been almost totally overlooked—so complete has been the dominance of the history of the subject by bibliophiles and book-listers. Yet all the early writers on British insects allude to him; and several go out of their way to pay tribute to his friendship and encouragement and remark on the generosity with which he put his knowledge and his very extensive collection, ranging over many orders, at the service of beginners. His influence in these early years seems to have been all-pervading—and more constructive and enduring by far than that of Petiver, whose work on British insects, performed in a narrower spirit and prompted by a collecting mania directed almost wholly to private, rather selfish ends, has been allowed to overshadow that of his contemporaries quite unduly. By trade a pattern drawer for the manufacture of silks and a designer of considerable repute (a number of his designs have, in fact, recently been detected in the Victoria and Albert Museum), Dandridge lived near Moorfields (just round the corner, in fact, from his great friend Petiver) and, for a period, in Stoke Newington, which then lay in open country. Stories about his insect-hunting lived on in the latter place for many years after his death. The man with the net was an even greater curiosity then than today, and that a man of standing and substance should indulge in such antics must have baffled and amused his neighbours. A slightly redeeming feature, possibly, was that he also collected a great variety of objects of a rather more ordinary character: shells, fossils, birds' eggs, bird skins, and all manner of plants including even lichens and mosses. His collection of paintings or drawings of England's mushrooms and toadstools covered more than one hundred kinds; while his collection of English spiders and harvestmen comprised over one hundred and forty 'species', which he held could be divided into nine separate classes. A volume of meticulous water-colour drawings of these last, accompanied by careful notes on their appearance, life-cycle and habits, is now in the Sloane Collection in the British Museum; it dates from before 1710. The drawings and descriptions were made from life, since Dandridge knew of no way of preserving such specimens. In forming these collections he came into touch with the leading workers in each of these fields. He knew Petiver, Buddle and the Sherards; he must have known of the Temple Coffee House Club; he may well have attended some of the Apothecaries' excursions. Thus the notion (if indeed it was his) of forming a similar society for the Aurelians seems very likely to have been borrowed from the botanists.

Quite exceptionally, this is one society the date of whose ending we know with precision: March 1747–8. For this we have to thank the dramatic, indeed catastrophic, circumstances that unfortunately attended its demise. While the Society was in session, a great fire arose in Cornhill and quickly enveloped its meeting-place, the nearby Swan Tavern in 'Change Alley. The members barely escaped with their lives, many having to leave behind them even their hats and canes, while the Society's valuable collection of insects, its entire library and all its records and regalia were completely devoured by the flames. Moses Harris, the great entomological illustrator, had been introduced to the Society by an uncle of his about 1742, when a mere boy of twelve, and it is due to his graphic description in *The Aurelian; or, Natural History of English Insects* (1765) that we know anything at all of this melancholy event. 'Their loss so much disheartened them', he adds, 'that, although they several times met for that purpose, they never could collect so many as would be sufficient to form a society.'

———

Apart from these signs of energy in entomology the years between 1725 and 1760 are largely a blank for British natural history. But the same is true for British science in general. Following the death of Newton in 1727, the Royal Society went into a steep decline, admitting many Fellows of dubious merit and focusing its attentions increasingly on antiquarian matters. Martin Folkes, the president immediately after Sloane and Newton, set the tone by regularly going to sleep in the Chair. Deprived of the Society's leadership, the rest of the learned world gradually lost heart or lost interest. The torrent of new discoveries ceased; publications dwindled; clubs and societies one by one petered out.

At Oxford and Cambridge, in particular, a change of such marked extent and abruptness set in that a tidemark of decay is still visible. Foreign scholars who visited them in these years returned appalled. One German who went to Cambridge to study found the manuscripts at Caius dumped and neglected in a garret, while at Magdalene much of the library was slimy with mould. At Oxford, in 1730, William Huddesford, the President of Trinity, was elected Keeper of the Ashmolean at a salary of £50 a year 'whether he do anything there or not'. For thirty-six years, from 1747 till 1783, Humphrey Sibthorp dozed in its Chair of Botany, stirring only intermittently to put in some gentle work in the University Botanic Garden; throughout this whole period he published not a single scientific work, so far as is known, and delivered only a solitary lecture—and that a bad one (according to James Edward Smith, who admittedly disliked him and coveted his position). When Joseph Banks went up to Christ Church in 1760 as a Gentleman-Commoner and wished to treat himself to lessons in botany, he was driven to the rather drastic expedient of journeying to the Other Place and bringing back from there a leading amateur, Israel Lyons, to give him private coaching.

But at least Sibthorp stayed in residence, which is more than can be said for his Cambridge counterpart, John Martyn. After managing to seize all the lecturing from Richard Bradley, the much-abused but under-rated pioneer experimentalist—who had been forced into writing and lecturing on botany for a livelihood after losing his comfortable means in the bursting of the South Sea Bubble—Martyn went on to secure the Chair, not without some backstairs manoeuvring, on Bradley's death in 1732. Three years later his lectures ceased, on the rather slim pretext that the lack of a botanic garden made his task unduly difficult; and though he stayed away for close on thirty years, he failed to resign until 1762—and then only so that the Chair could pass on to his son.

Such posts generally carried no emoluments; but potentially, at least, they conferred prestige on their holders as well as considerable earnings from the writing and lecturing engagements that invariably resulted. More important, they were pulpits for the subject which any occupant of energy and vision could well have made good use of, to win for it a wider national understanding and a larger following. All such opportunities, however, the professors were more than content to let slip, compounding the neglect of their duties with the abdication of these wider, public responsibilities. In the absence at this time of any body of standing able to speak for the country's natural history as a whole, this lacuna in its leadership assumed a more than ordinary importance and its effect was the more crippling.

It becomes easier to understand the behaviour of men like Martyn and Sibthorp if we view it against the background of the abnormal morality then prevailing. The forty years following the Duke of Newcastle's arrival in power as Walpole's Secretary of State in 1724 are notorious for the unparalleled extensiveness of their corruption. Public posts were systematically reserved for those prepared to support the Whigs, to a point where the tentacles of patronage penetrated even to the humblest levels and anyone who sought advancement would have been expected to subscribe to the way in which matters were ordered—or find their path for ever blocked. In such an atmosphere it would have been extraordinary if a general mood of cynicism had not arisen. As a means of injecting into government a sorely needed stability it was a system that spectacularly worked: its effects more generally, however, can hardly have helped but be corrosive. This must have been pre-eminently the case in the world of learned pursuits. Where positions of esteem are no longer gained on the strength of ability, the basic authority of scholarship is undermined. In such soil scientific subjects cannot continue to flourish. They depend on an established consensus about what is true, if they are to be capable of moving forward. Without a conviction of cumulative achievement, they become emptily repetitive, mere exercises in observation and rational thought.

At the same time there was also a more positive antipathy to science abroad. It may well be that the very brilliance of the Royal Society under Newton helped to ensure an unusual violence in the inevitable reaction. Just as there are swings in interest from one branch of knowledge to another, so at times the swing can be away from empirical thought altogether. In an odd way, too, scientific genius tends to display itself in sudden, brief bursts of magnificent intensity, followed by long periods of comparative darkness. Through its sheer success and the widespread excitement and admiration it had aroused, the intellectual explosion of the preceding half-century must also in itself have been the cause of a certain pent-up rancour and envy. The habit of scepticism which the practice of science naturally engenders may well have contributed to this legacy of retribution too.

In this more generally adverse climate natural history had particularly severe problems of its own. Well before the Royal Society had entered upon its decline, a marked narrowing had occurred in its outlook. 'I find there is no room in Gresham College for Natural History', Walter Moyle, the Cornishman and ornithologist, had bewailed in 1719: 'Mathematics have engrossed all.' The reason for this was that death had caused a sudden, drastic reduction in the number of naturalists in its ranks. In the space of just a few years the best part of a quite exceptional generation passed from the scene and, disastrously, went without replacement. In 1720 we find William Sherard reporting to Dr Richard Richardson, the eminent Yorkshire naturalist, on a meeting held that spring at his London lodgings: 'Mr Tilleman Bobart was with me; and presently came Mr Manningham, with Mr Rand; and soon after that, Mr Dubois and my brother. It is the first time so many (for there are few more) have met together since I came into England.' Here is the sad, resigned tone of someone conscious of being but a last survivor. Nowhere was there anyone in sight to follow on.

Accordingly, in these middle years of the eighteenth century, just as in the 1920s, British natural history experienced one of its thankfully rare breakdowns in elementary manpower. The intake of recruits proved quite insufficient to keep up the tradition. Absorbed in their own activities, the giants of the heroic age now passing had neglected to train successors. Once they were gone, the indirect influence of their example, which could have done duty for this at a more favoured period, proved too weak on its own to cure the deficiency. In their place the new, up-and-coming men, who could normally have been relied on to inspire and stimulate the young, in far too many cases allowed themselves to be seduced by the 'strong infection of the age' and either spent their energies in manoeuvring for positions or, like John Martyn, sank from sight into the lurid depths of Grub Street journalism and filled their days with scurrilous lampooning. Though extreme, Martyn's extraordinary downhill career was all too typical of the period: a promising start, then a long, inexplicable barrenness. Significantly, like other leading teachers of the time, he produced not a single pupil who later adorned the subject—with the conspicuous exception of his son.

Naturalists, it is true, are probably seldom created *ab initio* by teaching; but they are at least 'confirmed' by well-timed help and encouragement. The first essential for a vigorous crop of newcomers is a suitable prevailing climate, for this in itself will produce that greatest of all stimuli: like minds of a similar age. The very fact that it was not from their contemporaries, nor even from their parents' generation, that some of the young, emergent figures of these years received their primary inspiration and assistance is sufficient proof of the precarious way in which the torch just succeeded in being handed on. Benjamin Wilkes, for example, had to acknowledge the eighty-year-old Dandridge as his 'principal mentor in entomology' when he first discovered the subject, around 1740. Edward Jacob, whose *Plantae Favershamienses* was later to be one of the earliest local Floras, owed his first careful field instruction when a youth to a fellow Kentish botanist, the Rev. John Bateman, a veteran of over seventy. Of the small handful of others most turn out, on closer investigation, to have had some vital personal contact in their most impressionable years with some member of the great

Ray-Sloane-Sherard-Petiver generation—to be indirectly scions, in short, of the Temple Coffee House Botanic Club. Thomas Gray, author of the famous *Elegy*, had caught his keenness for botany and entomology while a boy at Eton from his uncle and master there, Robert Antrobus, who in turn had been a protégé of an actual member of that club, William Vernon. John Martyn, as we have seen, received his first encouragement from Blair; while the young friends with whom he constituted his Botanical Society were in the main disciples of Isaac Rand, the Demonstrator of Plants for the Apothecaries, who as a young man had collected in the company of Petiver, Buddle, Du Bois and Plukenet. John Wilmer, Martyn's great friend, who some years later found himself entrusted with the Apothecaries' Garden at Chelsea, made a special pilgrimage to Oxford in 1719, at the age of twenty-two, to sit at the feet of the younger Bobart and though he found him helpless and decrepit, 'we had a great deal of talk, and I saw his collection of plants, insects, fossils, etc.'

In the absence of continuing interpreters much of the New Learning was forgotten. The great classificatory advances embodied in the work of Ray and his contemporaries, the foundation for the system based on natural structural affinities that was ultimately to triumph, fell into such disuse that the inferior 'artificial' system of Linnaeus was later able to brush it aside with little difficulty—and in the process considerably retarded the development of biological systematics. In much the same fashion the remarkably advanced thought of Robert Hooke, who had already conceived the outline of a theory of the earth based on a cycle of erosion by 1668, became wholly lost to sight and was not available for building on when James Hutton came to formulate, in far more compelling detail, the more or less identical theory with which in 1785 he laid the foundations of the modern science of geology. No one, either, appears to have seen fit to follow up an even more epoch-making assertion by Hooke: that the Biblical Deluge, that traditional stand-by of those who looked to recorded history for an explanation of the presence of fossils, was far too brief and insubstantial to have caused the formation of all the known fossiliferous rocks. Had his contemporaries heeded this, there might never have occurred that wholesale freezing of religious belief that was later to cause so much trouble for Darwin and his forerunners. For the chief casualty, above all others, of the eighteenth-century decline in intellectual inquiry was the necessary readjustment of theology to the new scientific findings of the Enlightenment. Instead, the old interpretations, outmoded though they were, failed to be dislodged; and the Church, suffering in its turn from the lapse in scholarly standards and the resulting poverty of contemporary critique, snuggled down once more into a doctrinal sleep. When at last it awoke, in the 1790s, the awakening came as a fright and a shock; and in the time-honoured way of the shocked and the frightened, attending only to self-defence, it responded by calling on the faithful to stand and close the ranks. The result, in the event, was doubly disastrous: on the one hand, an over-rigid stance of implacable hostility to science and, on the other, a painfully untenable insistence on the literal word of the Scriptures.

———

The languishing of formal societies did not mean an end of all organized natural history. Their function, as the vital sinews of the subject, was merely transferred for a time to that other, less visible social nexus, the semi-permanent circles of correspondents—or 'colliterations', as they might usefully be termed. Already far more important than today for spreading knowledge of new discoveries in the absence of a properly developed periodical literature, private correspondence now had an even greater role to play than ever before or since. The world of natural history, one might say, came to exist almost solely on paper. And though paper has perhaps always played the major part in the diffusion of ideas, especially of the more complex ones, it has its limitations. It is unlikely ever to match the effectiveness of personal meetings—as a way of introducing new techniques, as a means of evolving ethical standpoints, or as a method of evaluating reputations by submitting them to the instant testing-power of coterie opinion. With the temporary suspension of formal gatherings a certain slackening of conformity, a certain fraying at the social edges, a slowing-down of communications in various aspects of the subject was only to be expected.

To commit oneself to paper at this period, moreover, was to commit oneself to posts that were slow, costly and uncertain. To a quite maddening extent the letters of the early naturalists tend to be taken up—when they are not recounting all the grisly symptoms of their illnesses—with complaints of packages that have gone astray or with elaborate instructions regarding their dispatch. Merely to borrow a book from a friend could well involve the sending of a tedious list of suitable coach-times and naming one or more resting-places or agents to which it should be addressed. Even then it might not arrive; and even if it did arrive, it might turn up days, weeks, or months after it had been expected. 'I find occasions of transmitting boxes uncertain and unsure by the common carriers', wrote Sutherland to Richardson in 1702—in a masterpiece of understatement. Alternative means of transport could be almost equally unreliable: in 1755, when John Ellis chose to send a book by sea to the Rev. William Borlase down in Cornwall, the latter was moved to complain of the great time that it had taken—occasioned, so he was led to understand, by the excessive activity of the press-gangs, which so obstructed the navigation of the Thames that the ship that was carrying it had been long delayed.

Despite all these hindrances and risks, keeping up a correspondence was an inescapable necessity. Even at the end of the century three people out of every four still had their homes away from towns, and for almost all of these life was extremely isolated. Lesser gentry of reasonable education or medical men and parsons who found themselves with rural practices or parishes were condemned to be stranded for the whole of their lives without direct communion with fellow minds; and for those with scholarly leanings, for whom the normal round of hunting and shooting was distasteful or a bore, a well-stocked library, copious letter-writing and, if they were lucky, a neighbour or two of vaguely compatible leanings were generally their only solaces. The very expense of books and their mainly unhelpful character were hardly an encouragement to those who wished to pass on and explore fresh fields, and it says much for the pioneers of those days that they should have proved so successful when thrown so totally on to their own resources. Gilbert White, the contented chronicler of the *Natural History of Selborne,* is the classic example of one such person who triumphed over many of these difficulties. 'It has long been my misfortune', he lamented, 'never to have had any neighbours whose studies have led them towards the pursuit of natural knowledge; so that, for want of a companion to quicken my industry and sharpen my attention, I have made but slender progress in a kind of information to which I have been attached from my childhood.'

In writing this, White was being just a trifle disingenuous. His experience was by no means extreme, and indeed his case can hardly have been all that typical. For he moved around a considerable amount, spent part of his life in residence at Oxford as a don, and entertained at 'The Wakes' certainly more than one Metropolitan intellectual. But of alternative examples there is at least no shortage: Samuel Dale, Essex apothecary and botanist; William Kirby, Suffolk vicar and entomologist; Richard Pulteney, country physician in Leicestershire and Dorset, and student of plants and shells . . . The list is almost endless of those who maintained this long and very fruitful tradition of the parish scholar exercising his brain in the study of his immediate surroundings. Respected themselves, such men made their subject too seem worthy of respect and greatly raised its standing in the eyes of the local public.

The special attraction of natural history for the clergy, in particular, has probably never been underlined better than in this passage by J. C. Loudon, published many years later in the *Magazine of Natural History*:

> It would be altogether superfluous to insist on the suitableness of the study of Natural History for a clergyman residing in the country . . . Compared even with a taste for classical studies, for drawing, painting, or any other branch of the Fine Arts; or for amateur turning, or any other kind of a

mechnical employment; a taste for Natural History in a clergyman has great advantages, both as respects himself and others. It is superior, in a social point of view, even to a taste for gardening. The sportsman often follows his amusements to the great annoyance of his parishioners; the horticulturist exercises his gentler pursuit within his garden; and the classical or indoor student of any kind secludes himself in his closet or his laboratory; but the naturalist is abroad in the fields, investigating the habits and searching out the habitats of birds, insects, or plants, not only invigorating his health, but affording ample opportunity for frequent intercourse with his parishioners. In this way their reciprocal acquaintance is cultivated, and the clergyman at last becomes an adviser and friend, as well as a spiritual teacher.

Pursuits like this certainly needed the helping hand of respectability in the face of the normal crudities of life that prevailed in eighteenth century Britain: a period when the common reaction to anyone or anything at all out of the ordinary continued to be aggressive and even violent. People were ragged for being cripples; strangers were jostled and hooted at; fashionable finery was a target for mud. Solitary walkers, in particular, invited general contempt or hostility, for the only people who moved freely abroad in this way were, it was well known, either footpads or paupers. Inn-keepers, accustomed only to 'carriage company' or riders, never ceased to be suspicious. When one traveller from Germany asked why Englishmen never wandered abroad like him on foot, he was assured they were 'too rich, too lazy and too proud'. A man's mode of travel advertised his economic status. If he appeared in public walking, this was a certain sign he was too poor to run a stable or to own a carriage. If the gentry felt the urge to stretch their legs, then they did this in decent privacy on their estates: Englishwomen, indeed, had won a reputation on the Continent for strolling excessively in their gardens—the French claimed it gave them big feet.

Travelling on foot, besides, had definite dangers quite apart from the mere inconveniences. For everywhere lurked thieves—even as close in to London as the road from Kensington Palace to Westminster. As late as 1749 Horace Walpole lost his gold watch to two highwaymen armed with a blunderbuss in Hyde Park. The wilder parts of the country were even more unsafe. Edward Lhwyd, who ventured farther afield than almost anyone in search of plants and what he termed 'formed stones', was constantly harried in his travels by local troubles of this kind. 'I wish [the Irish plants] had been more, and better', he wrote to Richardson in 1701; 'but we came out of Ireland too soon, and the Tories of Killarney in Kerry obliged us to quit those mountains much sooner than we intended.' The previous year, in Cornwall, he and his companions were repeatedly molested, being generally taken for Jacobite spies. And when spies seemed too far-fetched, the country people still convinced themselves that they were 'employed by the Parliament in order to raise some further taxes'. The Jacobite scare continued for years. Dr Caleb Threlkeld was one naturalist out of many who met with reason to complain of it: in 1707, while planthunting at Tynemouth, he recorded, 'because I clambered up the rocks, and kept not the highroad', he was quickly pounced upon by the locals as a spy. And even Sir Joseph Banks, in his younger days, while poking about in the hedges near Hounslow in 1760, was seized on suspicion as a highwayman and hauled before Sir John Fielding at Bow Street before the error was exposed.

Travelling by coach or carriage was not a pleasurable luxury. Inns were often filthy and grossly overcrowded (it was still not unknown for travellers to sleep several to a bed, quite unclothed); and until the advent of the turnpikes after 1751, even main roads were often in an appalling state and sometimes proved impassable. Add to this the expense of coaches, their unreliability, and the continual swaying that made so many of their passengers sick—Gilbert White being one notable sufferer from this—and it is hardly surprising to find that many preferred to avoid them, at least in summer, and made their journeys on horseback instead. Ray and Willoughby, Pennant, Gilbert White, Lhwyd, Lightfoot—the great majority of the early naturalists—regularly traversed the country in this way. And provided the weather was fine, it must have been both healthy and pleasant. 'Almost all my tours were performed on horse-back,' Pennant writes in his autobiography:

> to that, and to the perfect ease of mind I enjoyed in these pleasing journies, I owe my *viridis senectus* . . . I consider the absolute resignation of one's person to the luxury of a carriage, to forebode a very short interval between that and the vehicle which is to convey us to our last stage.

But horseback did not suit everyone. James Sherard, for example: 'I cannot go into the North nor West of England but on horseback, who am but a very indifferent horseman, and not provided with an easy one fit to carry me such a journey', he grumbled to Richardson in 1724–5. His usual mode of travel, instead, was a light chaise and pair, with a servant riding a third horse 'to change or put to as occasion serves'.

Carried on like this, by solitary mounted figures criss-crossing the length and breadth of Britain, by isolated scholars jotting down their observations in their private libraries and studies, by parcels of specimens and books shuttling to and fro around the country from one collector to another, the organization of natural history at this period must have seemed to a contemporary bafflingly ethereal. With next to no societies or periodicals to give at least an appearance of substance to the subject, its devotees might have been forgiven for concluding that no serious work was being done and that no one at all was interested in the data that they went on uncovering. The weight of treasure from those years that we must have lost in consequence—in unpublished notes and records, in naturalists of great potential who, unencouraged, failed to stay the course and left no name— is too unbearable to contemplate

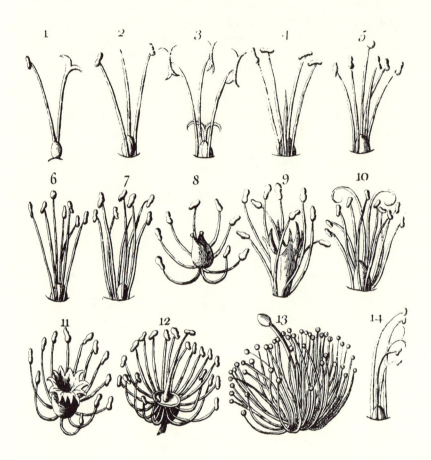

CHAPTER TWO

The Rise to Fashion

ABOUT the very time when natural history as a scientific study was entering upon its temporary period of decadence, a marked rise of interest in the subject began to take place, paradoxically, in the fashionable salons. The two developments, probably, were not unconnected. The general relaxation that overtook society and loosened the New Learning from its hold unleashed as well a major change in mood and attention that was to bring some compensating benefits. As Sense gave way, Sensibility strode in.

People put on easier clothes; gardens became less angular; baroque curled up into rococo. If the deaths of Hooke in 1703 and Ray in 1705 can be viewed as the beginning of the end of an era, just three years after this William Stukeley, sighing over his first ruin, can surely be said to have opened a fresh one. Ten years later Pope was to design the first informal garden and Robert Marsham, of Stratton Strawless in Norfolk, was to start his hobby of tree-planting—the hobby which, in a letter to Gilbert White, he was to refer to as his 'mad string'. By 1728 Batty Langley was braving the world to ask: 'Is there anything more shocking than a stiff regular garden?'; and by 1731 a craze for pseudo-rustic simplicity announced the arrival of the seventy-year reign of the 'Country Look' in dress. Something quite new in history was making its presence known: the collective enjoyment of the scenery of nature for its own sake and in its original, unmodified condition.

An admiration for nature—of a kind—was not new. In the history of Western civilization it can be traced back at least to the fifteenth century and arguably all the way to the Greeks and the Minoans. In ancient China such a high level had been attained in this direction that a system of rules had even been evolved for the proper viewing of scenery as an aid to meditation. A taste for nature, in fact, seems to arise of its own accord at a certain point in the maturing of civilizations. It seems to come whenever men have grown suffciently knowledgeable and secure to free themselves from ancient fears, and are able at last to look at nature with eyes that no longer see it as an invisible, menacing presence lapping all around them and harassing them at every moment of their lives.

But, though admired, nature till now had been treated as essentially an appendage to human handiwork. Where the eighteenth century was to foster natural woods, the seventeenth century had planted artificial groves and even stocked them with artificial birds. Nature had been something for people to point to proudly and remind one another that they had tamed it and turned it to serve their purposes. They enjoyed it only so long as they could be sure it would behave. They were still just a little afraid of its wild streak, and thought it safer to confine or restrict it—to the menagerie, say, or the walled-in garden.

It was the Enlightenment, with its ultimate triumph of dispassion and objectivity, that finally gave them this confidence. By dispelling superstitions and accustoming people to view themselves and their surroundings with detachment, it brought about a fundamental change in attitude. Stripped by science of its outward mysteries, nature gradually assumed a fresh and entirely different mysteriousness, intriguingly elusive and pleasurably unfamiliar in the way in which it teased not just the intellect, but the senses. The long, slow process was beginning in which natural objects were to lose their crude, straightforward power to overwhelm and even terrify, and to gain instead a far more subtle effect, by serving as the reflectors of inner human strivings and intuitions: moving to a less dominating role, becoming controllable and even optional, but by no means losing their ability to appeal and influence.

In this process the eighteenth century was a period of transition. In its earlier years we can watch people playing with nature, treating it like a newly purchased toy. Later, as they become accustomed to the novelty and learn to react with less and less unease, we see their boldness grow. Eventually, as the century ends, we find them helplessly in love with it. These first stirrings of activity represent the gropings of minds still only half-opened, moved more particularly by nature's glints and surface shimmer: the excitement of sudden, eye-stabbing colour, the calming pleasures of perfect forms, the thrill of fluttering wings. Many of its converts, significantly, prove to be professional painters, and especially painters of miniatures: Eleazar Albin, Benjamin Wilkes, Moses Harris—even Dandridge, we find, was a prominent designer. Albin does indeed confess that he owed his first attraction to the study to the brilliance of insects.

It was presumably thanks to this appeal of the exquisite that entomology was able to count among its followers at this time a remarkably high proportion of women. Mrs Eleanor Glanville (of the Glanville Fritillary) is the best known and was certainly one of the first of these, receiving much encouragement from Petiver. Another was Mary Somerset, the first Duchess of Beaufort, the chief patron of Albin and inspirer of his earliest book. It was she who first told Richard Bradley that every species of butterfly and moth has its own special food-plant: 'I believe [she] has bred a greater variety of English Insects, than were ever rightly observ'd by any one Person in Europe', he wrote admiringly in 1721. A volume of drawings of English lepidoptera is still preserved in what was once her library at Badminton. Rather later, in the 1740s, we find the Hon. Mrs Walters mentioned by Wilkes as a breeder of rare moths. Indeed, out of over a hundred persons listed by Wilkes as subscribers to or 'encouragers' of his principal work, women comprise no less than a quarter.

This suggests that flowers were not yet the particular preoccupation of the female sex that they were later to become—and that the study of botany was thus still spared the markedly feminine connotation that has since been its doubtful fate. Certainly, it was not until 1749 that the great botanical artist G. D. Ehret first began to give lessons in flower-painting to the Duchesses of Norfolk and of Leeds and to the daughters of many of the nobility, although he may have had predecessors of whom no record has survived. As far as botany in the more rigorous sense is concerned, the Duchess of Beaufort, again, would appear to have been the principal forerunner. In her gardens at Badminton and Chelsea, helped and advised by the leading botanists of the day (including William Sherard, who for a year or two was tutor to her son), she built up almost unrivalled collections of rare exotic plants, of which she left a large herbarium.

As a collector, however, none could begin to compare either in scale or munificence—if we exclude Sir Hans Sloane—with Lady Margaret Cavendish Bentinck, the wife of the second Duke of Portland, whom she married at the age of twenty in 1734. For the next fifty years most of her time and energies and more than all of her very substantial fortune went to the forming of an immense collection not only in natural history, in all its conceivable branches, but also in realms of the fine arts such as porcelain.

The collection was certainly the largest in Britain, quite possibly the largest in Europe: its eventual sale by auction after her death required thirty-eight days. The museum that contained it was housed in her great mansion at Bulstrode, in Buckinghamshire, in the grounds of which she also kept a botanic garden and a considerable menagerie. So far as the natural history of these islands was concerned, Bulstrode was probably even more important than the British Museum (which arose out of Sloane's great collections and was opened to the public, in a rather grudging manner, only in 1759). Naturalists thronged to inspect it and were always made welcome by the Duchess, a person of abundant charm and kindliness. Many of them, all over the country, were engaged to collect for her—James Bolton, the Halifax naturalist, a typical contributor, was sending lichens from Craven 'in an apartment in one of her Grace's boxes' in 1781—and a small, select few were entrusted with the daunting tasks of cataloguing and arrangement. The chief of these was the Rev. John Lightfoot, an expert botanist who held the near-by living of Uxbridge and whom the Duchess cunningly recruited as her librarian and domestic chaplain. Employed by her to collect as well, Lightfoot was dispatched to relatively remote and little-known areas like the Highlands, which resulted in such incidental, wider benefits as his pioneer work, *Flora Scotica*. Others who were prevailed upon to assist at the museum included Daniel Solander (who was made its official curator in 1779), Richard Pulteney and, to take charge of the insects, Thomas Yeats. Ehret came to paint her plants, the equally fine zoological artist William Lewin to make his superb illustrations of her British birds and eggs. King George III and Queen Charlotte, with their genuine fondness for such things, were among her more frequent visitors.

This supreme example of private patronage, a source of comfort and encouragement to a very wide circle of naturalists at a period when organized, cooperative endeavour hardly existed, was the unintentional outgrowth of a purely private passion fed by a distinctly bowerbird mentality. 'Have got the prettiest fly that ever was seen', she writes in one of her letters. Another time, as she writes about her shells ('. . . *all my beauties*'), we catch her in the act of what seems suspiciously like gloating. But at least she was human, endearing even; and if she did indulge herself more grandly, at least she was franker than most about the weakness that she constantly fell prey to.

The majority of rich collectors, by comparison, had little thought for science. Towards the end of the previous century, a cabinet of natural (and artificial) 'curiosities' had come to be regarded as one of the essential furnishings of every member of the leisured classes with claims to be considered cultivated. When the New Learning and the new, thrusting spirit of inquiry that accompanied it eventually faltered and finally petered out, the motive of science—never, at the best of times, particularly strong—tended to deteriorate into a mindless hoarder's lust and the motive of instructive exhibition into self-aggrandizement. When we read at this time of the rise to influence of the cabinet-naturalist, we must therefore be chary of accepting this as evidence of any very meaningful spread of interest in natural history. The main functions of the wealthy collector were to prime the subject with money and to build up a wide selection of the raw material for later systematists to study. Natural history, in the true sense, gained for the most part only incidentally.

It gained, in effect, in two main ways. First, the very fact that persons of the highest rank—and in France these included numerous courtiers and noblemen—considered such a subject worthy of their notice and a fitting one to allow themselves to be seen engaging in, succeeded in making it immensely respectable. As a result, the collecting of natural objects was pulled on to the stage of Fashion; and natural history became subject to its whim, in a century renowned for fads and crazes, to an extent that has never occurred since. With few social or financial checks to abort or constrict them, fashionable tastes were able to receive their fullest expression. That mysterious force that we term the 'spirit of the age' for once spilled over from the arts in strength and wrought its effects as well in the field of natural history. Subjects came and went in popularity not in any rational sequence, reflecting their relevance or otherwise for science, but seemingly in time with the ebb and flow of major styles in taste. Dr Joan Evans, in her monograph on *Pattern* (1931), has remarked on the faithfulness with which the fashion in France for shell-collecting ('*conchyliomanie*') 'rose and fell with the cognate style of decoration'—that is, the shell-like motif known as *rocaille*, which first began to reveal itself in 1719. An equally telling parallelism occurred in flowers. A marked rise in interest in botany and horticulture can be shown to have coincided with an outbreak of highly naturalistic floral designs on silks, a trend which began in the late 1720s and which originally came from Lyons. Kitty, Duchess of Queensberry, is said to have become famous around this time for a dress so perfectly representative of nature's beauties that it gave her the appearance of a walking botanic garden.

This fashion has been attributed, over-optimistically, to the influence of the early writings of Linnaeus. At that period, however, these were little known—at least in Britain. Even after Linnaeus had paid his famous visit to this country in 1736, we find Dillenius, in writing to the veteran Dr Richard Richardson, having to spell out who he was and why he seemed to merit some attention. 'A new botanist is arisen in the North', he reported prosaically, 'founder of a new method, on the stamens and pistils, whose name is Linnaeus. He is a Swede and has travelled over Lapland.' British botanists on the whole received his new Sexual System of classification without enthusiasm. Ray's *Synopsis* had become their standard handbook—particularly after 1724, with the publication of a third edition completely revised by Dillenius—and the use of the Natural Classification was consequently well entrenched. They were reluctant to abandon a native, well-tried system for a new (and, in truth, rather weird) foreign one. Some of them, even, waxed indignant at the thought. Thomas Knowlton, one-time gardener to James Sherard, was particularly outspoken in his views:

> As for Linnaeus' new method 'tis imposable for him or any other man whatsoever to go beyond a Ray, a Tournefort, etc., who have chose the flower and fruit, which are the princepily parts; as to a single part of the flower it is, in my opinion, altogether whimsicall and ridiculous, separated from the whole composure of them.

There are signs that the taste for botany was in any case well-developed before Linnaeus appeared. Richard Bradley, the leading writer on plant life of his day, turned out no less than twenty-four books and pamphlets on the subject, mostly of a popular nature, in the years 1714–30. After 1720 he was, we now know, writing to salvage himself financially; but the publishers would hardly have taken so much—or pirated his works so liberally—had there not also existed a comfortable market. One later outcome of this, no doubt, was the issue in 1744 of Ray's *Synopsis* translated from Latin into English: an encouraging portent.

From making collections of shells it was a small step to making collections of fossils, which for the most part were the same objects merely puzzlingly aged; and from collecting fossils a small step further to collecting samples of minerals and any other intriguing terrestrial phenomena. As the century opened, the true nature of fossils, as the preserved remains of animals and plants once living—a fact first recognized by the Greeks— was not yet universally accepted. Edward Lhwyd, one of the first to collect them assiduously, the creator of a notable 'lithophylacium' (or cabinet of fossils) at the Ashmolean Museum at Oxford and author in 1699 of the first book exclusively devoted to those of Britain, throughout his life had a largely wrong idea of what they were. Some at least, he supposed, 'are formed in the ground where we find them', and cited stalactites in support of this argument. In the view of Martin Lister, in 1671, they were '*lapides sui generis*', and never were part of an animal, produced by some influence within the rocks themselves. Robert Plot suggested that the earth gave rise to them as ornaments for its hidden parts just as flowers ornament its visible portions. Others supposed that they were the early 'misfires' of the Creator, cast aside in due course when He had learned enough to make the forms of life now extant. More and more, however, beginning with Hooke in *Micrographia* in 1665 (and Christopher Merret in his *Pinax,* quite independently, in the very next year), were coming to believe in their organic nature, a view which was to be general by the middle years of the century. The customary explanation was that they had all been drowned in the Noachian Flood. But Ray, in his travel diary as early as 1671, had refused to accept this belief, having observed, in the course of the previous ten years spent prowling around quarries, that many of the creatures preserved in fossil form were of species now extinct.

Whatever their explanation, by general assent fossils were 'curious' and deserved to be collected. Accordingly, all through the century this work went on, unobtrusively and without any obvious interruption. William Stukeley, a typical collector, recalls in his memoirs that in 1704, while up at Cambridge, he and various of his fellow students of medicine 'used to range about once or twice a week the circumjacent country and search the Gravel and Chalk pits for fossils'. Samuel Dale, at the same time, was engaged in exploring Essex and describing the various new species he encountered. In 1730, in an appendix to *The History and Antiquities of Harwich and Dovercourt,* he was able to furnish an accurate geological section in giving an account of the local cliff.

'Harwich Cliff abounds with several kinds of fossil shells', two collectors later discovered afresh, in 1748, when they 'troiled and also searched the shore' for their present-day equivalents. One of these was Emanuel Mendes Da Costa, a merchant of Portuguese extraction and the owner already of a large and valuable collection of shells, minerals and fossils. With the aim of augmenting this still further, Da Costa had built up by the middle of the century, as his published letters reveal, a wide network of correspondents scattered around the country whom he regularly succeeded in persuading to explore their local quarries and to send him some at least of the spoils from these that resulted. His instructions have an impressive, modern-sounding ring: each fossil was to be carefully wrapped in a separate piece of paper and a note inserted of where it had been found; if the species in question constituted a stratum, the depth of this should also be recorded, and if not, a note made of the stratum in which it lodged. 'I have made vast collections', he was able to boast by 1761; 'but my Collection of Fossils is reckoned equal, if not superior, to any private one in

England.' Two years after this he was able to extricate himself from commerce on successfully landing the post of Clerk to the Royal Society. His good sense then deserted him. After only a brief tenure he was found to have purloined for his own purposes nearly £1,500 of the Society's funds, and for this he was dismissed, tried and sentenced to a five-year term in prison. This was the end, presumably, of his valued correspondence—but not, even so, of his personal zeal for the subject, for even while 'inside' he still somehow managed, it appears, to give several lectures on 'The Fossil Kingdom'.

Da Costa has left us a list of some of the leading collectors in his field who were active around the middle years of the century. That this extends to a considerable number, in addition to his own private force of scavengers, would imply that collecting fossils as a hobby was a good deal more widespread at this period than we have been accustomed to imagine. These 'fossilists' (as they termed themselves) ranged from humble labourers up to men of rank and wealth like Thomas William Jones, whose shells and fossils, sold up with his house in the Strand in 1750, were the earliest Da Costa could remember having been disposed of by private auction—a useful index in itself of the current strength of fashion.

Another interest of these years whose prevalence, likewise, seems to have been underestimated, due to the general obscurity of the private collectors concerned, was the building up of collections of stuffed birds. Moyle, Sloane, Richardson and Dandridge were all exchanging skins—as well as eggs—in the early years of the century, following in the footsteps of the Tradescants, Willoughby, Sir Thomas Browne and doubtless others. Martyn and Blair, both primarily botanists, extended their attentions to birds not long after. Their letters to one another reveal that Martyn began by toying with the idea of boiling his eggs in order to preserve them, 'but now', he reported in 1724, 'I found the meat may be blown out' (the blow-drill was not to be invented till around 1830). Blair, up in Lincolnshire, engaged a professional birdcatcher to secure his specimens—with the aid of nets and a decoy whistle—and after that to stuff and mount them—an art on which the man dearly prided himself. Though asked by 'Noblemen and other curious Gentlemen to put them in a sitting posture', he made it his practice to mount all his birds in a much more realistic manner, raising their wings so that they appeared to be on the point of taking flight. Through Blair he offered to make Martyn's collection 'as curious in a year or two as any in the Island', promising to supply along with his notes on 'which are birds of passage and which are not, where and how they build their nests, the number of eggs, etc., in all which [Blair adds] he seems to have been very inquisitive'.

British collectors and stuffers were backward in their methods compared with the Continent. It was, for example, a schoolmaster in Berlin, J. L.

Frisch, who was responsible for the important innovation of keeping each bird in a separate, tightly closed glass case, thereby excluding harmful pests. His specimens, too, like those of Blair's bird-catcher, were mounted 'nach dem Leben'. At Paris the museum of the Comte de Réaumur, physician, polymath and a leading influence on the natural history of this period (and after whom the Paris Metro has named a station, in answer to Sloane Square), is known to have contained around the middle of the century three rooms filled with birds remarkable not only for the naturalness of their attitudes, but even more for the excellent, lifelike colours retained by their plumage. Unfortunately the preservation method that gave such splendid results was kept the closest secret, to which only a few naturalists were ever to be admitted—and none of them, it seems, collectors in Britain. It must have been quite a scoop, then, for the *Annual Register* for 1763 to be able to announce a 'New Method of Preserving Birds, with their Elegant Plumes, Unhurt'. The author, who sheltered behind a pseudonym, reported that he had tried for some years to hit on a method to give results as excellent as Réaumur's and now at last had succeeded, having lately in this way preserved some scores of birds, 'all of which come as near real life as possible'. His prescription was a mixture of common salt, ground pepper and powdered alum, then two days' hanging, followed by drying in a frame for a month or more. During this final process the specimen was braced up in a natural posture with threads.

The very fact that a publication of such obviously broad appeal should be prepared to devote space to so specialized a matter suggests that a fair number of country gentlemen had begun to collect examples of what they shot and had experience of some of the problems involved. The rising tide of employment that these activities doubtless brought to the stuffers probably did as much as anything to bring about the notable improvements in taxidermy that occurred at this period. These led to the sweeping away of such old and inefficient practices as 'drying' birds by gradual heat in an oven, pickling them in alcohol, or even dipping them in varnish. More pleasing results in mounting encouraged larger and more numerous collections. And more specimens in existence, with their characters more perfectly preserved, meant that descriptions, increasingly, were based on these and not, as so often before, just on published pictures.

The second main way in which the patronage of the wealthy and the fashionable benefited natural history at this period was in supporting the production of sumptuous illustrated works on the subject: the 'coffee-table' books of that display-conscious era. As Knowlton wrote of them, in his usual crusty manner: 'These books are made for pompe, to fill a library, and more for outward show than real use, etc., having very little within.' The first exponent of the genre, at least in Britain (for there were ancestors abroad), seems to have been Eleazar Albin, who began to work as early as

1713 on the plates that were eventually to constitute *A Natural History of English Insects* (1720). The figures in this are poor and the colouring has been described as childlike; nevertheless it must have sold, for it was to run to a fourth edition by 1749, and the author was emboldened to bring out further works on similar lines. In the meantime, in 1728, John Martyn had launched his *Historia Plantarum Rariorum,* illustrations of various plants newly introduced to Chelsea Physic Garden, a series which was to last out for eight years and fifty-two plates before proving financially non-viable. Most of the drawings for this were done by a Dutch artist, Jacobus van Huysum, reflecting the great flower-painting tradition of seventeenth-century Holland of which this new vogue in Britain may be viewed as the partial offspring. It was in the 1720s, too, that the zoologist George Edwards began to find his coloured drawings of animals fetched encouraging prices. After gaining a permanent position, thanks to Sloane's customary influential patronage, as librarian of the Royal College of Physicians in 1733, he was able to start on a four-volume illustrated work, *The History of Birds* (1743–51), which was later continued, for three further volumes, as *Gleanings in Natural History* (1758–64). Edwards had a far better knowledge of birds than Albin and was one of the very few naturalists in Britain at this time to maintain a correspondence with Linnaeus. His advent marks the start of a meatier, more scientific role for such books, which up till then had sold almost entirely on their illustrations.

In 1755 a prosperous merchant in the City and another correspondent of Linnaeus, John Ellis, interestingly chose to publish his learned *Essay towards a Natural History of the Corallines* in this same deceptively lavish format, with fine plates by Ehret. Three years later Moses Harris, a lepidopterist of much experience as well as an artist of considerable talent, started to bring out *The Aurelian; or, Natural History of English Insects,* which combined great beauty with a valuable body of accurate information. And three years after that Thomas Pennant, a North Wales landowner of ample private fortune, encouraged no doubt by the successful reception already accorded to Edwards, issued the first number of *British Zoology*—with its lucid descriptions, essentially the first handbook on the birds of Britain since Willoughby's *Ornithology* of almost a century earlier.

At the same time, as with the collections, so also with these illustrated books: it is dangerous to accept their popularity as a fair measure of the popularity of natural history as a constructive endeavour with pretensions to scientific ends. Equally, we must be wary of pronouncements that seem to tell us what we want to hear, like William Sherard's assertion in a letter to Richardson in 1720, that 'Natural History of all sorts is much in demand'—meaning, probably, only the demand for rare and expensive books on the topic—or the statement in 1746 by the Quaker merchant Peter Collinson, in a letter to Linnaeus, that 'we are very fond of all

branches of Natural History; they sell the best of any books in England'—
which, again, viewed against this insubstantial background, can only be
taken as a judgement made within the narrow terms of reference of a book-
seller or librarian. Nevertheless, the important thing is that these tastes at
least existed, shallow and ephemeral though they often were. Out of the
aimless skills and the casual curiosity a disciplined purpose could at any
time have emerged. All that was needed was a sense of direction, an intellectual compass which could first set them moving and then continue to
guide them on their way.

In the event it was the collections themselves that supplied the missing
impulse; for, as the eighteenth century wore on, they tended to increase so
much in size—and, still more, in variety—that they began to become unmanageable. Britain, France and Holland, each with extensive overseas
possessions and with a large and flourishing maritime trade, had long attracted to themselves most of the unending inflow of pets and ornaments
and keepsakes for ever being brought home by voyagers from distant
lands. As collecting rose to fashion, the knowledge that some objects were
preferred to others and that for these good prices might be paid gradually
spread among seamen and travellers, and encouraged them to return with
something a little less ordinary than the usual chain of cowries, the sticks
of sugar-cane and the occasional talking parrot. Collectors learned to hang
around the docks, making friends with the crews of outgoing vessels and
pressing on them sheets of instructions on how to go about their searches
and, even more important, on how to bring back in the best condition
possible whatever they might succeed in finding.

In these activities no one was more assiduous than Petiver. 'Wherever
you go ashoar, or into the Fields or Woods', runs one of his broadsheets,
'carry with you the Collecting-book (to gather the samples or specimens
in, which you must shift into this book the same day, or within two or
three at farthest after you have gathered them).' For a ship's surgeon about
to sail for foreign parts in August 1696 he listed—in his usual peremptory
language:

. . . The following Things to be taken with you when you go abroad,
viz.

Collecting books etc.
A Quire or two of Brown Paper
A Flagg Baskett
Two or 3 Cloath or Linnen Baggs for Shells
Several wide mouth'd Vialls or Glasses

A box for Insects
A Pincushion and Pins
Brandy or spirits for preserving fleshy worms, etc.

Almost everyone who was known to be going overseas, especially anyone with some claim to education, was liable to be pestered by Petiver's entreaties. A person of immense, almost inhuman industry, his hunger for new material was apparently insatiable. Specimens poured in on him from all around the globe; yet their very number and variety only served, it seemed, to drive him on to still more furious efforts. The result was entirely predictable: the sheer extent and bulk of these endless acquisitions in the end overwhelmed and swamped him, and the quality of all he begged, bought or otherwise procured—never at the best of times his strong point—became eventually lost to sight beneath the urge for quantity.

In his final years, in 1710, a wealthy German savant, Zacharias von Uffenbach, paid a complimentary call on him in London and came away profoundly disillusioned: 'We expected to see a paragon of learning and refinement,' he protested in his journal:

> but he was quite deficient in both. For he appeared to be wretched both in looks and actions and he had no parts, speaking very poor and deficient Latin and scarce able to string a few words together . . . As soon as he gets any object of the least value he immediately has printed a short and insipid description of it, dedicating it to any person with whom he has some slight acquaintance; and then he takes a present for it. Everything is kept in true English fashion in prodigious confusion in one wretched cabinet and in boxes . . . He offers all foreigners who come to him a sample of his collection; but he takes care to ask a vast sum for it, so I declined with thanks . . . They say that he has the charge of the physic garden of the apothecaries but treats it right scurvily, allowing no plants to multiply but either sticking them into his books or sending them away in exchange for others.

This, surely, was over-harsh. Petiver was mercenary, admittedly, indiscriminate in what he took and careless in how he kept it; but at least he hummed away like a dynamo and gave the natural history of that age a stimulating background of never-resting energy. And many others, too, were no doubt moved by his example, even if their grasp was less wide-ranging and their activities a good deal more restrained. He may have over-played his role, but it was a role that needed to be played at that particular moment.

Amassing the material was simple, however, compared with the problems of processing it to serve the needs of science. Names were cumbrous for the most part, usually consisting of a long string of Latin words which attempted to epitomize the features of the species, and difficult to memorize in consequence; and as it was still far from easy for naturalists of differ-

ent countries to keep in touch with one another and to exchange specimens and books, it repeatedly happened that the same species had
different names bestowed on them by different authorities. To add to the
chaos, hardly any two persons observed the same system of classification.
Inventing systems, indeed, might be said to have been one of the century's
fashionable amusements: it appealed to that liking for formal elegance and
order that expressed itself in the arts in the taste for Palladian architecture
or for the music of Bach and Mozart; it also reflected a weakness for the
grandiose and a sublime belief in the attainability of perfection. That patterns existed in nature was clear to anyone with the patience to look at all
closely: how these related to each other, within some wider, all-embracing
plan, was altogether more arguable. Possible solutions were proffered in
plenty—as Thomas Martyn was moved to complain to Pulteney, 'the
system-madness' was truly 'epidemical'. Most systems had something to
recommend them: the trouble was that none of them had quite enough.

The search for some scheme, if only to allay this rationalist daemon,
found its fullest expression in France. In 1732 there appeared in that country a massive, nine-volume work entitled *Le Spectacle de la nature,* in which
the doctrine of natural theology (already expoumded by Ray, some forty
years before, in *The Wisdom of God Manifested in the Works of the Creation*)
was set forth in the form of a conversation between a count, a countess, a
prior and a knight. The author was the Abbé Pluche. The reasoning was
shallow, the illustrations poor, but the style readable and lively. It was to
become natural history's first bestseller, passing into eighteen editions and
into translations in several languages—an English version appearing, as
Nature Displayed, in 1736–7—and was credited, some twenty years afterwards, with having been the greatest single factor behind the rush of interest in the subject that took place in France about that time. The literary
public, evidently, in so far as it wanted books on nature, wanted big books
which looked as if they embodied big ideas. It wanted works that would
sweep it off its feet, lifting it up from the humdrum realm of minor detail
on to an altogether more exalted plane of wonder.

Such a work it was to find, in 1749, in the first number of the great
Histoire naturelle of Georges-Louis Leclerc, later to be ennobled as Comte
de Buffon. This monumental creation, which ran to forty-four volumes
and took in all fifty-five years to complete (with the aid of several eminent
naturalists), was conceived as a description, in the finest possible literary
style, of the entire world of nature known at that time. Dressed in full
Court costume, complete with orders, Buffon toiled at the task without
respite for eight hours a day for forty years. It was an immense success
from the first, the initial printing selling out in six weeks. The whole of
Paris Society read it—or, just as important, claimed to have read it—and
for a time at least natural history overtook all others as the principal topic

of intelligent discussion. The work appealed by reason of its scope and style: its impact as a work of science was, by comparison, minor. The public, in the words of William Swainson, 'gathered the flowers, without probing for the honey'. It was the grandeur they were after, not the detailed information.

When, within a decade, much of the world was converted to Linnaeus, the French stayed faithful to Buffon. There was room in their pantheon for only a single master-mind of nature. They had no head, besides, for the plodding empiricism of the Swedes, the Dutch or the English. In their approach to natural history they put entrancement before utility: Buffon wrote like a dramatist; Linnaeus, for all the efficiency of his method, like some icy, impersonal machine.

The Linnaean System, in short, did not sweep in like some irresistible force: it penetrated faster in some countries than in others, and fastest of all in those that chanced to have an ideological vacuum. The British, as we have seen, clung as long as they could, like the French, to their own native hero—in their case John Ray. Even as late as 1766, during his famous sojourn in this country, the handbook that Jean-Jacques Rousseau had to guide him in his plant-hunting was a copy of Ray's *Synopsis*.

Britain began to turn to Linnaeus only after the final establishment of binomials—names of two words only (the name of the genus followed by just one solitary word to designate the species) being the one arguable improvement that Linnaeus could offer over Ray and over every other predecessor. This crucial innovation, so obvious and simple in retrospect, appears to have had its origin in Linnaeus' efforts, in preparing the *Hortus Cliffortianus* of 1737, to devise a more convenient method of citing references to books. Gradually, in a steady series of publications, he introduced a comparable system for referring briefly yet precisely to different kinds of animals and plants, inventing and putting into currency more and more standardized, one-word abbreviations of the Latin names of the species. This had the double advantage of saving space, in an age when printing costs were frequently prohibitive, and of making the names far simpler to remember. For many years, however, he failed to make use of binomials consistently, for every single species; and in the case of animals, in which his name-making—and his personal interest—lagged behind that in plants, he was anticipated by just one year by the Frenchman, Michel Adanson.

In the same way, his so-called Sexual System, a method of classifying the plant kingdom according to the number of male and female organs and the way in which they are arranged inside a flower, had a closely related forerunner in a system devised by the French botanist Tournefort. The unique achievement of the Swede lay in linking the simplicity of binomials to one classificatory scheme in particular which, if not ideal, could be shown at least to function adequately. To help in securing their adoption he was able to wield, furthermore, an admirable flair for precise description, an overwhelming productivity and a passionate belief in his own correctness, which combined over the years to wear down most of the doubters and resisters. There can be little doubt, besides, that the very possession of such a system, complete unto itself, conferred on those who subscribed to it a great tonic confidence which many came to misinterpret as intellectual infallibility. There rallied to Linnaeus, in consequence, an ardent train of disciples who sought a cause to champion and felt impelled to treat his works like holy writ; and by the sheer intensity of their fervour his methods won support to an extent which their merely scientific quality can hardly have justified.

Even so, it was as well that Linnaeus and his followers persevered; for what was needed then most urgently of all was one single filing-scheme that was easily comprehended and capable of commanding universal acceptance. Linnaeus himself conceded that it took too little account of the palpably close relationships between certain families and others, but he felt convinced that his primary task must be to reduce to manageable order the ever more bewildering diversity of nature then being steadily disclosed. Any method which, for the moment at any rate, proved both simple and workable seemed to be thoroughly deserving of a welcome. A move closer to Utopia could be left till sometime in the future, when the flood of undescribed material at last subsided and science needed no longer to concern itself with the mere threat of being overwhelmed. And indeed, while, in theory, the dominance of a system so entirely artificial must be regarded as retrograde, nevertheless, in practice, it did permit a unified concentration of effort and enabled the foundations to be laid for the outburst of systematic work that underlay all the Evolutionary enlightenment yet to come. More important still, by its very simplicity it brought an intellectual approach to natural history once again into fashion, and in so doing brought into being a wide public that felt it could keep abreast of science in this one area at least and was to persist in this belief until the rise of professional biology rather more than a hundred years later.

Undoubtedly, it was open to a native genius in this country to have grafted the advantageous use of binomials on to the stem of the traditional Natural System. But, possibly because of the general stagnation in learning at this time, no such candidate came forward. The British, accordingly, gradually began to adapt their thinking and their writing to the novel Linnaean methods, following upon the publication of the *Species Plantarum* in 1753. This was the key work which finally introduced the consistent use of binomial names, without supporting reference numbers, for seed-bearing plants—in the same way that, five years later, the tenth edition of the *Systema Naturae* introduced them for animals, making these two works the official starting-points for botanical and zoological nomenclature.

The first occasion on which the British public learned of the merits of this great work was in December 1754, in a long review in the *Gentleman's Magazine,* in which Sir William Watson lauded it as 'the masterpiece of the most compleat naturalist the world has seen'. The real process of conversion did not begin till some five years later. According to James Edward Smith (who can surely be relied on, for he must have studied these developments with the eye of a closely interested party), it was Richard Pulteney's *A General View of the Writings of Linnaeus* that 'contributed more than any other work, except perhaps the *Tracts* of Stillingfleet, to diffuse a taste for Linnaean knowledge in this country'. The work of Stillingfleet referred to appeared in 1759, and it was largely through his enthusiasm that his friend and neighbour, the London apothecary William Hudson, was induced to cast in a fully Linnaean mould his new and important handbook, the *Flora Anglica* of 1762. Another well-timed and influential work was James Lee's *Introduction to Botany* (1760), essentially a translation of the *Philosophia Botanica* of Linnaeus. In 1763 the Professors of Botany at both Cambridge and Edinburgh (respectively, Thomas Martyn and John Hope) started to give lectures on the System. In 1766 Daniel Solander, an ex-pupil of Linnaeus who had come to this country at the instance of John Ellis and Peter Collinson and thereafter worked as an assistant to Banks, spread the gospel to palaeontology in his text for Gustavus Brander's *Fossilia Hantoniensia,* a work on the Tertiary mollusca of Hampshire. And in 1769 the first volume of John Berkenhout's *Outlines of the Natural History of Great Britain and Ireland* signalled the arrival of Linnaeus in British entomology—though it was only with the publication of *The English Lepidoptera* by Moses Harris six years later that his methods can be said to have become permanently incorporated into the literature.

An immediate accompaniment of this outburst of publicity was a marked leap in interest in natural history, manifested in a great variety of ways. The automatic assumption is that these were wholly cause and effect. But while much of the lift in popularity at this point was specifically Linnaean in inspiration, it is hard to tell the real size of this for the reason that a strong revival of activity, seemingly quite independent in its origins, was under way in this country already.

―――――――

This revival was evident in a number of entirely separate quarters. One of them, extraordinarily, was at the very topmost level in the land: the accession of George III in 1760 had among its many effects the minor and rather freakish one of placing at the nation's head, for the brief space of just two and a half years, a trio of enthusiastic botanists. These were the Queen herself, whose interest in the science was certainly real enough to lead the King to buy her Lightfoot's herbarium as a present; the King's mother, the Princess Augusta, whose hobby of raising plants was to lay the foundations for what is now the Royal Botanic Gardens, Kew; and, keenest of all, the Earl of Bute, the King's chief minister, unquestioned idol and closest friend. Bute's interest in botany dated from his earlier days on his Scottish estate and extended to field-work round London, to collecting together a herbarium and a very large library of botanical books and paintings of plants, and to financing the printing of a massive new system of classification intended as a rival to that of Linnaeus—on the last of which he allegedly lavished the absurd sum of £12,000.

The King and Bute, for years, had had to endure a frustrating political impotence. Their arrival at last in power brought to the surface their long-nursed resentment of the late Court and its governments, and sent them brimming over with offices and favours for their own special cluster of friends and hangers-on, many of them disaffected ex-supporters of the outgoing régime. One of those to benefit as a result, in return for botanical services to Bute, was the versatile and much-maligned John Hill, who promptly found himself Master-Gardener at Kensington Palace (at what was reputed to be a lavish salary). A protégé of Hill's, a nurseryman of scant experience named William Young, in turn had bestowed on him the office of Queen's Botanist—in which capacity he was to succeed in doing serious injury to the scientific exploration of North America, by effectively depriving his compatriot, William Bartram, of crucial letters of introduction to the governors of Florida. Doubtless there were others, yet to be uncovered and no less obscure up till then in the world of natural history, who owed to this purely political upheaval a temporary ascent to influence and notice.

Almost simultaneously a small-scale reawakening of interest was taking place at Cambridge. This appears to have come about merely from the chance presence there at that time of a larger-than-usual number of undergraduates and others with a common thirst for natural history, and to have owed little or nothing to the University officially. The pacesetter was a young mathematician, Israel Lyons, who having taken up botany in 1755 was soon seized by the challenge of finding and adding to the localities for the rarer plants recorded by Ray in his early Flora of the area. The challenge was infectious, and a distinct circle of fellow recorders presently emerged. One of these was Thomas Martyn, the son of the errant holder of the Chair and himself by this time an experienced field botanist. The year which now saw him succeed his father, 1762, also witnessed another long-overdue Cambridge event: the opening of a new and enlarged University Botanic Garden. Most appropriately, the person appointed to run this was the son of John Martyn's old ally, Philip Miller, the eminent Gardener to the Apothecaries at Chelsea. Among the first of the Garden's regular visitors was the timid Thomas Gray, now well launched on his career as a poet but lately repossessed by his old schoolboy passion for collecting butterflies and moths. The new superintendent befriended him, and the two quickly found their way into the now fast expanding local circle.

At much the same time another small group, even more certainly pre-Linnaean in its origins, was to be found not far away, over at Norwich. Most of the members of this were men in humble life, employed in particular as weavers and tailors, and true to a tradition for long stubbornly and mysteriously characteristic of the followers of those trades they 'amused themselves in herborizing in the country' and did the best they could to identify what they found from the quaint and antique plates of old herbals that had lingered on in their possession. According to James Edward Smith, to whom we owe our knowledge of their existence, their activities crystallized at length into a definite society, 'founded many years ago' and still in being at the time when he wrote, in 1804. Back in the 1760s, Smith recorded, these long-undisturbed ways received a sudden jolt: a rush of newcomers swept in, their interest in the subject undisguisedly the product of the much-publicized Linnaean methods. In this corner of the country the latter were thus the cause of a kind of fault in the layering of tradition, an obviously unrelated stratum being abruptly superimposed on the ones that previously existed.

This pattern at Norwich was probably repeated, to a greater or lesser extent, over much of Britain. The Linnaean current merely added speed of flow and strength of direction to a tide that was running fairly strongly already in favour of natural history. Without some pre-existing influence it is otherwise hard to see how a journal like the *Critical Review* could have dared to proclaim so boldly, as early as 1763, that 'Natural History is now, by a kind of national establishment, become the favourite study of the time'.

The confluence of the two strong streams quickly restored some life to the desert of organized natural history. The first fresh growth appeared around 1762, with the resurrection (though only in name) of the Aurelian Society by Moses Harris. The records of this second society of London entomologists, like those of its predecessor, have not survived; we merely know that Harris acted as its secretary and that its members included Dru Drury, the wealthy silversmith in the Strand who acted as his patron and sometimes accompanied him on moth-collecting forays. It lasted, we are told, only some four years in all, before it was ruined by dissension among the members. At much the same time a 'society of literary and scientific men', without any formal title, was meeting weekly at a certain coffee house in Soho; its chairman about 1765 was John Hunter, the famous anatomist; Banks, Solander, Captain Cook and Dr George Fordyce, a leading medical lecturer of the day, are known to have been among the members. By the 1770s a small natural history society is said to have been established at Eccles, in Lancashire; early in 1782 James Edward Smith, while a medical student at Edinburgh, pulled together a handful of his friends into a 'Society for the Investigation of Natural History' (later, less vaguely, the Natural History Society of Edinburgh), which held meetings every Friday evening in the University museum—and gave Smith an early start in ceremony by electing him as its first president; and for some years around 1785 Erasmus Darwin and certain of his neighbours were entitling themselves the 'Botanical Society of Lichfield'. This last-mentioned body has secured its own small niche in history by virtue of its sponsorship of Darwin's brilliant poem expounding Linnaeus' sexual system, in which the stamens were designated 'husbands' and the styles 'wives', resulting in such felicities as 'Husbands live with their wives in the same house, but have different beds' (the definition of monoecious plants).

In October 1782, while Smith was busy with his society up at Edinburgh, a rather more substantial body, the Society for Promoting Natural History, was founded at 'Mr Dean's, the Corner house by the Turnpike, Pimlico' by, among others, William Forsyth (after whom *Forsythia* is named). Forsyth was Philip Miller's successor at the Physic Garden at Chelsea, so this is yet one more achievement to be credited to the Apothecaries. This society limped along, rather ineffectually, for as long as forty years before finally being displaced by its own offspring, the august and still flourishing Linnean Society of London.

The Linnean Society was the brainchild principally of Smith, who (along with others) had quickly grown dissatisfied with the poor way in which the Society for Promoting Natural History was conducting its affairs. More particularly Smith was in search of a lustrous corporate surround with which to highlight the attractions of the large and very valuable collections, manuscripts and books of the great Linnaeus, which he had managed to purchase, while still a student, and currently had in storage down in Chelsea. The Society was conceived in all but fact in 1785–6, but for personal reasons Smith had to delay the formal proclamation till February 1788, when seven founding Fellows met together for the purpose at a coffee house by Smith's home in Great Marlborough Street. The Linnean Society is thus the oldest body in the country exclusively devoted to natural history with an uninterrupted existence—just as its *Transactions,* first published in 1791, constitute our oldest purely natural history periodical.

From the first, Smith seems to have treated the Society as very much his private fief, and candidates for Fellowship of whom he happened to disapprove were liable to be blackballed (one such victim being poor J. E. Gray, an emment all-rounder on the staff of the British Museum, who was alleged to have sinned unforgivably on one occasion by missing out Smith's name in referring to 'Sowerby's *English Botany*'). Those honoured by being admitted were expected to observe the full Linnaean creed, down to the last capital and hyphenated epithet; to revere Smith as the chosen apostolic successor, as the defender of the one true tradition no less than as the guardian of the sacred relics. Linnaeus had left behind a legend: Smith and his admirers turned it into a contemporary intellectual bludgeon. And for all the pious utterances about their unique and indispensable character, Smith was deplorably high-handed in the way he treated the collections themselves. Some of the shells (at least) were given away as presents, all the minerals were disposed of by auction, many more of the original specimens disappeared mysteriously while in his possession. He further impaired their usefulness for study by mixing in with the types more recent material of diverse provenance. When, in 1796, he married and departed from London to live in Norwich, he took the entire collections with him and—as if to emphasize his disregard for the Society—persisted in continuing as president, even though he deigned to turn up at less than a quarter of its meetings.

For over thirty years the Society was condemned to stagger on, headless and all but bodyless, until Smith's death in 1828 finally released the collections for purchase—and the cost of these, by a heavy irony, thereupon almost crippled it and proved enfeebling for many years to follow. Smith's true memorials are his *English Flora* and his text for the much-admired *English Botany*. He provided the Linnean Society with a crucial *raison d'etre*, without which such a body might never have materialized; and, in so doing, he provided natural history as a whole with a central platform of respect and a formal medium, at long last, for the regular publishing of scientific discoveries (although, as George Montagu was heard to grumble, it could take at times four years or even more to get into print in its *Transactions*). But it was little thanks to Smith that the Society survived. That it did in the end succeed in prospering was mainly due to Thomas Bell, a dental surgeon and leading zoologist who became its president in 1853, five years before the move to its present home in Burlington House.

A Scottish counterpart of the Linnean Society, the Wernerian Society of Edinburgh, came into being some twenty years later, in 1808. Its founder, Robert Jameson, the new Professor of Natural History in the University, had recently returned from studying under Werner, the great German mineralogist; though his sympathies were wide, his prime interest was undeniably geology, and for the first few years at least the Society tended to be overweighted by ponderous speculations about the earth and its origins.

Like Smith, Jameson was the president from the start and stayed in office till the very end though in this case the end was not his death but the demise of the Society itself, after some fifty years, and its absorption partly by the Royal Physical Society of Edinburgh and partly by the Botanical Society of Edinburgh (both of which, happily, still continue).

Along with this restoration to the scene of active societies there occurred a remarkable efflorescence in the literature. The 1780s, in particular, were outstanding in this respect. Foremost among the numerous works that issued in those years was William Withering's *Botanical Arrangement,* a deliberately 'popular' manual which was written—at long last—in English. This became the standard text on British plants for at least a generation, passing through three editions in the author's lifetime and several more following his death. Withering, a successful Birmingham physician, is much written about today as the first expositor of the value of digitalis for treating diseases of the heart; he also deserves to be remembered, however, as the pioneer of the non-specialist guide (by no means a simple art) and as the first person in print to introduce the great majority of British botanists to the value of the screw-down plant-press and the tin vasculum.

The publication in English of works that till now had traditionally appeared in Latin implies an extensive new readership among people without any formal academic background. Many of these, undoubtedly, were women. Withering, for one, was well aware that these would constitute no small proportion of his readers:

> From an apprehension that botany in an English dress would become a favourite amusement with the ladies [he wrote in his preface], many of whom are very considerable proficients in the study in spite of every difficulty, it was thought proper to drop the sexual distinctions in the titles to the Classes and Orders.

The price of popularity for Linnaeus was thus not an unfamiliar one: to have his works purged of much of their essential content on account of their potential power to embarrass. The bugbear that was to complicate life for the Victorians so much was evidently just emerging: the female reader as a being set apart, that Perfect Lady to whom nature could be issued only under censorship, lest in the course of admiring its sweet and gentle beauties she should also happen to catch a sight of its raw and bloody underside. A work with the ominous title *The Young Lady's Introduction to Natural History* had made its appearance already in 1766 (the *Critical Review* went so far as to suggest that 'even grown gentlemen may profit by the perusal of it'). Not long afterwards the prevalent feminine interest began to be hymned in gushing dedications: the Rev. Charles Abbot offered up his *Flora Bedfordiensis* 'To the Fair Daughters of Albion', the Rev. Thomas Martyn his translation of Rousseau's *Lettres elementaires sur la Botanique* . . . 'To the Ladies of Great Britain; no less eminent for their elegant and useful accomplishments, than admired for the beauty of their persons'.

When we read lines like these, it is not always easy to remember that at the very time their gallant authors were penning them, regiments of very different-sounding women were meeting and displaying intellectual talents of what must have seemed by comparison a quite unnerving competence. Natural history probably owes a great deal more than it realizes to the famous drawing-room hostesses of that period, Mrs Vesey, Mrs Ord, Mrs Montagu and Mrs Boscawen, who about 1750 headed a revolt against the manners of their day by instituting parties—'petticoteries' Horace Walpole dubbed them—at which talking was to be the sole occupation and the tedium of the card-tables forgotten. At these 'conversations', or *conversazioni,* informal gatherings of up to several hundred, men and women met together, either for breakfast or at evening receptions at which tea and cakes, or coffee, lemonade and biscuits, were dispensed as refreshment. The one and only qualification required of those invited was the ability to talk intelligently, a qualification which for once applied equally to either sex—for the main, if unstated, purpose of these functions was to enable clever women to exercise the brains for which the conventions of the day refused to give them credit. Such women made learning fashionable for the hitherto unlearned sex; and it is pleasant to recall that the name 'bluestocking', which was hurled at them and stuck, derived from the eccentric garb in which one of their most prominent friends, Benjamin Stillingfleet, regularly came to the parties to discourse (we may presume) on botany and explain to them the delightful parlour-game lately invented by Linnaeus.

Leading naturalists, we may be sure, were favourite 'captures' at these gatherings; for the hostesses can hardly have helped but view themselves as at least the counterparts of those Parisiennes who currently lionized Buffon. The genial Solander, certainly, frequently showed his face. Pulteney, we know, was a guest at Mrs Montagu's in 1764, for it was there that the Earl of Bath acclaimed him as a kinsman and appointed him—abortively, alas—as his domestic physician. The Duchess of Portland, that queenly collector, was a regular attender; so, too, was Mrs Delany, who shared her home and hobbies; and likewise Hester Chapone, who exchanged poems with Gilbert White and often stayed at Selborne. Although the talk passed largely unrecorded, these names alone are assurance that natural history was not neglected as a topic.

This, finally, was the world—busy, excited, energetic, moderately crowded, more and more organized, by no means without sophistication—into which was born, in 1788, just a few months after the founding of the Linnean Society and just a few months before the fall of the Bastille, *The*

Natural History and Antiquities of Selborne, the one literary classic, universally acknowledged, that the subject in all its years of existence has so far managed to produce and (apart from *The Origin of Species*) its one native sacred text.

Superficially unattractive, a mere volume of letters, the book was slow in achieving popularity. The Rev. Leonard Jenyns recalled that when he went up to Eton about 1815, he came across a copy on the shelf of a friend: 'a book I had never seen before nor even heard of', and he was so delighted with it that he copied most of it out and learnt much of it by heart. Edward Newman, on the other hand, born in 1801 of Quaker parents who, like so many others of that sect, were both keen naturalists, claimed to have been brought up on *Selborne,* which was the favourite book of his whole family. Charles Darwin, too, was fired by it when a boy at school around the year 1820. But it was only with the publication of Sir William Jardine's edition of 1827 that the real vogue for the book seems to have started and its literary merits to have become widely appreciated.

It is difficult to account for this. One possible explanation is that the style of the writing was too Augustan to appeal immediately to a public accustomed to a diet of Romanticism. It was not till the late 1820s that a new, no-nonsense, mainly middle-class audience eventually emerged, able to discern the one great quality in White that has helped to bring his book such permanent renown: his gift of empathy, his ability to infuse deep feeling into what he described and recorded so carefully and soberly. He was perhaps the first writer on natural history in Britain to display this much more modern gift, and for that reason alone *Selborne* is of special historical significance. White's preference for patient observation, in an age when most people stopped merely to collect, is, similarly, far in advance of its time. But over and above even these there still remains that one ingredient without which no work attains the status of an irresistible classic: somehow, it enshrines a portion of our necessary collective mythology. Lowell came very close to the truth in calling *Selborne* 'the journal of Adam in Paradise'. For it is, surely, the testament of Static Man: at peace with the world and with himself, content with deepening his knowledge of his one small corner of the earth, a being suspended in a perfect mental balance. Selborne is the secret, private parish inside each one of us. We must be thankful it was revealed so very early—and with such seemingly unstudied simplicity and grace.

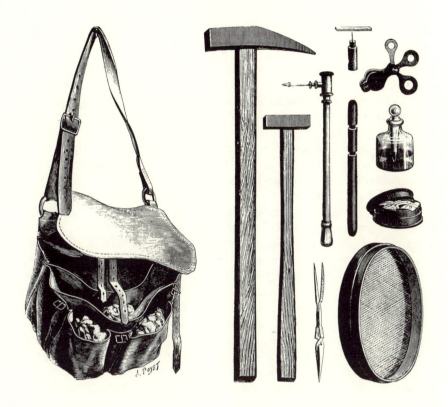

CHAPTER THREE

Wonders of the Past

The Natural History of Selborne must also be viewed within the wider context of its time. If there were few as yet willing or able to look at nature with the extraordinary maturity of Gilbert White, there were many gradually awakening to the attractions of natural scenery—if not always to the details which largely concern the naturalist—and learning to respond with steadily increasing assurance. The playful rusticity of the 1730s was turning into something much deeper and at the same time more ecstatically pleasurable and more disturbing. These emotions were finding their expression in the arts and, in keeping with the fondness for system of that age, giving rise to new and complex formulas of taste. Wealthy noblemen, returning from the Grand Tour with their standard quota of Italian masters, began to discover a preference for one or two artists in particular, Claude and Poussin and Salvator Rosa, who had chosen to paint scenes of nature: landscapes of the Roman Campagna, in which for once human figures, if present at all, were subordinate. From this the notion took hold that natural scenery too, if looked at according to certain simple rules, if arranged and composed in the mind's eye just as in a painting, could be relied on to induce a mood of gentle, pleasing melancholy. Nature, by this new criterion, was most admirable when most amenable to imitation by art, when most 'picturesque'—a term already used for several years by the time William Gilpin's essay *Upon Prints* in 1768 finally brought the principles of landscape analysis into general notice. Gardens, traditional testing-grounds for such ideas and already under pressure from the mounting tide of informality, now succumbed wholesale and fell prey one by one to 'Capability' Brown and the professional improvers. Trees were carefully grouped for effect, vast rockeries constructed, lakes filled in, anything that failed to conform with the painterly canons ruthlessly altered or eliminated. And tours, the preserve of earnest fact-finders, like Pennant, since before 1740, now became tours in search of 'views': little fragments of rural beauty, contemplated from behind, maybe, through a 'Claude-glass' or painted down in words after the manner of Bernardin de Saint-Pierre's *Études*.

This discovery of the Picturesque, we can now see, was the essential preliminary to that far wider, and subsequently far more profound, reformation in taste that we term the Romantic Movement. It represents the quiet exordium, the gentle *avant-propos,* even as the wilder outpourings of, say, the 1830s—to which some would restrict the term 'Romantic'—represent merely the over-inflated peroration. In so far as it reflects a very gradual restructuring of the mind, bringing about an entirely altered attitude to nature, the whole period forms a single continuum. In these early years the imagination was still being unharnessed, Reason still being renounced. These are the years of the cult of shallow Sentiment, of a lapsing into vagueness so enchantingly personified by Jean-Jacques Rousseau himself, the master of these ceremonies. Rousseau's extreme short-sight was such that at the best of times he saw the landscape only as a blur, while his wife, in similar fashion, never knew which day of the week it was and never even learned to tell the time.

By reason of its very character, involving a change in perception of the world all around, an interest in nature was a prime ingredient in the Romantic outlook. Never before or since has natural history been so much to the forefront in general aesthetic advance. (And never before or since, it might be added, has the average naturalist been someone of such all-round cultivated distinction.) It may well be that the quickening of interest in the subject that coincided with the acceptance of the Linnaean System in this country helped to bring on the new Romantic movement faster than might otherwise have happened. Certainly, it is noticeable how many of those who played a key role in propagating the new tastes and philosophy, particularly in the formative early stages, were also practising naturalists. Rousseau's lasting fondness for field botany is comparatively well-known, and it was from the precise study of natural forms that Goethe derived that notion of a certain ordered arrangement running through all living things that so profoundly influenced the thought of his contemporaries. Thomas Gray, another threshold Romantic, whose famous *Elegy* was published in 1751, had been accustomed since boyhood to hunting butterflies and plants. These were only the first of many for whom the study of nature as a science and the study of nature as an aesthetic exercise were to seem inseparable and remain subtly interfused.

The results of this for natural history were not altogether happy. In a few, rare cases the power of observation, and even more the later recording, remained as unclouded and undistorted as it did for Gilbert White. Far more often the eye misted over, the pen trembled, Sense gave out as Sensibility came in. The accepted approach to nature had become no longer to set down what one saw plainly and accurately; the aim now was to record one's reactions—and the livelier these reactions appeared, the more beneficial, the more exalting, the more 'tasteful' the contact with nature was assumed to have been.

By about the time of the French Revolution the Romantic Movement had worn its way down to a deeper, more elemental level. Rousseau, in his admiration of scenery, had looked enthusiastically at mountainsides but had rarely, if ever, extended his gaze above the treeline. In this new phase the ultimate, avoided part of nature was now to be examined. The cultivated mind had come to terms with the tamer enchantments of the countryside: it now had to confront the portion that still remained—that part 'below the threshold', which went by the name of the Sublime. With this, the dimensions changed. The primitive core of the earth had emerged into vision: the troubling Id of nature, with its wild, uncertain tempers and in all its boundlessness of space and time. With the Sublime, Romanticism finally struck rock: stark, rugged peaks and the bare floor beneath the valley-bottoms, the age-old realm filled with dark mystery, desolate, unexplored, and 'horrid'. And with this, natural history began to turn its main attention to the lately christened science of geology.

While Da Costa and his contemporaries, in the middle years of the century, were forming their great collections of minerals and fossils, at least two other individuals were active whose curiosity led them into making more careful, more properly scientific investigations. These two must rank among Britain's first genuine field geologists—as opposed to mere searchers for specimens.

The first, James Hutton, a man of powerful intellect, trained in turn for the law and for medicine, had inherited a farm in Berwickshire and, with his scientific mind, had seen fit to go south and take up residence in Norfolk for a time in order to learn the latest improvements in agriculture. While there, in 1752–4, he made numerous journeys on foot into various parts of England, studying the make-up of the surface deposits. In one of his letters he relates how he made a point at this time of peering inquiringly into every pit, every ditch and every river-bed that he chanced to come across. About 1768 he retired from farming and from his other business interests and gave himself full-time to a more congenial life of the intellect in the stimulating atmosphere of Edinburgh. Here, after thirty years of continuous reflection resting on a basis of rigorous field-work, he laid before the scientific world in 1785 his classic *Theory of the Earth*.

In this, laying stress, in a thoroughly modern manner, only on what was 'observable' (one of his favourite words), he propounded the doctrine of 'actualism'—or, as it came to be better known, 'uniformitarianism'—maintaining that all the changes that had taken place throughout the whole history of the earth were most readily to be explained in terms of the 'actual' processes occurring all around us every day. These processes—denudation, transportation, deposition, consolidation, folding, uplift—he saw as ordered in one vast cycle of ever-continuing change. In consequence, the time-scale of the world extended so immeasurably as to appear almost without limit. In the light of all he had perceived, he was driven to confess, he could detect 'no vestige of a beginning, no prospect of an end'.

It was a conclusion both heretical and (unwittingly, no doubt) redolent with Romantic allure. Dimly foreseen already by bold thinkers like da Vinci and Buffon, and later to be re-stated, in far more compelling terms, by Lyell, it brought to the surface a haunting awareness of unbounded time, a sense of breathtaking scale, a fatalistic mood of being but an instant in the slow, majestic unfolding of Creation's inexorable plan. Long, gloomy corridors seemed to open out, reaching back into eternity, echoing with bestial cries. The terrible other face of nature, the brutal truth that lurked behind the sentimental mask, was painfully laid bare by geology. And out from beneath it, gradually emerging into view, loomed a raw and far more harsh reality: a nether world of awesome precipices, of bottomless swamps, of terrible scaly reptiles floundering around in stygian gloom. The 'struggle for existence', that bleakest of concepts, was to be taken by Darwin not, as so many have supposed, from the pages of Malthus, but from those of a geologist—Lyell.

But the learned world, at first, was largely deaf to Hutton. Unhappily, his style was obscure and not immediately appealing. Few read the two weighty volumes that finally appeared in 1795, only two years before his death; and those who did read or listen were tempted to revile him as a voicer of dangerous thoughts, a free-thinker. It was left to John Playfair, Professor of Mathematics in the University of Edinburgh, to interpret his views in 1802 in prose that has rarely been surpassed, in his *Illustrations of the Huttonian Theory of the Earth,* a work which gained a wide circulation among contemporary readers of geology.

The Huttonian conception of a grand sequence of change occurring throughout the history of the earth appealed to the tidy-minded, who looked always for order and system in nature. It accorded well, in particular, with the regular succession of strata then being worked out and progressively mapped, primarily in France and Germany, based on the study of the mineral composition of the rocks and the relative positioning of the different levels—and without reference to fossils. This degree of regularity in the record seemed to the majority satisfactorily accounted for by the current volcanic theory of mountain structure. First, rudimentary attempts at classifying strata had been supplied by Buffon in France in 1749 and by Kant in Germany in 1755; and advance in this direction proved to be so rapid that by 1780 a mineralogical map of northern France, in forty-four sheets, was able to be published.

The other British field pioneer, the Rev. John Michell, was our lone contributor to this early pathfinding in stratigraphy. The years in which he came to maturity were those years when science as a whole in Britain was very largely stagnant. Woodwardian Professor of Geology at Cambridge in 1762–4, he retired to marry and to spend his last thirty, highly active years as rector of a secluded country parish in Yorkshire, occasionally journeying up to London, on horseback or by coach, to attend the meetings of the Royal Society. In 1760, in a lecture to the Society on the subject of earthquakes, he revealed sufficiently extensive knowledge to be able to list the main divisions of the bedded rocks occurring across the country; and in later years, as we know from his manuscript notes, he succeeded in elaborating this in considerably greater detail. Unfortunately, due to modesty or mere inertia, he published next to nothing; and these invaluable results, for all the arduous work put into obtaining them, were lost to the generation that particularly stood in need of them—a story, alas, which in the history of science is only too familiar.

Not long before the deaths of both Michell and Hutton another lone worker had embarked on a lifelong study of the country's stratigraphy. This was a young, self-educated surveyor with the appealingly John Bullish name of William Smith—'Strata' Smith, as he was later to be known to his fellow geologists. It was Smith's great achievement to provide the essential groundwork of knowledge that permitted the two quite separate lines of geological inquiry, the high-flown speculations of grand theory and the humdrum poking around for fossils, to be welded together into a unified tradition. This he did by establishing over a period of years, with the necessary wealth of supporting data, not only that the different geological formations succeed each other in a well-defined sequence of age and in a certain predictable order, lying upon each other all across the country, in his vivid phrase, 'like slices of bread and butter' (which, independently and unknown to him, the mineralogists had demonstrated earlier); but also that each stratum can be readily identified, wherever it may occur, by the presence of certain characteristic kinds of fossils, thereby enabling beds in different areas to be correlated without much trouble and the place of any bed to be located with confidence within any particular succession. This key concept of 'guide' fossils was to revolutionize geology. On the one hand, it gave a sense of constructive endeavour to the hitherto unanchored joys of fossil-hunting; and, on the other, it brought the previously isolated science into a meaningful relationship with botany and zoology.

Smith first formulated his concept in a fully developed manner in 1796, the same year in which he conceived the idea of writing a major treatise on the subject of strata. But for a long time his discoveries remained more or less unknown. He had got it into his head, unfortunately, that his data were of great commercial value, and he accordingly tried to keep them a close secret until his final *magnum opus* should appear (which he was sanguine enough to believe would bring him not only reputation but substantial riches). As with another great discovery later, the Wardian Case, news was leaked out only very gradually, in tantalizing fragments. The first ration to appear in print was an account of the succession of the local strata in his friend the Rev. Richard Warner's *History of Bath* (1801). By the time this was published, we now know, Smith had mapped the entire oolitic series as it runs through England, and in the middle of that very year prepared for his private use the first-ever map of the whole of England and Wales with the main formations hand-coloured on to it. The final version of this map, considerably more perfect, he did not release to the public till as late as 1815, three years after Greenough had exhibited a rival map compiled under the auspices of the Geological Society which threatened to steal his thunder (and indeed, when Greenough's map too was finally published, five years after his, it did effectively put an end to the sales of its predecessors).

The great treatise on strata, started at last in 1805, made exceptionally slow headway. Smith found writing far from easy, and publication on the grandiose scale on which he had set his heart threatened to be so expensive that he went so far as to try to sell the whole of his property in order to raise the necessary funds. His mind was undisciplined and he was constantly tempted to digress from his central, arduous task into easier and slighter alternative undertakings. The 'Great Book' fixation also set his mind against bringing out his knowledge by instalments, in the form of several, shorter contributions, in, maybe, a learned periodical. In the end, inevitably, this was what he was forced to, and between 1816 and 1819 two separate, smallish works, *Strata Identified by Organized Fossils* and *Stratigraphical System of Organized Fossils,* made their long-delayed appearance, embodying his detailed researches and following immediately upon his map. Only then did the full significance of his achievement begin to become generally appreciated.

This was not the end of Smith's public services. In addition to his national map he conceived the further idea of issuing for sale a geologically coloured map of every county in England and Wales, which when fully published would combine to form a complete geological atlas of the whole country. Twenty-one counties were duly covered in this way in the five years up to 1824, but financial difficulties then intervened and compelled him to cease further work on the venture. The plates of the maps so far published, however, were treasured by the printers, and versions of them continued to be sold till as late as 1911, when they were still much in demand by cyclists and ramblers.

Smith is significant for quite another, non-theoretical reason. He owed his original discoveries to the great network of canals then in course of construction in many parts of England, a disturbance of the country's surface on a scale and to a depth up to that time without parallel. His profession, in fact, involved him full time in their study, and it was while Resident Engineer to the Somerset Coal Canal Co. that he gathered the material for his earliest map. We know that Michell, likewise, was a sharp-eyed patroller of the brand-new canal cuttings during the 1780s; and it is pleasant to think that the two might well have passed on some bank or other—and each remained unrecognized.

The economic motive as a reason for the great upsurge of interest in the subject is traditionally made much of by historians of geology; yet it is difficult to decide on its precise effect at this early period. For the first time, certainly, men of education were able to make a living in this field by hiring out their technical knowledge: Robert Bakewell, for example, whose *Introduction to Geology* (1813) proved exceptionally popular, acted as an out-and-out consultant in the subject, providing the landed gentry with reports on the mineral and soil potential of their estates. It is obviously true that the massive excavations prompted by the great industrial expansion provided enticing opportunities, hitherto undreamed of, for hunting for fossils and for investigating sections. The occasional spectacular finds, of skeletons of mammoths or of a puzzling cluster of large and unknown bones, could always count on catching the headlines; and in the prevailing

Romantic atmosphere, with its fashionable interest in the past, they no doubt attracted many fresh workers to the subject. It is also true that the regular anxieties aroused by the Benthamites about the 'usefulness' of such pursuits as natural history must have been most helpfully allayed by the blatant commercial potential of geology. Even so, it seems too much to assume that all, or even most, of the great new interest in the subject was mercenary. The sheer intellectual fascination, the wonderment caused by the freshly opened vistas, the greatly enhanced appeal of one of the longest-established collecting hobbies: all these are reasons enough in themselves to account for its popularity.

Yet the confident feeling that, at base, the subject was of great practical importance may well have played a part in winning the remarkable following that geology gained from the first among the aristocracy and the upper echelons of the gentry. There was nothing remotely effeminate about it; it fostered noble speculation; it made a man seem forward-looking and economically constructive. As geologists, men could see themselves as princely benefactors and at the same time as lords of learning: well-rounded personalities in true Renaissance style. By means of this science it was possible to parade both a lofty, dignified brow and commendable horny-handedness.

This social elegance that the subject quickly came to acquire can scarcely be stressed enough. A glance at its early most prominent figures is telling in itself: Greenough sat in Parliament at the same time as he directed the affairs of the Geological Society almost single-handed; De la Beche, Murchison and Lyell each received a knighthood (the second and third of these rising further still to baronetcies); Buckland and the younger Conybeare ended up as Deans. Murchison, the grandest of them all, was steered into the subject by an intellectual wife after retiring early from the army and his very fashionable regiment with the ending of the Napoleonic Wars. The news of his appointment as the Geological Survey's next Director-General was received in the Commons, we are told, with 'general cheers'; and at his funeral the Prime Minister, Mr Gladstone, was among the very many who paid honour to him by accompanying his bier to the grave.

These men, it should be noted, were not the mere titled ornaments with which many a subject or society customarily chose to elevate its social stature, but the accepted leaders of the science, who had personally earned their standing by the long and steady toil of their hammers. Geology attracted men not merely of mental distinction but, almost more important, of personal weight and influence. Even if themselves at a loss, they generally had friends in all or most of the appropriate places, very often personal connections by blood or marriage. One Member of Parliament was both the brother of Leonard Horner, a secretary of the Geological Society, and the uncle by marriage of Lyell; another, Lewis Weston Dillwyn, himself a leading botanist, had a son married to De la Beche's daughter. In the Commons of that day there was clearly the makings of a powerful geological lobby.

Herein lay one reason, at least, for the head-start over all the other branches of natural history that geology was to have in winning effective government backing. Men like De la Beche and Murchison lay already conveniently to hand: they were known quantities to those who had the decisions to make in such matters: and they were able to match the experience and dedication of professionals in an age that preferred to see its institutions headed by reassuring gentlemen-amateurs.

As an organized entity, geology had its birth in the two or three years immediately after 1800. Its start was abrupt—and surprisingly fully-formed from the first. In 1804, at the age of thirty, very soon after returning to this country from a prolonged immersion in the over-seductive teachings of Werner, Robert Jameson, the son of a prosperous soap manufacturer, found himself appointed to the Chair of Natural History at Edinburgh. Here he at once set to work to found a school of mineralogy directly modelled on the one in Germany that his master had made so celebrated. Amongst the items that this involved was the introduction of formal field classes, on the pattern developed already by Werner with great and continuing success. These were the first such classes in this science in a British university (if we except the informal outings with his pupils that Lhwyd was in the habit of making in the Oxford of the 1680s)—though there were, of course, several precedents in botany, some of them even at Edinburgh and as recently as 1801, under John MacKay. Among the many students who, over a period of many years, were thus to hear Jameson lecture in the open air at Arthur's Seat or Salisbury Crags—or even, on occasions, as far afield as the Western Isles—were Charles Darwin, Sir William Jardine, Hugh Falconer, Charles Daubeny (Professor, successively, of Chemistry and Botany at Oxford), Robert Grant (first Professor of Zoology in the University of London); many leading geologists such as Charles Maclaren, W. H. Fitton, the Swiss Necker de Saussure and the Frenchman Ami Boué; and, by no means least, great numbers of the surgeon-naturalists and explorers sent out on government expeditions, which Edinburgh long held the lead in supplying from among its former students of medicine. William MacGillivray, too, evidently found these field classes useful enough to introduce their counterparts at Aberdeen, when he went there as Professor of Natural History in 1841. 'These excursions', one of Jameson's obituarists was later to affirm, 'did more towards the making of geologists than any instruction that had been given within the century'.

In these early days, at the peak of his energies, Jameson appears to have been a stimulating teacher, full of quiet enthusiasm, if rather pedestrian and unimpassioned; but compelled, for financial reasons, to hang on to his Chair for far too long, he found his influence eventually tapering off and ended, miserably, in a bumbling dotage. Already, by the mid 1820s, Darwin found his lectures insufferably dreary: 'that old brown dry stick' he called him impolitely. Carlyle, the historian, another of his students, was no more complimentary. By the fifties, when Ramsay was to write of him in scathing terms as 'just like a baked mummy', he had finally grown so frail and doddery that his lectures were having to be read for him by a deputy. It was a pathetic finish to what started out as a career of much gusto and vigour which almost amounted at times to a crusade. For, from the first, in his early years of office, Jameson had conceived it as his duty to try to convert all and sundry to the so-called 'Neptunist' doctrine as enunciated by Werner. These ideas (which were actually older than Werner) demanded the existence of a once-universal ocean, out of which the earth had emerged by a process of crystallization. In the waters of these primordial seas a long series of sediments were assumed to have been deposited; and these, it was held, explained the successive strata now to be observed in the rocks.

To the Neptunists the rival explanation current, born in 1756 and lately stated afresh so forcibly by Hutton—that the earth had been mainly formed through the action of volcanoes—was complete anathema. It found a no less vigorous champion, however, in the person of Jameson's colleague and arch-enemy, John Playfair, who by then had exchanged the Chair of Mathematics for the rather more pertinent one of Natural Philosophy. Playfair and all who shared his views were dubbed, for contrast, the 'Vulcanists'. For several years they were a decided minority. Jameson had the chance to mass-indoctrinate his students in a manner hardly open to his opponent; he was able, furthermore, to use the *Memoirs* of his new Wernerian Society as a kind of stentorian mouthpiece for relaying his creed to a far wider public. Not content with this, he also propounded Werner's teachings in book after book, beginning with a three-volume *System of Mineralogy* (1804–8). 'No devotee ever more zealously maintained the infallibility of the Pope than Mr Jameson has done that of his master', the *Edinburgh Review* observed acidly, in noticing the first volume.

Despite the uneven struggle, the very whisper of two rival professors locked in a gladiatorial combat without apparent end was enough to set the whole University agog. Few things appeal to Youth so much as the sight of two of its elders hurling abuse at one another—and especially if these elders are its teachers and it senses a certain intellectual stake in the outcome. For a period of years, in consequence, geology at Edinburgh roused a quite exceptional enthusiasm, as student after student was drawn towards the subject by the sound of academic gun-fire.

Though Jameson's views were wrong and succeeded in retarding geology at least from a theoretical aspect, the great benefits he brought to the science as a teacher and a publicist easily outweighed the temporary harm he may have caused otherwise. It was entirely due to him, for instance, that the University Museum was built up to its very substantial size. He made great use of this for teaching, holding classes there several times a week. In 1819, with Sir David Brewster, he also started the *Edinburgh Philosophical Journal*, which published much of value on natural history generally and of which for many years he acted as sole editor. In short, he instituted an enduring tradition. As Edward Forbes, his successor, was to ask rhetorically in his Inaugural Address in 1854: 'Where else in the British empire, except here, has there been for the last half-century a school of Natural History?'—a broad school, that is, and one not merely confined to geology.

In the meantime a pronounced revival was taking place at Oxford. In 1805 John Kidd, the Professor of Chemistry, began giving lectures on mineralogy as well, and a group of enthusiasts who attended these proceeded to band themselves together into a small club. The mainspring of this was the Rev. W. D. Conybeare, later to win great fame in the subject; while among the others were his elder brother, the Rev. J. J. Conybeare, soon to be Professor of Poetry at Oxford, and a young student of theology who had come up in 1801, William Buckland. Buckland had been a keen collector of birds' eggs as a boy and had moved on from these to fossils by a kind of natural progression. Remaining in residence at the University and continuing to display a highly active interest in the science, he was duly rewarded with the Readership in Mineralogy in 1813 and six years after that became the first holder of the newly-endowed Readership in Geology.

Buckland's lectures—which owed, it seems, more to the stage than to normal academic usage—quickly became a legend. According to Lyell, he 'would keep his audience in roars of laughter, as he imitated what he thought to be the movements of the Iguanodon or Megatherium, or, seizing the ends of his long clerical coat-tails, would leap about to show how the Pterodactyl flew'. The description reminds us at once of a certain kind of schoolmaster most of us at one time or another have encountered: the self-dramatizing 'character', the ham actor in a gown, who manages to use to quite brilliant effect as a teacher a certain quirkishness of personality that in almost every other walk of life would be reckoned a serious handicap. His is not behaviour that at once commands respect, but it is behaviour that can hold the eyes and ears of an audience where all other approaches fail.

Some people found Buckland's perpetual posturing distasteful. To Darwin, for one, he seemed 'a vulgar and almost coarse man', 'incited more by a craving for notoriety, which sometimes made him act like a buffoon, than by a love of science'. Many a Victorian—in spirit if not yet in fact—with the earnestness that increasingly characterized the age, found it all too hard to accept that such a justly serious subject received no injury from so unserious a style of treatment.

Buckland worried people, too, because he lacked altogether the demeanour of the typical geologist: there was no hint of distant reverberations in his personality, no suggestion of ageless time, no ring of iron on stone; all people saw was a kind of learned clown. And in many ways he was undeniably a very curious person: an oddly truncated man, who appears to have trimmed intellectually and, as though in compensation, kept himself in mental health on a diet of wordly plaudits and a constant traffic in eccentricities . . . He sported childish jests and puns, devised peculiar contraptions, went in for the weirdest kinds of food. It was typical of him that he drove around in a special kind of carriage, strengthened in an ostentatious manner for the heavy loads of minerals and fossils that it regularly had to bear and fitted on the forepart with a furnace and implements for carrying out assays and analysis—probably the first really substantial piece of specialized equipment in the annals of natural history. It was typical of him that he carried around a mysterious blue bag, out of which, at opportune moments, he would draw bone after thought-provoking bone, like a conjuror at a party. It was typical, too, that he led his students on excursions into the field wearing quite incongruously formal clothes.

The field lectures that he instituted, like Jameson, as an adjunct to his course were perhaps his supreme accomplishment: an outdoor setting must have been best fitted to his histrionic talents, toning down those parts of his performance that indoors would have seemed too contrived and forced. 'The next lecture,' he liked to startle a roomful of his students by announcing, 'will take place in the fields above the quarry at Stonesfield'; or 'Tomorrow the Class will meet at the top of Shotover Hill at ten o'clock.' These lectures were sometimes conducted on horseback—and were then known as 'geological rides'.

In June 1832, when the British Association held its annual meeting at Oxford, Buckland laid on one of these rides in its honour. Gideon Mantell, who happily captured the occasion in his journal, relates that a large concourse of people began assembling on the bridge at the London entrance to Oxford, some in carriages, some on horseback, the rest on foot. The party then set off for Shotover Hill, where tents were pitched, refreshments taken, and fossils purchased off the local labourers, while the Professor of Geology regularly discoursed on the scientific sights to the crowd.

At a later meeting of the Association, at Birmingham in 1839, Buckland attracted an audience totalling several thousand for a lecture in the famous Dudley Caverns, specially illuminated for the occasion. Carried away by the general magnificence, he was tempted into rounding off with a shameless appeal to the audience's patriotism. The great mineral wealth lying around on every hand, he proclaimed, was no mere accident of nature; it showed, rather, the express intention of Providence that the inhabitants of Britain should become, by this gift, the richest and most powerful nation on earth. And with these words the great crowd, with Buckland at its head, returned towards the light of day thundering out, with one accord, 'God Save the Queen!'

Cambridge, not to be outdone, eventually replied in kind—with field lectures by Adam Sedgwick, Buckland's friendly rival. Sedgwick, a mathematician by training, had been invited in 1818—one year before Buckland's Readership—to take the Woodwardian Chair of Geology (till then a notorious sinecure), despite the fact that it was a subject about which, as he frankly admitted, he knew absolutely nothing whatsoever. Declaring 'Hitherto I have never turned a stone: now I shall leave no stone unturned', he was soon to make amends for the somewhat outrageous manner of his appointment and more than justify the astonishing faith of those who sponsored him.

In 1835, after a great deal of field experience acquired in various parts of the country, Sedgwick started the practice of giving lectures out-of-doors, on horseback, which at once proved extremely popular. Parties of up to seventy mounted students would regularly turn out and go cantering across the Fens, to listen in the course of the day to five different lectures— the last of which, on fen-drainage, was traditionally delivered from that matchless point of vantage, the cathedral roof at Ely. The idea for these occasions was doubtless inspired more immediately by the antics of Buckland; but field classes were in fact an established practice at Cambridge already in the sister science of botany, introduced at the instance of Sedgwick's fellow professor and lifelong intimate, Henslow. Interestingly, we have it on the evidence of a fairly near contemporary, Professor T. G. Bonney, that in the Cambridge of those days riding by undergraduates was not general, for only a limited few could afford the expense involved. As Henslow's botanists (and, often, entomologists too) were in the custom of hiring a stage-coach for their outings or a barge down the river to the Fens, or, failing these, made do with a long tramp there and back on foot, the much more dashing mode of conveyance that the students of geology went in for is yet one further indication of the distinctly more elevated social level attained by this study.

The other important event of the first years of the new century was the founding, in 1807, of the Geological Society of London. This arose out of the gatherings of a small group of mineralogists who had formed the habit of meeting together occasionally for breakfast. Humphry Davy, one of their number, had been driven to propose a change of time to the evening:

> The chills of Novr mornings [he objected] are very unfavourable to ardor in the pursuit of science, and I conceive we should all think better and talk better after experiencing the effects of Roast Beef and wine than in preparing for tea, coffee and Buttered Buns.

At one of the dinner meetings that duly resulted, at the Freemasons' Tavern in Great Queen Street (where the Linnean Society also dined, once a year, to celebrate its anniversary), a Geological Society was formally constituted, on the thirteenth day of November, in the presence of thirteen persons—which, for the superstitious, can hardly have seemed a promising start.

To have begun in this manner was a strange reversal of the traditional train of events. Most of the large London societies gave rise to dining clubs as subsequent offshoots, but it was almost unheard-of for formality to be born from informality, for learned papers to materialize out of relaxation and gossip. That it should have happened at all, and in so contrary a fashion, is perhaps some measure of the urgency of the need then felt by geologists for a regular forum in the Capital.

At the Society's first session it was resolved that the members should dine together at the Tavern on the first Friday of every month from November to June inclusive, at a cost on each occasion of fifteen shillings per head. Because of the expense of the meal on order, any member unable to attend had to notify the secretary three days beforehand or else incur the massive fine (for those days) of ten-and-sixpence. 'Dinner', read the rules, was 'to be on the table at five o'clock precisely', to be followed by the business of the evening on the dot of seven. The high cost of belonging, despite the fact that most of the founder-members were under forty, indicates a high average social rank. And it may have been on this account that for its first few years the Society was subjected to fairly severe pressure from the Royal Society, which evidently saw in this body an unnecessary and potentially dangerous new rival.

The first president, George Bellas Greenough, a young man of twenty-nine who had inherited a large fortune while still a schoolboy, was himself largely responsible for the Society's early rise to influence. Though he published very little, study of his numerous letters has recently made clear that his work behind the scenes, on the Society's behalf, was not only energetic and wide-ranging, but conceived with foresight and intelligence. Under his guidance the Society was spared the sterile Neptunist-Vulcanist disputes and steered instead into a much more promising channel: no less than the first attempt at nation-wide cooperative research ever to be undertaken by a natural history body.

From its earliest days the Society saw as one of its tasks 'ascertaining what is known in [the] science and what yet remains to be discovered'. To this end, within five months of its founding, a series of questions—compiled by Greenough and a chemist, Arthur Aikin—was drawn up and printed, and distributed to all members in the form of a small booklet with the title *Geological Inquiries*. Thus was born 'network research'. The method itself was not entirely new: a few years before, Dawson Turner and Lewis Weston Dillwyn had circulated around the country a printed four-page questionnaire in seeking records for their valuable *Botanist's Guide* (1805), a handbook to localities for rarities, and there is an obvious parallel in the lists of questions sent round to local clergy and gentry by Pennant on his many fact-finding missions earlier in the previous century. The Geological Society's project, however, was the first to be initiated by a permanent, organized body—with the implication that, if successful, it could be perpetuated indefinitely and that there were properly qualified persons ever to hand who could be relied on to handle the material sent in and see that it was made available in a fitting form for the general benefit of fellow workers in the science.

The Society's booklet amply served its purpose and a great deal of information on local deposits flowed in to Greenough from its recipients, by no means all of whom were members. By way of following this up, he then made numerous tours around the country calling on these local informants, no doubt partly to satisfy himself about their competence and accuracy, but partly also to put them into touch with the London-based Society. Seeing the need to build up a national chain of observers, inexperienced though many of these might be, he made it the Society's policy to enrol as many as possible of these local workers as formal members. The Society was thereby enabled, in a very short time, to acquire a reasonable outline knowledge of the geology of much of Britain. In the process, almost accidentally, it turned itself into a large and flourishing body with a keen national following instead of, as might well have happened otherwise, a tight little London clique more concerned to ostracize unwanted strangers than to foster the wider spread of learning.

———

Around 1820 a pronounced shift of interest away from its former preoccupations began to become visible in British geology. Seas and earthquakes, the bleak elemental forces working to mould the surface of the planet, ceased to be the dominant, overriding concern; in their place, fascination began to grow for the myriads of creatures, often eerie and unfamiliar, that had once populated the earth in the earlier phases of its existence. With this, geology turned more and more into a kind of petrified zoology; and a new name, 'palaeontology', was coined in 1825 (by Cuvier's disciple, de Blainville) to take the place of the more restricted 'oryctology', by which the study of fossils, in a non-dynamic sense, had up to then been commonly denoted.

While Smith's discoveries and mapping still remained virtually unknown, several other works on fossils had been making their appearance, which subsequent historians, with eyes only for the well-known and weightier volumes emanating from France, have been led into seriously underrating. The earliest, and the most important, was James Parkinson's *Organic Remains of a Former World* (in three volumes, 1804–11). The first popular work to be devoted to fossils, providing the reader with ample illustrations and descriptive matter and including a careful discussion of their nature, its publication has lately been acclaimed 'the outstanding event in the history of our scientific knowledge of British fossils'. It cannot have met with overmuch success, however, for Gideon Mantell refers to the subject in 1811 (when Parkinson showed him his cabinets) as being 'a department of natural knowledge at that time but little cultivated in England'. Undeterred, in 1822 Parkinson brought out a second book on the topic entitled, rather forbiddingly, *Outlines of Oryctology.*

Parkinson's pioneering work was gradually joined by others. *Outlines of an Attempt to Establish a Knowledge of Extraneous Fossils on Scientific Principles* (1809), by William Martin, an ex-actor and drawing master, was the first true textbook on the topic; it was also of special interest for anticipating William Smith in print by a good seven years in drawing attention to the usefulness of fossils as a means of dating the stratified rocks. *The Mineral Conchology of Great Britain,* a lengthy series of attractive plates of fossil shells, started by James Sowerby, the founder of a well-known dynasty of natural-history draughtsmen and dealers, and later carried on by one of his sons, began its thirty-four-year existence in 1812.

In that same year the French anatomist Georges Cuvier published his *Récherches sur les ossemens fossiles de quadrupèdes,* a work which was quickly to have a profound influence on thought in Britain, in that it confirmed, in no uncertain manner, the inkling that Ray had obtained many years earlier that a good many of the creatures occurring as fossils belong to species now no longer extant. A firm believer in the fixity of species, Cuvier sought to explain this awkward fact in terms of a number of severe 'catastrophes' which he saw as having overwhelmed the earth at certain periods in its history. On each of these occasions, the most recent of which was the Biblical Deluge, he suggested that the extinction of life had never been absolutely complete, just sufficient creatures escaping to be able to re-populate the world anew.

This theory seemed to reconcile, once and for all, the findings of geology and the teachings of orthodox religion, and on that accounts it gained unusually wide publicity in Britain. The immediate result was that people now felt freed to study fossils without any tormenting pangs of conscience. Indeed, as Buckland contended in his much-read volume, *Reliquiae Diluvianae* (1823), on the fossil relics of what he supposed to have been the Biblical Flood—and again, even more unequivocally, in his famous Bridgewater treatise of 1836—the researches of geologists appeared to confirm the early history of the earth as recounted in the Scriptures in such gratifying completeness and detail that inquiry into these long-lost periods of our past might well be regarded as a mere extension of religious duty.

Unfortunately not everyone saw it quite like this. For many years a large body of British public opinion held to the absolutist view, typified by George Bugg and his *Scriptural Geology* (1826), that the sole account of the early history of the earth that could possibly have any validity whatever was that to be found contained within the covers of the Bible. A wordy pamphlet-war long continued in this vein; and though it must have troubled a few consciences, the fact that this caused a larger and larger section of the public to try to keep within earshot of the developing science suggests that no real harm to geology resulted.

The 'Catastrophist' theory was taken up with gratitude by Buckland, Sedgwick, Murchison and other giants of the science, attracting also a very big following among amateurs. Throughout the 1820s and 1830s it formed the central topic of geological discussion, and its proponents and adversaries lined up in battle with much the same intensity—and, more usefully, with much the same publicity—as in the now-expiring Neptunist-Vulcanist contentions, the theological undertones of Catastrophism making up in fervour for the absence of quite so sharply personalized a drama. Once again, tempers were frayed; once again, outsiders poured in to sample the science in order to discover what could possibly cause such turbulence and clamour. As Lockhart, the editor of the *Quarterly Review,* who made a habit at this time of attending the Geological Society's meetings, used to remark to his friends: 'Though I don't care for geology, I do like to see the fellows fight.'

To help in holding this already exceptionally attentive audience, British geology at this point had a further piece of luck: the turning up, in reasonably quick succession and with mounting attendant publicity, of a series of desirably horrible prehistoric monsters.

The first, the Ichthyosaurus, entered the full glare of science some time before the others, in 1805. Four years earlier a skeleton of one of these had been discovered in the highly productive Liassic cliffs near Lyme Regis, by the young son of a local cabinet-maker who, before his untimely death, had introduced his children to the delights of hunting for fossils. The eldest of them, Mary Anning, had taken to collecting, and used to offer specimens for sale to visitors, displaying them alongside the fresh fish in her mother's tiny shop in Lyme. It seemed natural to her to excavate her brother's find, and the sale of this to the lord of the manor for £25 spurred her on to further searches.

In 1821 she had her due reward by discovering the first nearly complete skeleton of a Plesiosaurus, which this time was sold to the Duke of Buckingham—for the startling sum of £200. The evident cash value of her pursuit, the scientific importance of her finds, the fact that she was a young girl and not a greybeard professor, and her use of the earnings from her fossils to help to support her widowed mother, all made perfect copy for the press and brought the study to the attention of people who up till then can never even have heard of it.

Almost simultaneously, in a book on *The Fossils of the South Downs*, news was leaked out of the bones of 'one or more gigantic animals of the lizard tribe' that had lately been discovered in the Weald of Sussex. The author, Gideon Mantell, a busy surgeon in Lewes, had received his early encouragement in the study from James Parkinson and was, thanks to his medical background, a more than capable comparative anatomist. In 1824 he recognized that some teeth found locally two years earlier by his wife closely resembled those of an iguana. Cuvier, to whom these had first been submitted, had dismissed them carelessly as the teeth of a rhinoceros; and so it was not without some boldness, in the face of such weighty authority, that Mantell proceeded to describe them as those of an entirely new creature. This he called the *Iguanadon*. Conceived of at that time as merely a gigantic form of lizard, its subsequent discovery in further places, combined with finds of other, obviously related forms, gradually made it clear that this was a completely different type of reptile from any now existing. The collective name *Dinosauria*—or 'Terrible Reptiles'—was accordingly coined for them by Richard Owen (in 1842): a name, with its flesh-creeping suggestiveness, perfectly chosen to evoke a modish Romantic flutter.

Luckily, besides being a palaeontologist of real ability, Mantell was also a man of verve and enormous restless energy: he needed, it is said, no more than four hours' sleep each night. He was also a compulsive showman—with a weakness for flourishing his personal coat-of-arms and given to lashing out beyond his means on domestic magnificence and a fashionable carriage. Knowledgeable, eloquent, endowed, above all, with the precious gift of enthusiasm, he made a superb public lecturer, in which capacity he was soon greatly in demand. Latterly, he was also the author of a predictably best-selling work, in two volumes, *The Wonders of Geology* (1838)—in his own words, 'the *romance* of the science', which he had it in mind to try to capture on paper. *The Medals of Creation, or First Lessons in Geology* followed in 1844. In the long run his influence as a winner of converts to the subject may have outstripped even Buckland's.

One final reason for the popularity of geology still remains to be mentioned. This is the almost uncanny way in which the more progressive thinkers of the age—and even the unprogressive, prompted by a kind of intellectual prurience—scented in the dust from the subject's seemingly unglamorous chippings the warfare over Evolution which was yet to come. Lyell's great classic, *The Principles of Geology,* a massive work of synthesis set forth in glorious prose, published in three volumes in 1830–3, was the cornerstone of Darwin's eventual theory. It has been described as *The Origin of Species* minus only the Natural Selection hypothesis. Geology, of all branches of knowledge at this period, seemed to be advancing fastest and farthest towards the bedrock of ultimate, incontestable truth. Those who felt compelled to enter on this journey took care, accordingly, to place themselves among the van.

CHAPTER FOUR

The Victorian Setting

THE NINETEENTH CENTURY, while less complex than the eighteenth as far as natural history is concerned, was by no means so uniform as is commonly supposed. Nevertheless, certain of the basic strands that went to form its distinctive pattern did manage to last out unbroken for what seems in retrospect an impressive period of years and gave to the greater part of it an easily perceptible unity which greatly helps us in our study of it today.

These strands constitute the essence of what we have come to call 'Victorianism', even though they were recognizably in being for the most part a full decade or more before the Queen's accession. They were partly new and partly adaptations—in some cases almost out of recognition—of various dominant concerns inherited from the previous era. They held together because they sprang from an inner consistency, from a set of assumptions founded in a certain well-defined emotional-cum-religious attitude which, for want of a better word, we may identify as Evangelicalism—using the word in a non-sectarian context.

The Evangelical Revival, which had made its presence felt in the closing years of the eighteenth century, most notably in the speeches of William Wilberforce and in the crusades of the Clapham Sect, was in reality a mere recrudescence of the powerful Puritan strain so long embedded in English life which had lain beneath the surface for the previous hundred years. Its corpus of beliefs, which was more a series of emotional reflex actions than a worked-out system of ideas, carried itself by the very strength of its convictions into every corner of middle-class English life and quickly imparted to that key segment of the nation a forceful new morality.

If there is any truth in the notion of 'challenge and response' in history, the Evangelical Revival is a most suggestive instance. For the rising tide of industrialism found itself accompanied by a new ethical code perfectly suited to its furtherance and by a concentration of energies which greatly speeded its progress. The moral and the useful became, increasingly, intertwined: pursuits like geology could be justified, in the self-same flickering of conscience, as a means of revering the earthly grandeurs of Creation— the Natural Theology as re-enunciated by Paley and now taken up in a ceaseless chant in every preface—and as a means of prospering materially. Any pursuit, on the other hand, without an ostensible core of usefulness but which all the same exercised a compulsive fascination, whether it be climbing mountains or forming collections of flowers, had to be defended from the barbs of soulless Utilitarians; and the simplest way of doing this, a way which was ordinarily unanswerable, was to discover some moral content and so proclaim its edifying character—as it were, as a kind of afterthought.

Those transcendental moments of ecstasy which earlier Romantics had seen as the workings of the life-force were now reinterpreted in orthodox, theistic terms. Nature's magical enchantments still continued to be acknowledged, as fully and freely as before, and to be valued for the obvious bounties that they brought to human minds; but the uplift that men received from them (like the experience of delight that they received from art) was envisaged no longer as sensuous and neutral, but as spiritual and prescriptive: the *vis medicatrix* became conceived as a sacrament.

For the most part all that resulted from this was mere emotional relabelling. The new middle class laid claim to the playthings of its predecessors and received them with an awed respect, hardly altering their outward appearance even though they used them inevitably in a somewhat novel fashion. Just as they acquired the taste for Gothic and redirected it from old and crumbling ruins to rising modern edifices, so they retained the Rousseauist view of nature and translated it into an earnest religiosity. The 'horrid' came to seem virtuous, the vistas were sanctified: those 'legends in flowers' that had so bewitched their predecessors gave way, almost without being noticed, to equally obsessing sermons in stones.

By the 1830s the true Romantic inspiration, its roots increasingly obscured, was growing less and less familiar, the so-called Romanticism that usurped it more and more patently a pose. The tasteful exercise of sentiment, so long and generally accepted as the hallmark of a cultivated gentility, tended to lie beyond the reach of minds dulled by industrial routines or by the no less stunting effects of a too literal fundamentalism. Increasingly, it turned instead into a feigned emotion: into Sentimentality, the mere sop to fashion of those who could not or would not commit themselves in the fuller way required—a debased substitute which by reason of its very shallowness was able to travel much faster and much farther.

By the 1820s this had made its début in France, under the name of '*l'amant de la nature*'. Little sentimental works, most of them on flowers, gushed forth from the presses in response and were soon selling in their thousands. One in particular, Charlotte de Latour's '*Le Langage des fleurs*' (1833), with charming illustrations by Pancrace Bessa, proved so overwhelmingly popular that it was translated into English and thus spread the infection across the Channel. Among Britain's chorus of replies were Mrs Hey's *Moral of Flowers,* Miss Twamley's *The Romance of Nature* ('I love flowers, as forming one of the sweetest lines in the GOD-WRITTEN Poetry of Nature'), Willcock's *Flora Poetica* and such later outpourings as *Butterflying with the Poets* by Joseph Merrin. For a time it became all but obligatory to work into every book or article on natural history a quota of lines from Wordsworth. Even sober works of science were not immune from this, one or two, for the sake of an easier sale, pandering to the current mode so that they ended up, like Webb and Coleman's *Flora Hertfordiensis* of 1849, as ludicrous half-breeds, their solemn text liberally spangled with snippets of assorted verse.

Although we may deplore its effects, we must be grateful for this final surge of would-be Romanticism, for it came just at the moment when the new middle classes were succeeding to dominance and thereby helped to keep their gaze firmly on nature. Without its existence—or confronted with a purer version of the taste, which might well have seemed too high-flown and rarefied to imitate—perhaps they would have turned instead to more accessible, less rural diversions or at least not discovered the aesthetic potential of the countryside with the same immediacy. The very speed and smoothness with which the wholesale handing-down of the established interest in nature took place must not tempt us into assuming that this was at all a necessary event. Rather, we owe the massive strength of Victorian natural history largely to a cultural accident.

The natural history that now emerged was in its whole essence an Evangelical creation, and like every other aspect of life lucky enough to be assimilable to the new preponderant mental type it swept in with an overpowering pervasiveness. Indeed, the subject in its novel, revised form was so faithful a reflector of many of the facets of the nation's make-up that it can even be regarded as a kind of mirror. In their study of nature the Victorian middle classes gazed out upon their own image: natural history exercised so compelling a fascination throughout that era for the reason that it offered to the Evangelical character an unrivalled range of outlets for its expression.

For a start, the subject was pre-eminently fitted for the discharge of those often uncomfortable results of the puritanical short-circuiting of emotion. Victorian sentimentality arose partly from the forced conjuring-up of an expected emotional response when none initially was there, and partly from the sheer misfiring of constantly under-utilized passions. Either they could not register their reactions with a desirable preciseness, or else they felt far less than they should and had to pretend to an excitement supposedly in line with the best aesthetic canons. Both activities resulted in mawkishness.

At the same time that marvellous Victorian self-discipline which, by contrast, was one great benefit derived from this cause was equally liable to be carried to excess and turned into an almost masochistic delight in privation. Robert Dick, for example, 'the Botanist of Thurso'—by trade a baker—made it his regular practice to walk all day, for up to forty miles, with one ship's biscuit as his only sustenance. George Don the elder, the pioneer of Highland botany, used to leave his home in Forfar for a week at a time, sleeping out in the open in the mountains wrapped in a plaid and living off hunks of bread and cheese and a bag of oatmeal. William Mac-Gillivray, in his earlier years, also frequently slept out—after supping on a piece of oatcake and a few mouthfuls of water from a spring. All these three, admittedly, were Scotsmen, reared in a long tradition of self-denying austerity. But Englishmen could be no less brutal in their treatment of the flesh: Babington, out in North Wales in 1830, subsisted on only 'a crust of bread and some cheese'; Tyndall would climb the highest mountains with merely a flask of tea and a single sandwich.

Maybe it was this same compulsion that led so many of them, too, to behave towards the countryside as if it was a testing-ground for more muscular forms of endurance. Tyndall, almost throughout his life, indulged himself in fifty-mile-a-day walking tours; the elder Hooker regularly managed sixty miles with ease; Henslow, as a young geologist, once walked all day for forty miles with his hammer and his specimens on his back and then danced the whole night following at a ball. Such feats, admittedly, are not extraordinary even in these modern days among those inured to dependence on their legs: the Victorian ones, however, were more general, more individually consistent, and probably also kept up through a longer period in life.

Certainly, it is hard to believe that there has ever been anything in recent times to compare with William MacGillivray's amazing tramp of 1819. The naturalist was then twenty-three, very poor but desperately impatient to set eyes on the matchless bird collection in the British Museum. What he did have in superabundance was energy. This led him to decide to make his way down to London entirely on foot—a distance of over 800 miles. He started off on 7 September—having risen, in fitting style, at approximately half-past four in the morning and breakfasted around five. In his knapsack and his pockets he carried 'a penknife, a small ink piece with pens, a small itinerary of Scotland, a glass for drinking by the way, and a trowel.' 'To my dress or clothing', he noted in his journal, 'I have added a great-coat and a pair of old gloves. Of money I had just ten pounds sterling.' He subsisted on barley bread.

Choosing initially a most circuitous route—west and then south, by Braemar, Strathspey, Fort William and Inveraray—he succeeded in covering some 500 miles in the first thirty days. At that point he had spent half his money. Undeterred, with the five pounds remaining he pressed on south: 'Bread and water will do very well for the greater part of my journey.'

But to his dismay, on entering Cumberland, he found Scottish banknotes were refused because of suspicion of forgeries and he was unable to purchase food or lodging before reaching Keswick. He slept under hedges, among heather, in barns, more often than in beds. By Manchester, he had to report, 'my trousers are ragged . . . plastered with mire . . . my shoes are nearly worn down, and my stockings are fairly finished.' By Northampton his total funds were down to one and three halfpence, so he decided from there onwards to dispense with breakfast. By the time he had struggled on to St Albans he was being obliged to sit for a time every two or three miles, to ease the appalling soreness of his feet.

He finally entered London on 20 October, six weeks after starting out—appropriately, in a torrential downpour. The very next day, refusing to admit his exhaustion, he duly inspected the British Museum. He stayed in the capital a week (presumably on borrowed money) and then returned to Aberdeen by steamboat.

Some twenty-five years later, when Professor of Natural History in his native city, he liked to take his students out on field excursions and would walk even the most active of them, it is recorded, 'into limp helplessness'. His death in the end was due to the effects of exposure.

This extreme physical doggedness was matched by astonishing displays of intellectual stamina. In virtually every field of study the Victorian age produced figures of such many-sided energies and accomplishments as to leave us today open-mouthed in wonderment and make us feel weak merely reading about them. Natural history had its full share of these. Beside a Pugin or a Paxton it could set a Lindley or a Loudon: men of equally prodigious output and quite invincible in their dynamism: Lindley—who until the age of fifty never knew what it was to feel fatigue and never took a holiday before he was fifty-two; Loudon—who at one period of his life was editing five different monthly publications, generally took no food at all between a seven o'clock breakfast and an eight o'clock dinner, spent most of every day standing in the open directing a team of horticultural draughtsmen and then went in to write till as late as two or three in the morning. So superhuman was Loudon's strength of will and so obsessive his determination that he pressed to be allowed to return to work straight after having had a surgeon amputate his arm.

The Rev. F. O. Morris, in the early fifties, produced, simultaneously, regular monthly parts of *A Natural History of British Birds* (1850–57), *A Natural History of the Nests and Eggs of British Birds* (1851–3) and *A Natural History of British Butterflies* (1852–3)—all the time while coping with a very substantial parish and raising a large family. The Rev. Miles J. Berkeley, another country vicar, found time to describe over 6,000 new species of fungi, a group on which he became an acknowledged world authority. J. E. Gray, for thirty-five years Keeper of the Natural History Department of the British Museum (and thus endlessly bothered by routine inquiries and administrative trivia), is said to have published no fewer than 1,162 papers and articles on a great variety of subjects, his interests being 'by no means confined to zoology or even to natural history, for he took an active part in questions of social, educational, and sanitary reform, and he claimed to have been the first to suggest (in 1834) a uniform rate of letter postage, to be pre-paid by means of stamps'.

Of the Rev. J. G. Wood, another of the great mid-Victorian popularizers, his biographer has written:

> His power of work was simply astonishing . . . He was always at his desk by half-past four or five o'clock in the morning at all seasons of the year, lighting his own fire in the winter, and then writing steadily until eight. Then, in all weathers, he would start off for a sharp run of three miles over a stretch of particularly hilly country, winding up with a tolerably steep ascent of nearly a quarter of a mile, and priding himself on completing the distance from start to finish without stopping, or even slackening his pace. Then came a cold bath, followed by breakfast.

And so the day went on. Fully twelve hours, out of the twenty-four, we are told, were spent with pen in hand, 'recreation being reduced to a minimum, and indeed almost to the vanishing point'. With all this, it is not perhaps surprising that throughout his life he suffered greatly from dyspepsia.

Work for such men was more than just an interest that absorbed them; it was a compulsive discharge of effort. Brought up to feel guilt at idleness and an utter abhorrence of sloth, recreation for them could never mean relaxation. 'How many, many persons,' the author of one local Flora can be found ejaculating, 'for want of some agreeable and instructive employment of their time, turn to idle and vicious habits, and perhaps finally come to ruin!' Every single moment needed to be filled with some useful activity, and that productive power which so impresses us today owed much to the meticulous way in which the Victorians learned to plan their time.

Many an amateur owed his achievements largely to schooling himself to rigorous early rising. Edward Newman regularly rose in summer at five, four or even three in the morning to do his natural history work, and much of his ceaseless flow of books and articles was written (like Trollope's novels) before sitting down to breakfast. H. T. Stainton, similarly, rose at five every morning to seize some hours for entomology, as Gideon Mantell did for geology and Ward (of the Wardian Case) for botany. So finely timed were these stints that some naturalists, like Sir John Lubbock and G. C. Druce, even made a habit of wearing elastic-sided boots, however out of fashion, expressly to save a few precious moments in their hurry to reach their work-table each morning. On page 72 is the programme of self-improvement that Joseph Prestwich, the geologist, set himself for his hours of leisure as a young man in about 1830.

The single-mindedness that they gave to their studies could at times be almost inhuman. Philip Henry Gosse, for instance, became so lost in his work that he registered the birth of his only child with the remarkable entry in his diary: 'Received green swallow from Jamaica. E delivered of a son.'

This delight in industriousness gave a distinctive slant to all Victorian learning. Books came to be judged on their very size and solidity, as if the work and effort poured into their creation—the expression of their author's moral strength—was their overriding merit irrespective of their readability or accuracy. Those who wrote for commercial publishers tended to be pressured into voluminous prolixity, and the habit of this had an ill effect on the type of contribution produced for struggling learned journals. Many of the early societies crippled themselves quite unduly through the absurdly over-elaborate character of so much of the material that they published. Many books, from the same cause, were much more expensive than they need have been, and in the absence of public libraries or of ready access to the shelves of learned bodies must have lain well outside the reach of many who could have made the best use of them.

The idea of work for work's sake also introduced a new note of fervour into the hitherto rather inconsequential pastime of collecting. As with the books, the very size of a collection came to be regarded as worthy in itself, implying the strong-minded devotion of many hours of loving toil and effort—and brought to bear, what is more, while gazing all the time 'through Nature up to Nature's God'. In this way the pious could comfort themselves that their activities were virtuous, however greedily they shot or netted or uprooted and however oblivious they remained of the true needs of science. Collecting, in short, received religious sanction. At the same time, just because it had become more earnest, it also became distinctly more efficient. System was brought to bear on it: the coverage was made more intensive, specimens were preserved more conscientiously, the labelling was done more scrupulously. Proper working tools, in place of artistic creations, thereby resulted.

The blind piling-up of facts—the unquestioning seeking-out and garnering of data—accorded equally well with the prevailing academic temper. All through British science a sudden thirst arose in the 1830s for massive amounts of factual material, the reflection perhaps less of rationally perceived requirements than of emotional convenience—but coinciding with the birth of a new professionalism.

In place of a handful of grasshoppers the landscape all of a sudden seemed to be swarming with ants. The new Evangelical climate hatched out brood after brood of natural lexicologists and list-makers, of counters and comparers: prizers of minor accuracy who excelled in the unsubtle pedagogic virtues. Such men functioned best between the shafts of some well-established system; they were strong on staying-power, weak by comparison on speculation and insight. Their minds were of the sort that would automatically prefer the cosy sureness of the Fixity of Species to the upsetting fluidities of a never-ending Evolution.

Not very surprisingly, a noticeably high proportion of the key people of this period—Dawson Turner, J. E. Bowman, Edward Forster, G. S. Gibson, William Brand, even Yarrell in his early years—earned their daily bread by working in a bank. There was something about the counting-house mentality, with its punctilious sense of order and its skill in executing business with complete correctness and despatch, that made it well suited to the ceaseless roster of minor, yet demanding and sometimes back-breaking tasks in the intellectual housekeeping that forms so large a part of the work of natural history.

This new seriousness of purpose had its roots in the Evangelical attitude: part *pietas,* part *gravitas;* partly an awesome reverence, partly a patriarchal sense of dignity and personal honour. From the former arose an unswerving sabbatarianism so all-pervasive and so extreme that MacGillivray, on the verge of complete exhaustion, in the course of his long tramp to London, could still find energy to register disgust at the shame-

Rise at a quarter to 6	6 to 7	7 to town time	To tea	8.30 to 10	10 to 11 – bedtime
Monday	Arranging my cabinet	Attend to mathematics	German	Natural philosophy	Miscellaneous reading
Tuesday	Chemistry	Miscellaneous reading	Chemistry	Read mathematics with Bella	Do.
Wednesday	Miscellaneous experiments	Attend to mathematics	Geology	History	History
Thursday	German	Chemistry	Chemistry	Chemistry	Miscellaneous reading
Friday	Label, trim, arrange my fossils and minerals	Miscellaneous reading	Natural philosophy	Read geometry with Bella	History
Saturday	Miscellaneous experiments	Attend to mathematics	German	Miscellaneous reading	Natural history
Sunday	Rise at 7; then read Paley's *Natural Theology*, Milton's works, Bible, etc., until church-time.			To Nature's God through Nature's works	

less way the shops in English country districts stayed open on a Sunday; and that Buckland, when geologizing in Scotland upon the Sabbath, should have found it expedient to conceal his hammer. From the second arose a morbid self-righteousness, ever watchful for vague affronts, which repeatedly exploded into the pages of journals and caused much waste of energy and of expensive print.

But these attitudes had some beneficial counterparts. People projected the sense of dignity on to the activities they felt called on to perform. In this way many a petty institution or ritual was made to seem majestic and ennobling; many a turgid lantern-lecture and boring field excursion came to appear enlightening and uplifting. Their high mindedness made the Victorians wondrously tolerant of hard wooden seats and ill-lit, draughty halls. Nurtured on sermons, they made the devoutest possible audiences and put more into and took more out of such occasions than is the case today. Their readiness to listen and their sense of rational responsibility shored up many a learned society that in laxer times would long since have been swept into oblivion.

At the same time the grave cast to their general countenance was frequently offset by a certain levity. So long as they thought no one was likely to be looking, the Victorians were capable of a frenzied unseriousness, a totally abandoned sense of fun, seen at its best in the nonsense literature of Edward Lear and Lewis Carroll (so well described as 'inverted sermons'). Natural history was one domain where they felt it safe to unbutton. As a result, many of the periodicals of that age that had no great pretensions to weightiness are a good deal less ponderous than their present-day equivalents—and not necessarily any less useful or accurate. Which of the journals of today will read as well in a hundred years' time as Loudon's *Magazine of Natural History* or Stainton's *Entomologists' Weekly Intelligencer?* Their irresistibility lies not merely in the period quaintness or the high literary standard of so many of the individual contributions, but in their charming candour and their unselfconscious enthusiasm.

For this the comparative smallness of their world was also in part responsible. It was easier for everyone then to feel that they were writing just for one another—a browse through these old journals often leaves an uncomfortable sense of listening in to a private discussion. The great majority of naturalists in those days shared the same ideas about the purpose of the subject and were happily oblivious of potential alternative attitudes. Professionals, moreover, were sparse, and as yet there was little fragmentation by language.

This almost total absence of a separate world of professional science was one way in which the first half of the Victorian age differed quite sharply from the second. Apart from the British Museum and a handful of minor institutions (such as the museum of the Honourable East India Company in Leadenhall Street) the only full-time posts at first were the Chairs in natural history subjects, under very varied names, at the six or seven English, Scots and Irish universities. In these, professors sat in isolation, without staffs: in T. H. Huxley's words, 'an army of generals with no privates'. Lacking colleagues to share an interest in their work, a clear-cut student following or any wider public to give them a hearing (or to breathe down their necks), how hard they worked at their duties depended largely on themselves. In 1834 the Chair of Natural History at King's College London was formally done away with, due to a sheer dearth of students—for whom the subject was merely an optional, and no doubt seemingly valueless 'extra', which none in any case would ever have been likely to adopt as their profession. Of Cambridge ten years later a leading zoologist was forced to report: 'Natural history is discouraged as much as possible, and regarded as idle trifling by the thousand and one mathematicians of that venerated University.' Had it not been for the inspiring teaching of so fashionable a subject as geology and the apparently accidental demand (as we shall see) for instruction in botany by the students of medicine, the whole field would probably have continued to languish, as it had for most of the previous century, at the nation's seats of higher learning.

On the other hand, if the formal teaching of these subjects often went by default, the influence of individual professors who happened to have a personal keenness for their subject could still be very great on a purely informal basis—and possibly all the greater for being imparted 'out of school'. This was helped by the fact that so many of the professors of that age stayed all their lives in one place and could thus build up over many years a smoothly functioning social milieu—like the weekly evening meetings at his home that Henslow introduced at Cambridge for all persons interested in science, whether dons or the rawest undergraduates ('a step of immense importance in diffusing a taste for science', in the view of one of his obituarists); or like Alfred Newton's later famous Sunday evenings there for the 'bird men', into which freshly arrived enthusiasts could be fitted more or less immediately and to their infinite advantage. The very low stipends that went with teaching as such—or, even worse, as in Scotland, the slender and unreliable fees to be extracted from students—ordinarily meant that professors depended on their private means (combined, if they were lucky and at Oxbridge, with the income from the fellowship of a college). The effect of this on a university could sometimes be against its interests. As late as 1877 T. G. Bonney, on election to the Chair of Geology in University College, decided that its income was 'too small to justify the expense of housekeeping in London' and instead travelled up regularly by train from Cambridge.

Only the rashest of men embarked on a career as a teacher at a university without some auxiliary source of finance. One who did so was Robert

Jameson—with the pitiable results in later years that we have seen already. Another was Edward Forbes, who found himself obliged to take the uncongenial post of Professor of Botany (for his field by then was primarily zoology) in King's College London in 1842, after his father had unexpectedly gone bankrupt. So paltry was the salary—well under £100 a year—that he was forced to take on simultaneously the Curatorship to the Geological Society, for a further £150, scuttling to and fro from one to the other, and augmenting the combined amount in what little leisure he then had left by writing for the popular papers with his very able pen. 'Both offices are hard work, no play, and little pay,' he complained to a friend, not unreasonably. The types of post that were all that lay open to him invariably belied their grandiose titles; founded originally as resting-places of honour for amateur scholars comfortably off already, their salaries fell below subsistence level, and the brilliant men of science who were now compelled to occupy them received much less in pay than secretaries and clerks. So we find Forbes writing, in a no doubt passing mood of bitter self-reproach: 'People without independence have no business to meddle with science. It should never be linked with lucre.'

Posts within the Government service did not pay much better and normally involved even greater drudgery. This, too, often had results that went seriously against the general interest. When W. E. Leach, a physician by training, thankfully blessed with ample private means, joined the staff of the British Museum in 1813, he found the zoological collections in an appalling state of chaos and neglect, due quite simply to the fact that his predecessor, Dr George Shaw, had had little or no means beyond his tiny salary and had thus had no choice but to give virtually all of his official time to 'writing for the booksellers'. The backlog of work that had resulted was so overwhelming that Leach, in his turn, failed to cope; and his health giving way, he was forced to retire prematurely. One man, in any case, could hardly make much impression on collections of so vast a size left untended over such a lengthy period. William Swainson, writing some years later, described the basements in Bloomsbury as resembling 'the catacombs we have seen at Palermo, where one is opened every day in the year, merely to deposit fresh subjects for decay, and to ascertain how the process has gone on' during the year preceding.

Swainson himself had particular reason to grumble on this matter, for, on Leach's retirement, he had entertained every hope of being appointed his successor, on the strength of his great experience and reputation and backed by a sheaf of the most impressive testimonials. Instead, to his chagrin, the post went to J. G. Children, a chemist by training and lifelong inclination who knew no natural history at all up to the time of his appointment. It was a case of placemanship typical of the age. Until the advent of competitive examinations, in 1855, the Home Civil Service was manned exclusively by patronage, most of it political in character, with the result that no matter how able and conscientious a man might prove himself in many a junior position, he had to resign himself to the knowledge that most of the coveted senior posts were normally reserved for outsiders.

The reasons for this situation were various. Partly we may blame public apathy, partly academic and official conservatism, partly the strength of entrenched socio-political reaction. But most of all, the nation as a whole had a deep *laissez-faire* repugnance to bestowing public funds on any subject or activity, however worthy or constructive and however much it offered promise of yielding general wealth or national economic advantage. Government effort, in consequence, stayed feeble and amateurish. Starved of money, institutions seldom grew—and then only through the drive of exceptionally single-minded individuals. The Royal Botanic Gardens, Kew, that marvellous monument to the foresight and industry of the Hookers, father and son, from 1841 onwards, is a particularly fine instance of what it was possible to achieve even under these adverse conditions, always provided the right man was put in the right position in the first place.

Inevitably, the failure of the Government to give practical encouragement to science and technology, especially in the light of rival countries' efforts, attracted searing criticism from certain quarters. The Scottish philosopher, David Brewster, in an unsigned diatribe in the *Quarterly Review* in 1830, was outspoken:

> There is not a single philosopher [he claimed] who enjoys a pension, or an allowance, or a sinecure, capable of supporting him and his family in the humblest circumstances! There is not a single philosopher who enjoys the favour of his sovereign or the friendship of his ministers! . . . So thoroughly is the spirit of science subdued, and so paltry are the honours of successful inquiry, that even well-remunerated professors, and others who. . . are highly fitted by their talents to advance the interests of science, are found devoting themselves to professional authorship, and thus robbing their country of those services of which it stands so much in need.

In much the same vein was Edward Forbes's 'Sonnet to the British Public', sung to the 'Red Lions' (a rather boisterous body which he had helped to found in 1839), at one of the early meetings of the British Association:

> Oh, you learned Societies, Colleges, Schools
> You dullards and pedants, you asses and fools
> You thing called the British world scientific,
> You mob in the d—dest of folly prolific;
> Here are four 'rising young men', a hardworking crew,
> Have been slaving their souls out for you—idiots!—you.

Although all this public agitation and pressure must have played a part, in the event it was the activities behind the scenes of certain well-placed individuals that proved to have the greatest effect in bringing about a change. In the particular case of natural history this achievement can be credited very largely to just one man: Henry Thomas De la Beche—the master 'operator' of the nineteenth-century scene, the worthy heir to the line of grand interventionists that descends from Sir Hans Sloane and Sir Joseph Banks.

De la Beche, as we have seen already, started off with two very great advantages: he was personally well connected, and he could speak with unquestionable authority on behalf of the currently most respected of the sciences. His efforts were also greatly aided by the fact that his field was one into which the Government had chanced to make some first, wary steps already, thus making itself vulnerable to arguments from precedent.

To see the story in perspective it is necessary to go back to 1791. In that year the Government of the day had set up the Ordnance Survey, charging it with the task of producing a one-inch map covering the whole country—a type of work which, under the auspices of the military, had in fact become accepted as an official responsibility since the time of the 1745 Jacobite Rebellion. The first sheets of this Ordnance Survey map, covering the south-east corner of England, eventually reached the public in 1801. De la Beche, then Secretary of the Geological Society, was commissioned in 1832 to put on to this the detailed geological data relating to their mining districts; and in view of its manifest economic value saw fit to ask the Government to make a grant-in-aid towards the cost. When £300 speedily materialized, he was probably as surprised as anyone.

Seeing his chance, he proceeded to canvass the idea in the appropriate quarters of adding to the Ordnance Survey's permanent strength a small team of professional geologists. In urging this he was able to point to the state-supported geological surveys already at work in parts of France, Germany and America. In 1835 this advocacy eventually succeeded—and, appropriately, he himself was appointed the new section's Director.

Following up this success, De la Beche went on to secure the founding, in impressively quick succession, of a Museum of Practical Geology (which subsequently evolved into the Geological Museum, in South Kensington); a Government School of Mines 'and of Science applied to the Arts' (which was later to become the basis for what was—in effect, if not in name— Britain's first technological university); and a Mining Record Office, which under a different guise still lives on in Whitehall.

An important further factor in the later of these successes was the personal interest and backing of Sir Robert Peel—more particularly during his second Ministry of 1841–6. Peel's active sympathy for science was well known, and that this was no mere political pose is testified by the accounts left by some of the leading scientific figures of the period. In 1844, for example, at a soirée given in honour of the King of Saxony, he startled Edward Forbes by revealing a working knowledge of his dredging research in the Mediterranean. He was also, Forbes recorded, 'marked in his attention to Yarrell, seeking out the little man among the crowd, shaking hands with him, and telling him what pleasure his books had given him. These doings were the more notable as the minister did not talk to everybody.' Some four years later Gideon Mantell revelled in being asked to a private dinner-party at the Peels' at which almost all his fellow guests were geologists. 'Took my microscope, and shewed a few specimens to Lady and Miss Peel', he noted in his journal.

There is good reason to believe that it was their shared keenness for science that helped to bring together Peel and Prince Albert in the years after 1840, thereby reconciling the Queen to the Tories after the fall of her beloved Melbourne, and so avoiding serious constitutional embarrassment.

The Prince Consort's own role as a patron of science has been sufficiently celebrated to need no further stressing here. Perhaps less well known, though, is his fully developed taste for natural history in particular, acquired in boyhood and never entirely lost (he was, for example, a subscriber to the Ray Society at the time of his death). Reputedly, it was this proclivity of his (and not merely the general fashion of the time) that we have to thank for a whole succession of leading naturalists—Richard Owen, Charles Kingsley and Philip Gosse among them—being summoned from time to time to the Palace to give the royal children instruction. While satisfying his own deep conviction of the value of the subject, such a gesture was clearly also an immense publicity asset, confirming the previously hesitant taste in this direction of innumerable Victorian households.

Inevitably, it was geology that was the more immediate beneficiary of the Prince Consort's patronage. As the supremely 'safe' science of those days, it offered the perfect vehicle of entrée into the world of learning for a public figure who had natural history inclinations already. Before long he was able to count the great Lyell among his friends and was mingling with confidence with the cream of the Geological Society at the Marquis of Northampton's frequent sumptuous receptions. So energetic was this display of interest that the title which the firm of Tennants in the Strand so raucously proclaimed in its advertisements—MINERALOGISTS TO HER MAJESTY—may have had some rather more than nominal justification.

The politics of scientific influence at this time are difficult to disentangle. They cut across all lines of party, religious affiliation and professional solidarity. One most active force, if somewhat indistinct in its substance and coherence, has lately been distinguished under the useful name of the 'Cambridge Network'. This was essentially a pressure-group, formed from 'a loose convergence of scientists, historians, dons and other scholars, with a common acceptance of accuracy, intelligence, and novelty'; not tightly knit, but held together mainly by the agency of the personal letter. Its dominant aim was the professionalization of English science; apart from this it struggled to uphold freedom of speech and freedom of thought. It was against the conservative, aristocratic element that still controlled the Royal Society, against anything, in fact, that seemed to smack of amateurism in learning. Among its leading members were the geologist Sedgwick and the botanist Henslow. One of its several enlightened coups was the selection of Darwin for the *Beagle* voyage in 1831, his name being passed through to the Admiralty by a chain of Network men which terminated in Henslow—who put forward his favourite pupil.

Of more immediate relevance to natural history, however—and a good deal less machiavellian in their functioning—were those closely meshed dynasties of scholarly minded kinsfolk that Noel Annan has termed the 'Intellectual Aristocracy'. These came into being from the twin tendencies that developed, as the century wore on, for certain families to intermarry, sometimes again and again, either for strict sectarian reasons or through a common professional and recreational background.

The best-known one, and the most obviously wide-ranging in its influence in the world of natural history, was the great interlocking complex of leading Quaker families: the Buxtons, the Gurneys, the Hoares, the Lubbocks, the Barclays, the Cadburys. Most of these, happily, still continue to send forth a steady stream of naturalists, in response to long family custom and a certain educational predisposition in favour of these peaceful studies.

Another outstanding cluster was formed by the families of devout Evangelicals descended from the original Clapham Sect. Two of these lines in particular were highly productive of naturalists. The first, the descendants of William Arnold, included in the first generation a keen amateur geologist in the person of Dr Arnold of Rugby and a sister of his who married the brother of his old Oxford mentor, William Buckland. Subsequently, two generations later, this produced a link by marriage with the Huxley family (with the result that Sir Julian Huxley was a great-great-nephew of Buckland's sister-in-law). The second line was centred on Zachary Macaulay, the father of Lord Macaulay, the historian. One of the latter's sisters married into the Trevelyan family, a prominent member of which, Sir Walter Trevelyan, was a noted fern-collector and geologist. But, more important, an aunt of Lord Macaulay married Thomas Babington, whose nephew became the famous Professor of Botany at Cambridge and whose grand-daughter married the son of W. D. Conybeare, the geologist and

Dean of Llandaff. Professor Babington—whose own father, a great friend of William Wilberforce, was also something of a botanist—had another uncle, Thomas Gisborne, who made contributions to the *Flora of Staffordshire,* while a first cousin, the Rev. Churchill Babington, gained the Chair of Archaeology at Cambridge, collected shells and plants, and wrote *The Birds of Suffolk.*

But the largest dynasty of all, amounting to a kind of royal line running all through British natural history, is that which radiated from the Hookers.

Sir William Jackson Hooker, his son, Sir Joseph Dalton Hooker and then the latter's son-in-law, Sir William Thiselton-Dyer, kept the Directorship of Kew continuously within their family for sixty-four years. The older Hooker's wife was the daughter of Dawson Turner, the botanist and antiquary and Hooker's father's business partner—and they were both in business, as well, with the Gurneys, the Norwich bankers, Quakers and naturalists. Dawson Turner, himself an expert on seaweeds, had a brother who worked on lichens, a daughter who drew and engraved mosses, a wife who was herself an accomplished botanical illustrator, and a nephew, Thomas Palgrave, who made a name as a bryologist. He also had another son-in-law, the Rev. John Gunn, who became president of the Geological Society of Norwich.

The younger Hooker, going one better than his father, made two marriages which both brought links with numbers of prominent fellow-naturalists. The first was to a daughter of Professor Henslow, the Cambridge botanist. Henslow's own wife was the sister of the Rev. Leonard Jenyns (later Blomefield), a leading all-round naturalist, who was connected in turn with Professor Daubeny, the holder of the Oxford Chair of Botany, with the Rev. Leonard Chappelow, another very keen naturalist, and with another famous scientific family, the Wollastons. A second Henslow daughter married a leading Gloucestershire botanist and archaeologist, while his son became Lecturer in Botany at London University.

The younger Hooker's second marriage was to the widow of Sir William Jardine, the leading zoologist. She herself was the daughter of the Rev. W. S. Symonds, a geologist, author of *Old Stones* and founder of the Malvern Field Club. Symonds owed his interest in geology largely to H. E. Strickland, who besides being an ornithologist and conchologist was sufficiently adept at their sister science to be appointed Buckland's deputy at Oxford. Strickland, who had two aunts who were excellent botanical artists, married Jardine's daughter. The late Sir Norman Kinnear, the authority on Indian birds and Director of the British Museum (Natural History), was their great-nephew—thus providing a personal link by marriage between the heads of two of our foremost national institutions devoted to natural history.

This by no means exhausts the full list of naturalists belonging to this one all-pervading octopus. Its extraordinary reach is explained in part by the strong Nonconformism of at least the earlier members of the clan. But one suspects that another reason was the conspicuous eligibility of so many of the daughters, who, quite apart from their other attractions, had a lengthy, first-hand experience of natural history and so could be relied upon to be tolerant of the sometimes trying behaviour of naturalist husbands.

Though there were none quite to compare with these in extensiveness, there were many other family groups and connections by marriage that played a role in the world of Victorian natural history. Even among the group who founded the British Ornithologists' Union in the fifties one can find two examples: Canon H. B. Tristram was a cousin by marriage of his field-companion, Osbert Salvin; while H. J. Elwes married the sister of his great friends, the Godman brothers.

At first sight the frequency of this is not surprising. The range of choice of a marriage partner was far narrower then than now. Regard for social rank severely pruned the possibilities; strict chaperonage, poor transport and sometimes straitened family means combined to keep girls out of circulation. Marriage was the privilege of an envied mere majority, and there must have been a continual temptation for daughters with apparent charms or prospects to be dangled in front of likely young men who came to call on their fathers or brothers.

These circumstances all the same were hardly novel. It was, however, only with the advent of the Victorian period that naturalists came to intermarry with such impressive frequency and along so broad a front. At no time, in fact, has there occurred between the different branches of the subject such widespread miscegenation. Thus never before or since has natural history as a whole maintained such a closely knit corporate existence; and certainly never since have the various individual studies that compose it had so large a number of devotees in common.

This degree of interlocking conferred on Victorian natural history certain advantages. For a start, it ensured a continual traffic in news; one field knew for much of the time what was occurring in another and, in the process, often drew on its ideas or copied features of its institutions. It brought, too, an underlying stability in morale. The consciousness that he worked within an accepted family tradition freed a naturalist from social isolation and rendered him immune to accusations of eccentricity. It even had administrative convenience. The passing of scarce jobs from fathers down to sons—and then even on to grandsons—as happened with the Hookers or the Sowerbys, at least guaranteed a singular continuity of outlook and, in an age when poor men in ill-paid posts were so frequently undependable, meant that certain standards of probity and rectitude could be relied on to be observed simply out of regard for family tradition.

The role of these family networks as job-securing agencies, even so, must not be exaggerated. Most of them consisted largely or wholly of amateurs, among whom considerations of this nature can therefore not have arisen. Only two, in fact, were predominantly professional: the Grays, four of whom, in the space of three generations, worked on the natural history staff of the British Museum; and the Sowerbys, ten of whom, over four generations, were botanists or conchologists and gained their living as natural history draughtsmen, as dealers in specimens or—in one line, spanning three generations—as secretaries to the Royal Botanic Society (which owned a garden in Regent's Park).

Reflecting this greater sense of intimacy, perhaps partly helping to create it as well, was the great undergrowth of private entertaining that gradually grew up over and above the steadily increasing opportunities for bon-homie provided by the formal societies and clubs. In an age of spacious houses and plentiful domestic help this brought great benefits. At one extreme were magnificent receptions like those given by Sir Roderick Mur-chison and his wife, at which the leading figures in science regularly found themselves moving among the leaders of Society and fashion. Slightly less overwhelming were the dinner-parties followed by a conversazione that the wealthy laid on for their scientific friends—a usage that lasted right up until the death of Lord Avebury in 1913. There were also leisurely breakfast-parties, of the kind long since made famous by Sir Joseph Banks. It was out of a regular series of gatherings of this type that the Geological Society crystallized; while as a form of entertaining it can be found linger-ing on even today at some of the universities.

At the lowest level of formality there was a particularly useful custom known as 'open house'. This was normally on a Sunday evening, when servants were excused from cooking, the ladies of the house contented themselves with a cold supper and the menfolk conventionally took refuge in their clubs. Certain naturalists would let it be known—maybe, like Stainton, by inserting an announcement in one of the specialist journals—that they welcomed at such times anyone who cared to come along. Those who did were provided with refreshments, often on a lavish scale. Among the best-known hosts in this manner were Edward Newman, J. F. Ste-phens, J. S. Bowerbank, and the benign and generous N. B. Ward, the inventor of the Wardian Case, who used to refer to such evenings as his 'stitching parties'. It was from these last, in 1839, that the Microscopical Society was born, thanks to the enthusiasm for the microscope that Ward shared with his neighbours in Wellclose Square, the brothers Edwin and John Thomas Quekett. There is no doubt that natural history today is much the poorer for the disappearance of so simple a social device.

CHAPTER FIVE

The Fruits of Efficiency

THE NEW earnest, bustling breed of men who arrived on the scene in the 1830s—so strangely similar to that other earnest decade, the 1930s—were well pre-Victorian in origin. Their prototype was George Montagu, the methodical, vigorous, immensely painstaking lieutenant-colonel in the Wiltshire Militia who fought as a young man in the war with the American colonies and was later court-martialled and drummed out of his profession for causing trouble among his brother officers with some provocative marital skirmishing. When a long list of eager, searching questions from this unknown ornithologist arrived on the table of Gilbert White, shortly after the appearance of *Selborne,* the old spirit of restless, probing field inquiry, the spirit of Ray and Willoughby, was reborn in British natural history.

Montagu's *Ornithological Dictionary,* published just within the new century, in 1802, transformed the scientific study of birds in Britain. Just as

another military man, General Pitt-Rivers, was many years later to revolutionize archaeology, Montagu injected into the subject a brisk efficiency
and a down-to-earth, no-nonsense approach that verged on the graceless
and chilly. He was immune to the usual distractions and biases of fashion
and, like any experienced officer, well trained in assessing intelligence, ag-
gressively distrustful of all unsupported allegations and hearsay. His great
contribution was to establish scrupulous standards in the acceptance of
evidence which for many years were not to be surpassed. This was precisely what such a subject needed at that particular stage in its history: a
man without blinkers, prepared to charge about the country making certain of his facts by looking at them with his own eyes.

Hard on the heels of Montagu's massive compendium came another
influential work written in a similar spirit: A. H. Haworth's *Lepidoptora
Britannica* (1803–28), the first really comprehensive account of the British
butterflies and moths, which was to remain the standard text throughout
the first half of the century. Interestingly, in the pattern of his career Haworth mirrored the great botanical systematist George Bentham, co-author
of the later counterpart for students of British flowering plants: both were
trained as lawyers, but, possessing ample private means, preferred to devote the rest of their lives to writing scientific monographs. One important, unintended result of the continuing popularity of such a work was
that the English names employed in it also came into standard use in the
process. As the scientific nomenclature of the lepidoptera proved chronically unstable, collectors were able to make themselves consistently intelli-
gible by resorting to the vernacular equivalents.

While 'Haworth' was still in the process of appearing, James Edward
Smith also brought out his *English Flora* (1824–8). This in its turn set a
new high standard for works on plants. For a lengthy period afterwards all
similar publications are reputed to have drawn on its exceptionally full and
accurate descriptions, and by providing at last a text that could be relied
upon, it gave, in the view of a near-contemporary, 'a decided impulse to
the study of British plants, by presenting a standard and authoritative
work in our own language'. It was not to be totally superseded for many
years.

Such monster works merely continued an established tradition. Like
Albin's showy tomes or Pennant's *British Zoology* they were aimed at the
shelves of affluent gentlemen-scholars. They were not working manuals;
and the high price that went with their temptingly lavish character put
them beyond the reach, as usual, of many field-workers who genuinely had
need of them.

By the late 1820s there was a substantial unsatisfied demand for inexpensive works of identification. It was thus a singular stroke of luck that
just at that point there should have occurred a breakthrough in publishing
economics.

The prohibitive cost of printing just after the end of the Napoleonic Wars had acted as a serious brake on the progress of learned societies. In 1822 an estimate for the publication of one volume of the *Transactions* of the Geological Society of London came to no less than £369, an appalling figure for such a body to have had to contemplate. The development of steam-driven printing-presses in 1810–14 soon altered the position completely. By the end of the next decade presses could produce up to twenty times as many impressions an hour as in 1810 and costs had begun to fall accordingly. The election of the new Reform Parliament of 1832 then brought to a head the long-standing liberal objection to 'the taxes on knowledge', so deeply offensive to the passionate belief in salvation by rationalism; and within four years the heavy tax on paper and the stamp duty on newspapers were both reduced significantly, permitting a great expansion in press and periodical publishing.

A rash of natural history journals broke out as a result, along with 'numerous cheap and elegant pictorial manuals' and pocket libraries of popular instruction. Many naturalists who might never have contributed to the highly technical Transactions or Proceedings of one of the scholarly societies were now encouraged to commit themselves to print. Underpaid professors and curators found themselves agreeably harried with requests for books on this or that topic with a wide and sure appeal, and a few succumbed to the extent of becoming virtually full-time authors. More than ever before, it began to prove possible to earn a livelihood by turning out a steady flow of printed work on this and the various kindred subjects classed under the general head of Useful Knowledge.

All the same, to succeed in this, a man had to be prepared to accept harsh limitations. He could not specialize: he had to display, without hope or respite, a bogus omniscience and reckless versatility. Among the titles credited to one such writer, G. W. Francis, the author of several fairly learned works on British plants including the book (in 1837) that officially launched the great fern craze, were chemical and electrical texts for students, *Favourites of the Flower Garden* (1844), *A Manual of Practical Levelling for Railways and Canals* (1846) and *The Art of Modelling Wax Flowers* (1849).

Most of the periodicals devoted partly or wholly to natural history that were launched at this period did not last for longer than the first few issues. Runs of most of them tend to be very scarce today in consequence. Usually they were subsidized at first by some generous, if over-sanguine, well-wisher, who soon grew impatient when losses mounted, proceeded to interfere with the running, feuded with his editor and finally departed hurt. Even those that were well-conducted suffered from an intractable problem peculiar to subjects of this kind: if they were ever to pay, they had to be pitched in a sufficiently popular vein to draw and hold the largest possible audience, for naturalists in the strict sense were too few in number as yet for publications exclusively aimed at them to be commercial. Unfortunately the only people who could normally be depended on to produce regular and accurate contributions were the relatively learned workers who hungered to have their findings placed on permanent record in print. In consequence, by a kind of remorseless law, journals gradually rose above the heads of the main mass of their potential purchasers, sales then fell off and the venture quickly ended. Both the *Magazine of Natural History* and the *Magazine of Zoology and Botany*, the two worthiest productions of the period, eventually succumbed to this frustrating cycle.

The *Magazine of Natural History* was started in May 1828 by that amazing man, John Claudius Loudon. Loudon had a flair for journals of this type and made a fortune out of a similar enterprise, the *Gardener's Magazine*. Published by Longmans, this highly novel venture (for it was the first popular periodical exclusively devoted to the subject) appeared at first every other month. For three or four years it was in great demand, especially among the beginners and schoolboy naturalists to whom it was addressed in the first instance. From all parts of the country letters flowed in to Loudon, praising him for this unexampled service to the natural history community. 'Every succeeding No. makes me more and more enraptured with it,' a leading botanist, J. E. Bowman, confided to his neighbour, J. F. M. Dovaston, 'and I confidently predict that it will slowly and silently but effectually work an amazing change in the pursuits of the rising generation . . . and draw them off from the low and grovelling objects that at present form the recreations of the majority.'

In 1834, encouraged by remarks of this kind, Loudon decided to publish monthly. This proved a disastrous mistake. Many of the better contributors, like Dovaston, who had made the earlier issues so useful and readable, were already beginning to tire of the effort; the very success of the magazine, too, was now tempting into the field a growing number of rivals. Material was increasingly unforthcoming or inadequate, and the standard of the editing, insufficiently supervised because of the innumerable calls on Loudon's time, noticeably declined. After the installation in 1836 of a new, more competent managing editor, Edward Charlesworth, a professional museum naturalist of some standing, it quickly acquired a more earnestly scientific slant, and in this very useful—but, alas, unprofitable—form it limped along for a few years further. But eventually in 1840 a merger had to be arranged with another learned invalid, the *Annals of Natural History* (itself a recent hybrid product, from the merger of two earlier journals), and with this its independent existence finally came to an end.

But the journals were not the only popularizing force at this period. Something has been said already of the books that were also pouring forth, and among them a particular place of honour must be reserved for the long series of works on zoology, forty in all, that made up Jardine's *Naturalist's Library*. These appeared at intervals of every three months or so from 1833 to 1845, fifteen of them written by the conceiver of the series, Sir William Jardine himself, and were placed on the market at a much lower price than was normal then for natural history books (at least of their quality). Swainson's account of the Flycatchers, for example, with over thirty coloured plates, sold for six shillings, 'not one third of the price at which many works of no greater scientific value have been and are still published', according to the *Magazine of Natural History*.

Another important development was the introduction of lithography. Invented in Germany between 1796 and 1798, this method of drawing in ink or crayon on a certain kind of limestone allowed more subtle effects to be attained by way of illustration and, more important, brought greater speed and economy in printing. Its first appearance in this country in a work of natural history was probably in 1812, when Ackermann's *A Series of Thirty Studies from Nature* was published with lithographs. In 1815 there was still only one exponent of the method at work in the whole of Britain. Two years after this John Phillips employed it for reproducing a number of geological sections in colour, which he offered for sale at a shilling each. This appears to have been the earliest use for a strictly scientific purpose. The first major use in this respect was by William Swainson for the first series of his *Zoological Illustrations* (1820–23). The process then was still uncertain, and it was necessary to draw the same subject several times before the printer succeeded in obtaining a satisfactory impression. Gradually it came into use as an accepted alternative to copperplate engraving (the method favoured, for example, by the Sowerby family) and eventually overtook and largely superseded it. John Gould became its best-known exemplar, early adopting it for his marvellous illustrations of birds because, by enabling the artist's work to be transferred directly to the plate, it allowed the most minute details of the plumage and colour to be preserved. The bulging picturebooks which had been produced so generally till then for people with more cash than knowledge—or even literacy—thus came at last into their own as scientific tools of the requisite precision and exactness; and the great increase in accurate coloured illustrations in natural history works which occurred in consequence helped to stimulate still more interest in the subject.

In the light of all these encouragements—a growing and readily available literature, a regard for nature dictated by fashion, a prevailing ethic that sanctioned, if not sanctified, collecting—it is not surprising to find many a writer at this time testifying to the striking growth of interest that could be seen. In an article entitled 'Proofs of the Increasing Taste for Natural History', *Blackwood's Magazine* as early as 1818 was insisting that the subject, 'at one period so much neglected in this island, has now become a general study. The man of business, as well as the philosopher, takes an interest even in the details of this delightful branch of knowledge'. By 1831 this same magazine reported that 'the works of genuine naturalists, such as White's *Selborne* and Knapp's *Journal of a Naturalist,* are selling by thousands, and will continue to sell to the tune of tens of thousands'. Around the same time George Samouelle, in the *Entomological Cabinet,* wrote with awe of the 'wonderful progress in England, much beyond what the author could have expected', that had taken place in just this one branch of the subject in the ten years since 1820.

It was the tremendous access of interest in birds that came in more particularly for comment. In that golden age of game-preserving it would have been remarkable indeed had there been no non-sporting side-effects, and the forming of collections of stuffed birds and, increasingly, of birds' eggs was enjoying a great expansion. But there was, besides, a deeper current: an aesthetic awakening brought about by the gradual discovery of *Selborne* and by the much-admired woodcuts in the works of Thomas Bewick, the humble Tyneside engraver whose labours were infused with a profound and lifelong love of nature. 'I have, all my life, busied myself with feeding Birds', Bewick once disclosed to a friend—a singular practice for that period, and part of the secret of the vitality and accuracy of his illustrations. Of his books he himself confessed:

> I did not ever think they would have been so singularly noticed by such numbers of people grown up to maturity . . . My efforts were directed to the rising generation and my object was to inveigle youth onwards by the vignettes to the study of natural history, up to nature's god.

Bewick was, first and foremost, an artist; his concern with recording scientific facts was, by comparison, not great and his behaviour in this respect at times cavalier. His *History of British Birds* became the textbook of a generation *faute de mieux* and its author insufficiently appreciated this extra, all-important role he had accidentally come to fill. When, in 1823, a group of Shropshire naturalists sent him the extensive harvest of many years of unusually careful observation for inclusion in the forthcoming sixth edition, he expressed his thanks—and proceeded to ignore it almost entirely, thereby seriously discouraging them and probably stunting the progress of field ornithology in this country.

Bewick, even so, had laid a vital groundwork, and it was on this that successive authors all through the rest of the century preferred to build. The next storey, erected by William Yarrell—with the very same title, to emphasize the continuity—appeared in 1837–43, at two-monthly intervals in thirty-seven parts. With good plates and tolerably accurate, it quickly became the standard handbook, with progressive extensions over the years until its culmination, in 1889, in the guise of the classic *Manual* of Howard Saunders. Unhappily, so great and complete was its success that it quite overshadowed a much more profound work of the same title, with a drier, more academic content ('all guts and gizzards', as its author put it, wryly), that was brought out almost simultaneously by MacGillivray.

Besides these literary and sporting influences there may have been a further one of which we know tantalizingly little. Our principal source of information, once again, is Swainson, that invaluable fount of comment on the period. In a passage tucked away in the middle of a treatise on taxidermy, published in 1840, he remarks in passing:

> In nothing has the growing taste for natural history so much manifested itself, as in the prevalent fashion of placing glass cases of beautiful birds and splendid insects on the mantel piece or the side-table. The attention of the most indolent is attracted, the curiosity of the inquisitive awakened.

His implication is that converts to natural history were being won simply by repeated exposure to such displays.

There is something about this fashion that is mysterious and suggestive. It coincided with, maybe even antedated, the first wave of enthusiasm for filling drawing-rooms and window-sills with Ward's new closely glazed cases of ferns and other greenhouse exotics. That widespread taste for bottling up natural objects under glass which we think of as quintessentially Victorian, clearly started earlier than is generally supposed; it must, in fact, be pre-Victorian. Quite suddenly, it seems, people felt the urge to surround themselves with choice extracts from nature in the interiors of their homes. There was no change just then in the price or availability of glass; and collections of birds in individual cases had been known since early in the previous century. Was there, then, some more elusive motive? Was this, perhaps, the first reaction of the newly emergent urban middle classes to their permanent exile from nature by the ugly sprawl of industrialism? Can the great growth of interest at this period in birds and insects—in particular—be interpreted as a protest by an unhealthily deprived subconscious?

The new fascination for insects was even more striking than that for birds. That the two occurred together—as was to happen again, much later, in the 1890s—may have been no accident. In place of the flowers and shells, the static, stylized, pretty-pretty edging that formed the principal appeal of nature to eighteenth-century man, the nineteenth century seemed to feel the lure of wings, needed to gratify itself with something closer to flesh and blood, with more life-like souvenirs of the starkly elemental. The swing to birds and insects, it may be, was at base a switch of symbols.

Stirrings of an amply rational kind, even so, are evident in British entomology at this period. For a start, the subject had its full share of disputatious excitement. W. S. Macleay's Quinarian Theory, introduced in his *Horae Entomologicae* (1819–21), served much the same attention-winning function for this science as Catastrophism was doing for geology. Like Catastrophism, too, its origins were French. The son of another distinguished entomologist who was for many years Secretary of the Linnean Society before being appointed Colonial Secretary of New South Wales, Macleay had spent several years in Paris as attaché at the British Embassy and made many friends among the leading naturalists of France. From there he had returned to England steeped in a peculiarly Continental strain of Romanticism and convinced of the truth of a semi-mystical system of classifying nature somewhat akin to the theories propagated by Goethe. According to this, all life on earth was organized in terms of the number five, conveniently allowing the myriad animals and plants to be grouped together on this basis. So bizarre a theory was bound to be irresistible to many. What is more, its proponent was a man of no small academic stature and the very extensive data put forward in its support demanded that it be taken seriously by scholars. Even more convincingly, two fervent champions presently appeared in the somewhat unexpected persons of N. A. Vigors and William Swainson, both of them in the forefront of contemporary systematics. As a result the theory was argued over fiercely and at length. In the end, inevitably, orthodoxy prevailed; but we have Swainson's own word for it, many years later, that the controversy, scientifically sterile though it proved, did at least give the subject a vigorous winding-up and started it off on a climb to popularity.

This climb was helped by a number of unusually attractive books. Of these, the most influential were the delightful volumes that made up the *Introduction to Entomology*, by the Rev. William Kirby, a country vicar in Suffolk, and William Spence, a businessman in Hull. Kirby had won renown already with a monograph on English bees, and the two had entered into correspondence arising out of this in 1805, the year of Trafalgar. They found they both keenly felt the need of an accurate and comprehensive guide which would help and interest beginners; and four years later they were able to meet in person and start to plan its writing. The first volume was published in Waterloo year, 1815, and at once proved so popular that it had passed through several editions by the time the third and fourth volumes were ready to be added in 1826. Few semi-technical works on natural history can be read and re-read with such unchanging pleasure. Most attractively written, it captures the spirit of the old collectors in a way that has probably never been rivalled. It is not hard to believe that many new converts to the subject—converts, at least, from the usual listless and transient schoolboy collecting—were won from a happy reading of its pages.

Very soon, many other authors were tempted into trying to emulate the huge success of Kirby and Spence, but none succeeded in achieving quite so irresistible a flavour. Edward Newman, that excellent writer, probably came closest.

There was certainly a strong inducement all over England (though hardly at all in Scotland, which long remained comparatively uninterested). An enthusiasm for entomology had sprung up, so powerful that it even threatened to swamp natural history's other branches. Of Cambridge in the late 1820s the Rev. Leonard Jenyns was later to recall:

> Never before . . . was natural history so much in favour in the University; nor has it ever since held the place it then occupied . . . So numerous were the Entomologists in particular . . . that several persons among the lower classes derived a part of their livelihood during the summer months from collecting insects for sale, especially in the fens which abound with so many rare and local species.

Among these undergraduates so badly bitten by the bug were Charles Darwin and the subsequent Professor of Botany, C. C. Babington, who became so besotted with the order Coleoptera as to acquire the temporary nickname 'Beetles'.

A predictable result was the reappearance in entomology of specialist societies. A third Aurelian Society had been formed as far back as 1801 and, after a shaky start and a change in name, this had flourished to the extent of publishing *Transactions*. But it now lost out to another, more recent body, which was able to put on a show of sufficiently greater vigour to deprive it of most of the newcomers; and before long it had gone the way of both of its predecessors. The usurper was the Zoological Club of the Linnean Society. Its founders had originally had in mind a further, independent society devoted to entomology; but to allay the hostility of the Linnean to the creation of a potentially powerful rival, it was decided to function under its nominal aegis. The relationship proved from the first an uneasy one. It also had a conspicuous absurdity, in that one of the Club's main supporters, J. E. Gray, could never formally be enrolled as a member as he was permanently excluded from the Linnean by Smith and his lackeys. For six years, nevertheless, the Club persisted as a society within a society, producing what amounted to its own separate periodical, the *Zoological Journal*.

This situation, however, could not last. The Club's notably greater liveliness began to arouse the resentment of the remainder of the Linnean Fellows, who saw it turning into a cuckoo that would surely end up appropriating their nest. The members of the Club, in turn, began to give thought to transferring their allegiance elsewhere.

In 1826 this, in effect, is what they did; for the Zoological Society of London that was brought into being in that year, primarily at the instance of Sir Stamford Raffles, noticeably drew on the Club for its initial set of officers. Support for the Club now quickly dwindled, its journal became spasmodic, its funds ran out, and eventually, late in 1829, its death was formally pronounced. In the very next year the Zoological Society (the founding of which had not incurred the Linnean's displeasure, because it revealed no plans to publish learned papers) set up a scientific committee, began to hold scientific meetings and proceeded to embark upon a programme of publication. Although its relevance for the study of the natural history of these islands has always been at best marginal, the success of the Zoological Society established an important precedent. In future, the trend towards greater specialization could find its embodiment in new national societies without being credibly accused any longer of endangering the unity of the subject. The result was that the 'centre', represented by such societies as the Linnean, experienced a serious draining-away of supports to the 'wings', which merely served to intensify its already inturned and uninvitingly lethargic character.

The Zoological Society was not to benefit as the main home of British entomologists for very long, however. Already, in 1826, while it was still in the process of being founded, four keen London collectors, including Samouelle and Newman, had banded themselves together as an Entomological Club, meeting in each other's homes in rotation one evening every month. In 1832 Newman launched the *Entomological Magazine* to serve in effect as the journal of this body, and this managed to last out for as long as seven years. The Club purposely kept itself minute, in order to preserve its atmosphere of cosy camaraderie; this prevented it from growing too ambitious and thus saved it from the fate of so many of its predecessors. After being reorganized once at least in later years, it ultimately enjoyed a very marked revival after 1887, when G. H. Verrall, the official Starter at Newmarket and a leading authority on flies, turned it into a vehicle for large annual Suppers at which he delighted to entertain the pick of British entomology entirely at his personal expense. These gay affairs have continued down to the present and are known as Verrall Suppers in honour of their founder. The Club, too, still survives, and though no more than a dining-out appendage to the Entomological Society, it can fairly lay claim to the title of the longest-continuing association in the world exclusively devoted to entomology.

It is sometimes asserted that it was the Entomological Club that gave birth to the second (and still thriving) Entomological Society of London, but there is no evidence for this. If there was a clear parent, it was, rather, the Zoological Society. For the entomologists, who had abandoned their club within the Linnean Society in order to give this new body their wholehearted support, appear to have become speedily disillusioned; and in May 1833 a group of nine met at the British Museum and decided, after all, to set up a society exclusive to their study. The creation of just such a body in Paris in only the previous year may well have served as the final trigger.

Two features of the Entomological Society of London are worthy of special note. First, of the nine people who attended the original meeting, no less than five were professional naturalists (almost all of them on the staff of the British Museum). This was thus the earliest natural history society to be launched preponderantly by professionals—even though, almost at once, they crept away into the background and left the running to the amateurs. Three of the founders in particular were old hands by now at managing the affairs of such societies. They were, indeed, the linchpins of organized natural history at this period, turning up at the head of one body after another like a miniature stage army. Natural history owes them a great debt and their names deserve to be remembered: Vigors, an ex-Grenadier Guards officer and an advanced liberal in politics who by this time had entered Parliament, was also a founding member and first Secretary of the Zoological Society, a Council member of the Linnean, a main promoter of its Zoological Club and co-editor of the later volumes of its journal; J. E. Gray, of the British Museum, also an instigator of the Zoological Club, was soon to help found and for many years preside over the Botanical Society of London; and Yarrell, who ran a newspaper agency just off Piccadilly and acted as Treasurer of the new Society for eighteen years, was also Secretary for a time of the Zoological Society and Treasurer of the Linnean. Only Stainton's roll of office can compare: Secretary, at various periods, of the Ray Society, the Entomological and the Linnean, and for one short term even on the Council of the Royal Society.

The second point worthy of notice, singled out for comment by William Swainson, was the relatively informal atmosphere of the Entomological Society's meetings compared with those of almost all other London bodies at this period. In this respect its forerunner, the Zoological Club, had also differed quite sharply from the eighteenth-century ponderousness of its adoptive parent, the Linnean. The entomologists, people noticed, were much younger on the average and more obviously ardent. The subscription was fairly low. The library and collections were freely accessible, without the formalities and delays so often complained of elsewhere. No persons secured election merely on account of their name—that is to say, the Society was free of the prevalent obsession with rank. And finally, the membership was an effective one, not, as with so many other societies, to a great extent nominal: there was, in Swainson's words, 'no quackery in its composition'.

Within the first eighteen months of its existence the Society acquired more than a hundred members. Quite a number of these seem to have come from the ranks of the Cambridge entomologists, and two of those who joined at once were Babington and Darwin, both of whom kept up their membership for the remainder of their lives. But from then on progress was slow. The numbers grew by only 52 per cent over the space of fourteen years and in 1840–43 the membership more than halved, dropping to a mere eighty-eight, clearly due to a severe weeding-out of the large number who had failed to keep up with their subscriptions—a singularly drastic change on which the official history of the Society is oddly silent. By 1849 it found itself seriously in debt; but, thanks to Stainton, a successful membership drive was mounted and publication of the Society's *Transactions* fortunately escaped suspension. It is clear nevertheless that the Society at this time was very far from being properly representative of the country's entomologists.

In the world of botany, in the meantime, events had taken a completely unexpected turn.

The underlying cause of this has long remained obscure. As so often in social history, the particular circumstances at the time that we most want to know about must have seemed to contemporaries so commonplace or so utterly apparent that it occurred to hardly anyone to refer to them explicitly. The one clue so far traced is contained in a little-known book published in 1816, *The Botanist's Companion*. The author, William Salisbury, had been first a pupil and then the partner of William Curtis in a private teaching establishment which the latter had launched in 1770 after resigning from his post with the Apothecaries. The core of the enterprise was a small botanic garden—at first almost on the site where the Festival Hall now stands and ultimately in Sloane Street—in connection with which courses of lectures and field excursions were offered for a fee to the London medical students, clearly in straight imitation of the long-established Apothecaries' tradition. Salisbury wrote his book partly to advertise the fact that he had just made plans to institute a full-scale herbarizing school, 'a recent act of the legislature [in his words] having made [a knowledge of plants] indispensable to all the younger branches of the medical profession'.

This startling statement refers to the Apothecaries' Act of 1815, long conventionally cited as one of the great turning-points in the history of medical education in this country. In reality, however, as some recent research has made clear, the Act was highly retrograde, the quite unintended result of a legislative muddle. What its main protagonists *meant* it to do was to control the dispensing of drugs throughout England and Wales. What it actually ended up by doing was to confer on the Society of Apothecaries, a hitherto purely London body, the monopoly of licensing all the general practitioners in the country (except for Scotland and Ireland), none of whom, however highly qualified already, were henceforth allowed to practise without having first served a five-year apprenticeship to an apothecary. As it failed even in its original aim of preventing ignorant quacks from prescribing or dispensing drugs, the Act was thus a disaster for medicine and pharmacy in general—even though that reactionary body, the College of Physicians, welcomed it as a means of acquiring a metropolitan stranglehold on all the country's medical education. For botany it was a no less unexpected, but quite unprecedented, windfall. For it meant that from then on every single medical student—including even those at Scottish and Irish universities, should they contemplate practising in England (as so many of them did)—had to work up at least some minimal acquaintance with British plants.

It was this freak happening, more than likely, rather than the example set by the geologists in the persons of Buckland and Jameson, that lay behind the remarkable burgeoning of field classes in botany that suddenly took place in several British universities about this time—in itself possibly the most important development ever to have taken place in the history of organized field botany in this country. Regular field classes (attended almost entirely by medical students) were started at Glasgow by the elder Hooker in 1821 and almost simultaneously at Edinburgh by Robert Graham. Seven years later Henslow introduced them at Cambridge. All three professors, we know, were closely in touch with one another and, almost certainly, this was not coincidence but straight imitation. In all three places the excursions aroused tremendous enthusiasm, and perhaps most of all at Edinburgh, where Graham quickly proved himself another Thomas Wheeler. Several detailed accounts of his classes have been left on record by his students. They show quite clearly that the Edinburgh excursions resembled those of the London Apothecaries with a very suggestive exactness, down even to quite small details. A deliberate copying, again, is highly likely—and, in view of the Apothecaries' age-old reputation in this matter, perhaps only to be expected.

Just how important these field classes were to prove for the future of British field botany can be glimpsed from the names of some of those who attended them in these early years. Hooker, we find, took out David Douglas, later to win fame as a plant-collector in America, Dr Walker Arnott, later Professor of Botany at Glasgow, H. C. Watson and the leading student of mosses, William Wilson—these last two as extra-mural guests, several of whom often joined the Glasgow or Edinburgh parties on their lengthier, weeklong excursions into the remoter and unexplored parts of the Highlands. Henslow's flock at Cambridge included Darwin, Babington and the great mycologist Berkeley. At Edinburgh Graham taught his successor, J. Hutton Balfour, as well as several other incipient teachers who carried the torch far afield as they moved on elsewhere: Edward Forbes, for example, who started Grahamite excursions for his botany students at King's College London in 1843, 'alarming the neighbouring villages by an invasion of twenty or so *vasculiferi*' and winding up the day at an inn, 'with lots of punch (in moderation) and good songs'—a typical piece of Forbesian conviviality. It was Graham's excursions, too, which fathered indirectly the Berwickshire Naturalists' Club, the parent, as we shall see, of a vast brood of local field clubs which were to populate the landscape of mid-Victorian Britain.

Apart from introducing generation after generation of students to the secret delights of field-work, these classes also popularized—and in the process standardized and cheapened, thanks to the large and steady market they created—various kinds of field equipment. Foremost among these was the botanist's stethoscope, the vasculum. At Edinburgh and Cambridge, already in the 1820s, vascula were apparently carried universally, every student being expected to provide himself with one before attending an excursion. The long Highland explorations also fostered much experimenting with drying methods (and led to the discovery of a better kind of paper for this purpose) due to the need for extreme simplification under the highly primitive conditions that were regularly encountered. There were so few inns in the areas visited that Hooker on one occasion supplied the party with a single large marquee, which was transported in a Dutch wagon pulled by a Highland pony. Another time the whole party had to sleep elbow to elbow on a large bed of heather spread out over the floor of a cottage.

It was expressly for the students on such classes that Hooker wrote his *British Flora* (1830), which was later to be merged with another, more popular handbook to become the famous 'Bentham and Hooker'. The standard contemporary text, Smith's *English Flora*, was far too voluminous for the field as well as impossibly expensive for students. By pruning it severely, Hooker was able to produce a single octavo volume. Whilst this met the needs of the more persevering beginner, it was nevertheless unsatisfactory for the more experienced; and for them Babington devised his *Manual of British Botany* (1843). Both books ran to numerous editions, continuing all through the century.

The exceptional *esprit de corps* built up among Graham's students bubbled over into the founding, first, in 1823, of the Plinian Society of Edinburgh, a general scientific society which organized occasional field excursions; and later, in February 1836, of the much more important Botanical Society of Edinburgh, the chief promoter of which was Edward Forbes.

This new body, from the start, resolved to make one of its primary functions the organized exchange of specimens on a national scale—'a new feature in the constitution of such a society', as the *Magazine of Natural History* observed. Rather more than six years before, a blueprint for such a scheme had appeared in that very same journal, over the initials of H. C. Watson: apparently the first foray into print, at the age of twenty-five, of the man who was shortly to become the acknowledged leader of Victorian field botany. In this note Watson had proposed a kind of commodity exchange, to which collectors could send their surplus specimens and receive in return others that they particularly wanted, paying the equivalent of a brokerage commission on all exchanges effected or, alternatively, an annual subscription or entrance fee, to make the whole undertaking economic. The best plan, he thought, would be for people to mark their desiderata in certain standard publications which would serve as catalogues, each item being marked in such a way as to indicate its rarity or other criterion of value.

This master-concept, a grand information-exchange embracing the whole of natural history, lay at the centre of Watson's thinking for the rest of his life. And although the Edinburgh Society was founded some three years after his departure from that University to take up residence in the south, there can be little doubt that it was to his fertile brain that the Society owed the central idea which led to its success. Certainly, it is significant that in the very first year of its activities it was Watson who made more use of its exchange facilities than almost anyone else. The Society also followed his blueprint faithfully by issuing a special catalogue of British flowering plants and ferns, which members were urged to use when sending in lists of their desiderata. Furthermore, the fact that a contributor was able to specify what specimens he wanted—and have reason to expect them in proportion to the amount and value of what he contributed himself—was a vital aspect of Watson's original scheme (and not necessarily one that would have found its way into anyone else's). Watson's characteristic far-sightedness can be recognized, too, behind the Society's ordinance that a record of all labels sent in with material for exchange was to be preserved, with a view to their use in the compiling of local Floras and, ultimately, of a complete Flora of Britain. Thus was born the first 'network research' within the field of botany.

Five months later, almost certainly stimulated by the Edinburgh Society's example, a meeting was convened in the English capital which speedily gave rise to a Botanical Society of London, on virtually identical lines. Daniel Cooper, a nineteen-year-old medical student and the author in that year of a small Flora of the environs of the Metropolis, appears to have been the prime initiator, helped and encouraged by J. E. Gray and a number of keen local amateurs and by some of the lecturers in botany at the hospital medical schools. The medical world, in fact, was for many years heavily represented in its make-up: in 1839, for example, two fifths of the council and officers were drawn from the ranks of this profession. By the end of the first year the membership had reached sixty-five and continued to rise steadily, passing 250 at the end of the next decade—a markedly different pattern from the violent ups and downs of the Entomological Society.

Unlike the entomologists, the London (and Edinburgh) botanists made a special effort to expand their membership in the provinces, distinguishing such recruits as Corresponding Members and even going so far as to designate quite a number as Local Secretaries (the London Society had no less than twenty-five of these by 1839, comprising fully one quarter of the total membership). The purpose of this, plainly, was to build up a country-wide network of collectors, who would send in a plentiful supply of specimens from the lesser-known outlying parts and so make the central principle of exchange that much more appealing and effective. Essentially, this was the same policy that the Geological Society had pursued some years earlier under Greenough, but there is no reason to suppose that the botanists were influenced at all by the geologists or were even aware of their pioneering efforts. Indeed, they seem to have started out with very vague ideas of what they hoped to achieve by this novel kind of cooperative activity.

For the first five years or so the youthful and energetic Daniel Cooper did his best to cope with the mounting burden of the annual Exchange, making up and sending out the many parcels of duplicates from the Society's herbarium in an order of size designed to match the value of the specimens which each collector had contributed. But well-meaning though he was, his methods were slapdash; and the frequency with which specimens became separated from their labels and then, maybe, attached to wrong ones, was sufficient to cast serious doubt for ever afterwards on the trustworthiness for scientific purposes of this key aspect of the Society's work in these earliest years. It was not altogether unfortunate therefore that Cooper presently decided to enter the army as a surgeon and in consequence resigned the office.

In his place, by a stroke of great good luck, the Society was able to obtain the services of no less a person than the system's original conceiver—H. C. Watson himself. Watson had moved down to live near London some ten years previously, but until then, it appears, had played no part at all in the Society's activities. A lifelong bachelor, subsisting on a small private income, his whole time was given over to his lengthy and detailed studies of the distribution of the flowering plants within the British Isles and of the factors controlling their spatial occurrence, a new science which he made very much his own and which he pursued with the full intensity of any true professional for, quite apart from one, seemingly half-hearted attempt to secure a Chair at an Irish university, he worked away all through life with an outlook so uncompromisingly scientific and with a dedication so total and continuous that it hardly makes sense to class him as an amateur. By 'professionalism' we mean, in effect, a certain rigour of application and intensity of emotional commitment; and these qualities need not always be associated with the holding of a full-time paid position.

At the same time Watson subscribed to a personal code of conduct that was almost shackling in its severity. It made him touchy to a fault, at times preposterously stiff-necked; but it also held him to a course of action unswervingly once he had decided this was necessary and correct. On such occasions he would give of his utmost, without thought of any reward or honour, and, as far as possible, anonymously. It was from some such motive, we can be sure, that he consented to serve the Society as its new 'Distributor', and it was typical of him that he should have insisted on holding the office strictly unofficially—and relinquished it, eventually, as soon as he found that the rest of the Society did not wholly share his opinion of its sovereign status and potential.

In no time at all he overhauled the existing methods and made them a model of efficiency. He ensured that all gatherings of new, unknown or otherwise difficult entities were submitted from now on to appropriate national experts for comment, thus immeasurably increasing the value of the material sent back to contributors under the Society's label, and introduced the practice of publishing the more interesting of these remarks in print in the country's leading botanical periodical. He bullied the Society into bringing out a standard checklist, known as the *London Catalogue of British Plants*, so that all who sent in plants could be made to observe the same common system of nomenclature and thereby provided British botanists in general with a cheap and handy list of the latest accepted names, which did much to bring about a helpful uniformity of reference. He also contributed extensively to the Exchanges himself, and thereby received in return a great mass of invaluable material which enormously aided him in his own researches.

By his efforts, Watson claimed, he had saved the Society from almost certain extinction. Never a man to mince his words, he publicly advanced the view that the exchange activities were the one function by which the Society had so far justified its existence; and he deplored the obsession of so many of the members with holding meetings and with building up a large library and reference herbarium, for which the Society had neither the funds, the skilled labour nor the necessary resident knowledge. Instead of these over-grandiose, wrongly centripetal aims—of trying to turn itself into a specialized version of the Linnean Society—he saw it as serving a far more useful purpose by cultivating a centrifugal, non-localized approach, thereby catering for the country as a whole and not just for a handful of privileged London members. '*Tempora mutantur:* the object for which scientific societies used to be instituted', he wrote, 'are now better effected by periodical literature, by travelling, by correspondence, and by exchanges.' A remarkably prescient, if somewhat premature, statement for the year 1849.

One further development for which he was probably responsible was a notable improvement in the quality of the Society's annual intake—quite abruptly, in 1846, and coinciding very suggestively with Watson's final work on the first volume of his *magnum opus* on plant distribution, *Cybele Britannica*. It seems very probable that in seeking out more and more local workers scattered all over the country, to whom he could send his copies of the Society's checklist for marking up in it the species occurring in their areas, he took the opportunity, as Greenough had done with his local geologists, to interest them in the Society's facilities and so usefully incorporate them into the existing national network.

Not long after this, however, Watson resigned as Distributor. About the same time the meetings grew less regular and the entering-up of the minutes suddenly developed marks of negligence. For several years thereafter the reports of the Society's activities which had long regularly appeared in a variety of periodicals also virtually ceased. Eventually, late in 1856, a winding-up meeting was announced, the books and collections were sold to pay off arrears of rent, and the Society was pronounced defunct. The surplus from the liquidation, a mere thirty pounds or so, was given to G. E. Dennes, the honorary secretary, a solicitor by profession, who (according to one of Watson's letters) was 'in a starving condition' and is believed soon afterwards to have taken ship to Australia.

What exactly happened remains a mystery to this day. Quite possibly Watson's strictures in 1849 proved only too well-founded, and the Society's growing ambition over-reached its never very well-lined pocket. The minutes in the forties show that even then the Society subsisted in a permanently precarious financial condition, to the extent that if more than even a few members fell into arrears with their subscriptions, activities in general had to be trimmed down correspondingly. It seems odd that the Society (and others like it) failed to launch a once-and-for-all appeal in order to place itself on a permanently secure footing, or that it failed to enjoy any private benefactions and endowments. The Geological Society, by comparison, had such ample ancillary sources as the much-prized Wollaston Fund—to be used in 1834 to bring over a leading foreign scholar like Louis Agassiz and put him to work on the fossil collections in the country's leading museums.

From the wreckage of the Society the exchange activities, mercifully, were rescued more or less intact. These carried on, without any serious break, at first from a base in north Yorkshire and later, after 1865, again from London. Stripped of all its real estate, the Society now became perforce the purely postal body long since urged by Watson, and entered upon a lengthy convalescence under the more restricted name of the Botanical Exchange Club.

The Edinburgh Society, meanwhile, had been even more creative. For a start, unlike its London sister (which only ever rose to a single number of its *Proceedings*), it issued annual reports and *Transactions* in an uninterrupted manner. It gained a great deal, too, by being closely associated with the university which was generally accepted at this time as the leader in the field of botany and which had among its teachers and students of the subject a quite exceptional array of gifted individuals. One of these in particular, William Brand, an ex-student of Graham's who by this time was a fledgling lawyer, played a most important role which has been undeservedly neglected.

In 1838, in trying to devise the most satisfactory method of logging the vast amount of distributional data that was starting to flow into the Society through its exchanges, Brand hit upon the idea of dividing the British Isles into 42 numbered 'districts', roughly equal in size and based on the existing counties grouped as far as possible to reflect the main river-basins. In making up a looseleaf register of the Society's collections, he was then able to rule the pages of this into 42 columns, so that the presence or absence of species in each district could be pinpointed at a glance. A map showing his districts was exhibited by Forbes that September at the annual meeting of the British Association, with the suggestion that some such common base-map should be used for recording the distribution of all British species—animals as well as plants. A special committee was accordingly set up and entrusted with the task of having a sample set of maps of this type lithographed. Copies were circulated in proof to a variety of naturalists for comment, and the agreed version finally became available for use in 1842.

In the very next year, in the latest in his series of major works on British plant geography, Watson published 'provincial distribution maps' for 39 different species of flowering plants. These maps were based on a subdivision of Great Britain into 18 broad areas, named after their principal rivers. Though the concept was strikingly similar to Brand's, there is no reason to doubt Watson's assertion that he had acted entirely in ignorance of the Edinburgh work.

In the event, it was Watson's system that prevailed. Apart from the wide influence he commanded through his books, he alone refused to treat this first, gross dividing-up of the country as a permanent solution. As more and more data accumulated, he switched over without compunction to progressively smaller units, until in 1873–4, in his culminating grand

compendium, *Topographical Botany,* his original 18 'provinces' had dimin-
ished to as many as 112 'vice-counties' (as he had in fact anticipated in
print some twenty years before). Had he only lived, there is no doubt that
even these would have been abandoned by him in time for that ultimate in
biological cartography, the dot distribution map. Certainly, in an article on
map construction in the *Magazine of Natural History* as early as 1836, he
had envisaged this as the ideal—even though at the time he had rejected it
as hopelessly impracticable.

As it was, the 'vice-county' system became so popular and generally accepted as the basic unit of recording in this country that it ended up by
considerably outstaying its usefulness. Watson's death left such a hiatus in
forward thinking on the topic that it was not until 1936—exactly a hundred years after its initial foreshadowing—that a dot-map of the full
known range of a British plant was eventually published. By that time
maps of this kind had long been in use on the Continent (since as early as
1860 in Germany), and it was impossible to pretend that our failure to
take to them was due to lack of awareness of their superior potential. It was
simply that the Watsonian system had been allowed to set solid and British
methods of recording had become so chronically committed to it that a
change by then seemed intolerable.

The reason why the 'vice-county' exercised so strong a hold is not difficult to understand. For the first time a unit had been sanctioned which was
small enough to offer almost inexhaustible scope for new records—and
thus, by his own reckoning, for demonstrable scientific usefulness—to the
ordinary, comparatively static local worker. From now on a naturalist need
not leave his own estate or his parish in order to feel that his hunting
served a purpose in the national scheme of things. A man could share pride
in his county: with his 'vice-county' he could identify individually. For
those who wanted a relatively undemanding pretext for combing the
countryside immediately to hand Watson had provided the perfect answer;
and throughout the final quarter of the century the task of filling in the
gaps that his preliminary cataloguing had disclosed supplied the study
with a great part of its momentum.

The search for better means of mapping distribution was not the only
way in which British field botany showed signs of anticipating the future.
A careful scrutiny of the literature reveals plenty of other thinking that
now seems astonishingly modern. Thus, in a paper read before the Botanical Society of London in 1836, Alexander Irvine proposed that the members should undertake a collaborative Flora of London, for which

> printed lists of species should be circulated among the Botanists of the metro-
> politan districts . . . Such lists having columns for the insertion of the precise
> habitation of the species, the nature of the soil where it grows, the altitude of
> its locality, the time of flowering, and such like.

Two years later, the members of the same Society were being urged to aim at much greater precision in the citing of localities, 'making the compass the companion of the vasculum'—in other words, as botanists have learned to do only fairly recently, furnishing their records with pin-pointing map-references. In 1844, in the *Phytologist*, there is a path-finding note by Watson 'On the number of botanical species to a square mile of ground'. And in the period 1840–47 the Rev. W. H. Coleman, a young Hertford schoolmaster, devised a set of methods in preparing a Flora of Hertfordshire that were essentially the same as those used over a hundred years later by the members of the Botanical Society of the British Isles in collecting the data for the *Atlas of the British Flora*. Each district was allot-ted to one or other of his various helpers, who, he found, 'having a local interest in the reputation of their respective districts, were stimulated to increase their diligence'. A register was prepared, divided into columns for each of the districts (the method pioneered by Brand) and the task of field recording then began.

These great strides in organized field study, which enabled botany, for a while, to take the lead in natural history, owed much to the special suit-ability of plants for straightforward distributional plotting and compari-son and to the special ease with which flat, dried specimens could be trans-mitted through the post. The organized exchange of specimens never caught on in any other field to the same extent despite the great improve-ments in the postal service brought about by the advent of the railways. On the founding of the Geologists' Association in 1858 such a function was included in the original statement of its aims; but it never proved successful, allegedly because the members found difficulty in agreeing about the comparative value of their fossils (and not, as one might have supposed, because of the cost and trouble involved in posting such mate-rial). But at least the geologists made an effort. The entomologists, by comparison, when someone in the *Intelligencer* in 1859 proposed a 'Co-operative Entomological Society', barely even responded—though years later, in 1890, an exchange club was at length started by the *Entomologist's Record* and for a time appears to have been successful.

One feature which the geologists do appear to have copied from botany was the appointing of local secretaries. These were adopted by a new asso-ciation launched in 1847 for the publishing of figures of all undescribed British fossils, the Palaeontographical Society. From this source the idea passed in turn to the Geologists' Association, which of all the national societies was later to lead the way in the setting up of local branches.

The Palaeontographical Society was itself partly modelled on another, rather similar body established three years earlier: the Ray Society. This materialized from the need widely sensed about this time for some means of bringing out learned works on natural history—particularly monographs on the more abstruse groups—that were unlikely to find a commercial publisher or otherwise had to be issued at a price that placed them beyond the average naturalist's means. At least three people thought up schemes along these lines independently and almost simultaneously. One of them, the ornithologist (and geologist) H. E. Strickland, first tried to interest the British Association in sponsoring such a venture. When this proved abortive he decided on the founding of a special-club, analogous to those already in existence for the printing by private subscription of books of interest to antiquaries, clergymen and doctors. His original idea was to call this the 'Montagu Society' (after the famous ornithologist) and to confine it to zoology. But meanwhile the ever-energetic George Johnston, mainstay of the Berwickshire Naturalists' Club and dominant in marine natural history, had started to canvass support for a scheme which was organizationally almost identical but aimed at a much wider spread of subjects. Sensibly, the two joined forces and it was agreed to name the body after a less specialized naturalist—of whom John Ray was far and away the most appropriate. Five hundred members, it was calculated, would be needed for success. A prospectus was duly printed and batches sent to groups of leading naturalists throughout the British Isles, asking them to recruit locally and among their friends.

Partly because of this rather makeshift mode of circularization, perhaps, and partly because of downright opposition from a few influential people who as usual saw danger in this for the established national societies, the scheme made slow headway and Johnston all but despaired of success. But after a further month, with enrolments doubled and a total of 157 already 'in the bag', the risk of formal establishment seemed worth taking, and Johnston was voted into office as the secretary. Now, at last, he exulted,

> I shall see new life and vigour infused into practical out-of-door naturalists, working zealously and well, seeing that their labour shall no longer be in vain; and I shall see the poor country apothecary and the priest with cheap and good Manuals in their hands, and I shall see popular bookseller compilations at a discount, and I shall see the neglected corners of our Fauna and of our Flora searched out, and all their hidden treasures described as well as are the lilies and the birds, and the gaudy shells of drawing-room amateurs . . . The meat and medicine have been too long dispensed only to the rich.

Still very much alive today, the enterprise has turned out one of natural history's lesser-known but most far-reachingly constructive success stories.

In the background to this and many another activity at this period, time and time again, we keep catching glimpses of that 'heavy uncle' figure, the British Association for the Advancement of Science. This had been founded in 1831, ostensibly on the model of a similar perambulating body started nine years before in Germany. Apart from providing the natural history world as a whole with a useful annual meeting-ground and forum, the 'B. A.' helped these studies in a more practical way by making grants-in-aid (all of which, up till 1903, derived exclusively from the annual subscriptions of the members). Geology was the prime gainer from these— not unreasonably, for the geologists had played a leading part in the founding of the Association and in its early years tended to loom disproportionately large in its counsels and proceedings. Between 1834 and 1843 their science was adroit enough in cornering no less than 15 per cent of the total £7,614 paid out, which was twice as fat a share as it was able to secure in later years. All told, in just under the first hundred years of its existence, nearly £28,000, or 30 per cent of the total funds awarded by the Association by way of grants, was to go to either geology or the biological sciences; but a high proportion of this was to be for projects overseas, and in reality very little indeed was ever devoted to furthering field-work on the flora and fauna of Britain. Even so, the very appearance on the scene of such a substantial grant-giving body was in itself noteworthy and helped to raise the morale of British scientists in general, compensating to some extent for the almost total lack of interest shown for so long by governments.

Ironically, the first major project of substantial interest to naturalists in this country to benefit from British Association support—the bird migration studies that began in the 1880—had been foreshadowed within three years of the Association's birth. In 1834 a contributor to the *Magazine of Natural History*, J. D. Salmon, actually proposed the noting of passage movements of seabirds 'by the cooperative agency of naturalists residing near headlands on the coasts'. He was, as it proved, a good forty years too early. British zoology, unlike British botany, had still to wake up to the possibilities of collective research.

Yet even then there were developments taking place in the study of birds that held promise of interesting things to come. Already fair numbers of ornithologists—Edward Blyth, Charles Waterton and J. F. M. Dovaston among them—were regularly abandoning guns for small spy-glasses or telescopes, by which means Dovaston, for one, had (according to Bewick, writing in 1826) 'acquired numerous points hitherto unknown'. A few had also made the discovery that to study a bird it was not always necessary to stalk it from afar: the bird could be enticed to come up close to the observer. This could be done, they found, by means of artificial nesting-holes and boxes (in use by various people in the 1820s and 1830s); by erecting 'hides', like the ones camouflaged with brushwood described by MacGillivray as in use by T. D. Weir in 1837; or by putting out food on some special contraption, such as Dovaston's 'ornithotrophe', sited conveniently outside the windows of one's home. Through this last means Dov-aston, an inveterate experimenter, found it possible to lure robins into a trap; and by marking and then releasing them he was able to report that 'all birds have their particular beats . . . and very rarely intrude on those of others'. He also accomplished some sketchy mapping of their territories, straying on to a rich field of inquiry which was otherwise to be overlooked till the work of Henry Eliot Howard many years later.

Thus, by the 1840s, in one field after another, the signs were multiplying of a distinct deepening in penetration. Comparatively suddenly, British natural history had become noticeably acuter in its inquiries and more ambitious in its organizational reach. At this rate it was destined soon to arrive at that crucial juncture in its growth that may be termed the 'take-off' stage.

A field science 'takes off' when a number of developments have been achieved in a certain critical combination. The first and most essential is the attainment of a sufficient, fast-rising popularity to produce an invigo-rating sense of growth and weight. This 'stimulus of mass' in itself pro-vokes more elaborate forethought and planning. A large following also yields a sufficiency of competent workers to provide a minimal coverage of the country. A second precondition is the establishment of a common so-cial code: that is to say, a wide measure of agreement must have been reached on at least the major aims and there must be a tolerance for the constraints inseparable from working as a team. Thirdly, there must have been evolved a degree of standardization in the principal *modus operandi:* accurate, not-too-expensive, preferably portable field handbooks; a com-mon system of nomenclature; and—if material cannot feasibly be de-manded to be sent in for checking—an acceptable general level of field-character recognition. Fourthly and lastly, there must exist at least one institution—perhaps a national society, perhaps a periodical—capable of acting as the receiver, processor and storer of the records, of furnishing the administrative staff, and of ensuring that degree of organizational stability that alone makes possible the essential continuity. For once the initial gearing-up has been accomplished, the type of research machinery that results is self-perpetuating. Its operators, emboldened by their first suc-cesses, proceed to set increasingly sophisticated targets; the experience of working together creates a lasting *esprit de corps;* habituation to a drill im-plants higher standards and thereby generates a supply of capable partici-pants. The field science, in other words, thenceforth builds itself up by means of its own internal dynamics.

For some reason, however, the 'take-off' of the early Victorians failed to be carried through. In botany, at least, the necessary ingredients seem all to have been present but somehow they did not fully jell and the final achievement proved elusive. The collapse of the Botanical Society of London must have been to some extent responsible. Its vital exchange activities, it is true, still continued to be carried on; but the débâcle removed the one national body closely identified with the forward-moving work of Watson and one of the only two capable of providing the necessary continuity of direction. The rift between Watson and the Scottish circle no doubt prevented the Botanical Society of Edinburgh from filling the vacuum. Watson's personality must indeed have been a seriously disabling feature. Impossibly prickly, ultra-fastidious, the wielder of a blistering pen, he was not at all the kind of man to whom a team of voluntary enthusiasts can easily be harnessed. To work with him a man would have needed a rare degree of stoicism and a clear-headed rationality so efficient and so bereft of blemish that it must be doubted if any such paragon could ever have been discovered.

At bottom, though, the prevailing mentality of the period was perhaps just too competitive and individualistic. For the great majority of naturalists the forming of bigger and better private collections was still the central focus of their energies and interest. Organized exchange proved successful merely because it chanced to be so mutually convenient, not because collectors sought a means of pooling their efforts in the interests of a more efficient gathering-in of knowledge. The field-workers of that time were still insufficiently rehearsed in the tact and forbearance necessary for undertaking cooperative projects successfully. In so far as they realized the potential usefulness of the cooperative machinery, invariably they saw its end-products as turned out to serve the needs of certain outstanding individuals; they did not conceive a research network as having any intrinsic value in itself.

If the 'take-off' failed in botany, then, in the other branches of the subject it can scarcely be said even to have begun. Greenough's brilliant start in geology seems to have been allowed to peter out, possibly because the main initiative for large-scale research was handed over so early in this science to the Government. In zoology there were no specialist national bodies for the study of either the British birds or the mammals, while the one body that did exist, the Entomological Society, proved itself a dwarf in giant's clothing and as a result could not offer the necessary national coverage. The chance of a great step forward was lost. And for many more years to come the dominant motivating impulse throughout natural history was to remain that of the private collector working on his own behalf.

CHAPTER SIX

Exploring the Fringes

THE 1840s, the 'Hungry Forties', those gloomy years of bad harvests, soaring prices and tightened lips and belts, were years of pride and hope as well. For they ushered in the Railway Age, the climax of a long-drawn-out, tremendous increase in the speed of travel.

The change had started first on the roads. In 1784 the introduction of the mail-coach for the specially rapid transport—at a price—of passengers as well as letters proved for the first time the true possibilities of a properly organized system able to depend on well-kept highways. The more ponderous stage-coaches, hitherto resigned to inefficiency and by long tradition leisurely, were forced to rise to the challenge, and their services in consequence improved quite dramatically. The journey from London to Manchester, for example, which had typically taken four and a half days in 1754, was reduced to a mere twenty-eight hours by 1788. Even so, it was still extremely costly.

Later, during the 1820s, a further spurt took place, under the impulse of the new surfacing methods of Macadam and others. Whereas in 1821 it had taken the palaeontologist Gideon Mantell no less than eleven hours to travel up to London from his home in Sussex, only a few years later he was doing the same journey in less than half this time and there was a choice of some thirty to forty coaches daily. Similarly, the journey from London to Edinburgh, a ten days' pilgrimage in 1750, had been brought down to as little as two days by 1830.

Once the highways had been improved, it was natural for attention to be turned to the secondary roads as well. This, above all, brought the country-side within reach of the towns and touched off the first conspicuous invasion of pickers and uprooters of attractive flowers. Well before the railways arrived, even in areas that were comparatively remote, local botanists had begun complaining of the depredation that had set in from this cause.

For naturalists, the steam-engine was by no means the conclusive instrument of rescue that it has conventionally been depicted. For a long time before, they had been able to move across country with acceptable swiftness and convenience. Many, indeed, held the stagecoaches in a particularly high regard, not least because of the unrivalled view of the scenery provided by a long-distance journey up on top. William Smith, for one, had found this an ideal means of subjecting wide tracts of country to a preliminary visual survey, and many of his maps had their genesis on windswept coach-tops, with the driver's whip cracking at his ears and the horn blaring out across the landscape. Entomologists who travelled in this way also found it a fruitful, if unexpected, means of netting occasional insects, and at least one list appeared in print of species taken on a single journey by this means. Even to botanists the coaches were not without their uses: one or two had the bright idea of placing their plants to press and dry underneath the cushions of the seats, thereby making free of that normally untapped source of helping warmth, the human body. Would they have been so bold, one wonders, in the more restrained and crowded atmosphere of the average railway carriage?

In fact, a new, impersonal note enters into British travel with the railways. The Rev. John Gunn, the Norfolk geologist, has left us the alert observation that whereas on the coaches the passengers had always chatted freely to each other, the passengers on the trains preferred instead to sit in silence. Perhaps people were simply dazed at first and then never lost the habit; perhaps the hiss of steam and clanking of machinery gave them the feeling of sitting in a factory instead of winding here and there, just one small group on its own, through the peace of an undisturbed countryside.

It was not so much the speed that impressed people: it was the sense of power unleashed, the miracle of energy harnessed. The railways were the single greatest symbol of industrial progress. Hence the mania for financial speculation, the Railway Overtures, the Odes to Steam, the readers of the *Iron Times*; hence the people who patted locomotives with affection as if they were creatures of flesh and blood.

The lines fanned outwards, appearing almost everywhere—and altering almost everything. In the space of a few years they destroyed for ever all idea of a pristine, undisturbed wilderness over much of Britain. At the same time, they brought the first realization of the harm that might occur if such developments were to continue unhindered. As early as 1837 Daniel Cooper warned the Botanical Society of London of the likely fate of Battersea Fields 'when railroads extend into this, the metropolitan Botanist's favourite locality, overturning and obliterating some of nature's choicest productions'. By 1844 a botanist was writing to the *Phytologist* from the Lake District to blame the railways (together with the spread of learned societies) for a serious reduction in the numbers of the rarer species. Such fears, of course, were much exaggerated, for the damage directly attributable to the building of the lines or to the greater numbers of collectors that they immediately discharged upon the country were as nothing compared with what later years would bring. Nevertheless, they were symptomatic. Naturalists from now on could hardly watch the spread of the railways without a certain uneasiness.

At the same time they made the most of the great new opportunities that the railways offered. Societies, in particular, found the radius of their activities extended quite markedly. When, in 1838, in the third summer of its existence, the Botanical Society of London decided to make its first field excursion, it chose Woking, some twenty-five miles out, as the base for explorations, just because of its easy access by the London and Southampton Railway. Thanks to the trains, excursions *en masse* now became much more feasible for such bodies, especially for those of fairly humble status with few or no members who were able to rise to the expense of either a horse or a carriage.

Plant-spotting from train windows became an entertaining pastime as long as the speeds still permitted. In the *Magazine of Natural History* we find William Christy reporting several interesting records made in this way in the course of a journey from Liverpool to Bolton in June 1832—'at a speed which almost precluded any botanical observation', he commented admiringly. This was just two years after the first passenger line in Britain had been brought into service.

But geology was bound to be the science most heavily affected. As had happened, years before, with the building of canals, the excavation of the cuttings brought great numbers of fresh exposures and gave a tremendous fillip to field research. It was while engaged in this activity, some years later, that H. E. Strickland, the rising hope of British natural history, was knocked down by an unexpected express and mortally injured—and he was not to be the last geologist in Britain to lose his life in this manner. In the years 1841–4 the British Association awarded over £360 in grants for the investigating of new railway sections. The surveyors and constructors, in their turn, leant heavily on such geological work as had been carried out already in the areas they were due to cover, and a good deal of unpublished data by this means emerged out of drawers or came down off shelves and ended up in unanticipated print. The pioneer map of Ireland, for example, drawn up by Patrick Gamly as long before as 1815 and used by Richard Griffiths in his lectures while Professor of Geology to the Royal Dublin Society, had publication finally bestowed on it in 1838—on a scale of one-inch-to-ten-miles—in one of the reports of the Railway Commissioners.

The speed and scale of the railway building were astonishing. In 1841 a mere sixteen hundred miles of track existed, linking London with Bristol and Newcastle but extending no farther. Within ten years this total had grown fourfold, resulting in a great entanglement of services stretching from Plymouth to Inverness. Travel became not only quick and easy, but, still more important, cheap. For the first time it began to be possible for large numbers of people, imprisoned till now in smoky towns and cities, to seek some break in the twelve months' routine to take themselves and their families away on an annual holiday—for preference down to the coast.

The seaside as a source of recreation had first achieved some popularity in the fifties of the previous century, following the appearance of Dr Richard Russell's two solemn tomes in Latin which had claimed for sea-water a highly beneficial influence on the glands. Sea-bathing had promptly become a vogue, both here and on the Continent. And as has been the case, no doubt, since time immemorial, those who found themselves beside the sea usually ended up at one moment or another by indulging in the gentle sport of beachcombing. As Richard Ayrton was to write in 1813 of the visitors to Hoylake, 'the pursuit of picking up shells and weeds every day is something to help on existence between breakfast and dinner'—to put it at its very lowest. Two tourists in the mid 1760s noted that at Margate, already, visitors went down on to the sands at low tide to collect 'pebbles, shells, seaweeds, etc.'—just as in more recent times newcomers to the countryside have been wont to gather bluebells by the armful, giving vent to some blind impulse touched off by a murmuring sense of wonder.

Long before then, even, a few naturalists had existed who took a special interest in the sea and in its animal and plant productions. In the late seventeenth century the Rev. Lewis Stephens, a Cornish vicar, had collected seaweeds and sent many local specimens to such distinguished cabinet-collectors as Du Bois and William Sherard. Sherard himself, in a letter to Richardson in 1722, mentions that 'a gentleman at Greenwich, of a plentyfull fortune, has lately fallen on this study . . . He has promis'd to send his *fuci* the beginning of next week: he keeps a pleasure boat, and sails about the coast in search of what he can meet.' This person, whoever he may have been, could well have been the first to collect his specimens by trawling for them.

Thirty or forty years later, with the onset of the sea-bathing fashion, marine natural history seems to have climbed in popularity. It was in 1751 that John Ellis started forming the collections of seaweeds that within fifteen years was to become, to the best of his knowledge, the largest in the country. He was introduced to the study by taking up a current fashionable pastime which consisted of making imitation landscapes from bits of seaweeds and corallines skilfully arranged on paper. In order to admire their beauty more minutely, he was led to examine them under the microscope and in this way found that corallines were not plants, as had been generally supposed, but animals. After he had made this discovery public, various naturalists who lived by the sea started sending him regular parcels of specimens. Other collectors soon joined in. The Duchess of Portland, to the fore as always, even recruited a Mrs Le Coq for the purpose down at Weymouth.

Around 1800 there was a further flurry of interest. Remarkably, three of the authors of the learned tomes that resulted were all at some time colonels in the militia: George Montagu (who, while best known for his work on birds, was also an expert on shells), Thomas Velley, and T. J. Woodward. The latter was joined as co-author of a work on seaweeds by Dr Samuel Goodenough, who was shortly to become Bishop of Carlisle. Another fellow-enthusiast was a Cornish squire, John Stackhouse, who is reputed to have built himself a castle, near Marazion, expressly as a base for shore-collecting.

Not long after, another member of this circle, the wealthy Norfolk banker Dawson Turner, began to bring out a comprehensive monograph on the British seaweeds under the austere title *Fuci* (1807–11) with a final volume, badly delayed, in 1819. His publisher, apparently under some misapprehension about its likely market, wrote to urge that the first part be hurried in order to appear by April, 'that it might come out in time enough for the ladies at the seaside'. We may laugh at this; yet his optimism was not so totally misplaced. For this was the period of the first of the great lady collectors: the dedicated Ellen Hutchins, of Cork (after whom that genus of attractive alpines, *Hutchinsia*, was named), an all-round cryptogamic botanist—'she could find almost anything', it was said of her—and the most famous of them, Mrs A. W. Griffiths, of Torquay, earner of a memorable tribute from W. H. Harvey: 'She is worth ten thousand other collectors; she is a trump.' It was the period, too, that produced the seaweed descriptions in 'The Borough', one of the many poems by that more than adequate botanist George Crabbe.

The real growth of enthusiasm for marine life seems to date from the 1820s. In January 1823 James Clealand, of Bangor in Northern Ireland, reported to G. B. Sowerby the First: 'My Patellas are nearly extirpated, they became so much the fashion that the Visitors who frequented Bangor, as Sea Bathers, during the two last summers, employed the children to collect them, and there is not one to be seen now.' Around 1825, on going up to Edinburgh as a student, Charles Darwin found several of his contemporaries wonderfully keen on marine zoology, and in his days there he often joined Robert Grant to collect animals from the tidal pools, for later dissection in the laboratory, sometimes accompanying as well the local fishermen when they went out trawling for oysters. 1830 witnessed the appearance of Greville's majestic *Algae Britannicae;* 1833 of Mrs Mary Wyatt's *Algae Danmonienses,* albums of fifty pressed seaweeds prepared under the supervision of her mistress, Mrs Griffiths; 1838 of Dr L. J. Drummond's classic paper on how to dry and preserve these attractive subjects; 1840 of Isabella Gifford's *The Marine Botanist,* a handily portable volume written in a pleasing style; and 1841 of W. H. Harvey's standard textbook, his *Manual of the British Algae.*

Thus far, seaweeds and shells had formed the principal items that people collected and studied. Both, it was generally acknowledged, were 'tasteful' as well as decorative. In the words of one magazine, conchology selected itself as 'a study peculiarly suited to ladies; there is no cruelty in the pursuit, the subjects are so brightly clean, so ornamental to a boudoir'. But for the new, earnest generation that presently took over, so light and frivolous an attitude was scarcely tolerable. And so, once again, we can spot all the tell-tale signs as these strenuous, efficient newcomers moved in on yet another hitherto half-hearted and desultory study. In their active hands seaside natural history was quickly transformed into a serious, thoroughgoing science.

The key to this development was a great increase in the use of the compound microscope. Until about 1830 the average scientific investigator had grown inured to having to treat this instrument in the same way as a priceless tapestry or a masterpiece of sculpture, too valuable and delicate to bring into use except on very special occasions. In consequence few people really understood it and students received no proper training in its handling. Then, in 1831, Robert Brown discovered the cell nucleus; and the enormous interest aroused by this led to rapid improvements in microscope design. In the next ten years prices fell fivefold. By the end of the period every student, amateur or professional, had within his reach a sound working instrument, of far greater efficiency than previously and very moderate in price.

Many developments flowed from this. Some, far-reaching in their eventual impact, needed time to come to pass: it was not until 1840, for example, that microphotography was invented—and not until 1852 that the invention was separately made in Britain, by J. B. Dancer, a scientific instrument-maker in Manchester and a keen naturalist from boyhood, who was also the first person to produce photographic lantern-slides. Again, though lapidaries had used a method to produce very thin laminations of precious stones for use as ornaments for perhaps two hundred years and a lapidary called Sanderson had actually prepared sections of minerals in this way for Sir David Brewster as early as 1818, it was not until 1851 that H. C. Sorby, a Sheffield geologist of independent means, drew wide scientific attention to the grinding of thin slices to the study of the minute structures of minerals and rocks and thereby revolutionized the study of petrology.

In other directions, however, the effects were felt immediately. Most notably, there took place a marked surge of interest in the lower organisms, which hitherto had had to be neglected. 'The old stagers in Botany', Dovaston was grumbling from Shropshire by 1834, 'are so damned larned, that they will not look at a phaenogamous flower. No. Nothing will go down with them but a Moss, Lichen, or Fungus. They are all Cryptogamists'. A big stimulus came from W. J. Hooker's cryptogamic supplement to Smith's *English Flora,* published 1833–5, (including a magnificent section on the fungi by Berkeley), and from R. K. Greville's excellent *Scottish Cryptogamic Flora* (1823–8). The number of species of fungi known to occur in Britain was to be multiplied fourfold during the reign of Queen Victoria, and for twenty years a quarterly journal solely devoted to cryptogamic botany, *Grevillea*, managed to flourish without involving its proprietors in any pecuniary loss. Similarly, there occurred in the thirties a marked access of interest in the detailed structure of various groups of small animals, including some of the earliest dissections of such off-putting creatures as spiders.

This general use of the microscope had the wider effect of bringing before people's vision an unsuspected realm of delicate forms and brilliant colourings. What had seemed drab and insignificant objects now revealed their splendour and held their beholders enthralled. Philip Henry Gosse, the loving painter and describer of the sea-anemones and starfish, emerged from his years waist-high in the rock-pools irremediably dazzled, to be caught up in later life by a comparable fascination for astronomy—and an equally profound obsession with celestial coloured stars. For Thomas

Moore and countless others ferns, as if by magic, ceased to be their previous humdrum selves and appeared instead as 'objects of exquisite elegance'. To Shirley Hibberd they seemed like 'vegetable jewellery', 'plumy emerald green pets glistening with health and beadings of warm dew'. 'I am absolutely filled with wonder and in an ecstasy of delight,' wrote J. E. Bowman, 'at the structure and contrivance of some of the extremely minute specis . . . How many beautiful and interesting productions we tread daily underfoot and pass by unnoticed!'

Time and again we come across such tones of awe; and we are surely mistaken if we dismiss them as factitious. Years of peering closely trained the eye in the admiring of minutiae, the intricate details, the lowly magnificence of Creation. With their microscopes, the Victorians found a means of penetrating to nature's furthermost recesses, of laying bare new aspects of the elemental. Is it too far-fetched to see in the 'microscopic Romanticism' that resulted a major contributory cause of that over-concern with details that so fatally injured Victorian art? Was there not, perhaps, too familiar and simply obtained a visual pleasure to be had by staring raptly at minuteness, which spoilt the senses and led them to be misdirected?

Besides the microscope, there were other tools that helped to uncover the secrets of the sea. In 1816 an army surgeon and one-time botanist, J. V. Thompson, dipped a muslin hoop-net into the sea off Madagascar and accidentally discovered the teeming world of the plankton. In the course of the next ten years, following his posting to Cork, he perfected the use of this as a tow-net, suspending it over the stern of a ship, 'occasionally drawing it up, and turning it inside out into a glass vessel of sea water, to ascertain what captures have been made'.

Another simple gadget, the naturalists' dredge, a coarse netting bag on a rectangular iron frame which was dropped and dragged along the sea-bottom, also revealed a hitherto hidden layer. A modification of the oyster-dredge of fishermen, this was first used by two Italians, Donati and Marsigli, in exploring the Mediterranean early in the eighteenth century. About 1786 William Curtis, the London botanist and entomologist, became interested in the dredging method used for taking oysters off the coast of Essex and drew and described the apparatus in detail; but whether he used it in practice still remains to be established. The Dane O. F. Müller is otherwise credited with its modern introduction, in 1799, and in the early part of the 1830s its use became fairly widespread in Britain, France and Norway more or less simultaneously. Its chief proponent in this country was to be Edward Forbes—whose name will ever be associated with this, his favourite field of study.

The true birthplace of modern marine biology could be said to be a large scallop bank some three to seven miles off the northwest corner of the Isle of Man, for it was here, about 1830, as a precocious schoolboy of fifteen, that Forbes, a Manxman born and bred, first discovered the deliciousness of dredging. He used to prevail on friends among the local farmers to row him out and, it is said, always took with him his microscope. The reports on the mollusca he collected—for he found the bank 'especially prolific in conchological treasures'—were written up in the autumn of 1834 and published shortly afterwards in the *Magazine of Natural History*. By that time he was a student of medicine at Edinburgh, but being assured (as he supposed) of ample private means, most of his waking moments were still given over to natural history. He continued to dredge regularly, and in 1839, after a series of spectacular hauls off the Shetlands, he persuaded the British Association to establish a permanent Dredging Committee and to set aside an initial sum of £60 to support such work. A great deal of valuable research was subsequently achieved by this Committee, much of it in distant seas.

Meanwhile from the shallower waters an ever-growing literary harvest was being extracted. The years around the middle of the century witnessed the appearance of several major monographs as well as many popular handbooks. Notable among the former was the *History of British Mollusca* by Forbes and Sylvanus Hanley, with such fine plates that they are still regularly referred to by shell-collectors—just as the somewhat later *British Conchology* of J. Gwyn Jeffreys has continued to be consulted for its text. W. H. Harvey, Professor of Botany to the Royal Dublin Society, similarly brought out his massive, four-volume *Phycologia Britannica*, one of a series of great marine Floras he succeeded in completing in his lifetime. In the middle of this he also produced *The Sea-side Book*, the kind of general, not-too-demanding introductory guide for which an immense audience had abruptly materialized.

A Popular History of British Seaweeds was another characteristic product of the period, fully living up to its title, for it ran to a third edition. Its author was the Rev. David Landsborough, the minister of Saltcoats, in Ayrshire, who had dredged a lot around Arran and the Cumbraes. One of the items of information incidentally disclosed in its pages is that the custom had grown up among many seaside visitors of preparing 'little collections of these marine paintings, to gratify their inland friends on their return'. Seaweeds, in other words, were now a part of the holiday industry. Numbers of people were even offering their services as gatherers of this raw material in return for a small consideration. This was a trade in which Landsborough's own children, he reveals, had already been deeply engaged for some years. As a result of their efforts many hundreds of sets of pressed specimens had been prepared under his guidance and sold in aid of his kirk and its schools. Before long, quite a proliferation of enterprise along these lines was taking place. 'I need scarcely refer to sea-weed baskets and pictures,' a later author was to write, 'or to the . . . books and maps of named species which are often sold at bazaars, and by means of which considerable sums have been raised for rebuilding churches . . .' It is a nice thought that the Gothic Revival may have been sustained in part on a diet of marine algae.

One of the most enthusiastic readers of Professor Harvey's volumes was the dauntless Margaret Gatty, a Yorkshire parson's wife (after whom, with a fitting touch of gallantry, he was to name the genus *Gattya*). In 1848, shortly after the birth of her seventh child, a serious breakdown in health had forced her removal down to Hastings for a period of several months. It was here that the local physician, casting around for something to hold an invalid's attention, introduced her to the subject that was to become her overriding passion. Two years later an entry in her diary reads: 'Set off for Filey, Alfred, self, seven children, two nurses and the cook. Arrived safely D. G. Went down to the sands and found sea-weeds.' Subsequently she visited the great Dr Johnston at Berwick and accompanied him on several of his expeditions. Johnston, no less gallantly, named a new marine worm in her honour: *Gattia spectabilis*. In 1863 she duly published the inevitable book, *British Seaweeds*, including in this a special section of handy hints on dress for fellow members of her sex. 'Any one really intending to *work* in the matter, must lay aside for a time all thought of conventional appearances,' she opened ominously. For the feet, she advised a pair of boy's shooting-boots, rendered waterproof with a thin coat of neat's-foot oil. Petticoats should never reach below the ankle, and cloaks and shawls were, if possible, to be avoided. 'A ladies' yachting costume,' she went on, 'has come into fashion of late, which is, perhaps, as near perfection for shore-work as anything that could be devised.' A hat was to be preferred to a bonnet, stockings of merino wool to ones of cotton, while a strong pair of gloves was, of course, indispensable. Finally, all fancy millinery-work 'must, and will, be laid aside by every rational being who attempts to shore-hunt'. Thus clad, the novice could decently set forth—always remembering, in the author's parting words, that a low-water-mark expedition is more comfortably taken under the protection of a gentleman.

It was on to this already active scene that there suddenly appeared, early in the fifties, that enormously popular invention, the marine aquarium.

For years people had been trying to find the secret of keeping animals permanently alive in jars of water, no matter whether fresh or salt. Some supposed that the reason why such creatures always perished in the end was that the water was allowed to become too stagnant and motionless. Richard Bradley, who advanced this view in 1721, suggested that collections of marine fish might be preserved by making at sea-level 'little Store-

Ponds to be fed by the Tides', in which two water-wheels could be placed 'to be turned by the Flux and Reflux of the Waters'. Alternatively, he thought a portion of a flowing river might be dammed off and its water salted artificially: in such a way, he claimed, Sir Hans Sloane had long managed to keep alive a marine turtle. Others supposed that keeping the water fresh was the one essential requisite. The traditional method, in that case, was to change the whole contents of the jar daily; and this was in fact normal practice in dealing with bowls of goldfish throughout the first half of the century. It was of course extremely tedious. Moreover, it was scarcely practicable if it was marine creatures that one was particularly keen to have. Sir John Dalyell managed to keep a sea anemone alive for twenty-eight years and numerous other marine animals for lesser periods, but only because he was wealthy enough to be able to arrange for a fresh supply of sea-water to be brought round to his house every morning.

In time, various people made the crucial observation that the animals survived, and the water remained much purer, if some plant life as well chanced to be included. But either they failed to grasp the full significance of this or else they kept the information to themselves. None merits the real honour as the inventor of the aquarium principle, which must surely be reserved for the person who not only first fully appreciated its importance, but also took the trouble to give the world the benefit of his knowledge.

Patrick Neill, a leading Edinburgh naturalist, furnished a typically truncated account: around 1831 he noticed that pieces of a water-plant floating on the surface of the tank made his pet Water-puppy considerably more lively and 'tended also to keep the water from corrupting'. Apparently his curiosity was not aroused further. At least Mrs Anna Thynne, who sixteen years later unknowingly repeated the discovery, had the good sense to revolutionize her goldfish-keeping by ever afterwards keeping seaweed in her bowls—even though the reason for its effectiveness entirely eluded her. The method must have been a welcome change after the singularly elaborate procedure she had been used to employing before, in trying to preserve her marine collection:

> I thought of having it aerated by pouring it backwards and forwards before an open window, for half or three-quarters of an hour between each time of using it. This was doubtless a fatiguing operation; but I had a little handmaid, who, besides being rather anxious to oblige me, thought it rather an amusement.

The true inventor of the aquarium, contrary to almost all accounts of the subject, was Nathaniel Bagshaw Ward, the Whitechapel surgeon who made that even more important (and closely connected) discovery, the preservative power of closely glazed cases. To be strictly accurate, Ward himself was the re-discoverer of the principle with which his name has become inseparably associated. For a few years earlier, about 1825, quite unknown to him, a Glasgow horticulturist named A. A. Maconochie had followed a rather similar line of reasoning and successfully constructed a glass case of this very same type, which he had put to use as a window-garden. Maconochie did not trouble to publicize the fact, however, nor did he appreciate the wider applications of his discovery, and there is no doubt that the full credit rightly belongs to Ward.

Ward's own discovery of the principle occurred early in 1830. He happened to notice that the seedling of a grass and the sporeling of a fern had sprouted in a little moist mould accidentally left behind with the pupa of a hawk-moth, which he had sealed up in a glass jar some few months before. Possessed of a keenly inquiring mind and an overwhelming passion for growing plants, it struck him that here was the way to create the luscious greenery that he craved in the face of the poisoned atmosphere that so permanently enveloped his home deep in London's dockland. By being enclosed in glass, it seemed, and rendered almost but not entirely air-tight, his plants would thrive indefinitely without any further need of watering, thanks to the moisture that they gave forth by way of transpiration which, in due course, was reabsorbed. Not only did this save enormously on labour, it also protected the plants completely from outside changes in temperature and from all noxious fumes, such as smoke and gas, which had had the further effect of exiling all greenery from the drawing-room and the parlour.

With the help of Loddiges, the famous firm of nurserymen, numbers of small glass cases—in effect, miniature greenhouses—were then made up according to his specifications, and soon his house was filled with these almost to overflowing. Loudon, who paid a visit there specially to see them, in March 1834, reported in excitement to the many readers of his *Gardener's Magazine* on this

> most extraordinary city garden we have ever beheld . . . The success attending
> Mr Ward's experiments opens up extensive views as to the application [of the
> cases] in transporting plants from one country to another; in preserving plants
> in rooms or in towns; and in forming miniature gardens or conservatories . . .
> as substitutes for bad views, or for no views at all.

With obvious reluctance, and doubtless after a good deal of pestering, Ward proceeded to set down on paper some brief accounts of his discovery, which found their way into print in four separate places. Possibly he found writing tedious; certainly, his professional duties took up most of his energies and left him scanty leisure. Whatever the reason, it was not until

1842, twelve years after his initial discovery, that he finally got round to writing a full-scale monograph on the subject: *On the Growth of Plants in Closely-glazed Cases.*

In the meantime the Wardian principle had been discussed, with much publicity and learning, at the meeting of the British Association in 1837 and by Michael Faraday in a lecture in the following year at the Royal Institution. The cases also received a special mention by G. W. Francis in his *An Analysis of the British Ferns and their Allies* (1837), the first book wholly devoted to ferns to appear for many years and which took almost everyone by surprise by its exceptional popularity. Ferns, as Ward and others had discovered, grew best of all in the cases, and very soon fern-growing and the adoption of the Wardian principle became very largely, if fallaciously, identified in the minds of the majority of people. Edward Newman, in his even more popular *A History of British Ferns and Allied Plants* (1840), did much to fix this confusion, at the same time puffing Ward unashamedly as 'the man who has clothed our courtyards, aye, even our windows, with a perpetual summer'.

By the beginning of the forties, if the contemporary accounts are not exaggerated, the Wardian case had at last been taken up by the leaders of fashion and a great number of people had pounced on the invention as a means of growing their own exotics without having to resort to the crippling expense of a hothouse. But after a year or two, all the evidence suggests, excitement faded as the novelty wore off. The cases continued to be used, but took on an aspect of ordinariness. And fern-growing, in turn, was relegated to the status of a specialized minority pursuit, mainly confined to a few field botanists, who vied with one another in building up collections in their ferneries of as many as possible of the forty or more hardy British species.

A similar absence of popular interest at the outset also occurred in the case of the aquarium; but for this Ward's disinclination for publicity can be blamed more directly. As early as 1836, in one of the first published notes on his original discovery, Ward had suggested that his cases might also be useful for bringing examples of the lower orders of animals to Britain from the tropics, as it was reasonable to expect them to confer the same immuniy to external changes of temperature on living creatures as they had been shown to do on plants. Five years later he duly confirmed this hunch, proving that his principle, the vital interdependence of plant and animal life, had almost equally far-reaching implications for zoology. He did this by putting a number of ornamental fish into a large tank standing in his fern-house (for his original small cases had given rise to some of quite massive dimensions) and showing that they flourished, without any change of water, thanks to the presence of the various aquatic plants that he also had growing in it. A robin, likewise, trapped by accident in the fern-house, furnished proof of the principle by living there quite happily for a period of six months. Later he introduced a chameleon and a Jersey toad; and both, once again, proved to thrive, the latter for as long as ten or eleven years, till it ended up by becoming quite a pet.

The resulting version of his case specially designed for housing animals came to be known as the 'vivarium'—and numbers of people were using this, especially for keeping snakes and amphibians, by the fifties—while its counterpart for water creatures was termed the 'aqua-vivarium', soon abbreviated to the simpler 'aquarium (both terms, 'vivarium' and 'aquarium', had actually long been in use already, but in a generalized sense only, for collections of plants or fish). One of Ward's great friends, the microscopist J. S. Bowerbank, borrowed his idea and proceeded to create what appears to have been the first ordinary-sized aquarium (complete with a piece of glass on top, to make it closely glazed) designed in accordance with a proper comprehension of the underlying principle. Unfortunately its date has never been disclosed. All we know is that it was this jar of Bowerbank's that attracted the attention of the Secretary of the Zoological Society and gave him the idea for the large aquarium that was eventually opened in 1853 in the Gardens in Regent's Park.

Before this happened, however, two further people had discovered the principle, each quite independently, and had begun to publicize it on a far more extensive scale than the self-effacing Ward had ever contemplated—though he did at least make known his original experiment in no less a place than the official catalogue of the 1851 Exhibition. The first of these was a chemist, Robert Warington, who started on a thorough and extensive series of experiments in 1849. The other was Philip Henry Gosse, who wrote on natural history for a living and is best known today as the appalling parent portrayed in that masterpiece of autobiography, *Father and Son*. In 1850 Gosse had noticed the strikingly beneficial effects that the proximity of certain aquatic plants had on freshwater Rotifera; and two years later, driven down to Devon by a bout of nervous dyspepsia, he took the opportunity of confirming that this also held true for species of salt water. As a result he devised a small marine aquarium.

Gosse was already well known for his immensely successful book, *The Ocean*, published in 1843. Ten years later he now repeated his success with *A Naturalist's Rambles on the Devonshire Coast*, in which he described the marine aquarium and forecast that it would soon be in mass-production for the parlour.

A great rush of books promptly followed—and a general advance on the beaches by a large section of the British middle classes. The aquarium, almost overnight, turned into a national craze. Ladies of fashion, it is credibly recorded, had palatial plate-glass tanks erected in their drawing-rooms; the odd corners of most of the newspapers were filled with notes for the would-be aquarist; a multitude of shops opened for the single purpose of supplying aquaria and their contents. And as if this was not enough, simultaneously an equally violent and widespread craze—and, by comparison, a considerably more longlasting one—broke out for collecting ferns and growing them indoors in cases like those devised by Ward.

Why was there this sudden upsurge? Why was it not until the fifties that such numbers chose to become so captivated by two inventions already put to use—if not, as in the case of the aquarium, also publicly paraded—a good few years before?

There were evidently two reasons, the first of them purely economic. The removal in 1845 of the onerous and much-resented excise duties on glass (partly as a result of agitation by Lindley, Ward and others, who emphasized the great impediment this meant for horticulture) had brought about a tremendous expansion in the use and output of plate glass, the price of which had dropped a great deal accordingly. Ten years earlier, crazes like these, more or less wholly dependent on glass for their expression, could not have taken place on so vast a scale on straightforward grounds of cost—nor could the manufacturers have supplied the quantities required for such purposes with anything approaching such immediacy.

The second reason was a social one. A new public for natural history had all of a sudden sprung into being, not merely far larger than ever before but of an appreciably altered character. Compared with the naturalists of the 1820s and 1830s this new wave was sloppier, less intelligent, more given to hysteria. Authors wrote down to them, unashamedly, much more. For this, more than a simple change of generation was responsible: a whole new stratum, the 'middle' middle class, had surfaced and exposed itself to cropping. The 1850s resembled the 1950s: after a lengthy period of depression there was a fresh lurch of prosperity and suddenly far more people with far more money to spend on leisure activities. And just as had happened previously, early in the 1830s, the accession of so many new adherents had a distorting effect on the pre-existing scene. What had been small and rather dilettante coteries became engulfed by huge crowds of zealots. What had been mildly eccentric pastimes ballooned into pursuits of fashionableness and respectability.

Yet, as so often with major social changes of this type, it is difficult to find allusions to it in the writings of contemporaries. One of the few exceptions, the renowned pupa-hunter, the Rev. Joseph Greene, writing in 1865, helpfully comments in passing on 'the spread of education, and . . . the vast increase of Entomologists' since twenty years before, which he noticed found reflection in a pronounced decrease in ridicule of the man with the net by the unenlightened and the boorish.

This 'spread of education' was no mirage. Between 1850 and 1859, as a result of the Kay-Shuttleworth reforms, Government expenditure on schools rose almost sixfold. Over the period 1832–61, compared with a national increase in population of 40 per cent, the number of pupils in day schools expanded by no less than 68 per cent. Illiteracy, as a direct result, dropped sharply, as evidenced by a sudden increase in the fifties in the numbers of people able to sign their name in the marriage registers. In the thirty years after 1832, similarly, the number of letters sent by post showed a sixfold growth and the circulation of newspapers almost trebled.

The adverse economic climate of the forties seems to have killed off the previous high level of popular intellectual striving while at the same time reducing incomes. In the middle years of that decade the sales of books and magazines of the Society for the Diffusion of Useful Knowledge, the enterprising publishers of the famous *Penny Magazine,* fell so badly that it was forced to cease. On the other hand, partly to make up for this, the spread of railway travel led to a marked increase in the amount of reading—if of a rather lighter character. The first railway bookstall opened on Euston Station in 1848 and publishers rose to the challenge with great numbers of special cheap editions the equivalent to today's paperbacks— expressly aimed at this new market. Technical improvements in printing and illustration also helpfully coincided.

One consequence of all this was the rise to prominence of a distinctive new genre in natural history publishing, accompanied by sales figures that must have astonished preceding generations. Many so-called 'classics' had their birth in this period—one of those crucial, and in a sense freak, periods when a hitherto untapped public for books abruptly thrusts itself upon commercial attention. At such times books of no outstanding merit may turn into runaway successes, due to the mere accident of entering a particular field as the market ripens. Their publishers, mystified but happy, persuade themselves that their offspring must possess some essential, if indefinable, ingredients of genius; and their blithe confidence in printing further issues, combined with the sheer omnipresence and familiarity of the books themselves, together succeed in ensuring for them a life-span as remarkable as it may be undeserved.

Flowers of the Field, published in 1851 (not 1853, as usually stated) at only half-a-crown and written by a Hampshire schoolmaster, the Rev. C. A. Johns, was possibly the first of this new breed of overvalued favourites. It ran into numerous editions, acquiring better illustrations as the years went by, and has maintained a place on booksellers' shelves right up to the present. Johns went on to repeat his success with *British Birds in Their Haunts* (1862), which likewise passed through many editions and is said to have exceeded in popularity even that far better-known, but no less indifferent work, Morris's *British Birds*. Also symptomatic were the long-continuing sales of a book quite unheard of today: *Wanderings among the Wild Flowers* (1854) by Spencer Thomson, a Burton-on-Trent physician. Slight, but humorous and intelligently written—typical 'secondary' literature, light reading for the already converted—it achieved three editions within two years of its appearance and continued to a tenth edition in 1866.

It was on to this abnormally fertile soil, too, in 1858, that George Bentham, a nephew of Jeremy Bentham and a brilliant full-time amateur systematist, was lucky to sow the fruits of his before-breakfast recreation. This was his *Handbook of the British Flora,* written in deliberately simplified terms—as he later confessed, 'for the ladies'. A volume of uncoloured illustrations was added in 1866, and 'painting one's Bentham' thus had its start as the alluring way into the subject that has held its popularity down to the present.

Of all these, however, none had sales that can compare with the sometimes amazing ones enjoyed by that other great name among popularizers, the Rev. J. G. Wood. His *Common Objects of the Country* (1858), one of a series of shilling handbooks written for Routledge, despite its seemingly unappetizing title, sold a hundred thousand copies within a week of publication. Admittedly, even the author accepted this as a freak. But set beside the *Self-Help* of Samuel Smiles or Mrs Beeton's *Book of Household Management,* each of which appeared shortly after and sold only twenty thousand copies or so in a twelvemonth, the figure is impressive.

These suddenly swarming book-buyers, then, were the people who rushed off in such masses in frantic search of sea-anemones and ferns. Unschooled in the codes and avid for these untasted pleasures, they succeeded in perpetrating the most extensive damage—damage which was to be compounded ever further in the years that lay ahead as their conspicuous obsessions passed on to even weaker brethren. Great stretches of the coast were largely stripped of their attractive inhabitants; whole areas were cleared of ferns, helped by professional touts who saw in this an easy means of turning the quick penny, filled up great cart-loads from the wilder parts of Britain, and sent them off to the London markets.

Then, at length, the enthusiasms faded. Nine out of ten aquaria were thrown out or abandoned; many of the shops folded up their shutters; 'to all appearances', in the words of the Rev. J. G. Wood, 'the aquarium fever had run its course, never again to recur, like hundreds of similar epidemics'. And the fern-fanciers, similarly, found that their interest began to flag as commercial growers proceeded to glut the market with deformed trash. The much-thumbed albums gathered dust and were presently consigned to attics; the ferneries slipped from sight as a pall of weeds closed in. Even then, many more years had still to pass before those sections of our native fauna and flora that had been so misguidedly victimized and mutilated in the process were fully able to recover.

CHAPTER SEVEN

Deadlier Weapons

EVEN WITHOUT the wholesale recklessness that characterized these two collecting crazes the enormous swell of interest in natural history must surely have given rise to considerable misgivings. For, by now, the classic instruments of the naturalist-collector had advanced to such a stage of high effectiveness that, unless used with considerable discrimination, they were liable to prove quite lethal.

Until this point, no one had had much cause to worry about such matters. Naturalists had seemed so few and far between; the countryside lay still unspoiled and its natural riches appeared to all observers comfortably inexhaustible, materially no less than intellectually. A steady increase in the scope and scale of collecting implied automatically a steady pushing back of the boundaries of knowledge. It would have been heretical indeed to have queried the advisability of any of the outward signs of such manifest all-round progress.

The severest threat, undoubtedly, came from the developments in fire-arms. Wildfowl had been killed with guns in England since the early six-teenth century, but for years the weapons had remained extremely ineffi-cient, very awkward and downright dangerous to use. In 1807 all this suddenly changed, when the Rev. Alexander Forsyth patented the detonat-ing or percussion principle—generally regarded as the most important in-novation in fire-arms since the original discovery of gunpowder. Forsyth, a minister in Aberdeenshire with a passion for duck-shooting, had become so infuriated by the way in which the ducks invariably dived at the sight of the flash before the shot had so much as a sporting chance of reaching them, that he had accordingly undertaken experiments at the Tower of London (where a plaque now stands to commemorate his efforts) to find a detonating chemical to replace the traditional steel spark and flint. By the end of the Napoleonic Wars the copper percussion cap had been intro-duced and with its general adoption by sportsmen by the mid 1820s a weapon had arrived at last with powder that could no longer be dampened by rain. It was this novelty that Edward Newman enjoyed trying out, ap-parently with good effect, on the sea-birds of the Isle of Wight in 1832.

In 1851 there came a further marked improvement, with the introduc-tion from France of the first efficient breech-loading shotgun, with self-contained cartridges. This was safe, economical, and very accurate. Even so, many people still preferred to use a muzzle-loader; and it was not until 1861, with the introduction—again from France—of the less clumsy central-fire cartridge, that modern breech-loaders eventually came into general use in sporting circles. Even then, for some years yet, muzzle-loaders persisted among the less well-off.

It is sometimes said that the arrival of the breech-loader 'ushered in the golden age of game-preserving'. It all depends on what one means by this. Gamekeepers, though unofficial, were commonplace by the year of Water-loo, and the *battue,* with its wholesale slaughter, was well established be-fore 1837. Long before the middle of the century the sizes of the bags reported had already begun to look a good deal more than just imposing. On the Duchess of Sutherland's Highland estate as early as the years 1831–4 no fewer than 224 eagles and 1,155 hawks and kites were claimed to have been killed, to say nothing of 900 ravens, 200 foxes and 900 wild cats, polecats and pinemartens. (Such figures, however, are not altogether reliable, for the fact that gamekeepers largely depended on the bounties for their living tempted them to exaggerate.) It was thus that, with the passing of the Game Act of 1831 and the legalizing of the status of the game-keeper, the death-sentence was finally confirmed on a high proportion of the bigger birds of prey that still survived in Britain. At the same time access to the countryside became much restricted—though this was not wholly injurious, in so far as it meant preserves became reserves and many of the smaller creatures that might well have suffered grievously at the hands of the non-sporting fraternity thereby enjoyed some measure of protection.

Organized sport, moreover, focused its sights on only a restricted range of species. Far more damage, almost certainly, was perpetrated by followers of the unorganized pursuits—such as punt-gunning. Punt-guns were fowling-pieces notorious for their massive 'over-kill'. One Norfolk exponent of this sport is said to have once picked up 603 Knot, 9 Redshank and 5 Dunlin as the result of just two shots from a range of about eighty yards.

Nor was the shooting necessarily disguised as sport. Richard Townley, in his Isle of Man *Journal,* was complaining already in 1790 of 'so many foolish fathers that permit their booby sons, mere boys, to ramble about with guns; and . . . with such urchins, blackbirds and thrushes are choice game'. He did not comment on the risk to the youths themselves in putting the ill-tempered flintlock into their undertrained, impatient hands. On the canals in Yorkshire, Charles Waterton was moved to protest in 1835, 'not a water-man steers his boat along them but who has his gun ready to procure the Kingfisher'. 'If I may judge by the disappearance of the Kite, the Raven, and the Buzzard from this part of the country,' he continued, 'I should say that the day is at no great distance when the Kingfisher will be seen no more in this neighbourhood, where once it was so plentiful.' His was not a lone voice; though there were few enough who troubled to remonstrate like this in print. One who did, Richard Pigott, a Norfolk ornithologist, had his letter to Neville Wood's *Naturalist* in 1838 published under the headline: 'Impropriety of Wantonly Shooting Birds' apparently the earliest call for moderation to be accorded such prominence.

This great increase in killing did have one useful side-effect. Private collections began to grow in size so much more rapidly that better means had to be devised for storing and displaying them, and the outbreak of experimenting that this induced led to several valuable discoveries. Some of these came in fact at the hands of the most ruthless collectors. William Bullock, for example, a Liverpool goldsmith, whose most famous single exploit was the hunting down in 1812 of the last Great Auk in the Orkneys from a six-oared boat and who built up a very fine 'London Museum of Natural History' which he put on public exhibition at the Egyptian Hall in Piccadilly, was the inventor of a special box for relaxing bird-skins. He also discovered a marvellous way of skinning and stuffing fish, which he apparently refused ever to make public. His zoological specimens, if Swainson is to be believed, set a new high standard for museums in general—a standard, moreover, which became abundantly familiar to the public by virtue of the supreme accessibility of the Bullock collections, and which must accordingly have hustled rival collectors into seeking better methods far faster than might otherwise have been the case.

More numerous specimens and proportionately fewer wealthy collectors both worked against the earlier, grandiose principle of one bird to one case. About 1820 the practice began to come in of displaying whole groups of birds together, with details of their natural surroundings added as a setting. A few, less trophy-minded, went even further: cases were done away with altogether and the skins merely placed in drawers in a cabinet, spread on cotton and protected by camphor. When Swainson adopted this far more convenient practice around 1818 it was, he records, 'to the great surprise and disapprobation of our scientific friends'; but by 1836 it had become almost general. Associated with it, as Swainson strongly urged, was the practice of attaching to the specimens numbered tags (pieces of thin lead) corresponding to a number in the collector's notebook in which were recorded colours, sex, and other appropriate details. Thus slowly museums changed from mere private hoards or public peep-shows to storehouses of carefully preserved scientific records.

This trend also found reflection in the growing readiness to keep specimens in spirit, instead of resorting to various inferior and often dubious processes purely in order to produce exhibits. Since Robert Boyle's first discovery of its value in 1663, spirit had become the grand preservative for almost all objects of manageable size. But till now collectors had been inclined to treat it primarily as a rough-and-ready field method, as a means of keeping the specimens in a fit condition until such time as they could be taken out and mounted. Only certain kinds of organisms, fungi, for example, had been deemed so intractable as to require permanent embalming in this fashion. An additional deterrent, quite possibly, was cost. As pure alcohol was found to destroy colours and alter the consistency of objects, unless diluted, the preferred medium had come to be spirits of wine. Distilled spirits were usually dismissed as much inferior, but in countries where these largely took the place of wine collectors were more or less forced to use them, and in practice their preservative powers proved quite sufficient. Specimens from the West Indies or South America, where rum was cheap and abundant, arrived in good condition, while Yarrell found that fish sent to him from Scotland and Ireland travelled equally well in whisky.

But much more prohibitive than the cost of the liquid was the cost of the glass required for containing it. The sudden fourfold increase in the tax on glass in 1812, imposed when the country was running up huge debts in waging war against Napoleon and—as so often with wartime taxes—carefully not repealed by a persistently hard-pressed Exchequer, hit science and medicine severely because of their heavy dependence on laboratory and dispensary glassware. The repeal of the duties in 1845 accordingly brought these fields equally sharp compensating benefits, which quickly found reflection in natural history collecting. Within two years specialists in the small creatures such as spiders and worms had begun to adopt series of small corked glass tubes and used them on the principle of one for each individual capture—in place of the previous practice of putting numbers together in a single bottle, which often led to serious blunders. It is probably not without significance that the two earliest-known exponents of this in Britain, George Johnston of Berwick and R. H. Meade of Bradford, were both medical men, for it was doubtless in the world of medicine that this newly feasible profligacy with glass found primary expression. Until then, equipment of this kind had been much too expensive to be diverted in any quantity to such marginal pursuits as natural history, even for purposes of museum display—much less for being taken out into the field and exposed to the risk of breakage.

The greatly lowered price of bottles probably also played a part in the general swing-over to new types of killing-agents in entomology. But in this the more immediate spur was the need for methods that were both more convenient for the field and less obnoxious to the tenderer consciences of the new generation of collectors.

Until the 1820s the usual way of dispatching the larger insects was either 'pinching' (a quick nip between the thumb and forefinger applied just beneath the wings) or else stabbing the thorax with a pin. For most purposes either was speedy and efficient. But there were unfortunately exceptions: dragonflies, in particular, as Edward Donovan was forced to admit in 1794,

> are extremely tenacious of life . . . We have seen one of the larger kinds live two days on the pin, and even shew symptoms of life twenty-four hours after being deprived of its head. The most expeditious method of killing those creatures [he added, with a show of compassion] is to run a red hot wire up the body and thorax, for they will live a considerable time in agony if you attempt to kill them with aqua-fortis [concentrated nitric acid].

This was altogether too crude for the squeamish; and in order to avoid having to cope with a still-struggling insect before applying the final *coup de grâce* on reaching home, various methods of asphyxiation were developed, which seem to have proved quite popular despite being often highly cumbrous and primitive. Insects were held over lighted sulphur matches (despite the fact that this badly injured the colours, as several writers pointed out) or had tobacco smoke puffed over them, or were subjected to the hot air from a fire or an oven, or to the steam from a boiling pan, or, more sensibly, put in collecting-boxes strongly impregnated with camphor. A further refinement on this, adopted in Germany and England in the 1820s, was the 'death-chamber' method: imprisoning the insect in a hermetically sealed container (popularly known as 'the stifling box') and immersing this in boiling water.

But although some of these practices continued in use among the conservative, the coldly callous or the followers of outdated books down to the fifties or even later, the altered needs of the times combined with the advance of technology to bring to the fore a steady series of fresh killing-agents which were often more effective, if more dangerous to use, but—much more important—were also ethically more acceptable. Ether and ammonia were both in use by the end of the 1820s, the latter on occasions in the more domestically convenient form of common smelling-salts. Chloroform, however, until it succeeded in capturing the headlines in 1847 with its first introduction for surgery, failed to attract much interest: its wide adoption during the decade following (which also saw the invention of special chloroform killing-bottles) nicely matched the spread of its reputation as an instrument of mercy for human beings. As one clerical collector insisted, 'the old plan of red-hot needles, boiling water, steam etc., gives an idea of much cruelty, but since the introduction of chloroform these practices must be dispensed with'—for all the world as if it was a change from the bad old days of medicine of which he was setting himself up as the advocate.

Chloroform causes stiffening in insects, which makes them hard to set. Ammonia avoids this drawback but tends to alter colours; bottles of this substance, furthermore, are liable to explode from the heat of the sun. Bruised laurel leaves, which emit prussic acid gas, have none of these irritating defects, and some ten years after J. F. Stephens had first announced their effectiveness in 1835, they came into widespread use, even for ridding stoves and greenhouses of injurious pests (if a note recommending them for this purpose to the Horticultural Society in 1838 was indeed ever acted upon). Their one disadvantage was their slowness; but later still, in 1854, an even faster and deadlier agent was reported, and in turn adopted: potassium cyanide. This chemical, 'now so extensively used in the arts', as G. Bowdler Buckton pointed out that summer to the British Association, could kill insects in anything from two minutes down to forty seconds; it was inexpensive and would keep indefinitely in a stoppered bottle. But it, too, had a tendency to make specimens stiff and was, besides, a risky substance to put into the hands of a youthful novice. When someone ventured to recommend it in the *Entomologists' Weekly Intelligencer* in 1859, adding that it was 'already in the hands of every dabbler in photography', the editor butted in with a stern rebuke, maintaining that it was altogether too dangerous to merit general adoption.

These less messy modes of killing salved the conscience and improved the general condition of the specimens that were captured, but they had little or no effect in increasing the size of collections. This was remedied, however, by the simultaneous invention of 'sugaring'—the most dramatic tipping of the scales in favour of the hunter till the advent of the mercury vapour light-trap in the mid-twentieth century.

Like the aquarium principle and the closely glazed case, 'sugaring' was one of those momentous discoveries that could have been made much earlier, if only people had been more alert to the possibilities raised by certain casual observations—and readier to act on them. In the late 1820s and early 1830s, coinciding with the great increase in the numbers of entomologists, several collectors noticed that certain sugary substances held a pronounced attraction for moths, especially for the less familiar nocturnal species. These 'sweets' included ripe yew-berries and the bottles filled with sugar and water (or, alternatively, beer) traditionally hung against walls in gardens to tempt wasps away from fruit. About 1832 two young brothers, Edward and Henry Doubleday, who worked under their father in a grocery business in Epping, noticed that moths were attracted in quite unusual numbers to some empty hogsheads of the dark-brown, strong-smelling West Indies sugar commonly known as 'Jamaica Foots' which had recently been put outside their warehouse. Taking the hint, they proceeded to experiment with placing several of these hogsheads in open places in the neighbourhood, near gardens and out in fields; and, much to their gratification, they caught by this means no fewer than 69 species, some of them quite uncommon.

Unfortunately the Doubledays failed to grasp the full implications of their discovery, and for some years they seem to have treated the method merely as an amusing curiosity, assuming that it was necessary to trundle heavy hogsheads about the place in order to benefit accordingly. Despite a note on the subject published in Newman's *Entomological Magazine* only one other collector appears to have been sufficiently intrigued to give the method a serious try. This was P. J. Selby, a Northumberland squire and one of the foremost ornithologists of the day, who in 1835 had taken up entomology with great enthusiasm—probably to treat himself to a refreshing change after slaving for a good ten years on a monumental work on birds. Sugar-casks were not readily procurable in his part of the country, so he used an empty beehive, generously smeared on the outside with honey. In a letter to the Rev. F. O. Morris in April 1837, which the latter considered of sufficient general interest to send for publication in Neville Wood's *Naturalist,* he reported that the hive was best placed

> on a forked stick at the most convenient height for taking the insects with the clippers. I set it immediately after sunset, and visit every half hour till ten or eleven o'clock, during autumn and summer . . . The Moths are generally so

engaged in sucking the honey, as to allow themselves to be easily taken if quietly approached. A candle or lamp is used, but not left standing with the hive.

(Selby was thus the originator of the collector's regular tour of inspection, which came to be dubbed the 'sugar-beat'.) On a favourable night in July, he added, he had seen the whole outside of the hive completely covered with moths and taken on it at one time eighteen to twenty different species. With praiseworthy farsightedness he suggested this might well serve as an excellent means of studying the seasonal duration of different species as well as the fluctuating ratio of the sexes—an interesting parallel to Dovaston's virtually contemporaneous idea of utilizing his special feeding-device as a means of studying more precisely the varying incidence of different birds.

In the same letter Selby made a further, even more discerning comment. 'Anointing the trunks of trees,' he remarked quite casually, 'would no doubt have the same effect as exposing a hive, but it would require a much greater consumption of honey, as wasps, bees, and other insects would devour every particle during the day.' From his words it does not sound as if this potential alternative had taken his fancy sufficiently to be put into practice; and although ten years later he was certainly brushing honey 'or syrup of sugar' on to the trunks of trees on his estate it is likely that he subsequently switched to this method under the influence of the prevailing fashion.

It was not until 1843, in a note in the *Zoologist,* that the details of the invention were properly made public for the benefit of collectors in general. Even after that, for a year or so, adoption of the method was singularly slow and scarcely spread outside the privileged circle of London collectors, who presumably had received first-hand demonstrations of its efficacy at the hands of the sociable Henry Doubleday. Many of the provincial collectors, it seems, imagined at first that ordinary white household sugar was enough and, on achieving no success, concluded that the method was a fraud. It was only after 1844 that knowledge of the correct formula spread up and down the country, in no time at all effecting a veritable revolution in the range of species represented in the average collector's cabinet. Rare nocturnal moths, which up to then had carried a price on their heads of fifteen shillings each or even more, were now all at once taken in plenty—and the dealers faced a catastrophic decline in their livelihood.

Every moth-hunter has his own favourite recipe for 'treacle' (as 'sugar' has since become better—and more accurately—known), brewing his concoction in a treasured 'treacling-pan' much as a *chef de cuisine* sets apart a

special pan for his omelettes. Here, as an example, is the mixture prescribed by one late-Victorian collector: Take a quantity of the strongest-
smelling brown sugar, add hot water (or, even better, beer) and mix to the
consistency of treacle; then stir in rum, or alternatively methylated spirit,
and flavour to taste with aniseed or essence of Jargonelle pears; then 'serve'
by smearing on the trunks of trees or on posts, in likely situations, with a
painter's brush—and at dusk, before the moths emerge. To light his progress while he went his rounds,—but at the same time to free both hands
for his essential purpose, the collector was further recommended to wear a
lantern suspended from his neck or attached to his waist by a belt—a
device sported by certain of the London collectors as early as the 1820s
and mentioned in the pages of Kirby and Spence.

The French were reported to 'sugar' with decomposed soap-suds, and
rotten apples also had their vogue. One collector even tried adding gin to
the ingredients, but did not repeat the experiment, as the insects fell from
the trees and lay about on the ground quite stupefied before the preliminary brushing had even been completed. All manner of substances, in fact,
seem to hold attractions for night-flying moths. The problem, rather, is to
find an ideal solution that will not only function most effectively as a bait,
but also prove resistant to 'sugar's' two eternal enemies: heavy rain, which
washes the mixture off the trees; and earwigs, which consume it.

The panoply of entomology—of all the branches of natural history the
one most cluttered with unavoidable equipment—otherwise survived
these years of such extensive change with little disturbance. Indeed, so
slight have been the adjustments to most of the main weapons of the chase
over a very long period that it is easy to forget how ancient so many of
them are.

A remarkably high proportion of the traditional implements of British
entomology in fact receive mention in the preface to Benjamin Wilkes's
The English Moths and Butterflies (1748–9) and in his even earlier supple-
mentary sheet to his *Twelve New Designs of English Butterflies* (1742), the
earliest publication wholly devoted to entomological methods in any language. These show that already collectors used at least two kinds of nets,
beating-sticks and -sheets, pill-boxes (for putting over insects when captured), cork-lined pocket collecting-boxes, pincushions (for holding the
pins—in the days when specimens were always 'pinned' in the field), cork
setting-boards, card 'braces' for setting, setting-needles, breeding-cages
and even special trowels (purloined from the bricklayers) for the time-
honoured practice of digging under the roots of trees for pupae. Wilkes
also knew of the technique commonly termed 'assembling'—he called it
'simbling'—first discovered by Ray in 1693 (and also practised by the Chinese from early times), which involves hiding a female moth in a box or
cage and then merely waiting for the males to arrive in swarms from up to

half a mile around. On the other hand, the phenomenon of 'stiffening' seems to have nonplussed him and he appears to have discarded quite needlessly all specimens that had undergone desiccation or *rigor mortis* in the interval before they could be taken out for setting.

Even at this early period there are signs of the intense conservatism in the matter of equipment ever displayed by British entomologists. The disdain for the bag-net (or ring-net), the much more convenient type of net prevailing on the Continent from the seventeenth-century onwards, is the prime instance of this. The reason, just conceivably, is that collectors in this country failed to discover the special knack required for its proper use. Swainson, in 1822, seems to have been the first to refer in print to the needed 'sudden and abrupt twist, accompanied by a forward jerk'; while J. C. Dale, sixteen years after this, implied that it was still a mystery known only to the French. As their principal weapon the British clung instead, apparently without exception, to the heavier and far clumsier clap-net or 'batfolder', which was borrowed from the armoury of the fowlers, who had long used this implement for trapping small birds at night. It differed from the modern kind of net (which is essentially the bag-net) by being worked up under the insect, which was 'clapped' in by bringing the two rods together simultaneously. By 1766, we learn from Moses Harris, such nets were sufficiently widely in demand to be stocked by fishing-tackle shops, where they went under the name of 'butterfly traps'.

It was not until after 1850 that clap-nets began to give way to their handier Continental rivals. Even then they did not vanish overnight, and some diehards persisted in using them until the end of the century. Today, somewhat ironically, no single example of one has survived, even as an antique curiosity.

It seems to have needed the more cosmopolitan temper of the later Victorians to sweep away this insular, not to say chauvinistic, attitude and to allow the introduction of this and several other more than reasonable foreign usages. For at much the same time, in the 1860s, the grooved setting-board also finally arrived in strength from across the Channel and the first box-trap for moths was introduced to a British audience from America. Before that date British collectors had always set their specimens low down, with the wings depressed so as to touch the wood of the setting-board. They defended this out-of-step practice as being more pleasing to the eye, as it made the insects—or so they claimed—more lifelike in appearance. (They flinched from changing, too, as flat-setting was one simple way of telling apart non-British specimens, so that by adopting this they risked throwing doubt on the authenticity of their captures.) In consequence they used shorter ('English') pins, and their setting-boards were made without a central groove.

This had an important side-effect: low-setting meant that the specimen

left no room for, or at best completely concealed, the requisite ticket recording the place and date of capture. As a result the great majoriy of
British entomologists were additionally tempted into excusing themselves,
quite unforgivably, from this utterly essential scientific practice. Thereby
most collections of insects, until a comparatively recent period, were rendered valueless as records: they merely served to advertise the prowess of
their owners, to gratify their urge to shine in competition, or to please
their senses with a splash of brilliant colour. The most that could be said
for them was that they helped to show the range of variation existing
within each species.

The first true moth-trap appears to have been invented by Townend
Glover, the first Entomologist to the United States Government. This consisted of a lamp shining through plates of glass arranged diagonally in a
box. The moths, attracted by the beam, entered the box and then could
not (or at least did not) manage to escape. It was a rather complex piece of
machinery and thus, inevitably, expensive. H. G. Knaggs, one of the editors of the *Entomologist's Monthly Magazine,* was responsible for introducing it to British collectors in an article in that journal in 1866, shortly after
meeting Glover in London. This 'marvellous moth trap', he announced in
excitement, 'will catch moths all night long without any trouble to the
owner'—in other words, for the first time collecting had been rendered
automatic. Subsequently, simpler and cheaper versions were marketed, for
as little as five shillings. Nevertheless, despite the great increase in technical
sophistication that such an invention implied, this further exploiting of the
drawing-power of light did not begin to compare with the discovery of
'sugar', either in the degree of magnification of destructiveness or in the
fillip provided to collecting as a whole by the novelty and utility of the
device. Nor is it possible to see in this clustering of new developments in
the sixties anything much more than a belated catching-up with progress,
certainly nothing like the social challenge-and-response effect that recognizably occurred in the thirties.

Technological conservatism is not peculiar to entomology. It is to be
found in every branch of natural history, and partly arises from the fact that
the tools of naturalists also serve as their insignia and mutual recognition
symbols. In order to fulfil this secondary function, they need to be stereo-
typed and so must retain substantially the same appearance over lengthy
periods.

This pull towards distinctiveness has a useful side-effect. The very fact
that their pursuit tends to appear weird and eccentric to outsiders inclines
naturalists to make a strength out of a defect and seek to emphasize their
apartness. In the process they also strengthen their sense of belonging, as
naturalists. The ritualized character of their methods and equipment helps

in this direction; and in fact, without them, it would be much more difficult to generate a shared mystique. A further ingredient, but a subsidiary
one, is no doubt a dash of that ordinary, whimsical delight in oddity which
is so exceptionally well developed in the English.

The combined result is a mild theatrical streak running all through British natural history: a self-conscious cult of the frankly quaint and the defi-
antly archaic. Entomologists continued to take the field in formal top hats
long after these had passed out of fashion, on the absurd pretext that when
lined with cork they formed the most convenient collecting receptacle that
had ever been devised. Why else, except as a complicated private joke,
should Professor D'Arcy Wentworth Thompson, the author of the classic
work *On Growth and Form,* have insisted on regularly using a battered old
umbrella for chasing Lepidoptera—when butterfly-nets of every size and
description could be had for almost nothing? Why else should Samuel
Brewer, an early eighteenth-century moss collector, have 'contrived [ac-
cording to John Hill] a dress on purpose for herbalizing, and had a mask
[specially made] for his face, and pads to his knees, that he might creep
into the thickets'?

The inverse of this is the naturalist's everlurking sense of embarrassment
—at being seen with such curious or suspicious-looking paraphernalia, or
at being caught in socially dubious or downright disreputable activities.
'With all your implements about you,' Kirby and Spence rightly warned
the beginner in 1826, 'you will at first be stared and grinned at by the
vulgar.' However, they added 'they will soon become reconciled to you,
and regard you no more than your brethren of the angle and of the gun.
Things that are unusual are too often esteemed ridiculous'—a sentence
which deserves to be nailed over every naturalist's mantelpiece.

Until the advent of the modern bird-watcher and his quite exceptional
achievement of total respectability, this strain of embarrassment was inseparable from the study. The literature, admittedly, contains few allusions to
it; even so, we can be sure that it was always there, if only from the clearly
furtive trend apparent in the design of so much of the old equipment. In
order to avoid insulting remarks or irritating glances, naturalists often used
to hide their equipment from public view . . . hammers worn in a belt
beneath the jacket, the hoop of the butterfly-net doubled up and carried
under one's clothes or in a pocket. ('When we first began Sea Weeds,'
George Johnston once confessed to Mrs Gatty, 'my wife carried a larger
muff than the present fashion would commend, and many a heavy stone
and well-filled bottle has therein been smuggled.') Alternatively, and more
cunningly, they dressed up their tools in disguises to make them seem
more commonplace. Net-cases were strung across the back to allow moth-
hunters to pass as anglers or men out shooting. Nets were designed to

look like umbrellas—even though, when the rain came down, the entomologist looked far more ridiculous walking around with one still obstinately furled. Collecting-boxes were camouflaged as books, even sometimes beautifully bound and with a title on the spine, which explains their standard size today—determined by the height of the average bookshelf.

In some cases the need for concealment prevented or delayed desirable innovations. In botany the small tin candle-boxes which Stukeley and his fellow students took out on their rambles around Cambridge in the summer of 1704 continued to serve as the standard specimen-containers throughout the eighteenth century, even though plants of any size, to be fitted into them, required to be doubled up and were ordinarily so squashed that they made execrable material for herbaria. Their one great asset, of course, to which they clearly owed their long survival, was their diminutive size, which allowed them to be tucked safely out of sight inside a pocket. Similarly, although most people seemed to be agreed that the sensible colour for the clap-net was white, in as much as this enabled small insects to be far more easily discerned, green muslin remained the fashion; for—as Edward Newman put it explicitly—this had

> the merit of being less conspicuous, which under some circumstances is an advantage, for instance, in those country lanes where the pedestrians are unused to such an exhibition, the white never fails to attract a little crowd, which causes some slight inconvenience to the entomologist, as well as loss of time, for he is invariably under the necessity of explaining to the bystanders what he is doing.

It may well have been because of the embarrassments likely to arise from so much indispensable impedimenta that the ranks of entomology, all through its history, have never acquired so markedly aristocratic a composition as have, at different periods, geology, botany and ornithology. For there was one further serious social barrier with which, until well on into Victorian times, the would-be naturalist had somehow to contend. This was the convention that a gentleman did not carry tools or heavy burdens or betray any other evidence suggestive of manual labour. To circumvent this, the lordly—taking a lead from sportsmen—often resorted to the caddie principle, hiring small boys to take on the obvious drudgery. Thus Sedgwick in the 1820s rode round exploring the geology of the Lake District with a miner's boy permanently *en croupe,* ready to do the heavier hammering. Swainson's *Naturalist's Guide* of 1822 suggests that the canvas knapsack holding the entomologist's equipment 'may be carried . . . by a little boy'; and again, in connection with birds: 'A little boy may carry the basket or box which is intended to hold the game.' The wholesale entry of the Victorian middle classes put an end to this practice, though there remained the odd moneyed individual who, for show or out of sheer convenience, still refused to abandon it. Wilfred Huddleston, a leading palaeontologist, habitually took with him on field excursions his manservant, whose task it was to carry the bag into which went every specimen: 'Put it in the bag, John,' he would forever be saying, until it turned into a catchphrase among his fellow geologists. Even as late as the 1930s Mrs M. L. Wedgwood regularly toured the country collecting plants in a large car driven by a liveried chauffeur, who as often as not was deputed to do the actual gathering.

Nothing illustrates better the New Order that came into being in the 1830s than the general swing among botanists to a much larger type of vasculum for ordinary, everyday purposes—so novel that Greville thought it deserved a special name and proposed that it be christened the 'Magnum'. Instead of one tiny tin in the hand or in a pocket and a second vast and very heavy one for lengthy excursions, the new generation compromised with just a single one intermediate in size, which they were also happy to wear from the shoulder by a strap with an assured, near-professional nonchalance. These new vascula, unlike their predecessors, were roomy enough to take specimens of a satisfactory size for proper scientific study, to say nothing of the far larger quantities on average demanded by the increased greediness that had lately begun to overtake collecting; they also matched in length the larger size of herbarium sheet just then becoming standard. Thanks to large-scale commercial production, made possible by their being prescribed for field classes by the various universities, they ousted the previous models remarkably speedily.

The commercial sale of special drying-paper followed, beginning about 1845. There was much experimenting with better methods in this direction too, which culminated in Thomas Twining's announcement in the *Botanical Gazette* in 1850 of 'A New Botanical Drying Apparatus'. He had rediscovered the efficacy of artificial heat for this purpose; and recommended, in particular, an airing-cupboard as used for household linen, which he found saved 'the troublesome expedient of continually changing the sheets'. Unfortunately, the botanical world seems to have been surprisingly dilatory in acting on this very useful hint.

The standardization of equipment—that typically industrial achievement —which formed the outstanding feature of the early Victorian period, was accompanied by a certain standardization as well in clothing and in provisions. In place of the frock-coat in the field came the shooting-jacket popularized by sportsmen, with its very welcome numerous pockets. Kirby and Spence were urging its adoption as early as 1826 and Newman, some years later, insists on its having 'ample cross pockets outside, on the hip; also several breast pockets, particularly two (at least) very small ones, for glass vials containing spirits to stand upright in'. Its present-day counterpart is plainly the anorak. This is the nearest, perhaps, that the ordinary naturalist has ever come to wearing anything remotely approaching a uniform. The only known example of a true uniform, in fact, is the one which the staff of the Geological Survey were required to wear in the field during the first six years of its existence, up to 1845: blue tunic and trousers, brass buttons and a top hat.

The standardized packed lunch, another under-celebrated achievement, took curiously long before it became based on sandwiches. The usual field sustenance for most of the first half of the century seems to have been bread and cheese or hard-boiled eggs, washed down by a flaskful of diluted brandy. The Thermos flask lay far in the future, coffee was much dearer than today and tea cost some three times as much as in Edwardian times (before the country had the benefit of the Indian crops); even so, many of Graham's students opted for cold tea as their refreshment. Sandwiches, an English invention of the 1760s, were sufficiently widely carried by sportsmen by 1817 to have brought into being the term 'sandwichbox'; but the first naturalist to mention them specifically appears to have been the Rev. C. A. Johns, who had a packet with him down in Cornwall in 1831 during the hair-raising adventure which he later so graphically described in *A Week at the Lizard* (1839). After that date allusions to them become more frequent. This point is of slightly more than academic interest, for it seems to have been British botanists' repeated use of their vascula for holding and preserving sandwiches—to such an extent that J. C. Dale, in 1838, actually dared to recommend, quite unequivocally, 'a vasculum (for sandwiches)'— that caused the standard design of this implement to be heavily influenced by that of the sandwich-box, and so led to a British vasculum that is still markedly different in aspect from the usual models on the Continent. The British way of eating, one might say, appears to have produced a neat case of technological endemism.

Perhaps it would have been better if only more people had used the vasculum as a resting-place solely for their sandwiches. For, like the accurate breech-loaders, like the entomologist's baits and traps, the botanist's aid to collecting had become by mid-century so readily obtainable, so widely disseminated and so fatally easy to abuse that there was a serious danger that the countryside of Britain would become irreparably injured by the very people who were among its keenest admirers. The advance of technology, as so often, had outstripped the social attitudes appropriate to its use. An endless stream of accoutrements and gadgetry rained down upon the naturalist and tempted him to suppose that he earned the name merely by donning, discharging or deploying them. There grew up a kind of mechanical fallacy: a half-conscious, wholly false analogy with the onward thrust of industrialism that was everywhere so triumphant. Natural history thus began to suffer from its own insidious brand of the doctrine of Progress; and collectors continued to fan out across the countryside with their often murderous devices with much the same blind energy and diligence as the excessively house-proud are wont to wield their dusters and their brooms.

CHAPTER EIGHT

The Field Club

THERE was one other Early Victorian invention which was to have a more far-reaching influence and bring more benefits to more people than all of the rest put together. This was that masterpiece of social mechanics, the natural history field club.

Local societies had existed, as we have seen, long before the Victorian era. Some had been specialized, others had ranged over the whole field of learning, taking the Royal Society as their implicit model. One of the earliest of the latter, Spalding Gentlemen's Society, came into being in 1710. 'We deal in all arts and sciences,' its founder was able to claim, 'and exclude nothing from our conversation but politics, which would throw us all into confusion and disorder.' Other 'gentlemen's' societies followed, mainly in smallish country towns. Later in the century, after most of these had passed away and been forgotten, a fresh wave of essentially similar bodies, the literary and philosophical societies, gradually spread across the new industrial areas of England: from Manchester in 1781 to Newcastle in 1793, to Birmingham in 1800 and to Leeds in 1819. These in their turn acted as the models for a further wave, the first local societies devoted specifically to natural history—and to the subject as a whole—which were founded in most of the leading towns and cities of the British Isles in those two buoyant decades, the 1820s and the 1830s. The Ashmolean N.H.S. of Oxfordshire, which still flourishes today, is the oldest survivor of these, dating from 1828.

These new institutions all had certain basic features in common. In the first place, reflecting the superb faith of their members in the power of Reason, in mere discourse as an instrument of discovery, they required a debating-chamber to serve as the forum where the best brains in the community could meet and grind together. Secondly, to ensure that their collective wisdom was duly placed on permanent record, they needed to publish a weighty series of Transactions. Thirdly, as inheritors of the eighteenth-century faith in the educative value of 'cabinets of curiosities', they placed the forming of a museum high among their priorities. Fourthly, if only to complete the academic ambience, they sought to build up a library of rare and expensive volumes.

Such objects were costly. A meeting-hall of the necessary dignified dimensions entailed a substantial rent. A library and collections meant extra rooms and, ideally, a full-time curator to keep them orderly and dusted. The publishing of Transactions brought heavy printers' bills. In consequence, subscriptions were high and only the well-off could afford the price of membership. Whether they wished it or not (and probably they often did wish it), these institutions tended to be exclusive, and many of the humbler and keenest grew up regarding them as altogether outside their concern.

Simultaneously, and by comparison almost invisibly, societies of a very different type had sprung up in several of the blackest of the manufacturing districts, particularly in the area where Lancashire, Cheshire and Yorkshire all meet. These bodies, which concerned themselves largely or wholly with botany, were remarkable for the fact that all their members, without exception, were manual workers, most of them factory operatives or jobbing gardeners. All too little is known about their beginnings. Around Manchester they dated back to the 1770s at least, evidently generated in that same stratum of enthusiasm that produced the very similar, pre-Linnaean botanical society described by Smith as having once existed among the Norwich weavers. Loudon, in his *Encyclopaedia of Gardening* (1822), makes the arresting observation that in both Scotland and England 'wherever the silk, linen or cotton manufactures are carried on . . . the operatives are found to possess a taste for, and occupy part of their leisure time in, the culture of flowers'. It may be that as the new textile industries developed in the north, the skilled hands attracted there from the waning factories of East Anglia took with them this special, deeply entrenched tradition—which they in turn, perhaps, had originally acquired from the immigrant cloth-workers from Flanders. Intriguingly, a parallel passion for collecting colourful insects long flourished among the silk weavers of Spitalfields. Whatever the explanation, it is certainly remarkable that a keenness for botany—and, even more, for precise plant identification—should have persisted so long and so strongly in such apparently inhospitable surroundings and often in the face of the most discouraging personal circumstances. James Crowther, for example, one of the most energetic of these botanists, was born in a Manchester cellar, the youngest child of an unlettered labourer. Another, John Horsefield, a hand-loom weaver, about the time of Trafalgar is said to have been so keen to memorize the various classes of the Linnaean System that he had them written out for him on a slip of paper attached to his loom-post and repeated the names to himself as he drove the shuttle.

It has long been the custom in such districts for all those sharing some special interest to meet at a particular public house. The botanists were no exception. There they exchanged specimens and reminisced and pooled their slender earnings to buy some of the latest books. These regular gatherings sometimes crystallized into formal clubs, then typically took their name from the public house where they met. This produced such bizarrely titled bodies as the Independent Oddfellows Arms Botanical Society and the Black Cow Botanical Society. These met regularly every Sunday, the only free day that their members enjoyed. Most of the time they kept independent of one another, each going its own way; but now and then all the societies for miles around would link up and mingle together at a conversazione at some place convenient to everyone concerned. So they went on, flourishing for a time, then declining and dying out, then being revived again, right up to the turn of this century, their end only coming with the general revulsion against collecting and the rising lure of weekend sport.

From these two quite separate stocks, the one rather avidly academic but with a well-proved role in promoting the advancement of knowledge, the other unambitious and convivial with its roots in the field, the equivalent of a natural hybrid, with all a half-breed's vigour, arose spontaneously in the year 1823. This was the Plinian Society of Edinburgh, a general scientific society which luckily happened to have its birth just as field classes had become all the rage at the two southern Scottish universities—and which, accordingly, made history, apparently almost without noticing, by including in its programme from 1825 at least occasional excursions into the surrounding countryside on foot.

Among the members of this Society were three students at the University: two brothers by the name of Baird and an aspiring surgeon, George Johnston. When all three took up their respective professions in their native Berwickshire, they continued to meet from time to time and renew their friendship with the communal rambles that they had come to enjoy as Plinians at Edinburgh. Out of these grew the idea of starting a local body on similar lines; and an inaugural meeting for this purpose, attended by nine people, was held at Coldingham on 22 September 1831 (just three years before the ending of the long tradition of instructional 'herbarizings' by the Society of Apothecaries). Thus was born the original ancestor of the great majority of local natural history societies existing in this country today: the Berwickshire Naturalists' Club.

The Berwickshire Club had several novel features, which attracted a good deal of comment at the time. To begin with, its meetings lasted a whole day and were not just in the evening; moreover, they were always in the field, not in a stuffy and uncomfortable room. So far from being at the same place, they were also held in different parts of the district in turn, thus suiting the convenience of outlying members. This nomadic character liberated the Club from the traditional necessity of permanent premises and deterred it from attempting to own any library or collections. In consequence, its expenses were slight and the annual subscription could be kept down to a mere six or seven shillings, thereby bringing it within the reach of those of slender means. Even more revolutionary was the fact that ladies were admitted—although the Club revealed some self-consciousness in this by allowing them only as honorary members.

Until that time, curious though it seems, people appear to have had the utmost difficulty in conceiving of a successful corporate entity without visible substance. According to the contemporary social creed, status was founded on property—and a propertyless body, it was assumed, must be no less contemptible and ineffective than a propertyless man or woman. The advent of the 'floating' (as opposed to the 'static') local learned society was symptomatic of the rise to prominence of the new middle classes and the start of the erosion of this hitherto accepted, purely aristocratic standard. Like a limited-liability company, a field club proved that it was possible to have strength without magnificence. That it was the Border Country in which this new institution first arose may have been no coincidence; for here, more than in most parts of Britain, the hierarchical divisions in society have for long been untypically ill-defined and loose. What would have been hard for others, and particularly for Englishmen, the men of Berwickshire doubtless found comparatively simple.

The pattern of the Club's outings also deserves some notice. The members would start the day by assembling at eight or nine o'clock and breakfasting together at an inn. Thus fortified, they set about their work, splitting up into sections to study the subjects in which they variously happened to take a special interest. Collecting would go on till four o'clock or so, after which everyone met again for dinner, where the customary toasts were drunk and the company tucked into a fine salmon sent over for the occasion from Berwick. After this would come discussions of the day's finds, with perhaps a comment or two by the appropriate expert, and this would be followed by short papers on relevant subjects of interest.

It was a highly successful formula and, nourished by the intense local patriotism of that particular corner of Great Britain, it was soon being sedulously propagated by the members and gradually spread to other districts. Johnston himself persuaded his trawling friend, the Rev. David Landsborough, to start a similar club in Ayrshire. Another member, Ralph Carr, helped to originate the Tyneside Club in 1846; and in the same year Sir Thomas Tancred, a former member who had moved south to live in Gloucestershire, helped to found the Cotteswold Club. Thus infected, the Middle West of England erupted in a rash of these bodies, each of them dominated by one, or maybe two or three leading local naturalists, who were mostly on friendly terms with their opposite numbers in other clubs and, in some cases, even interrelated. Thus, the Rev. W. S. Symonds, who founded the Malvern Field Club, was a connection of the founder of the Bath Field Club, the Rev. Leonard Jenyns; and similarly, to take a more long-range example, Robert Garner, the mainstay of the North Staffordshire Club, was instrumental in persuading the husband of a niece of his, Philip Kermode, to carry the creed to his native Isle of Man and there start up a successful replica.

This mouth-to-mouth chain of enthusiasm proved invaluable. The wholesale copying that went on meant that the majority of local natural history societies acquired from the first a common structural form—in some cases, even, a total constitutional identity—as well as an underlying consensus in behaviour and outlook. This meant, in turn, that a naturalist could leave one club for another on moving to a different district and at once feel at home.

Furthermore, the strong identification—as happened so often—with one particular founder produced a much heavier investment of concern and energy than would have occurred in the case of clubs originating more or less anonymously. The individuals in question, mindful that their local reputation was staked on the venture, made an extra effort to ensure that they were not associated with failure. Many clubs that might have failed were thereby kept afloat indefinitely, and sometimes, against all likelihood and expectation, turned into an undeniable success.

In extreme cases, under the influence of this motive a society could take on a character that was uncomfortably paternalistic. The Richmond and North Riding Club frankly admitted that it owed much of its success to the princely support of its president, Edward Wood, who generally organized all the excursions himself and met all the requirements out of his own pocket. On one occasion, when the Club had made a special trip of over a hundred miles to visit Flamborough Head and the members had missed the return train due to a mistake in the arrangements, the president chartered a special train to take them from Scarborough to York entirely at his personal expense. The Holmesdale Club at Reigate, which had an equally wealthy and benevolent president, is another, more recent instance.

Not all societies had to depend for their founding on the initiative of naturalists with some degree of local eminence already. In several cases, at Leeds and Northampton for example, the instigators were all young men in their twenties, who merely invited some much older man to preside over their meetings as a figurehead. It was not unknown, too, for a society to be conceived more or less accidentally, by a kind of collective combustion, and in the most public manner possible: in the columns of a local newspaper. The Bedfordshire Society arose in this way out of a very lively correspondence over the status of the Sweet Flag in the County—rather as the body which has since become the London Natural History Society, now by far the largest of its kind in the country, had its origin in 1858, in a most inappropriately hole-in-corner fashion, in a short letter to that very chatty periodical, the *Entomologists' Weekly Intelligencer*.

Many of these societies also took in archaeology. For much of the Victorian era, when archaeology was still regarded by some people as just another form of field collecting, to combine this with natural history in a single society seemed both sensible and natural. 'The liaison of a sprightly young damsel with a sober and mature husband,' was how Robert Garner once justified the practice. Such a marriage, however, was not without its strains, chiefly because of the rather different kinds of people, with rather different inclinations, the two studies tended to attract. Local antiquarians were often wealthy collectors of *objets d'art,* for whom the subject was an exercise in Taste rather than a scientific study; or they were fashionably Romantic and loved to drone about grottoes or give themselves the shudders by imagining horrible druidic rites; or else they were overbearingly 'county', with a passion for genealogy that could lead to quarterings and lengthy extracts from parish documents crowding natural history out of the society's Transactions. The 'Ants', furthermore, were always stoutly Tory, while the 'Nats', according with the radical inclinations of science, tended to be more Liberal in outlook—which may explain a curious rule observed by Leicester Literary and Philosophical Society, according to which the office of president had to be filled alternately from among the adherents of one or the other of the two main political parties.

Around 1860 the field club, by now flourishing mightily, succeeded in back-crossing with the grander of its parents and producing yet another distinctive type of society, peculiar to the larger towns and cities. This differed most obviously from its predecessors there in offering a programme of the now indispensable field excursions.

In Liverpool, Manchester and Bristol, almost simultaneously, societies were founded which differed at once in the enormous size of their membership and the correspondingly lavish scale on which they were conducted—with, as a result, rather high subscriptions. Nearly four hundred people joined Liverpool Naturalists' Field Club in the first few months of its existence, and of this number at least half turned up regularly for the Club excursions. The Manchester Field-Naturalists' Society recorded an attendance of no fewer than 550 on one of its outings (surely an all-time record?), due in part to its audacity in advertising its meetings in the local papers. Such mammoth parties were defended as allowing the hire of a special train, so that the serious core was enabled to visit places of interest at a considerable distance that would otherwise have remained beyond reach. At the same time, it was easy to criticize them as far too large for proper scientific study or instruction, and the suspicion that they were merely a cloak for a lot of frivolous junketing was not allayed by the glittering soirées that were held in the winter evenings.

Another source of suspicion was the novelty of so many women at these meetings—in the Liverpool Club as many as a third—and the tendency in consequence for excursions to become leisurely and short, starting after lunch and stopping for a substantial dinner-tea around five o'clock. All the same, they were undeniably gay affairs; and the Liverpool Club was clearly right in congratulating itself in its first annual report on its 'pleasant picnics' and in attributing much of its success 'to the opportunity it affords of pursuing a pleasing study in company with that sex whose presence doubles the enjoyment both of rural rambles and of scientific investigation'.

Several other societies appear to have succumbed to this trend, among them the Leicester Literary and Philosophical Society; and a particularly charming account has been left on record (significantly, not in the Society's publications, but in a local paper) of an occasion in 1861 when the members went on a Picnic to Bradgate Park. The proceedings started at about three o'clock, when some seventy or eighty members and their guests assembled at the gates and, after being officially welcomed by the Mayor, marched into the Park with the Volunteer Rifle Band at their head. Following a short address by the President and the inspection of a ruin, lemonade, apple wine and sherry were freely distributed, the band struck up a lively air and a number of the company danced. An open-air lecture on 'The Geology of Leicestershire' came next, for which the speaker was given three cheers. An excellent tea was then 'partaken of with vigour' at a near-by inn, after which there was another lecture (three cheers again) followed by more dancing; until, finally, towards dusk, no doubt thoroughly exhausted, the party broke up and the members made for home.

Much of the success of such societies was due to the fact that their members were drawn from a single social stratum; but sooner or later, particularly in the smaller towns, the problem had to be faced of bringing together people of widely different backgrounds who had never been used to mixing on any but the most formal occasions. That it was solved so soon was due very largely to the reforming zeal of two individuals—one of them an apprentice in pharmacy, the other an eminent divine. Two county towns, especially notorious for their cliques and their rigid social divisions (for which bitter sectarian differences were even more to blame than differences in wealth) selected themselves for such an experiment: Northampton, at the hands of G. C. Druce, an astute diplomat with all the charm of the youthful enthusiast; and Chester, at the hands of Charles Kingsley, the radical and Chartist, the preacher of 'muscular Christianity'.

Northampton in the seventies, like many other towns at this period, was a warren of separate social groups and sub-groups each riven in turn by political and religious differences held with an intensity that today is barely comprehensible. The last, in particular, were such a powerful divisive force that when the idea of forming a local natural history society was broached, it was recognized that it stood no chance of attracting a truly representative membership unless the backing of the various local churches could be secured. This problem Druce overcame by deliberately recruiting as founder-members the clerical headmaster of the Grammar School, a Baptist and two Congregational ministers, and a Roman Catholic priest. At a special preliminary meeting it was further resolved (and formally laid down in the Rules) that the Society should be conducted on a strictly non-sectarian basis. Despite vocal scepticism in many quarters that so socially heterogeneous a collection could work together even on formal occasions, much less in the informality of the field, from the first it proved a success, striking an important blow at the petty intolerance which had previously undermined all wider social activities in the town.

The Chester Society of Natural Science, Literature and Art, by contrast, owed less to diplomacy than to the dominating personality of one of the city's leading figures. 'I wish that side by side with the debating society', Kingsley had said as early as 1846,

> I could see young men joining natural history societies; going out in company on pleasant evenings to search together after the hidden treasures of God's world . . . and then meeting, say once a week, to debate, not of opinions but of facts; to show each what they had found, to classify and explain, to learn and wonder together.

A quarter of a century elapsed before he found the opportunity of putting this dream into practice.

In 1870, shortly after coming to Chester as Canon, Kingsley started a botany class for young men; and as he was a born teacher, with wide sympathies and an enviable power of exposition, the sixteen clerks and shop-assistants with whom he had started soon increased to an audience of several hundred, of both sexes and drawn from all social levels. From this it was an easy step to converting the class into a formally constituted Society, so that it now ran itself, arranging its own meetings and publishing reports, with Kingsley to continue to lead and guide it as president. Indeed, it was still Kingsley's classes in all but name: on the excursions it was still the Canon's enthusiasm that kept up interest, and everyone continued to hang upon his every word. He not only headed the Society, but moulded it according to his personal convictions—'high and low, rich and poor, one with another'—so much so that when on some of the more distant excursions the party had to take a train, rather than risk the affluent travelling First Class and the lowly Third Class, he insisted, with a compromise of genius, on bundling everyone into Second Class compartments. By such skilful social engineering he was able to break down many of the barriers that had formerly existed, and so succeeded in his more immediate aim of uniting Town and Cathedral.

This sort of problem seems to have been a peculiarly English one, for in other parts of the British Isles the different classes had met and mixed freely without any tension. In Scotland, for example, in the seventies there were societies like that at Alloa, in Clackmannanshire, where the president was an earl; the vice-presidents a doctor, a grocer and a wine-merchant; the councillors a clergyman, a bank agent, a barber, an architect and an ironmonger; the treasurer a druggist; the secretary a physician; the curator a blacksmith; and the librarian the governor of the local prison.

As if tension between the sects was not enough, to this presently was added a serious heightening of tension between the sexes. For the first time women began to demand a say in the running of societies, insisting on their right to be admitted to positions from which they had all along been excluded. 'Excluded' is an appropriately ambiguous word that sums up the attitude of most nineteenth-century learned societies. Women were either left out, ignored, only brought in on festive occasions, because they could scarcely be seriously interested; or else they were deliberately kept out, because science was a man's business and the club a kind of intellectual stag-party where a male rattled his antlers: a place reserved apart for him, like his study, where women should never be allowed to intrude. Women were patronized, told that their achievements in botany were splendid, even (as in the Liverpool Club) offered special prizes to compete for; but secretly no one regarded their presence as much more than decorative. It was accepted that they undermined the seriousness of the proceedings. Kingsley, indeed, had been disturbed by suggestions that his botany class should be extended to include a sprinkling of young ladies: their presence would distract the young men and spoil their work. However, he could hardly send away the wives, daughters and girl friends who flocked to the excursions of the Chester Society. He bore their presence with an ill grace and was once heard to remark in despair, with the slight stammer he never quite lost: 'Those good ladies quite spoilt my day—but what can you do? When they get to a certain age you must either treat them like duchesses or sh-sh-shoot them!'

But apart from the Victorians' suspicion of free intermingling of the sexes and disbelief in women's intellectual capabilities, the women themselves were in some ways to blame for their exclusion. For a start, they turned out in impossible clothing: flimsy shoes, precious hats, voluminous skirts. In the sixties, when the crinoline had swollen to its largest proportions, one club included in the advance notice of a meeting a special warning that the minimum stile-gauge to be encountered in the course of the afternoon's excursion would be 1 ft—this in an age when a grown man needed little more than the glimpse of an ankle to make him pass out with excitement. The women, too, acquiesced in the exaggerated ideas about their fragility. The Berwickshire Naturalists refused to allow them on their excursions in the genuine belief that the distances would prove too much for them; and their descendants, the Cotteswold Club, held a special 'ladies' meeting' once a summer, when the terrain was carefully chosen. In spite of such precautions there were often awkwardnesses, to which the Liverpool Club, one of the most venturesome, seems to have been particularly prone: in 1890, on a visit to Ingleborough, the members had to pass through the series of caves, 'each carrying a lighted candle on the end of a stick, and as they moved along in single file in the deep gloom the effect was very weird. Taken altogether the experience was novel, but to many of the ladies not very pleasant.'

When some societies specially removed the barriers in a consciously liberal effort to attract women members, the response was generally feeble. When the Natural History Society of Glasgow decided in the sixties that women were eligible as members, only one woman took advantage of the fact. About the same time the Geological Society of London experimented for a year or two with admitting women to its meetings as visitors, but again the response was so poor that the innovation was quickly dropped—though, admittedly, the less highbrow Geologists' Association had a rather richer haul after expressly allowing for women members at the time of its foundation, in 1858.

In the seventies and eighties the mood noticeably changed. Women's Rights began to nag, women's magazines began to carry intellectual articles, and women in great numbers began to take an active interest in scientific pursuits. One by one the leading provincial societies opened their doors. At Leicester, when in 1886 it was at last decided to admit women to full membership, thirteen were elected immediately. 'The present change of practice', read the Society's annual report, 'appears to be a natural outcome of the alteration which is taking place in the English mind with regard to the position and education of women'. By 1907 the Oxfordshire and Northamptonshire Societies had even elected women presidents.

The attitude, however, was very different in the case of the old-established national societies based on London, with their more academic traditions and their Clubland exclusiveness. The Zoological and Botanical Societies, which both admitted women on the same terms as men right from their founding, long stood out here as very much the exceptions. For most of the century the prevailing ethos was doggedly anti-feminist. By 1896 the Royal Society had relented enough to arrange a special Ladies' Conversazione, but in the following year a woman was prevented from sitting on a committee of the British Association despite nomination. The Linnean and Geological Societies also struggled hard against electing women Fellows, the former being finally stormed single-handed by the determined Mrs Ogilvie Farquharson, who quite literally battered her way in and after repeated petitioning eventually brought the Society's Council to its knees, opening the way for formal surrender on 17 November 1904.

Once the women were in, the children soon followed. In the nineties several societies organized special lectures for schoolchildren and offered prizes for collections; and the societies at Newcastle upon Tyne (in 1897) and at Croydon (in 1900) started admitting Junior Members at a specially reduced subscription. Even before this, some societies must have accepted non-adults for membership, but they had refrained from formally drawing attention to the fact.

For many years school natural history societies had been in existence, some of them of considerable distinction. There was one at Belfast Academy as early as about 1830, but generally it was the Quaker boarding schools that led in this: that at Bootham, founded in 1834, still continues to flourish and is easily the oldest school natural history society with an unbroken existence. The major public schools mostly followed suit in the sixties. Marlborough's society, the first, dates from 1864—its founding is said to have raised a storm of protest, for fear that it would harm the school games—Repton's from 1866, Rugby's from 1867. Many of these, from the first, had lectures and excursions and issued impressive printed reports (alas, prohibitively expensive to imitate today).

Even where there were not formal societies or clubs many school-children received instruction, singly or in groups, in or out of school hours, from masters who happened also to be naturalists; and there are instances on record, going back to 1790 (in Ireland), of lessons in the subject being included in ordinary school courses. Despite the omnipotence of Classics more science than is generally appreciated was taught in British schools—intermittently, it is true—from a surprisingly early period, and a high proportion of this was botany, zoology or geology. On the whole, therefore, the embryo naturalist was not being neglected, and the fact that he appeared so late as a recognizable entity on the books of the adult local societies shows a lack of definite organization in such matters rather than any deliberate cold-shouldering.

In 1873, a survey disclosed, there were at least 169 local scientific societies in Great Britain and Ireland, of which 104 (rather less than two thirds) were professedly field clubs. Most of the latter had come into being since 1850. A second survey made at the end of the century estimated that the combined membership of all natural history societies totalled nearly 50,000.

From the point of view of a healthy community life this was admirable; but from the point of view of science it was tiresome and confusing. Far too many little groups of naturalists were now giving themselves a dignified title and publishing lists of their finds in obscure, privately printed volumes of Transactions—so obscure that sometimes not even compilers of the most exhaustive local Faunas and Floras were aware of them.

To remedy this, a slow process of rationalization was set in train, aimed at a closer degree of cooperation, and, better still, where feasible, a pooling of energies by means of broader regional groupings. The first step in this direction had been taken in 1864, when six small societies in one of the industrial parts of Yorkshire amalgamated as the West Riding Consolidated Naturalists' Society (adopting as their official motto 'Union is Strength'). In the following year they launched a new journal, *The Naturalist,* primarily to serve as the organ of the combined membership now of three hundred; although it failed at first for want of support, it was revived in 1872 in time to become the perfect link for the twenty-seven societies which collaborated five years later to form the first, and probably most successful, of the various federal experiments: the Yorkshire Naturalists' Union.

Yorkshire patriotism was one thing: it was quite a different matter when it came to persuading societies in rival counties that there was something to be gained by travelling to distant towns and meeting and working with their opposite numbers two or three times a year. The first attempt of this kind was the Midland Union of Scientific Societies, an unwieldy body whose cohesion depended on little more than an annual convention. Even this can have been no light undertaking, to judge from the grand scale on which arrangements were made when, for instance, delegates of two dozen assorted societies met at Northampton in 1880: an official reception, a Great Meeting in the Town Hall, a meat tea at the Plough Hotel. That was the trouble: there was usually little time on these occasions for anything but eating, drinking and ceremonial. The different societies were mostly too remote from one another to mix easily, still less constructively, when they met so irregularly.

At the inaugural congress of the South-Eastern Union, in 1896, Dr George Abbott put forward a scheme for organizing the country's societies on a national basis which, though absurdly utopian, shows us the particular line of thought then being pursued. The country should be divided, he suggested, into fifteen or twenty districts, each with its own union, to which all the local societies would be afflliated. Each union would hold an annual congress, in a different town in the district and with a fresh president every year. Each would also be self-supporting, by means of small contributions from its member societies. Each of the latter would be responsible for a district within the area of its union, which in turn would nominate a member in every village to act as a local agent or registrar. At the top of this magnificent pyramid would be the British Association, directing, gathering in and processing the huge harvest of facts from every corner of the land. By some such means, wrote the editor of *Natural Science,*

> the control of experience and learning will be available to shield the ignorant and the beginner from the risk of publishing what is erroneous, of republishing what is already perfectly well known, or of hiding away in some obscure publication results that are really important.

When we recall that it was only four years later that Mendel's work was unearthed in just such a place, we can only applaud this concern with unblocking the lines of communication.

However, the natural history world decided it was not interested; and these plans were all left on the drawing-board and forgotten. Naturalists had already begun to have doubts about the value of purely local bodies, in the light of the new horizons for nation-wide activities opened up by the spread of mass communications. The swell of grassroots opinion which held every promise at that point of producing the equivalent for natural history of the Congress of Archaeological Societies (since evolved into the Council for British Archaeology) died away with the general change of temper; and the great, elaborate structure was left permanently unfinished for over half a century more, until the establishment of the Council for Nature in 1958. And, by then, the balance of vigour had so shifted that it was from the centre that the initiative finally had to come, not from the periphery. In the end the local societies had to be nursed into the wider pattern: they were not its creators, as they once had the chance to be.

––––––––––

It is not hard to see why the local field clubs throve as they did. Though some naturalists are solitaries, most of them are sociable beings. They share a special set of traditions not readily encountered in the world at large and which therefore makes them happy to seek out one another's company. The nature of the subject, too, calls for a modicum of social intercourse in the interests of efficiency: to listen to the experts, to glean the latest news, to learn and pass on tips. And for most people it is far pleasanter to have an interested audience for one's hobby-horses than to have to thrust them on the unenlightened.

Such compulsions on their own, however, while making for friendly gatherings, was not enough to bring about the smoothly functioning, un-ruffled, productive entities that so many of the field clubs succeeded in being. Two further factors must be invoked. In the first place, the very qualities that go to make a first-class naturalist—that instinctive love of order, system and detailed record; patience; unremitting care—were also qualities essential for the proper conduct of a society's affairs. Secondly, these often slight and fragile local endeavours were quickly buoyed up by that peculiarly British proclivity for covering all social activities in a heavy coating of ritual. They were saved by acquiring—in Walter Bagehot's phrase—a 'cake of custom'.

The British like to take their pleasures, not sadly (as foreigners will have it), but in a well-organized manner. Their social life is a curious mixture of gravity and gaiety, a blend of the formal with the informal. 'In the French societies,' William Younge of Sheffield wrote from Paris to his friend James Edward Smith in 1787,

> the members seem to have no regard to order, and the power of the president seems to extend no further than to the enforcing a momentary silence by making a more distinct noise than the members by means of a little musical instrument. But the great excellence of our societies in England consists in the exact limits drawn and observed between private and public business.

Smith's own society, the Linnean, early showed this native flair. As W. H. Harvey, taken to one of its meetings as an excited youth in 1829, reported:

> The President wore a three-cornered hat of ample dimensions, and sat in a crimson arm-chair in great state. I saw a number of new Fellows admitted. They were marched one by one to the President, who rose, and taking them by the hand, admitted them. The process costs £25.

In the same year the Linnean Society took steps to remove some of the severity from its meetings by providing those who attended with a cup of tea and a piece of cake. Taking their cue from this and from the lavish hospitality dispensed from time to time by individual members—as on the excursion of the Cotteswold Club in 1872 when 'a glass of sherry and a biscuit, which had been promised, developed into a splendid cold collation with champagne and all kinds of luxuries'—local societies gradually inaugurated dinners and soirées, dances and receptions, and exhibitions at which (to quote one annual report) 'the pleasant hum of conversation was interrupted by vocal and instrumental selections'. Typical of many is the following programme of a conversazione held by Oswestry and Welshpool Naturalists' Field Club & Archaeological Society at the Public Hall, Oswestry, in December 1864:

Hours	*Order of Proceeding*
6. 0	DOORS OPENED
6. 15	MUSIC (Instrumental): *Trio*—Flute, Violin, and Pianoforte; Mr. Whitridge Davies, Mr. A. Davis, and Mr. Oswald Davies.
6. 45	PAPER, by the President—On Ornithology. *Illustrated.*
7. 0	MUSIC (Instrumental): *Violin Solo*—Mr. Charles Eyeley.
7. 30	PAPER, by the Vice-President—How I learnt to see.
7. 45	MUSIC (Instr.): *Pianoforte Solo*—Mr. Sloman, Mus. Bac. Oxon.
8. 15	PAPER, by the Rev. D. P. Lewis—On Bronzes found near Pool Quay. *Illustrated.*
8. 30	MUSIC (Vocal): *Glee*—Sir Knight, Sir Knight—Glee and Madrigal Society.
9. 0	PAPER, by Mr. D. C. Davies—A quarter of an hour in Old Oswestry Gravel Pit.
9. 15	MUSIC (Instrumental): *Cornet Solo*—Mr. J. Evans.
9. 45	PAPER, by Mr. A. W. Dumville—The new metal magnesium. With *experiments*.
10. 0	MUSIC (Vocal): *Part Song*—O, who will o'er the downs so free—Glee and Madrigal Society.

GOD SAVE THE QUEEN

Nothing could be more misleading than the conventional picture of the Victorian learned society, with its rows of heavily bewhiskered gentlemen looking very stern and peering intently at the curate's sepia slides.

Above all, the local societies gained strength, in a way not open to national societies, by the very regularity with which the same group of people came face to face. The field clubs throve because they were, quite

simply, *clubs*. A man could join one in the knowledge that on every occasion, year after year, a high proportion of the people present would be
familiar—even if they never spoke to him or he to them. The annual programme was like the passage of the seasons: part of the regular cycle of life.
Lifelong membership was not uncommon. R. F. Towndrow, a botanist
and grocer of Malvern Link, probably set the record in this respect, attending the first meeting of his local field club as a schoolboy of fourteen and
continuing as its staunchest supporter till his death at ninety-two.

From this permanence of its membership and from the attractiveness of
so undemanding a pursuit for the self-effacing and those in search of a
social life but lacking the gift of surface sociability the local society derived
an extraordinary adhesive quality. A field club, by its very nature, proved to
be an extremely difficult thing to kill. Owning little, if any, property and
levying expenses from members as incurred, it was rarely troubled by
finance—and, when it was, all that needed to be done was to delay the next
number of the Proceedings. The type of studies followed called for no
rivalries in taste—and none, even, in skills which could not somehow be
avoided. The touchy therefore remained; and as there was ordinarily so
little to incite them, their remaining was not a cause of schisms. It was a
gentle world, a world full of tenacious loyalties, that could be dull and
uninspiring but that was normally sure of its usefulness and, come what
may, was nearly always busy.

CHAPTER NINE

The Parting of the Ways

AT THE VERY TIME that natural history was basking in high public esteem, events of profound significance were occurring off-stage. In 1858 Darwin had at last made public his theory of organic evolution, plunging the entire world of learning into a long-dreaded turmoil. Without question this was the scientific happening of the century. Nevertheless, as far as natural history in this country was concerned its immediate impact was relatively slight.

There was pride, naturally enough, that it should have been in this very field that an intellectual explosion of such palpable dimensions had taken place. Darwin, naturalists must have told themselves, was 'one of us'. In a sense, too, they were right: only a naturalist to the core would have carried in his head till the very end of his life the exact shape and colouring and place of capture of many of the beetles he had taken during his time as an undergraduate. Yet an essential basis of Darwin's genius was the combination in one man of two contrasting types that are normally quite separate: as well as a collector and an observer he was an experimenter and a theorist. In terms of the general run of naturalists he was thus highly uncharacteristic.

He was in fact the most illustrious representative of one tradition in British natural history that never acquired the wider following it deserved. He was one of a select group of men, almost invariably of independent means, who devoted their time and energies not to conventional species-logging and -describing, but to the formulation and testing of hypotheses in accordance with what has since become orthodox scientific practice. Many of them published their findings obscurely and some never published at all. Most therefore failed to receive proper recognition in their lifetime. A few even quite missed the significance of what they toyed with or reported—like Galton, in a letter to Darwin, suggesting the Mendelian system and ratios; or they lacked the technical skill or fundamental knowledge to check their hunches.

To all these Darwin stands out as the exception. He knew his subjects, he mastered the techniques, he published voluminously and prominently —and won deserved acclaim. As such he became the hero of generations of experimental biologists and field naturalists. And it was the field naturalists, at least to begin with, who formed the greater number of those who identified with him and claimed him as their own.

At the same time, just because it was their own special subject that had given rise to this terrible debate, those naturalists who found the claims of evolution difficult to reconcile with their religious beliefs experienced an agonizing conflict. Unlike others, they could not honestly deny the evidence or fail to comprehend its overwhelming suggestiveness. Their only refuge was to seek for some flaw in the accepted interpretations, whether doctrinal or scientific, and propound a comforting alternative (as poor Gosse rashly did, in his fatuous book *Omphalos*); or else to postpone all decision, hoping that the theory would be disproved or that some champion of the theologians would come forward with a palatable compromise.

Not all naturalists found the facts of evolution spiritually dismaying, and those who did reacted in different ways. There was no recognizable 'line' on the matter in natural history circles. If anything, because of the closeness of naturalists to the controversy's raw material, the spectrum of attitudes among them was even wider than in general. Most of those who grappled with the issues concentrated on the metaphysical or theological aspects: the naturalists, almost alone, could not avoid prolonged and fierce disputes over the scientific ones as well.

The bigotry was by no means all on the side of the religious dogmatists. Richard Owen, disagreeable and ever-disagreeing, snapped and snarled in defence of the fixity of species. No defender of the Faith, he viewed Darwin's theory with purely philosophical repugnance—and saw too closely aligned with it his arch-enemy, T. H. Huxley. Sedgwick wrote off the *Origin of Species* as in parts 'false and mischievous' and claimed that, when he read it, in places 'I laughed till my sides were almost sore'. Murchison, another of the leaders of geology, Thomas Bell, the then President of the Linnean Society, and J. O. Westwood, the prominent entomologist, continued as bitter anti-Darwinians to the grave. Men like these, despite the extensiveness of their learning, were of a naturally rigid temper, and many had allowed themselves to edge so far out along a limb of categorical denial that it was probably preferable by then to risk crashing down in pieces. Others, no less knowledgeable but free of such positions to defend, like Alfred Newton and the younger Hooker, found little difficulty in embracing Darwin's views. And comprehensive radicals, like H. C. Watson, predictably applauded from the first.

But for still others the matter was more complicated. Prominent men of science who happened also to be deeply pious sat hard on the fence (like Henslow) or were unwilling to look the facts in the face (like Henslow's Cambridge successor, Babington). Some, like Canon Tristram, the ornithologist, were enthusiastic converts at the outset but subsequently recanted—perhaps out of sheer fear of appearing too unorthodox. And some, like Lyell, thought Darwin's arguments not yet sufficiently convincing and on purely intellectual grounds preferred to adopt a cautious stance. These last, perhaps, were the most sensible. Finally, and doubtless inevitably, there were even naturalists on the outermost fringe: most notably the Rev. F. O. Morris, an out-and-out fundamentalist—who campaigned against the theory in innumerable pamphlets, couched in intemperate language, over many years.

For most naturalists the theory of evolution, in so far as it raised acute philosophical or religious problems, remained an essentially private concern. Of clear-cut factions, with contending rival ideologies, there was very little sign. But certain rough patterns of allegiance were distinguishable.

It was among the younger generation, for example, that Darwin found his strongest early support. Of the different branches of the subject, it was the ornithologists who tended to be most favourably disposed. Here Alfred Newton's influence told. The botanists, more divided, also supplied some keen adherents. The geologists, by contrast, remained aloof—it was left to A. C. Ramsay, when the brimstone had at last begun to cool, to bring round the leading doubters. Forthright opposition, on the other hand, centred on the insect world. 'The entomologists', Darwin complained to Lyell in March 1863, 'are enough to keep the subject back for half a century.' Their antagonism, indeed, lasted unmodified until the eighties, when the Entomological Society of London was won over largely by the single-handed efforts of Professor Raphael Meldola. We need look for no better testimony than this that the main constituent studies were by now largely self-contained.

Although sharing to the full in the general questioning and doubt, the naturalists were at least more fortunate than most in acquiring one inestimable boon, at first only dimly perceived, from the establishment of the theory of evolution: it conferred on their subject a unifying principle that, for the first time, was both intellectually respectable and emotionally convincing. In the Great Chain of Being, in the Quinarian Theory, above all in the doctrine of Natural Theology, they had indulged in successive gropings to discover the central secret, the elusive key to all organization and behaviour, that they had always sensed must exist. In Evolution this ultimate unity had been disclosed—and in that very fact they simultaneously gained a relieving sense of integration. Well might Alfred Newton later recall that the suggested explanation came 'like the direct revelation of a higher power'. A horrible fog had cleared. Paradoxically, deep down, naturalists could at last relax.

With this obsessing worry now resolved, a vigorous departure in some quite fresh direction was due. And inevitably it was the gaps in the evidence which Darwin had revealed that became the main focus of the next generation of scientific endeavour. Suddenly, once again, it was an intensely exciting time to be alive for those embarking on their careers. If Darwin's array of evidence was to be converted into proven fact, it was clear that much more attention than hitherto would have to be given to the study of phylogeny: to tracing the differentiation of species through time and plotting the closeness or otherwise of their relationship by the comparative study of appropriate organs and tissues. A tantalizing range of work here already presented itself. And there were other areas, less obviously accessible, that promised to offer problems enough besides. For example, how were so numerous and often such complex characteristics transmitted from parent to offspring? What exactly was the role of the environment? The first half of the century had been devoted to revealing the variety in nature; the second half was to be devoted to explaining how and why this variety had come about.

These new tasks required a new type of investigator. It was now necessary to probe beneath the surface of nature and explore processes and mechanisms: to leave the field and to neglect those scholastic niceties with which natural history had come to be erroneously over-identified. In place of the intuitive sense of pattern of the classifier what were now needed were delicate manipulative skills and a strong urge to take things to pieces.

The archetype of this new kind of scientist, The Biologist *par excellence,* was by common consent Thomas Henry Huxley. Huxley himself understood the distinctiveness of his bent more clearly than anyone: 'There is very little of the genuine naturalist in me,' he wrote, 'I never collected anything, and species work was always a burden to me; what I cared for was the architectural and engineering part of the business.' To become an engineer had, indeed, been his boyhood ambition. No one else could have personified better the up-and-coming laboratory craftsman—and no new creed could have asked for a more able champion and evangelist. His role as 'Darwin's bulldog', the chief public spokesman and in-fighter on behalf of the theory of evolution, has tended to make us forget that it was Huxley, more than anyone else, who in these same years spoke up for science more generally, and acted as the main driving-force behind biological teaching in Britain.

In 1854 Huxley had succeeded Edward Forbes as Lecturer in Natural History at the Government School of Mines in Jermyn Street, that brainchild of De la Beche. Here he was at once brought face to face with the vast technological revolution already being incubated in the scandalously few and ill-supported teaching establishments so far established to this end in what was then the world's richest country. To make a miserly nation face up to the stunting consequences of its neglect soon became a lifelong commitment. Year after year he spoke and wrote and lobbied to secure for science a greater share of the country's educational resources and, as a minimal measure, some instruction in at least its rudiments as a standard item in the school curricula. The lethargy that confronted him, however, was great and there were numerous entrenched positions to overcome. Science and scientists were distrusted—and the widespread public antipathy aroused by the very idea of evolution did not help. But gradually battles began to be won. In 1851 a degree in Natural Science was instituted at Cambridge. Fifteen years later, at Cambridge again, a new Chair of Zoology and Comparative Anatomy was created. In 1874 the great Cavendish Laboratory opened its doors.

It was the Education Act of 1870 that eventually brought the crucial breakthrough. Elementary science, said this Act, was to be taught as far as possible in all the government schools. This was magnificent and largeminded: the only trouble was that the necessary teachers did not yet exist.

At the Government's urgent request, Huxley at once set to devising a special 'crash' course in botany and zoology suitable for this training purpose. And in 1872, when the Natural History Department of the School of Mines moved to South Kensington and there was space at last for a laboratory and practical experiments, he introduced, with the aid of four demonstrators (Michael Foster, W. T. Thiselton-Dyer, Ray Lankester and W. Rutherford) the standard instruction in the general principles of biology which rapidly became the model for all such teaching throughout Great Britain and America.

The novelty of Huxley's course lay in the emphasis on practical work, on the use of the microscope and the laboratory, in the bypassing of most of contemporary systematics through the use of generalized 'types' in place of the normal bewildering variety of specific examples, and in the very strong bias towards anatomy and morphology—'the architectural and engineering part of the business'. This was the first time these last aspects had ever formed the centre of attention in any science teaching in Britain. They were the new glamour disciplines then unfolding on the Continent, and particularly in Germany; and inevitably they formed the focus of interest for Huxley and his band of young disciples.

In 1873 Huxley's health failed, and his place was taken by Thiselton-Dyer. One year later S. H. Vines joined as an extra demonstrator, and from then until 1880 the class-roll of the course included name after name that later became famous in British science. South Kensington served as the point of departure for a remarkable, nation-wide diaspora of brilliant young men. In this the teachers too were presently participants. Ray Lankester left to revolutionize the teaching at Oxford, while Michael Foster was appointed to a special new post in physiology at Cambridge, where he lost no time in introducing practical classes. He was soon afterwards joined there by Vines.

Apart from the newness of their subjects and their method of teaching, these men, by a historical accident, were the carriers of another quite new influence into British academic life. The cradle of the new biology was Germany, and it was during their stays in German universities while undertaking the now *de rigueur* spell of postgraduate study that they ingested an alien professionalism. This had become highly developed there for reasons peculiar to the German academic tradition, and it so chanced that certain elements in it were well suited to the advancement of the new type of science. Among its manifestations was a hierarchy of subordinate staff, whose services were exclusively at the disposal of the professor who headed their department—a pattern of military inspiration. In British universities, by contrast, professors had normally been staffless beings who taught and did research on their own, on the basis of one man per subject per institution. Now, whole teams appeared, with the function not merely of spreading the teaching load but of undertaking investigations in syndicate.

German scholarly usage also laid stress on the importance of priority and the consequent need to authenticate one's findings in print. From this the custom had grown up for professors to found their own specialist journals, to accommodate their personal output as well as that of their associated staff and pupils. We have seen an echo of this already in Jameson's activities at Edinburgh, which owed much to his experience in Saxony under Werner. Now, the new wave of Anglo-German graduates proceeded to adopt this same practice in turn, launching semi-exclusive new ventures, like the *Journal of Physiology* (in 1878) and the *Annals of Botany* (in 1887), as a means of encapsulating and proclaiming the freshness and vigour of their particular approach no less than of receiving the endless cascade of papers that flowed forth for publication from their work.

Thanks to their greater numbers, the new scientists were able to afford the luxury of a self-sufficient literature to a degree denied to all their predecessors. For the first time a large body of scholars had emerged who had no need to communicate with the laity. As a result their language became ground down, to serve as a stark, precise tool and nothing more.

The non-professional élite, accustomed hitherto to reading the raw scientific texts for their straightforward enlightenment, now found it increasingly impossible to keep up. The jargon was too dense and the accounts took too much specialized knowledge for granted in advance. For the first time people found themselves confronted with their own native tongue in a form that might just as well have been Urdu or Swahili. This, in an obscure kind of way, many resented. This deplorable pseudo-English seemed to them merely lazy and inconsiderate. Alternatively, and worse, it was a new private code deliberately designed to keep them out: a high-ring fence protecting the mandarin at his work.

There was further incomprehension—and sometimes further baffled fury—at the very dispassion of scientific writing and the blithe indifference of the new biologists to the aesthetic implications of their researches. On this topic no power on earth could have kept a man such as John Ruskin silent. In one of his ringing *pronunciamentos* Ruskin accused science of being inimical to art. And so weighty were his words with his innumerable admirers that Vines, just then appointed to Oxford's Chair of Botany, felt obliged to make a comparable public reply—even if it was a limp and feeble affair measured against the splendid torrent of vituperation from the Chair of Fine Arts.

Ruskin was articulating a fear widely shared by naturalists at that time (and he himself was a passable mineralogist and botanist, so as a spokesman he was not entirely unrepresentative). The new science, such people felt, was carrying the thrust of knowledge so far beneath the familiar surface that there must surely come a point where all the aesthetic landmarks would be erased. The new approach was thus subversive of man's capacity to benefit from nature emotionally. In the past, science had been thought of as merely a kind of lens, which magnified one's vision of the world and thereby enhanced one's enjoyment. But now it had become a violator. Unexpectedly, the biologists found their curiosity denounced as prurience: as a wilful desire to meddle with the inimical underside of nature. The view is one that has erupted from time to time, in various guises, ever since.

Yet these were not the only ways in which the layman and the professional were growing alienated. The new scientists too found ample cause to complain. Young men in a hurry, brashly assertive, they expected the walls of Academe to topple at the very first blast of their trumpets. When this failed to happen, and they ran up against the eternal immobility of the academic power structure, they felt aggrieved and frustrated. Their new fields, they had become convinced, called out to be explored with the very greatest urgency and deserved to be ceded absolute priority.

At Cambridge, the generally acknowledged pivot of their studies, the Chair of Botany, that supreme plum, had the misfortune to be occupied by an unsympathetic diehard in the person of Babington. Latterly too frail even to continue the taxonomic work on British flowering plants that had once been the inspiration of an army of amateurs, he still obstinately spent all the spare funds of his department on rare books for the Herbarium and refused persistently to set aside any sum for the furnishing of adequate laboratories. 'I remember about 1876', F. O. Bower has written, 'how I longed for a train of wagons to convey the Cambridge Herbarium away to Kew, and so to vacate for the New Botany the rooms that would have served its needs.' The new men had to content themselves, instead, with makeshift rooms and second-rate equipment; and their intense energy and zeal—typified by Marshall Ward, who talked with missionary fervour of 'the cause' and once even fainted at his bench from either sheer intellectual excitement or non-stop work—curdled into bitterness. Several decades had to pass before they were able to forgive. As the years went by, the rift acquired much of the gratuitous spite of a war between the generations. Systematics, natural history, even field-work as a whole became irretrievably identified with the mumbling, doddery Old Men. And when the last bastions had fallen and the biologists' turn eventually came, some of them were not slow to indulge in a certain vindictiveness on this account. Characteristic was the fierce, public attack on the British Museum and Kew by Professor F. W. Oliver—himself, significantly, the son of an eminent systematist—at the British Association meeting in 1906. In this these ancient institutions were belaboured for standing apart from 'the ordinary botanical current' and ridiculed for the uselessness of their vast collections.

In this way many of the new generation of scientists became not merely dedicated professionals, but militant anti-amateurs; in the study of nature, choosing to lead a cellular existence of their own, bent firmly over their microscopes and locked in their laboratories. In behaving thus, they robbed the field studies for many years of a much-needed intellectual dynamic, with the result that, as natural history moved on, it carried with it from this time some chronic damage to its tissues not the less severe for being largely unrealized.

———————

Amid all this ferment, Babington and Newton—settled and snug in their respective Cambridge Chairs, long-time friends, both staunchly conservative, both naturalists since boyhood who happened also to be dons—stolidly refused to be depressed, and acted for natural history as a whole by shrugging their shoulders and turning their backs. And, in a way, they were right: the new sciences had next to nothing as yet to offer the humdrum worker in the field. Some today, with the benefit of hindsight, would even contend that all but a fraction of the huge laboratory output of the last quarter of the nineteenth century was a terrible blind alley from which biology was only rescued after 1900 by the advent of genetics. If this is so, it is the more ironic that students of natural history at this period should have been made to feel like backward rustics inhabiting a cul-de-sac.

Compared with Babington, Newton was relatively open-minded. He was also more philosophic. In 1888 he was to write:

> I have watched the rise and progress of Morphology with the same kind of interest that may be excited in the mind of a lame man who watches a skating-party or a cricket-match, even though he can take no active share in the amusement; for I am too old to go to school again even under the tuition of my most brilliant pupils, and the new biological learning must be begun at the beginning.

Within a few months of these words being published Babington likewise had given vent to his feelings, at a meeting of the Cambridge Ray Club. He was more plaintive, more like a hurt parent:

> It is rare now to find an Undergraduate or B.A. who knows, or cares to know, one plant from another, or distinguish insects scientifically. I am one of those who consider this to be a sad state of things. I know that much of what is called Botany is admirably taught amongst us; but it is not what is usually known as Botany outside the Universities, and does not lead to a practical knowledge of even the most common plants. It is really Vegetable Physiology, and ought to be so called. It is a very important subject, but does not convey a knowledge of plants.

Babington, indeed, was doubly demoralized; for on top of the mass-desertion of the botany students in favour of the new methods as taught by

Vines, the regulation requiring the medical students also to be examined in the subject was abolished. In consequence the audiences at his lectures fell off drastically.

For most naturalists, however, such matters as yet were of slight concern. Having little, if any, contact with the new professional world of biology, they remained largely oblivious of all the abrasions and asperities. Darwin's great work, so far from deterring them or encouraging them to wander down new paths, had merely strengthened their adherence to their traditional preoccupations. As far as they could see, the fauna and flora of their native land still offered excitements in plenty and the amount of simple, straightforward record-making that they were aware still lay ahead promised to absorb their energies for many years to come.

But in their own way they, too, were now beginning to cut deeper. The remoter parts of the British Isles, those areas that were ordinarily out of reach or had merely been neglected while earlier generations concentrated on the ones that lay more readily to hand, were at last receiving their due share of attention.

A good deal of this very necessary work fell to professional collectors. Some of these worked on their own behalf and relied on making a profit from a trip from the sale of their specimens afterwards; others were employed directly by wealthy individuals or by learned bodies like the Botanical Society of Edinburgh. On occasions, some might even have several masters simultaneously, a number of private collectors having pooled their resources to dispatch them into the wilds on a subscribed share basis, in return for which each was assured of a *pro rata* portion of the spoils. (This ingenious device—the collecting syndicate—which, like the exchange club idea, was patently a straight borrowing from everyday mercantile usage, was apparently first resorted to by Lhwyd, round about 1700, and is still in wide use today in horticulture and archaeology.) As a trade professional collecting was, on the whole, an honest one, with a lineage stretching back into the seventeenth century, when Thomas Willisel, a Civil War veteran, had worked for Christopher Merret and later for the Royal Society. But it must also have been at the best of times precarious, appealing only to isolationists or the exceptionally rugged.

Among the main fruits of these more distant explorations was the discovery of many new local forms and distinct geographical races. This led to a proliferation in named subspecies and varieties, and to the eventual adoption by zoologists of trinomials (in recognition of the fact that regional versions of a species are often sufficiently distinct to be worth naming, while obviously not on a par with the major entities traditionally accorded a binomial). Among ornithologists, at least, these were at first highly controversial. Some disliked the massive coining of new names entailed; others simply found the whole effect ridiculous. On learning of the string of epithets produced by Hartert as the correct name for the British

Magpie, Abel Chapman is reported to have exploded: '*Pica pica pica!* just as one would call to one's housemaid!' He eventually resigned from the British Ornithologists' Union on this particular issue.

Even more new names were to result from the other great thrust of this period: the secondary exploration of areas already reasonably well known. These now were ripe for a follow-up stage of much more critical probing, a kind of work especially well suited to a type of naturalist that this era supplied in exceptional abundance. These were the stranded men, the voluntary or involuntary anchorites, the village parsons and country surgeons with a university education but who were rooted to one small district by their pastoral or professional duties for major parts of their lives. For such as these, if they happened to be naturalists, the compiling of as complete and exhaustive an account as possible of the plants or birds of their parish, district or county was a challenge, even a kind of reflex action. The second half of the nineteenth century was accordingly the period *par excellence* of the production of local Floras and Avifaunas (for some reason, the genre scarcely caught on in entomology), of a comprehensiveness and spaciousness scarcely matchable today in this age of prohibitive printing costs. Volumes of this general type had been appearing, of course, for a long time previously; but in the mid 1860s they suddenly took a big leap forward both in the bulk of the records presented and in the standard and range of the associated critical comment and introductory matter. From mere lists they had now graduated into large-scale scholarly monographs, often the distillation of the best part of a lifetime's experience and pondering.

Middlesex was the chosen proving-ground in this respect in both botany and ornithology: a county of manageable size and the one most readily worked from the Metropolis. J. E. Harting's *Birds of Middlesex* (1866) beat by just three years the still more massive *Flora of Middlesex*—accredited to two young men in their twenties, Henry Trimen and W. T. Dyer (later, as Sir William Thiselton-Dyer, to be Director of Kew), but certainly owing much to the painstaking work of the Rev. W. W. Newbould, a fine scholar but morbidly self-effacing. Virtually coinciding with Harting's book came H. Stevenson and T. Southwell's *Birds of Norfolk* and, following close behind, Alexander Clark Kennedy's *Birds of Berkshire and Buckinghamshire*, noteworthy also as the first bird book with photographs (four plates of stuffed specimens—hardly a captivating start) and for the singular youth of the author: a sixteen-year-old Eton schoolboy.

Publication of such compendia served a number of useful purposes. By alerting people to what was common and what was rare, it helped to ensure that finds of interest no longer passed unrecorded, that those which were not of interest were henceforth kept out of print and that novelties were not claimed or accepted without checking. It directed attention to understudied species and underworked districts, enabling those who followed to labour constructively and avoid duplicating the work of their predecessors. It presented newcomers to the study or the area with a nicely delimited target of work. Often it put neighbouring enthusiasts in touch—though usually only by letter, for in those days of bad or non-existent transport Floras and Faunas tended to be put together by essentially solitary workers, tramping for miles from convenient railheads or touring in a pony-trap hired by the hour. The modern team-efforts, with their committees and their recording squads, which today perform such a vital educative role, did not yet exist.

For many people, even so, the mere logging of localities proved insufficient for their skills and energy. Something more demanding was required. And this they found in the fine discrimination of closely similar entities—many of them, in the case of plants, the result of abnormal reproductive mechanisms producing large numbers of tolerably distinct, self-perpetuating strains—or in seeking out (but seldom, alas, breeding experimentally) the minor variants of the more readily separated species. Both activities had a modest scientific value, if only in providing pointers for later, more intensive professional research as well as valuable raw data for delineating the geographical affinities of smaller areas (about which the distribution patterns of the less recently evolved and thus more widespread entities have little to tell us).

This kind of work, while satisfyingly laborious and interminable, nevertheless had its dangers. The very time and patience required for mastering the specially complex groups tended to make their study all-absorbing. In consequence many of the best field brains were permanently diverted into essentially private preoccupations, of arguably sufficient scientific relevance. Non-specialists, moreover, lacking the necessary practised eye, found it difficult to see the subtle differences that the experts relied on and were often hastily contemptuous of the validity of the numerous entities they insisted on describing. The very multiplicity of the new creations—in some genera, like brambles and hawkweeds, running into hundreds—seemed a positive affront: a disturbing aberration from the pleasingly tidy pattern hitherto recognized in nature (an emotion which led to an excessive prejudice as well against the no less inconvenient hybrids). Botany, in particular, became divided into two long-warring camps, the 'lumpers' and the 'splitters'—a controversy which, though largely based on false premises and enduringly sterile, is by no means dead today.

There were some who prized these 'splits' and variants for other than a scientific reason. These were the collectors whose attitude to the raw material of their hobby was essentially no different from that of philatelists. Just as the latter set high value on errors, so these men, most of them entomologists, specially treasured aberrations. They bought, sold and swopped their specimens, regardless of the context in nature from which these came and without any pretence that they had gone to the trouble of procuring them from the wilds themselves. Just like stamp-collectors, some of them even clipped off butterflies' wings, mounted them in albums (painting in the thorax) or arranged them in tasteful patterns for hanging on the wall. Like 'fern-portraits', engraved birds' eggs and painted sea-shells, these merged insensibly into the decorative bric-à-brac of the Victorian parlour—there to join the stuffed birds and the wax fruit under glass domes as the mummified libido of that tortured, lace-trimmed Respectability.

To meet the heavy demands from this quarter there gradually developed a rampant commercialization with distinctly unsavoury fringes. Alongside the taxidermists and the small, specialist suppliers of naturalists' equipment there now appeared a new breed: the natural history dealer, the sharp middleman whose salerooms became a favourite resort for the new kind of customer—the dead-insect collectors, the wealthy purchasers of sets of botanical exsiccatae (like Henry Fielding and Charles Bailey, whose insatiable urge for amassing forced each to acquire an extra house, simply to hold their enormous collections) and all the other assemblers and re-assemblers of the fruits of other men's searching and field expertise. 'These collections', protested a writer in the *Entomologist* in 1877, 'have done us no good: they are broken up, sold, again distributed and used for the same purpose by others, who are glad of the chance of "doubling their series".' Worse still, he might have added, the specimens that changed hands were commonly unlocalized—or, if localized, of questionable provenance—so that any scientific value they might have had was thus nullified.

Fraudulence battens on ignorance. In the auction-rooms around Great Russell Street, London's naturalists' quarter, fantastic prices of up to several pounds each were paid for 'rare' moths or bird-skins the British origin of which rested merely on the word of a dealer for home-produced specimens invariably commanded a substantial premium. Even if a dealer was scrupulously honest, the vicissitudes through which the average specimen tended to pass made it rarely possible to make such assertions with absolute reliability. Some of the dealers were indeed dishonest—to the extent of importing quantities of insects at a cheap rate from France and Germany and claiming that they had been caught in Britain. Gullible collectors took what they offered—and threw lasting doubt on hundreds of other collections in the process. Sometimes the collectors themselves perpetrated frauds, claiming to have found or captured varieties in areas in which they were hitherto unknown, thereby gaining some cheap prestige for themselves and heightening the commercial value of the specimens. One such man exhibited a specimen of *Apatura ilia* (a scarce relative of the Purple Emperor) at a scientific meeting in 1880, claiming that he had taken it in Middlesex in the previous July. In fact, as close scrutiny soon revealed, it was of considerable age and had been pinned twice already. Last of all, and least easy to credit, as described by H. G. Knaggs in his *Lepidopterist's Guide*, there were even

> those ingenious delusions which may be classed as *post-mortem* varieties, and which are not infrequently indulged in by the unscrupulous, the sordid, and the envious . . . such practices as imitating varieties, or even rarities, by the aid of the paint brush and wasted talent, the manufacture of hermaphrodites, the clumsy artifice of dyeing by saffron and other agents, the conversion of greens into orange, bleaching by exposure to strong light or the fumes of sulphur or chlorine.

These years of increasing minuteness of study entailed greater specialization. One product was a further clutch of national specialist societies. The most typical of these was in ornithology—now becoming conscious of itself as more than just a branch of zoology. In November 1858 Newton's celebrated Sunday afternoon gatherings in his rooms in Magdalene eventually hatched out a scheme for a British Ornithologists' Union, the main aim of which was to introduce a periodical devoted exclusively to birds. The *Ibis* (which still continues) was the result, fledged in a matter of months.

Within a month of the founding of the B.O.U. the Geologists' Association crept into being in London. Formed 'with the view of placing the Science of Geology in the hands of that large class who have neither the time nor the money necessary for mastering the subject and becoming Fellows of the Geoiogical Society of London', it was the first essentially field society to function on a nation-wide scale—for, though some of the London societies had had organized field excursions in the past, these had never been more than desultory. This emphasis on the field, with its strong suggestion of informality and inexpensiveness, reflected the fact that the founders first met at the Working Men's College in Great Ormond Street—in marked contrast to their B.O.U. counterparts, who mostly came from landowning backgrounds.

Ornithology, uniquely among the major branches of the subject, had long been accepted as an extension of field sports, which enabled it to partake of their atmosphere and high social standing. While this was in some ways a strength, it carried the risk that the element of social exclusiveness would result in a scientific exclusiveness as well, isolating the students of birds from the world of natural history more generally. Accordingly, the fact that all but one out of the small group of men who constituted the B.O.U.'s original founding nucleus were ornithologists with no apparent allegiance to any other branch must be seen as ominous.

Yet some breaking up of the previous social unity was being made inevitable now by the sheer accumulation in knowledge, which forced people to specialize regardless of whether they really wished to. Increasingly, from this time on, the all-rounder begins to become noticeable merely on account of his fast-growing rarity.

Unhappily, this fragmentation was occurring just at a period when no one branch was outstandingly dominant and in a position to give a lead to the subject as a whole. Ornithology had not yet started out on its extraordinary rise in popularity; botany and entomology still more or less matched it in appeal, but both were marking time; geology, the erstwhile leader, had lost its momentum and even showed signs of losing ground.

A variety of reasons for this fading of interest in geology can be propounded. The exposing of Evolution had subverted its former *avant-garde,* slightly daring character: the sense of the past was being usurped by the rise of a more humanistic archaeology; prehistoric monsters had exhausted their initial power to horrify and shock. Even more, the primary task of systematic mapping, which in other fields was to keep great armies of amateurs happily busy for many more years, had been taken over and was beginning to be carried out, with quite unmatchable thoroughness, by professionals in the permanent employ of the government. The advance in knowledge that had occurred in this science was particularly extreme, moreover, and the ordinary collector was finding himself increasingly out of his depth. By 1886 the number of fossil species known from Britain alone was estimated at more than 19,000. 'Who but the specialist', complained the President of the Geologists' Association, 'dare put a modern specific name to an Ammonite or a Brachiopod, for their names are legion and their synonyms are every day increasing?'

Here, as elsewhere, the amateurs were becoming demoralized. For many of them even the traditional activities had begun to pall. Systematics, to all appearances, was now worked out. The countryside seemed to have been fully and conclusively explored. Everything had been accomplished: there was nothing to do now but sit and lament or else retire with the professionals to their laboratories.

This widespread failure of nerve had echoes in other, more surprising quarters. In the eighties no less a man than Lord Kelvin is reputed to have bemoaned the fact that all the discoveries in physics had now been made and that the only tasks remaining consisted of adjusting the last decimal point in certain measurements. Such notions can only have sprung from a wrong angle of vision, from an over-concentration on the palpable triumphs of the Victorian era in pushing to the uttermost limits of the visible world—that, and a certain cultural smugness besides.

Even so, something *was* wrong. Natural history seemed to be choking from a surfeit of dubiously useful data. The typical local worker had become, in the disillusioned words of Grant Allen, writing in 1901, 'the man who revels in the splitting of critical species, who discovers some new spot on a butterfly's wing, and who makes it his highest glory to have given his own name to this or that insignificant variety of the common stitchwort or the ordinary earwig'. Of Ireland the same author wrote: 'At the present day every nook has been explored zoologically and botanically, and the stations of every rare species of plant or animal exactly recorded.' Absurd exaggerations, of course—but in the circumstances, perhaps, permissible. Only harsh provocation, it must have seemed, could shift most naturalists from their infuriating torpor.

But though well-intentioned the Grant Allens of those years sought and preached a solution to the impasse that was premature. It was easy to insist, with one of the leading professors of the day, that 'there cannot now be a stable and progressive natural history which does not recognize the methods and results of morphology, physiology, embryology, and palaeontology'. It was less easy to see how this was to come about, as long as those trained in the new disciplines largely refused to associate with amateurs, and the amateurs themselves, even when prepared to listen, generally failed to understand. Even as late as 1914, on occasions when the two groups met, blank incomprehension was still the rule—if the following account of a meeting of the Entomological Society in that year (by the member and *littérateur* who wrote under the pen-name 'Barbellion') is anything to go by:

> It was really a one-man show, Professor Poulton, a man of very considerable scientific attainments, being present, and shouting with a raucous voice in a way that must have scared some of the timid, unassuming collectors of our country's butterflies and moths. Like a great powerful sheep-dog, he got up and barked, 'Mendelian characters', or 'Germ plasm', what time the obedient flock ran together and bleated a pitiful applause. I suppose, having frequently heard these and similar phrases fall from the lips of the great man at these reunions, they have come to regard them as symbols of a ritual which they think it pious to accept without any question.

The forced soldering together of the new biology and the old natural history was to prove futile, quixotic, totally misconceived. Proper time had to be allowed for true bridging studies to emerge and to win converts from both sides spontaneously. A subject like natural history proceeds at its own stately pace.

There were some, unusually perceptive, who even in these early years grasped this essential truth. Aware that was not all well with their study, they sensed all the same that the course that was urged from all sides—a wholesale switch to the aims and methods of the new biology—was dangerously facile and could not in the long term be a satisfactory answer. For such men W. B. Grove, an expert on microfungi, spoke, in the *Midland Naturalist:*

> The glory of the field naturalist has departed. The biologist or physiologist is the hero of the hour, and looks down with infinite contempt upon the luckless being who is still content to search for species. 'Tis but the swing of the pendulum, the fashion of the day, and like many another fashion, 'Made in Germany'. Soon will come the inevitable reaction; but it is, to say the least of it, decidedly ungrateful of the biologist to pour such vials of wrath upon the poor searchers of the past, who, if they did nothing else, at any rate provided the theorists with the foundations of their airy structures. For out of his own spinnerets, like a spider's silk, the closet-naturalist cannot evolve the species and genera with which he deals. These are the rewards of one who goes down upon his knees and patiently, hour after hour, turns over heaps of rotting twigs and leaves, or who tramps through woods and fields the lifelong day, and returns at night to his study with the spoil. The observations of the laboratory are, of course, right and proper in their place, but a world constructed out of them would bear but little resemblance to the glorious vision which the field naturalist has unfolding constantly before his eyes. *Liberavi animam meam.*

Had he only known, the way forward that he and others like him were then so painfully groping for had already been discovered.

The Works of the Lord are Great, Sought out of all them
that have Pleasure therein. Ps CXI. v. 2

1. Insect-collecting in the 1760s. Hand-painted frontispiece to Moses Harris,
The Aurelian, 1765

2. William Buckland equipped as a glacialist, from Sir Archibald Geikie, *Life of Sir R. I. Murchison,* 1875

3. The rapaciousness of Fashion, from *Punch,* May 1892

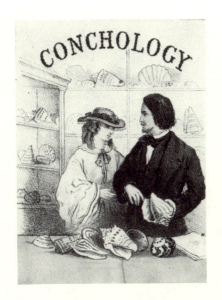

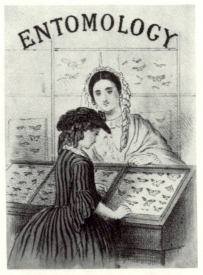

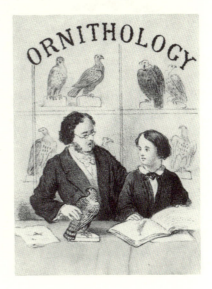

4. Children's playing cards, *c.* 1843

5. 'Seaside Sirens'

6. 'Collecting Ferns', from the *Illustrated London News*, July 1871

7. An excursion of the Liverpool Naturalists' Field Club, 1860

8. First admission of lady Fellows to the Linnean Society of London, 1905.
Painting by James Sant, R. A.

9. Members of the British Pteridological Society on their annual excursion, 1900

10. The photographic gun, from *Le Nature*, 1882

11. Bird photography under difficulties, from R. Kearton, *Wild Life at Home*, 1899

12. G. C. Druce (standing), with members of the Ashmolean Natural History Society, 1904

13. Nature Study class, 1923

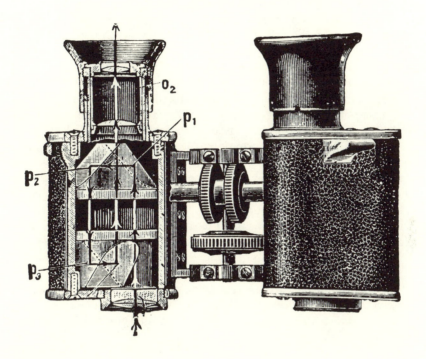

CHAPTER TEN

Dispersed Efforts

ONE summer's day in the early eighties a traveller along the road from London to Bristol might have seen a boy go pedalling by, mounted on a penny-farthing bicycle and all the while peering intently at the passing hedges.

Had that traveller been a naturalist, he might have been acute enough to recognize in this arresting figure a remarkable multiple portent. For not merely the boy's vehicle, but the ambitiousness of his journey, the fact that it was birds he was looking for (and not butterflies, say, or fossils) and that he preferred to watch instead of shooting them—all these might have given the traveller an inkling of the great changes that lay in wait for the subject as the nineteenth century drew towards its close. Had he also known the boy's identity and been able to visualize his future, he might also have obtained a vital clue to a major part of the pattern that was shortly to unfold. For the boy was Alfred Harmsworth, destined to become Lord Northcliffe and the prime arbiter of the tastes of the coming generation through his dominance of the new 'Yellow' Press.

Though few could then have suspected it, this was the brink of a period of turbulence. The long high summer of Victorian natural history may have induced a flagging of purpose but the appearance of languor was deceptive. Underneath, there were fierce, suppressed energics that would soon be demanding to be released.

The situation was not peculiar to the subject. This was a time of frustration in society generally. Economic recession had damped down the previous buoyant optimism; the radical hopes of the later sixties had largely been dashed; even overseas adventures had had an unaccustomed lack of spark, and a keenly expected war had failed to come about. All the swirling new currents that were to well up in the final years of the century and in the early years of the next—the hysterical nationalism, the strident assertiveness of women's suffrage, the sharp intensification in political division and social awareness—can be interpreted as due to protracted damming. People had grown desperate for action almost for the sake of action; and, when the time came, it was not surprising that this had a feverish quality and tended to be rather random.

Natural history reflected all this. These were years in which the subject suffered a basic lack of consensus about the direction in which it should be going, despite a widespread conviction that a fundamental shift of some kind was essential and imminent. In consequence people were left to follow the promptings of their own instinct. There started up a whole series of independent crusades, each of which constituted a rival answer to the current malaise. This element of competitiveness merely helped to strengthen the insistence with which the solutions were proffered, while imparting an added piquancy to the activities of the leading individuals.

Of these various crusades, by far the most far-reaching amounted simply to an inversion of the previous collecting tradition. This was the drive for Protection, later to grow up into the much more broadly based movement for Conservation. This particular story is too lengthy and complex to be recounted here in detail, and all that can be noticed are its overall features.

First, it already had a considerable past history. In the early years of the century that wave of humanitarian zeal which led to the abolition of the Slave Trade had also secured the illegalizing of bull-baiting and cock-fighting and produced the Society for the Prevention of Cruelty to Animals. While this failed to spill over in the direction of nature in any similarly concrete fashion, it clearly had some effect on the consciences of quite a number of individual naturalists. This was greatly helped by the prevalence of Quakers and leading Evangelicals in the following for the subject. In 1813, on returning from his travels in South America, 'having suffered myself and learned mercy', Charles Waterton began turning his Yorkshire estate into a sanctuary for all wild birds. Soon, one or two other landed gentry with equally strong natural history sympathies were doing the same, forbidding shooting and putting up artificial nesting-places. On a less elaborate scale initiatives of this kind date from very much earlier still. Colonies of sea-gulls, because of their sheer conspicuousness, were beneficiaries in particular. Local naturalists were making public protests at the regular slaughter of the kittiwakes at Flamborough Head as early as the 1820s, and there is one case at least of a temporary ban being placed on all shooting and molesting at the South Stack rock near Holyhead, during the building of the lighthouse there from 1808 onwards—as a result of which the gulls were seen to return to breed, 'as if aware of their security'.

One great obstacle to progress was the large number of naturalists who also relished field sports. Men like Yarrell, who, though one of the finest shots of the day, forswore the gun for ever on being converted to natural history in 1826, were for long exceptional. A further problem was the generally held belief that a bird, to be identified with certainty, needed to be shot—though already, as we have seen, the fallaciousness of this had been exposed by pioneers of 'hides' and field-glasses. Till quite late on, because of their specialized rapacity, naturalists themselves were the per-petrators of some of the worst of the damage. As late as 1870, when an osprey was reported over Tamworth, it was a member of the local natural history society who expressed regret that 'someone who should have known better let it go'.

The turning-point came half-way through the sixties. The immediate cause was the finally unbearable scale of the destruction wrought by the latest fashion in women's hats—which involved the wearing of substantial portions of the plumage of wild birds, more particularly gulls. Ironically, in view of the prominent part played by women in the struggle to counter-act it, this fashion appears to have been an obscure kind of echo of the seething frustration on the point of bursting forth as the campaign for Women's Rights. Following a barrage of protest led by that untiring pam-phleteer, the Rev. F. O. Morris, backed up by Professor Newton, Parlia-ment was successfully hustled into its first-ever piece of legislation on be-half of wild life. (A Yorkshire Association for the Protection of Sea Birds, specially formed in this connection, was similarly the first-ever wildlife conservation body in Britain, possibly in the world.)

But like later statutory measures this proved a disillusionment. Hardly anyone took the slightest notice and convictions were almost impossible to secure. In any case, it was not only sea birds that required the assistance of the law. Every other species was being harried, occasionally to extinction, by a ceaseless array of human foes: not only those who came at them with guns, but those who took them alive to supply the gourmet and cagebird markets, or who collected or ate their eggs. The Wild Birds Protection Act of 1880 in theory extended the law to cover most of these as well, but in practice it proved just as difficult to enforce.

It was in the decade after this that the cause at last acquired a substantial body of militants. The immediate trigger, again, was what the Americans by now were dubbing 'the Feather Fight'. There was a readily identified enemy, the plumassiers and milliners; and there was a single, clear-cut issue to help arouse emotions. This time round there were also far more people on the search for something to protest about. How much good their efforts did the wider conservation movement is a matter for doubt, but a large influx of supporters was essential to the galvanizing of public opinion on a scale that the small world of ornithology had no hope of matching. Inclined to hysteria, often absurdly impractical, the new abolitionists acted as a kind of Salvation Army band for British natural history, winning influence in quarters which could never have been penetrated by quieter methods.

Probably more important, they also succeeded in solidifying the protectionist front. In 1885, virtually coinciding with the birth of the Audubon Society in America, the Plumage League and the Selborne League were both founded—and, shortly after, joined forces. In 1889 a small group of women in Croydon began to meet regularly over tea and, christening themselves the Fur, Fin and Feather Folk, each took a pledge 'to refrain from wearing the feathers of any birds not killed for the purpose of food, the Ostrich only excepted'. Their rather sanguine hope was that enough other women could be induced to take the pledge to render the trade in ornamental plumage uneconomic. Out of this unlikely little body presently hatched the Society for the Protection of Birds (later, from 1904, 'Royal'). The taking of the pledge was continued and, aided by a subscription of twopence, membership bounded, producing a total above 5,000 before the first year was out. All of these without exception were women. Like its sister bodies, the R.S.P.B. at first deliberately excluded men as members, enrolling them, patronizingly, as 'honorary co-workers'—a sweet revenge for all the years of humiliating exclusion from so many of the grander learned societies.

The fact that women were kept out of the latter for so long (the British Ornithologists' Union, the most important in this connection, stubbornly resisted until 1909) did have one serious result. It meant that most of the pre-existing societies were isolated from the mainspring of protectionist activity, which, in consequence, went without the scientific injection that they could have given it, and rendered the anti-plumage bodies even greater hothouses of emotion than they might otherwise have been. Obsessed with propaganda, the R.S.P.B. delayed until 1902 before setting up a Watchers' Committee and the acquiring and wardening of sanctuaries seriously. By that time its transatlantic counterpart, the Audubon Society, had progressed further and, in the more violent American manner, had already lost three of its wardens to the guns of exasperated plume-hunters.

Like the R.S.P.B. itself, the idea of acquiring pieces of land and turning them into nature reserves was a product of the eighties. Despite Waterton's well-publicized initiative of many years before, it was only in 1888 that the Breydon Wild Birds Protection Society made this important innovation, in purchasing one of the choicest of the Norfolk Broads with a view to safeguarding its birds. The leap from the individual action of a private landowner to one by a group of people without the benefit of such a basis already was much bigger than it looks at first sight. Indeed it was not from the natural history world that the inspiration mainly came, but from the allied, but separate, amenity movement. This, like Protection, effectively dated from that radical interlude in the mid-sixties, when the Commons, Open Spaces and Footpaths Preservation Society had been formed. This spectacularly successful body was the equivalent in its day of the Society for the Protection of Rural England: with its unrivalled lobbying and legal expertise it acted as the natural coordinator of a wide range of other voluntary efforts. In so far as it was wholly or largely responsible for the saving of Epping Forest, Hampstead Heath and several other major London commons, all succeeding generations owe it an immeasurable debt.

The amenity movement derived its strength from the fact that it sprang from a number of separate motivating forces, which exerted their power in combination. The first of these was the straightforward recreational concept: nature as a necessary healing salve, as something which, like music, 'hath charmes'. The revulsion against the filth and squalor of the nation's cities that began to take hold about this time gave this motive added urgency. Secondly, there was the urge for preservation. Ever since the infamous General Inclosure Act of 1845 encroachment had been growing, and latterly it had accelerated. Out of this came the twin drives to prevent rare species being extinguished and to safeguard ancient monuments and buildings of historic interest. A third motive was the age-old lure of the sanctuary: the small area specially set apart and kept inviolate. 'Sanctuary' is cognate with sanctity, a deeply emotive word resonant with images of sacredness and privacy. 'Reserve', a much more neutral term with a hint of sensible economics, only supplanted it comparatively late. Fourthly, and closely connected with the last, there was the semi-mystical 'wilderness' concept. This was a pre-eminently American fixation—understandably, in a continent where true wildness still abounded and was not yet a modernist delusion. It rested on the conviction that some elusive innate virtue

resided in the pristine, uncontaminated outback: a Transcendentalist notion that may well have descended from Coleridge by way of Emerson. Its
first emergence can be dated to 1833, when George Catlin advocated in
the New York press the setting aside of portions of the unspoilt wilds as
national parks under the care of the state.

Overlying these basic motives, and by comparison mere materialist af-
terthoughts, were the economic and scientific arguments for conserving
irreplaceable natural resources, for instilling better methods of land-use
and for creating open-air laboratories. Probably because the seminal work
in which these found expression, G. P. Marsh's *Man and Nature,* was published only in 1864 and made little impact over here, this more sober
version of the cluster of attitudes that we have since come to recognize as
'conservation' was a regrettably tardy influence on British thinking and
missed inclusion in the ideological mix at this formative period.

Coexisting with these ideas, but independent of them, there also grew
up and flourished a new philosophical doctrine: Vitalism. This arose
largely out of the ruins of orthodox belief left by the triumph of evolutionary theory, though its origins were, in essence, pre-Darwinian. Refusing to
accept the bleak and pessimistic view of those who saw only the harsh
northern aspect of Evolution—the terrible inevitability of the Struggle for
Existence, the remorselessness of a Nature 'red in tooth and claw'—the
Vitalists built instead a positive and optimistic creed upon its other, warm,
south-facing side. Believing, with Bergson, in the supremacy of a creative
Vital Spirit, they put their faith in a quality of 'insurgence' inherent in
every particle of life, which, once harnessed, enabled an organism to sur-
mount all the constraints and pressures that opposed it. This led on to the
conviction that all life is equally deserving of reverence. Darwinism had
brought the cardinal insight that man is merely another biological species:
in and of nature, not above and outside it. The wanton taking of life in any
form or circumstances, accordingly, now seemed ethically wrong—a belief
that was to be far-reaching in its effects.

Furthermore, as Charles Kingsley in particular had insisted, for those
willing to look the workings of nature offered an alternative, more hopeful
interpretation than the sterile, mechanistic one prevalent among the majority. Everything in nature, those like Kingsley argued, depends on something else: cooperation, not competition, is the dominant rule. This is the
same basic Law of Help that features so extensively in the writings of
Ruskin, best set out in the fifth volume of his *Modern Painters* (1860): 'The
power which causes the several portions of the plant to help each other,
we call life . . . Thus, intensity of life is also intensity of helpfulness—
completeness of depending of each part on all the rest.' Reiterated by
William Morris and many others, this notion was to underlie the access
of interest in ecology (a term first used by the German zoologist Ernst
Haeckel by 1866) and in the social behaviour of animals and insects.

The Vitalist philosophy underlay much of the movement for social and educational reform in the late nineteenth and early twentieth centuries. It was the inspiration of such influential thinkers and teachers as Patrick Geddes and J. Arthur Thomson (who were to collaborate in writing a book entitled, simply, *Life*). Perhaps inevitably, it even had its own lunatic fringe.

Foremost among the inhabitants of this was Henry Salt. An ex-Eton housemaster turned full-time, multi-purpose campaigner—'an ist with a foot in every ism', as he once described himself—Salt contrived to spoil his case every time by taking extremist positions that only succeeded in making him look absurd. Where the average campaigner was content to call for the ending of the heedless destruction visited on wild life, Salt's answer was vegetarianism and the abolition of leather goods. *Seventy Years among Savages,* a ringing denunciation of the meat-eaters of Britain, was a typical product of his intemperance. By comparison, his *Animals' Rights,* with its suggestively modish title, probably gained many more converts.

If Salt and his like were to prove dubious allies, the overall contribution of Vitalism to the protectionist cause was nevertheless immense and even crucial. In retrospect it can be seen as the source of that sudden new current of energy that reinvigorated the campaign in the course of the eighties—even though few of those who then rushed in can have been conscious of owing their inspiration to it specifically.

At the same time its impact on natural history more generally was equally great. This occurred in particular through the drastic changes it presently succeeded in bringing about in the existing system of primary education.

Of all the areas of national life that Vitalism irrigated, none was more desperately in need of its enlivening influence. Equally, the typical mid-Victorian school, with its ramrod teaching and its arid, unimaginative curriculum, was a natural focus of attention for the advocates of such beliefs.

With Life as their central concern, it was also to be expected that the science of life—that newly popularized word, 'biology'—should come high among their instructional priorities. All children, they felt, should have their eyes opened to the wonders of nature while they were still at an elementally porous age and not yet smothered by concepts. But in so far as there was any teaching at all in this direction already, the emphasis had traditionally been on deadness: on forming collections and making museums. Natural history as practised at that time accorded ill with their principles.

It was with considerable relief, therefore, that they began to see possibilities in the knowledge of nature's processes that Huxley and his colleagues had for some years been expounding so enthrallingly to the many hundreds of teachers destined for the new Elementary Schools brought into being by the 1870 Education Act. Suitably watered down for juvenile capacities, this was developed into a totally novel subject, with a deliberately novel name: 'Nature Study'.

As contemporary educationists understood and defined the term, this was purely and simply 'intelligent intercourse with nature', 'the earliest and undifferentiated phase of all science'. It was designed to be taught specifically to children in the younger age-groups, as a generalized prelude to science in the formal sense, and the emphasis was on topics that could fairly be described as anatomy and physiology: the growth of seedlings, how sap rises, the development of frogs. These the children either watched and tended in the classroom or had pointed out to them on specially conducted rambles. Unlike traditional natural history, the subject involved no continuing, systematic exploration of the fauna and flora of a neighbourhood, the keeping of record lists, or even the concept of plants and animals as so many different species (the teachers relying, instead, on Huxley's device of 'types').

To begin with, the introduction of the subject depended on isolated initiatives. There were no standard courses, no books of instruction: the teachers merely drew on their old lecture notes and their personal observations and knowledge—or copied someone else.

One person they copied in particular was Sir John Lubbock (later Lord Avebury), for he was writing extensively on just the kind of topics that they most had in mind. Banker, Member of Parliament, voluminous author, celebrated amateur researcher, the philanthropist who gave us bank holidays, Lubbock was ideally fitted to be the foster-father of such a subject. Thereby Nature Study also became the grandchild of Darwin—for Lubbock had lived in Downe as a boy and had sat, doubtless literally, at the feet of the great scientist. At sixteen, it is recorded, he delivered a lecture on wireworms to an appreciative audience of villagers; and a special fascination for the everyday goings-on in the surrounding environment— a fascination shared with and no doubt partly inculcated by Darwin— remained with him all his life. When, in the seventies, he first launched on his lifelong efforts to arouse an interest in nature among children, his material was startlingly novel. Instead of telling them where and what to collect, like virtually all his predecessors, Lubbock unfolded before them the revelations of the microscope, the social life of ants, and the interdependence of insects and flowers. By 1882, the year of Darwin's death, he had become the country's leading popular expositor of the findings of science. From there he went on to achieve a still more spectacular success as a kind of parlour sage, recommending good books and dispensing advice on all manner of topics to the rising newly literate.

In 1897 the first teachers' manual on Nature Study was published in America (where analogous developments had been in train). Two years later, through the efforts of Patrick Geddes and J. Arthur Thomson, the subject was officially added to the curriculum of all the government schools in Scotland—and in the next year of all those in England too. This coming of age was celebrated in the summer of 1902 with a fortnight of exhibitions and conferences in London, attended by leading representatives of the academic world and a sprinkling of MPs. A few months afterwards, on the strength of the enthusiasm aroused, the School Nature Study Union was founded.

From the prolific outpourings that have come down to us from that time it is clear that misconceptions abounded. There was a lot of soggy idealism invested in the subject; many greeted it as if it was ushering in the Millennium. It is doubtful, as Stanley Coulter was to write of its equivalent in America, 'if any modern educational movement has been so hampered by definition, so obstructed by material, so deflected by sentimentalism'.

The sentimentalism was much the worst. At any other period in history the introduction of such a subject might have been comparatively innocuous. But this was the end of the nineteenth century, a time of peculiar torridness and of a secular rise in the social temperature too pervasive to be easily resisted. Children and their world had been well drenched in mawkishness already, and the publishers in this new age of mass literacy did all they could to pander to what they took to be the accepted taste. The study of life-histories, in particular, formed an easy prey for those who felt the urge to view the animal world in human terms, and before long anthropomorphism was rampant. Barbellion's 'diatomaniac' of 1908, with his 'pretty-pretty' slides, his lectures to Bands of Hope on 'The Butterfly's Life', his angry denunciation of biologists as moral perverts, was all too typical of the time. And books like *Insect Lives as Told by Themselves*, published by the Religious Tract Society in 1898, show what could happen when Nature Study was pressed into service as a kind of auxiliary Scripture.

The long-term effect was disastrous. A distorted idea of the study of nature (and so of the naturalist) was put into currency that was to prove as persistent as the 'Wordsworthianism' that has done no less harm to the image of poets and poetry. By making the study of nature a compulsory school subject, moreover, the damage was compounded. For it thereby acquired a fatal association with Lessons—and, even worse, with lessons for infants, and with topics (like tadpoles and chestnut twigs) that for some uncanny reason appear irredeemably risible.

The full enormity of the injuries inflicted on natural history as a consequence can best be appreciated from the failure of even the present-day vogue for bird-watching to blot out quite entirely this crippling taint of juvenilia. After Nature Study had done its work, a 'naturalist' for the average layman no longer conjured up a picture of a rather earnest-looking gentleman tapping on rocks with a hammer or peering at a plant through a lens—but of a grubby urchin with a jam-jar.

But possibly even worse, the propagation of the view that Nature Study was the one correct approach was divisive and impeded the efforts of those who strove to steer natural history on to a more progressive course. The well-meaning but uncritical thought they saw in it the answer to their quandary: the longed-for new dynamic that would revolutionize the old, sleepy, dry-as-dust study and put it on a completely altered basis. In a muddled kind of way, of course, they were anticipating ecology. Where they erred was in seeking to do violence to the facts of the existing situation and assuming that they could force an intellectual merger regardless.

Matters were not helped by the simultaneous emergence of a great new range of newspapers and magazines which competed in reflecting as faithfully as possible the tastes of the successive waves of children who now left the elementary schools. Nature Study, inevitably, came in for much attention and in the process had its life extended far beyond the schoolroom. The natural history of long tradition was squeezed out, and great numbers of people in consequence were given the impression that it represented an outmoded approach.

Still retaining his boyhood fondness for natural history, that archetype of the new press barons, Lord Northcliffe, was active in helping along the subject and indeed went a good deal further than most. It was due to his personal initiative that such consummate masters of popular nature writing as Henry Williamson and William Beach Thomas were engaged to write regularly for the Harmsworth publications and thereby guaranteed a readership numbered in millions. But his influence was not wholly benign. His efforts in such matters were subordinate to his instincts as a journalist, and here his grounding in *Tit-Bits* was hardly helpful. By inventing the Nature Note, he unwittingly imprisoned the subject in a chronically abbreviated format for the very fact that space was reserved for it in the form of a regular feature caused editors to exclude it from further (and fuller) coverage elsewhere. In return for this privileged position, it was thus its fate to have to endure for years almost total banishment from Fleet Street and a wholesale identification with a one-sided and increasingly obsolete approach to nature.

Under the combined impact of Nature Study and the deliberately less demanding style of the new journalism, popular writing on the subject soon became noticeably more diffuse. There was a drift away from plain factual detail towards a softened impressionism, echoing the contemporary trend in art. In place of the columns of exact and rather technical description that Charles Maclaren, the geologist editor of the *Scotsman*, had thrust upon his readers in the fifties, Northcliffe and his imitators prescribed a non-specialized diet, offered in a manner that good professional journalists, rather than good naturalists, were best equipped to accomplish. In this way the popular literature, too, lost touch with the established field tradition.

Not surprisingly the local societies, closely identified with the old, rejected approach, also began to fall out of fashion. In their stead, in keeping with the national mood of expansiveness that characterized the period, mammoth federations of naturalists became the vogue just as if, having tired of collecting specimens, people had merely shifted their energies to forming large collections of themselves.

Probably the first of these to appear was the Union Jack Field Club. By 1882 it claimed a membership of three thousand, mainly (and significantly) boys and young men, distributed among upwards of two hundred separate branches and linked by their own journal, the *Union Jack Naturalist*. Following this came the British Field Club, publishing *Nature Study* and describing itself as 'an amalgamation of nature-students in Great Britain and abroad', and the British Empire Naturalists' Association (still flourishing today, but with the 'Empire' tactfully dropped). The latter in turn gave birth in 1905 to an even more novel kind of journal, *Country-Side*, published weekly under the editorship of E. Kay Robinson, a professional journalist who had worked in India on the same paper as Kipling. *Country-Side*, in good Harmsworth tradition, cost only a penny an issue and was crowded with photographs. Just as these new nation-wide bodies presaged the mass-mindedness of the twentieth century, so their literature hinted at the visual age about to come.

CHAPTER ELEVEN

Recovery on the Coasts

DURING these same years, largely unnoticed, some highly promising steps in cooperative work were being taken. By coincidence, the two branches of the subject concerned shared the same natural habitat; but as luck would have it they were two which also had nothing in common and consequently had little chance of influencing each other.

At first sight it was not obvious that one of them should have been marine biology. There were, however, special reasons why this particular field gave rise to such developments. One of the most important was that it happened at this time to be at an innovative stage. As the variety of nature on land began to seem exhaustively investigated, it was to be expected that eyes should be turning seawards. Many of the best scientific brains of the generation found it intellectually exciting over and above its attractiveness as a working environment.

Despite the abrupt ending of the aquarium craze, interest in the sea continued at a more popular level as well. But reflecting the preoccupations of scientists, a shift from the shoreline out into the deeper waters increasingly became apparent, signalled near the end of the sixties by a widespread enthusiasm for dredging. In the short space of five years, according to the president of the Birmingham Natural History and Microscopical Society, the study of marine zoology had attained an interest 'second to that of no other branch of natural history'. Suddenly, the existence and habits of the denizens of the sea were being discussed 'as familiarly in the newspapers of the day as the events of social and political life'; while public enthusiasm for the marine aquaria established in various leading towns had grown so immense that 'the arrival of the octopus had attracted almost as much attention as the visit of a foreign emperor, and the death of a porpoise was mourned as a national calamity'.

Unlike working the shore, deep-sea dredging was no casual solitary endeavour; it was a collective enterprise, not to be embarked upon lightly, demanding careful planning, a lot of teamwork and a considerable expenditure of money. By requiring sea-going vessels, for the first time it came up against the problems of what has since come to be known as 'big science'.

True, these needs tended to be uncritically accepted and exaggerated. It was often conveniently overlooked that much effective dredging could still be carried out by individual effort, thanks in particular to the new, special throw-dredge invented by David Robertson, 'The Naturalist of Cumbrae', in 1868. Much smaller and lighter than the naturalist's dredge up to then in universal use, this was an ideal implement for catching the smaller creatures which were then, as always, most in need of being studied. Its smaller bag, of thin canvas or cheese-cloth, could be easily pulled up by one person, whereas the standard model was heavy work for even two.

Most collectors, nevertheless, were insufficiently experienced or self-disciplined to forgo the larger and more appealing species; doubtless they also preferred a party atmosphere and the opportunity to share with others the triumphs of the hunt. In general, therefore, dredging came to be regarded as an elaborate, communal affair, the prerogative of rich men with private yachts or the once-a-year treat of learned societies, beyond the scope of the ordinary collector except by joining up with a group of fellow-enthusiasts and pooling his resources.

It was this need for organization, no less than the cost and difficulty of transporting fresh material inland, that led to the device of the marine biological station.

Small laboratories established beside the sea are said to date from as early as 1843, when one was founded at Ostend. But it was not until the seventies, when governments in various countries began to realize the potential of their fisheries and could at last be looked to for funds for associated scientific research, that this institution really had its birth. Most of the first laboratories were small and makeshift, mere sheds or converted hulks, operational for only part of the year and—until the government or a university intervened—shakily funded. In marked contrast, the large aquaria in numerous towns and cities, essentially public spectacles (marine menageries, in fact), proved lucrative commercial ventures. The temptation was to try to arrange a marriage. The simpler approach, fastening on to commercial aquaria a programme of academic research, proved unsatisfactory all round: the two motives tugged in opposite directions, and the promoters, who inevitably controlled the budget, quickly grew impatient with activities which, however worthy, promised to drain away their profits. Many of these aquaria, moreover, were themselves no more than sideshows, risks built on risks, 'not to be compared in attractiveness to nigger minstrels, Zulu, or a Chinese juggler, but still useful as a bait to catch certain classes of the public' (in the words of a contemporary article in *The Times*); as such, they were eminently expendable. The contrasting approach—a primarily academic workplace with some fund-raising from the public proceeding on the side—had the even greater drawback of appearing to require a large initial outlay and, possibly, a lasting element of subsidy.

The solution to this dilemma was to be provided by a young German zoologist, Anton Dohrn. In 1867 and 1868, as one of the fanatical devotees of the new Darwinian biology, Dohrn had paid visits to this country from Jena in connection with his studies of a little-known group of crustaceans. One person here who happened to have done notable work on these was David Robertson, a one-time herd-boy turned Glasgow shopkeeper who for the sake of his wife's health had retired to live at Millport, on the island of Great Cumbrae on the Firth of Clyde, and now spent all his days studying the local marine fauna. Almost as a matter of course Dohrn was referred to him. At Millport, apparently for the first time, he came to realize the immense advantage of carrying out work of this kind with a supply of the requisite living material precisely located in advance (and observable if desired, *in situ*) lying permanently to hand.

In this way, quite unwittingly, Britain contributed the germ of a notion that was to become an ambitious scheme of international dimensions. For it was not long after his visit that Dohrn announced the idea of centres of marine research on a scale hitherto undreamed of. Consisting of a whole series of laboratories grouped around, and depending on, a large aquarium, these 'zoological stations' would be thoroughgoing academic establishments departing from the normal pattern only by being situated near the sea. As such, they would have a proper complement of fulltime scientists with all necessary supporting staff, including fishermen to assist with the dredging and to supply fresh specimens. The funds for this would come, as Dohrn saw it, from several sources, including fees paid by the public for admission to what would presumably be a high-quality aquarium, and one-year rents paid by visiting specialists for 'research tables'—a convenient shorthand term for the standard unit share of the overall running costs which each additional user of laboratory benchspace was estimated to incur. Created on a large enough scale, so that whole teams of research workers or complete classes of students could be accommodated at one time and thus enjoy the beneficial interchange of views in a university-type atmosphere, such ventures, Dohrn suggested, might well prove self-supporting.

On this model all subsequent field stations, marine and non-marine alike, have essentially been based. Few of them, of course, have managed to meet the full range of Dohrn's original criteria. Not many studies happen to be blessed with the scientific equivalent of beauty spots, with a pulling-power sufficient to bring in enough by way of residential fees to bridge the critical gap in overheads. Nor, in practice, have the expenses of the research workers themselves probably ever been sufficiently free of some degree of subsidy—from governments, from universities or from other learned bodies—to provide a proper test of the concept of a wholly self-financing scientific institute. Even so, in broad outlines, the model was well conceived and proved to have an enduring influence.

By virtue of its international scope, the scheme propounded by Dohrn had to be 'sold' to several countries more or less concurrently. In 1870, accordingly, Dohrn came over and delivered a report to the most obvious national forum here, the British Association. The B.A. responded, in the most decisive way it knew, by appointing a committee—'for the purpose of promoting the foundation of Zoological Stations in different parts of the world'. Dr P. L. Sclater, the Zoological Society's energetic secretary, is known to have played the leading part in this.

In coming up with the predictable recommendation that one such station be established somewhere within the British Isles, this committee had the good sense to point at one possible source of the necessary finance: the grant hitherto given by the Government for the upkeep of the Kew Observatory, but now—it was given to understand—to be discontinued. The type of institution it had in mind, the committee stressed, was the closest possible zoological equivalent to the observatories of astronomers; such a switch in funding, therefore, would be peculiarly appropriate. However, this appeal came to nothing, such funds as did prove forthcoming fell far short of what was needed, and for over a decade efforts in Britain to this end languished.

Ironically, one reason for this was the very success that Dohrn himself now had in translating his pipe-dream into reality. In that very same year, 1870, he began negotiating for the concession from the City of Naples of a highly desirable site on its water-front; and two years later, at a cost equivalent to some £20,000 in contemporary currency, the entire sum put up by his father, himself and a few friends (two of whom, Huxley and

Frank Balfour, were responsible for a small token contribution from Britain), he began to erect the world-renowned Stazione Zoologica.

It was the international basis on which this was conceived that was crucial to its success. The dispatch of specimens on request all over Europe proved to be an important source of revenue. The fact that more than just the one country constituted the catchment-area for subscriptions to the 'tables' also ensured a sufficient number of institutions likely to meet the cost of these *en bloc* to permit a relatively high charge (such as might well deter an independent research worker) to be imposed from the outset. Before long no fewer than fifty 'tables' were being subscribed for on this basis—three of them by institutions in Britain: the Universities of Oxford and Cambridge and the British Association. In this way the Naples Station became, as well as 'the Mecca of the biological world', a living monument to multi-national collaboration in the truest sense: not merely on the scientific plane (which was only to be expected), but, far more remarkably, on a financial one as well, to that extent foreshadowing such latter-day intergovernmental achievements as CERN and ESRO.

Naples, all the same, was a long way for British workers to have to travel. Nor did it help towards the much-needed investigation of our own coastal waters. Pressure therefore grew for a home institution on roughly comparable lines.

The holding of the International Fisheries Exhibition in London in 1883, and the considerable public interest that this aroused, served as the eventual stimulus. In the spring of the next year a meeting was convened in the rooms of the Royal Society, under the chairmanship of the ever-active Huxley, which resulted in the founding of the Marine Biological Association of the United Kingdom, with the establishment of a major station somewhere in these islands as its avowed immediate goal. Huxley was elected the first president, while Ray Lankester—already the cause's principal advocate—agreed to take on the secretaryship. A drive for funds was thereupon instituted.

With Naples now as a very solid precedent, the task this time proved less difficult: the Fishmongers' Company responded with a handsome £2,000, and on top of this a remarkably large sum was accumulated by way of small subscriptions from over 350 different organizations and individuals. More remarkably still, when the appeal had already been open some eighteen months, a fabulous grant of no less than £5,000 suddenly materialized from Her Majesty's Treasury, to be used expressly for the building of a large marine laboratory at Plymouth. At the same time—clearly, persuaded at last of the need for some support from public funds of national fisheries research—the Government undertook to make available a regular £500 for five years to help meet the running expenses of this institution, once its scientific programme had begun. With this munificent backing the future of the project was assured; and arrangements were at once put in hand for converting it into fact. Rather more than two years later, in the summer of 1888, the Plymouth Marine Laboratory formally opened its doors.

In the meantime a number of much smaller laboratories had sprung into being in various other parts of Britain. The first two of these were Scottish. In 1884, nine years after its Professor of Natural History had first publicly advocated such a step, St Andrews University was granted a small government subsidy for the equipment and upkeep of a station in a one-time fever hospital down by the shore. Almost simultaneously, an old barge was pressed into use as a floating laboratory in a flooded quarry at Granton, near Edinburgh, on the initiative of Dr (later Sir John) Murray and with the financial backing of—most notably—the Scottish Meteorological Society, which made over to this cause the sizeable surplus it had been presented with from the Edinburgh Fisheries Exhibition held two years earlier.

To this challenge the most marine-minded institution in the English university community—as always, Liverpool—was not slow in responding. In the spring of 1885 a group of local naturalists interested in dredging were brought together as the Liverpool Marine Biology Committee, largely at the instance of Professor W. A. Herdman, a man of tremendous charm and drive, a natural organizer and, above all, with useful contacts among the local shipowners. Through Herdman's influence vessels were placed at the Committee's disposal for days at a time entirely free of charge, and a series of highly productive cruises across Liverpool Bay duly took place that summer. After that, plans for a local marine station were well-nigh inevitable.

Up to this point the Liverpool story had been much the same as all the others: unworked seas, tantalizing spoils, a visionary academic . . . Now, quite by accident, it broke sharply with the pattern. In 1887, in the third season of its existence, the Committee managed to obtain the use of a derelict signalling station on Puffin Island, just off the coast of Anglesey. This was furnished and equipped, and a permanent warden was installed. With steamers from Liverpool regularly putting in across the way, a trickle of workers was soon arriving for stays of up to a week or two at a time. Students from colleges all over the North West were offered board and lodging plus the use of the laboratory for a charge of ten shillings a week all-in, and in those days of suffocating propriety in so many aspects of life the very austerity—let alone the adventure of the voyage—must have held a considerable appeal for many.

It was unfortunate that this experiment did not last. For what Herdman and his collaborators had accidentally created was a model not so much for a marine biological station (for in that capacity it soon showed itself basically unsuited) but for the kind of bird observatory that was eventually established in the 1930. That is to say, it demonstrated that remote outposts of this kind could be manned on a permanent basis and could depend on a sufficiency of visitors if operated on the hostel principle. As there were no ornithologists in the dredging community, however, knowledge of this precedent failed to reach them. But, even if it had, it would probably not have been put to good use, given the still undeveloped state of migration studies in the country at that period.

With this solitary exception, the marine stations can scarcely be regarded as 'field stations' as this term was later to be understood. They were really only outhoused laboratories, close to nature merely in the sense that they were sited on the very margin of the sea. Placed within easy reach of civilized comforts, their staffs could hardly sustain an image of privation. Even from a financial point of view their establishment was seldom a matter of great daring—with universities and even schools clamouring for places of this kind to send their students and pupils to and with governments generally alive to the economic value of their researches. And while it is true that, unlike their counterparts on the Continent, hardly any of those in Britain were steadily subsidized by the state out of educational funds, most of them did have assured government support for their applied scientific work.

In short, the marine biologists were coddled. They had their wishes realized with a minimum of struggle. Unlike other naturalists they had almost every advantage in their quest for a more effective operating framework and for well-located facilities.

———

By comparison, ornithology had scarcely any hope for support on the pretext of economics. It was a totally useless subject: the amateur's field *par excellence,* largely ignored by even non-utilitarian academics. No one entered it expecting to be given money and no one, for sure, had ever emerged with any. Yet despite this fundamental disability, it was here that organized natural history was to accomplish its greatest feats and the machinery of cooperative work to be brought closest to perfection.

Its secret lay in numbers. Birds had a breadth of appeal that no other branch of natural history could rival. The quantity of species likely to be met with in this country was small enough to be manageable, yet large enough to provide an appetizing ration of rarities. For most purposes Latin names could be dispensed with. And once guns had passed out of fashion there were none of the tedious chores of preservation inseparable from studies that revolve around collecting.

But numbers alone were not sufficient. The secret lay also in harnessing the enthusiasm of all these observers and turning it in constructive directions. In this process the character of the subject itself assisted immeasurably. Birds (unlike, say, plants) move about extremely rapidly, sometimes in enormous numbers. Studying them in the mass, with proper scientific objectivity, accordingly entails not only extensiveness of spatial cover—the straightforward distributional logging that Watson had already brought to bear so successfully on flowering plants—but in many cases, as well, the reporting of occurrences in widely separated areas as nearly simultaneously as possible. As no observer could be in two places at once, this could only be solved by collating observations of the same phenomenon made by different people in different spots—and the more numerous the better, not only to provide a more complete picture but to minimize the defects in the data resulting from individual vagaries. Certain kinds of bird study demanded sizeable networks of observers if they were to be carried out at all, with the corollary that with the appearance on the scene of far greater numbers of potential observers certain areas of the subject could be tackled with a degree of intensity that had not previously been possible.

That day had not yet dawned. Nevertheless, already a small handful of pioneers had at least started to prepare the ground. How far they were conscious of the implications for the future contained in the work that they undertook is not always clear. But it is perhaps significant that the two lines of inquiry that drew them in particular were among the very ones that held out the greatest possibilities of mass-participation: the compiling of a detailed picture of national distribution and the study of passage movements.

A third line of inquiry that might equally have attracted them for just this same reason—namely, census work—suffered near-total neglect. The explanation for this is simple: although so elementary, one of the last things it occurs to the average naturalist to do (without being prompted) is to make a count of the number of *individuals* comprising a particular population of any kind of bird, insect or plant. Obsessed with lists of names, which more readily appeal to the inclination to compile in his nature, the most that it will ordinarily occur to him to count is his current tally of the *species*. Even though some kinds of birds obligingly build their nests in eminently countable colonies, this traditional failure to acquire the true number habit meant that for a long time the taking of censuses went almost wholly by default. A few early naturalists, admittedly, like Gilbert White and Pennant, did try their hand at a certain amount; but their efforts were unsystematic and desultory. For the most part this remained one of natural history's extraordinary blind spots.

Ironically, the very few who did see the need for censuses tended to envisage them in national terms exclusively. Doubtless the periodic counts of the country's entire human population was the only experience most people had had of the term, and this fixed their thinking accordingly. But national censuses, it goes without saying, demand a far heavier commitment of time and effort than regional or local ones, and it was manifestly absurd to embark on a novel line of work in the most demanding manner possible.

Ornithology's chief mentor, Alfred Newton, was one person who was aware of the formidable amount of labour which even the simplest inquiry involved when mounted on a country-wide basis. He had found this out for himself, in the 1850s, when he compiled through correspondence a national register of all the then known heronries. His great friend, John Wolley, for whom the idea of a comprehensive census of all the birds in the British Isles had latterly become an obsession, must have been the cause of many a wry smile on that professorial face. 'A census of our birds', he warned the readers of *Ibis* in 1861, '. . . can only be taken by the co-operation of nearly all the ornithologists in the country.' And the country's ornithologists, in his considered view, were not ready for this. Before that generation was out, he thought, it was possible that the great task would have been accomplished; but for the meantime he advocated less grandiose undertakings. Local lists, he stressed, were still far too imprecise in the information they provided on relative abundance, and very little had been disclosed as yet about the dynamics of populations. One possibly fruitful approach might be to analyse the game-books of landowners for one or more species—and, appropriately, as the son of the owner of the famous Elveden estate in Breckland, he concluded his article by urging that some-one should make a start at this 'by polling the Partridges'.

These wise words were entirely ignored. Counting would have entailed setting aside the gun—and almost all students of birds at this period found the lure of feathered trophies irresistible. It was not till 1875 that the first thorough census of a common colonial land bird was eventually achieved, when J. A. Harvie-Brown, a one-time pupil of Newton's, circularized all the lairds in Caithness and asked them to report the number of rooks' nests on their estates—an inquiry which, in itself, constitutes an important landmark in the development of cooperative research.

By contrast, working out the broad distribution of each species across the country was much more straightforward and could be carried out, as the botanists had shown already, by a single person combining an exhaustive exploration of the literature with an appeal for records from an army of willing correspondents. This was merely county Fauna work promoted one rank upwards. And indeed, the man who duly came forward and happily assumed this burden was a compulsive compiler by temperament who already had impressive experience of this type of work, having collaborated with Watson (in so far, that is, as anyone could) on his *Cybele Britannica* and since launched forth himself on a companion volume for Ireland, *Cy-*

bele Hibernica. In his appetite for cataloguing grinds he was well-nigh om-
nivorous, a latter-day Loudon. Not content with transferring Watson's system from botany to ornithology, he also made a minor, experimental
attempt to apply it to butterflies, in a paper in the *Zoologist* in 1858. This
paper ended with an eye cast at other, still unpenetrated fields:

> We would venture to recommend Mr Watson's system to the consideration
> of those who are engaged in the study of other branches of British-Natural
> History; we have no doubt that it might be applied, with most interesting
> results, to the land mollusks and other *stationary* members of our Fauna; and
> the advantage of conforming to a plan already in use it is needless to enlarge
> upon.

To the land (and freshwater) mollusca it was indeed subsequently
applied—but by other hands, and not until 1881.

The name of this remarkable person was Alexander Goodman More.
Much of his life was spent in Ireland—and it is essentially as an Irish
naturalist that he is remembered today, if remembered at all. Of independent means, he was prevented by chronic ill-health from pursuing any full-
time profession—and his laborious compilations were repeatedly interrupted for substantial periods while he was compelled to retire to his bed.
Happily, this is just the type of work, easily taken up and set aside,
uniquely even-paced—the scholar's equivalent of knitting—that is perfectly suited to a life of protracted invalidism.

It was some time before 1860 that he first conceived what he termed,
quite explicitly, his 'Bird *Cybele*'. For this new venture More consulted
Watson on the best methods to follow and even took over the base-map
devised and used by him for his own pioneering work. But the immediate
stimulus probably came from elsewhere, for cooperative data-collection
was just then scientifically 'in the air' (due, no doubt, to the publication in
1859 of Watson's concluding volume): it was in 1860, for instance, that
two leading physical anthropologists embarked upon the first systematic
survey of the racial composition of Britain, circulating for the purpose a
remarkably sophisticated schedule to over three hundred people, most of
them country doctors. It was in 1861, at the British Association meeting
in that year, that a Dr Cuthbert Collingwood proposed recruiting the mercantile marine to the cause of dredging. And it was some time in the two
years following that David Robertson, drawing on his Millport experience,
capped this by pointing out the equally great potentialities for science of
organized collecting by the innumerable coastal fishermen advocating, at
the same time, 'a board of the leading naturalists appointed to name specimens', divided for convenience into county branches.

With such ideas circulating, it would have been remarkable if ornithology had remained unaffected. Nevertheless More must be given credit for

seeing that the work involved had value for reasons beyond the obvious scientific ones. 'What a chance of giving a fresh interest and a useful occupation to the many Field Naturalists, who think they have nothing worth recording,' he wrote to Newton in April 1861. And certainly, no one could accuse him in the end of having been neglectful on this score, for no fewer than ninety-seven correspondents were drawn on for a grand total of 118 county lists. The culminating work, a lengthy paper entitled, 'On the Distribution of Birds in Great Britain During the Nesting-season', was published serially in *Ibis* in 1865 and is said to have been extremely influential.

While engaged on this task, More had already begun to contemplate a similar mass assault on the elusive problems of bird migration. More than most, he was aware of the immense recording energies that were waiting to be released and had sound evidence that the results would not be so unusably inaccurate as sceptics maintained. What he particularly deplored, and wanted actively to combat, was purposelessness in natural history. As a good disciple of Watson, he had learned to appreciate the importance of system—not least for the sense of direction it provided for those who could not necessarily be expected to see the complete scheme of things. When, late in 1861, Newton disclosed his intention of taking up the study of migration in earnest, More's immediate reaction was to counsel him to 'lay down some systematic plans for taking observations; for hitherto observations seem to have been made in such a random manner as to lead to no result'.

In the upshot, it was not until his paper on distribution was out of the way and into print that he was able to give this next task proper attention; and when he did at last begin, about 1866, his approach proved as Watsonian as ever, merely consisting of collecting details on the seasonal frequency of various species from correspondents scattered around the country. He persisted with this for twenty years; but ultimately nothing came of it. For, in the meantime, a more promising, and far more imaginative, scheme had been evolved, in which More himself, almost inevitably, was to become caught up.

To see this new development in proper perspective, it is necessary to go back a good number of years. J. D. Salmon's far-sighted plea for a chain of coastal observers to plot the movement of sea-birds, made as early as 1834, has already been remarked on. Although there was no response to this in Britain, work along such lines did start on the Continent. In 1839 the Royal Academy of Sciences of Brussels sponsored the collecting of data on 'periodic phenomena'—of which migrating birds formed the major portion. Detailed questionnaires were sent to everyone who applied to take part; and as these came in, a large amount of precise information on dates of passage, departure and arrival for the first time found its way into print.

Soon other countries, notably Russia and Sweden, were following the example of the Belgians and copying their procedures.

Gradually, as experience accumulated, these attempts grew more ambitious, partaking in their own small way of the vainglorious competitiveness of Europe's rising nationalism. By 1875 it was the turn of the Germans to show off their scientific prowess. This they did by first drawing up a plan that involved the mobilizing of every single student of birds in their country and, within the space of a few months, with Prussian efficiency, launching them into action. Confronted with this, a suitable riposte from Britain must have seemed merely a matter of time.

As it happened, British ornithology did have in the making something suitable to reply with. For some time a number of people here, seemingly independently, had come alive to the first-class opportunities for studying the movement of birds around our coasts presented by the great chain of lighthouses and lightships that had gradually been building up. To the exceptionally powerful beams of these, it had been discovered, migrants in their hundreds were regularly attracted—and an appallingly high proportion died of exhaustion, dazzled. Clearly, if only those who manned these outposts could be induced to keep records (or at least send in samples of the fatalities) much of great value might be learnt.

Two fears, however, held people back. One was that the men might prove insufficiently persevering to justify all the effort and expenditure involved. The other was that if such operations were to yield acceptable data, they needed to be directed by persons of the highest competence, scientific as well as administrative. Such people were not only rare, but understandably reluctant to take on huge paper-work commitments which promised to keep them out of the field indefinitely.

One or two, fortunately, did exist. The first to make the attempt appears to have been the Norfolk landowner and naturalist, J. H. Gurney, Jnr (to give him his traditional suffix, to distinguish him from his identically initialled and equally prominent ornithologist father). His efforts, however, were on a small scale and soon came to nothing. It was only when John Cordeaux and J. A. Harvie-Brown entered the field in 1879 that a viable scheme developed. That autumn printed schedules were hopefully dispatched to 100 lighthouses and—to general surprise—almost two thirds of these made a return. 'So much willing co-operation, we confess,' the organizers reported, 'we could hardly have anticipated, especially on a first experiment.'

The success of this pilot project encouraged Cordeaux and Harvie-Brown to attempt a more comprehensive coverage, taking in a good part of both the British and Irish coasts. But this, they realized, would be beyond their capacities unaided, and they therefore looked around for an appropriate institutional sponsor. The natural first choice was the British Association, the only body with the funds for an undertaking of this size. The B.A., as usual, did not disappoint; and the customary committee was set up to place the scheme on the necessary formal footing.

The historic Committee on Migration consisted at first of Harvie-Brown and Cordeaux with—the best possible omen—Newton himself in the chair, to keep a fatherly watch over them. Subsequently two Irish representatives were added, in the persons of More and his star pupil R. M. Barrington; a well-known Berwickshire naturalist, James Hardy, to assist with the work in Scotland; and—alas, abortively (for he proved the lamest possible duck)—P. M. C. Kermode, the foremost worker in the Isle of Man. Half-way through, to restore their number to the requisite seven, Kermode's place was filled, on the strong recommendation of Cordeaux, by the young curator of the Leeds Museum (but shortly to move to Edinburgh), William Eagle Clarke. Throughout its eight-year life of data-gathering this Committee required only £175 in annual grants-in-aid to cover its general expenses. On top of this the B.A. met the entire cost of printing the substantial annual reports and, at a much later stage, awarded a further £95 to permit the huge mass of data to be worked up for publication. Seldom can there have been so energetic and productive a committee that has managed to subsist on such modest resources.

By 1886 the undertaking had become very complex. In that year no fewer than 126 lighthouses and lightships agreed to cooperate and were duly supplied with the standard schedules, letters of instruction and cloth-lined envelopes for legs and wings. Once again a sixty per cent response was obtained—and yet another very solid pile of data was garnered in. But by now the quantity of material was becoming an embarrassment; and in 1888, despite opinions that have been expressed to the contrary, there can be little doubt that the B.A. was well advised to bring to an end its support for the purely operational aspect of the work and formally charge the Committee with the preparation of a detailed digest of its findings. Barrington, evidently in dudgeon, refused to accept this as the effective close of operations and continued to soldier on in Ireland, producing a separate series of Irish Migration Reports at his private expense for a number of years longer. The rest accepted the inevitable and, dismantling their administrative machine, agreed to entrust the whole of the fearful burden of collation to the freshest of their number, Eagle Clarke.

Fifteen grinding years and five hefty digests later (to say nothing of a voluminous report by Barrington on all the Irish material) the project had still been completed, in Eagle Clarke's view, at the best in name only. Incomparably close to the data, he alone could see that it still contained important gaps and, not easily satisfied, he decided that these stood little chance of being filled unless he undertook the necessary further work in

person. As a result, from 1901 onwards, he journeyed to numerous remote lighthouses—beginning in style with the notorious Eddystone—
and stayed in these for forty-seven weeks, making regular observations at
first hand on a scale which no other British ornithologist had previously
dared to contemplate. Remote islands, too, came in for a share of his attention, St Kilda and Ushant (off Brest) in particular being accorded fourteen
weeks between them.

It was in the course of this island-hopping, in the autumn of 1905 (just
one year, ironically, after the final dismantling of the marine station building on Puffin Island), that Eagle Clarke stumbled upon a discovery that
was to result in the undoing of much of the contemporary benefits of his
work. This was the very remarkable and unique ornithological character of
Fair Isle, between the Orkneys and the Shetlands—'the British Heligoland', as he later proudly called it, in reference to the far-famed work on
bird migration carried out on that German island between 1843 and 1887
by Heinrich Gätke.

For the next six years this extraordinary migrant *entrepôt* continued to
draw Eagle Clarke regularly, accompanied on occasions by Norman Kinnear, a future head of the British Museum (Natural History). Together
they managed to interest one of the islanders in helping them with their
work; and after giving him prolonged training, in 1908 appointed him
their paid recorder on a day-to-day basis. This man, George Stout, was
thus probably the first-ever professional birdwatcher. What is more, he
was in effect the resident warden of what Eagle Clarke, in his ultimate
definitive work, *Studies in Bird Migration* (published in 1912) was to acclaim as 'the most famous bird-observatory in our islands'—in the process
establishing this as a new term in the language.

As a 'bird-observatory' Fair Isle at this time bore but a slight resem-
blance to the relatively sophisticated institution that was later to appear
under this name in the 1930s and begin colonizing our coasts; even so, it
constituted the essential nuclear idea. Already, Gätke on Heligoland had
devised one of the key operational features of subsequent observatories,
the daily census. The one crucial element still missing was the collective
residential effort. This the British were to learn very late, many years having to pass before the youthhostel concept finally spread here from Germany. With the advantage of this secret social weapon, the Germans were
able to make progress which looked spectacular by comparison. As early as
1903 they had the first bird-ringing station in being (at Rossitten, in East
Prussia), and by 1909 they were even ready to start on large-scale trapping
and ringing of migrants in specially designed traps at a fully constituted
observatory on Heligoland. By failing to link the two basic institutional
ingredients—Eagle Clarke's strategically sited outposts and the prototype
field station on Puffin Island set up by the marine biologists—the British

forfeited all chance of remaining in the van of innovation. In this respect, at least, the organizational leadership in natural history now passed decisively to the Continent.

Associated with this failure of imagination was a no less regrettable failure of intellectual stamina. Eagle Clarke had spelt out in as clear a manner as anyone could the superb opportunities presented by a place such as Fair Isle for mastering so many tantalizing scientific problems of long standing. 'The knowledge gained from the Fair Isle statistics', he declared in his 1912 book,

> has thrown a flood of light upon these important and in some respects obscure migrations, such as was never before possessed for the British Islands. It has been ascertained with a surprising degree of accuracy what species participate regularly in these great movements, and the dates between which they are performed at both seasons . . . [and] the island has afforded the opportunity of correlating the divers movements with the weather conditions.

Undoubtedly, stirring words. Indeed, largely inspired by his example, Miss E. V. Baxter and Miss L. J. Rintoul had already, in 1907, embarked upon their regular spring and autumn trips to the Isle of May, off the coast of Fife, out of which, in 1918, was to come the first formulation of the concept of migrational drift. 'The direction of the wind,' they wrote, 'has a great influence on the routes followed and therefore on the species which occur on our shores.' On the whole, though, they were lone pioneers. For all the contemporary acclamation of Eagle Clarke's work there was little serious follow-up of it in this country for almost fifty years.

The reason for this, once again, was the prevailing obsession with rarities. Quite fatally, in reporting his discovery of Fair Isle, Eagle Clarke disclosed that this and places like it were remarkable not merely for the sheer numbers of migrants that visited them, but also for the high incidence among them of species and races that otherwise in the British Isles are scarcely ever met with. In the mere six and a half years that he had known it no less than 207 species—or about one half of the total then on the British List—were recorded on 'this insignificant island'. This news was predictably riveting for a whole ornithological generation still overwhelmingly imbued with the collector's outlook (even if, increasingly, this was no longer expressed through the gun). At once, the challenging scientific potential of this long line of avian oases became very largely lost to sight beneath the overriding preoccupation with them as a new set of unsurpassed hunting-grounds. And British ornithology, almost as if in relief, succeeded in putting comfortably out of its mind all the elaborate theories and statistics which the Committee on Migration had so conscientiously brought together on its behalf.

Even so, the experience of that great project had not been for nothing.

It had demonstrated the possibilities of cooperative work so conclusively that the concept of network research at last took permanent root in this, the one field of natural history intrinsically most conducive to its rapid development. No other branch of the subject was blessed with so conspicuous a central mystery, which could serve as a focus for inquiry over many years and which could be grappled with effectively only by the coordinated efforts of great numbers of not particularly skilled observers. Only a problem of such scope, moreover, could be relied on to call into being methods of the necessary elaborateness to ensure that the kind of organization that resulted acquired a self-renewing character. Once proved in so popular a field, sheer prestige combined with force of habit could be expected to cause the methods to be adopted in other areas of ornithology and, in turn, other branches of natural history. It was in ornithology that network research was all along destined to enjoy its eventual efflorescence. The only question there had ever really been was how soon the prerequisite conditions for this would occur in the necessary lucky combination.

CHAPTER TWELVE

An Infusion of Mobility

THE MOST conspicuous feature of the nineties was the arrival of bicycles in strength. For the first time a cheap and highly flexible form of personal transport came within reach of the majority, and pursuits like natural history, traditionally a matter of short-term forays into ever remoter districts, were among the prime beneficiaries.

As usual, however, accounts of how individual naturalists responded to this crucial innovation are hard to find. Was their response, one wonders, always so forthright and uncomplicated as this general silence might lead one to suppose? This, from a Northamptonshire geologist, suggests that the reality was rather different:

> For a long time after bicycles were available we never made use of them; because we did not exactly see how they could climb walls, jump ditches, and scramble through hedges . . . Having bicycles altogether changed our usual plan of work; ten miles more or less was a small matter, and so our excursions were much more frequently one-day or half-day ones.

As soon as ownership of the vehicles became general—and while they still possessed a certain dash—the annual programmes of one or two of the societies were picturesquely affected. In 1898 the Geologists' Association began including some excursions specially for the benefit of its cycling members, under the energetic leadership of Professor J. F. Blake. The North London N.H.S. organized an annual Cycle Run, lasting a long weekend, for the odd year or two after 1900. Descending unannounced on some sleepy rural spot, in their straw hats and baggy knickerbockers, hammers at the ready or net-cases swinging at their backs, these intense-looking parties must have been fully as alarming to the locals as any of Edward Forbes's groups of 'vasculiferi'.

One great asset of this form of transport was its almost total silence. A number of people at this time remarked on the way that wild birds would allow a bicycle to pass within several feet where they would not tolerate a pedestrian within as many yards. So reassuring, indeed, does this first of the new machines appear to have been that it is almost in a tone of shock that someone reported to the *Selborne Magazine* in 1911 how he had recently watched some seagulls fly up in evident alarm as one of the strange new aeroplanes passed over.

That very year the dam broke. Motor-cycles, motor-cars, motor-coaches, in rapid and torrential succession, poured out on to the roads. The premature sense of relief was abruptly and brutally shattered.

The abruptness was made to seem even greater by the length of time that motor-cars had been around already, without impinging much on general notice. The first true one had come into being as far back as 1885. Even after 14 November 1896, 'Emancipation Day', when the law ceased to require them to be heralded by a man with a red flag, they had continued to be a rarity. Ironically, among the earlier homes in the country to boast one, by 1902, was Gilbert White's old house in Selborne, 'The Wakes'. At that period they were still a luxury confined to the very rich, an amusing variant on the everyday horse-and-carriage.

The ordinary run of naturalists probably became familiar with motor-coaches a good while before becoming accustomed to journeying by private car. The Folkestone Natural History Society held its first motor-coach excursion as early as 1908—the year in which the number of motor omnibuses on the streets of London exceeded 1,000. Admittedly, as a popular seaside resort Folkestone may have been alerted to the potential of these untypically early; at any rate, it was not until just after the First World War, when much faster and more comfortable models were introduced, that any great number of societies seem to have taken to them. By that time in some areas the ordinary country bus services were becoming good enough to be depended on for outings, so that a number of societies were able to switch to these and cut out the heavy cost of hiring altogether.

It was in 1911, when the first inexpensive cars began to be manufactured or assembled in Britain, that popular motoring had its birth. Their numbers at once suddenly bounded, reaching 150,000 by the outbreak of the First World War. After 1922, 'The Year of the Austin Seven', they speedily became a normal middle-class possession. By the end of the 1920s the country held a million, and a million more had joined these before the next decade was over.

One of the immediate results was a general rediscovery of the countryside. Motor transport encouraged people to visit this much more than when there had been only trains and took them into parts invisible from carriage windows or inaccessible from stations. At the same time it greatly accelerated the encroachment by building and touched off an epidemic of vandalism—the more blatant for never having affected such out-of-the-way places before. These in turn threw the newly realized attractions of the landscape into even sharper relief and aroused a much more widespread anxiety about its future. It was in the years 1924–31, in the midst of this outbreak of increased disfigurement, that a notable rush of further bodies added their energies to this cause: the British Correlating Committee for the Protection of Nature, Flora's League, the Council for the Preservation of Rural England (with comparable bodies for Scotland and Wales), the Society for the Protection of Wild Flowers and Plants, the Wild Plant Conservation Board, the National Trust for Scotland. The amenity movement, which had begun by battling in the suburbs, now fanned out over the country.

Along with the stream of vehicles came an energetic restlessness. Unlike the tours in search of the Picturesque of a hundred and fifty years before, the urge to explore the fields and the hills was this time not a matter of mental repose, but of stamina and muscle: it owed more to athletics than aesthetics. What H. J. Massingham christened 'Exodus Two'—the back-wash from the built-up areas, the drift back again to the land from the towns—consisted in remarkably high degree not of sedate onlookers in coaches, but of people with arched backs and wind-beaten faces, who preferred scrambling over rocks or hurtling down screes to the calmer, gentler processes of sketching or studying them.

Rambling, hiking, camping, mountaineering, caravanning: these were the pursuits that now came to the fore. In their emphasis on escape and on unfettered freedom to travel they echoed the mood of the time. Though some were crowd pursuits and others emphasized solitude, their common insignia proclaimed an underlying identity of outlook: the free-and-easiness of shorts combined with the toughness of the sleeping-bag and rucksack—the rebel uniform of the Wandervögel subtly intermingled with the craft tools evolved by earlier generations of Alpinists.

The ambiguity in appearance reflected an ambiguity in attitudes. On the one hand it stood for an aggressive break with the past and the defiance by Youth of Age; on the other hand it expressed a Rousseau-like yearning for the self-sufficient primitive and the reviving of eternal verities. It was a contradiction that was essentially Romantic.

Natural history, pre-eminently exposed to such influences by its very character, was deeply affected by both aspects. A 'revolution-by-rucksack' took place, which blew away the dust that had settled on far too many of the old-established local societies by then. The confrontations that occurred sound comical today, but they were often bitterer than they appeared on the surface. In an atmosphere of staid decorum it was possible to shock with only the mildest gestures. In 1920, when the stuffy Cambrian Archaeological Association wished themselves on to one of the new breed of earnest scientific investigators, they were aghast when their appointed Leader appeared before them clad in shorts. Even well into the 1930s there was one natural history society in the North in which any girl rash enough to appear in lipstick would be criticized to her face, and a young man flaunting plus-fours would find himself branded as a 'bolshie'. With such medievalism rampant, is it any wonder that some of the up-and-coming could not resist an impish tweak or two?

By contrast, the physical communing with nature was undisguised in its often passionate intensity. It went beyond an ecstatic sensuousness: it was a spiritual affirmation as well. A conviction that The Country, that ineffable, near-sacred thing, enshrined much that was somehow 'right' and 'good' was shared by very many, at varying levels of profundity and with differing degrees of coherence.

In large part this was no more than a recapitulation of one of the themes dominant in Romanticism—and which had already re-emerged across the Atlantic in the guise of the wilderness ethic. There it owed its stronger insistence to the vigour with which it had had the luck to receive its original expression, at the hands of Emerson and then of Thoreau. Thoreau's *Walden* had been written way back in the 1840s (though not published until 1854), but it was only now that the world had become receptive to its message. A careful and detached observer, no longer a deist and no mere treasurer of moods, Thoreau had been the first to attain that elusive interpenetration of intellect and feeling which is the eternal, ultimate goal of the naturalist in the purest sense—and the first consciously to proffer this as a worked-out creed. His legacy to the natural history of the twentieth century was a new, controlled lyricism, far more incisive than the now rejected sentimentality of the Victorians and given robustness by its intuitive source. For this a new literary vehicle was needed: something less constricting, better able to convey the core reality so easily lost to sight beneath the individual detail. The result was the nature essay.

Although Thoreau was the earliest to write about nature in this fashion, by the time his Journal came to public notice, in 1881, there were others who had begun experimenting similarly in response to the contemporary Vitalistic proddings, seeking to capture the essence while still remaining faithful to scientific actuality. Best known of these is Richard Jefferies, a Wiltshire farmer's son who struggled to make a living as an interpreter of country matters. While he triumphed in his quest for the new style, Jefferies was just too far ahead of popular taste to be able to profit from his efforts in his lifetime. It was to be a rather later wave, that school of nature essayists whom Joseph Wood Krutch has termed 'the Thoreauists', best exemplified in Britain by W. H. Hudson and in America by John Burroughs, that was eventually to enjoy a success that was more than just a creative one.

Hudson's achievement in this genre is the more impressive for being the work of someone who was not a native of the country he portrayed. Brought up on a cattle ranch on the Argentine Pampas—in itself symptomatic of the infusion that natural history was to receive from the New World at this period—it was not until he was a grown man that he chanced to read White's *Selborne* and experienced at once an overmastering urge to see with his own eyes the England that it depicted. To this alien background was perhaps due much of the freshness and intensity of vision that characterized his writing. Certainly, some have claimed to detect a faint Spanish cadence, while his attempts to capture simplicity that formed the essence of his style may have been aided by the fact that the language in which he wrote was not the accustomed one of his earlier years. 'Hudson writes as the grass grows', someone unkindly, perhaps enviously said; yet in reality the effect of utter naturalness that he managed to convey was won only by extreme fastidiousness and ferocious toil. What he aimed at was a studied casualness: a 'rambling' style, perfectly echoing the long, slow, unhurried tramping of his feet as he roamed through the gentle southern counties each summer, talking to the people, watching the birds, making a mental note of the scenes and often trivial experiences that came his way. The essays that resulted have been aptly described as 'the apotheosis of the townsman's "day in the country".' In their own special way they are historical documents, peculiarly redolent of those years when the people of England were walking, pedalling or driving out to rediscover their largely forgotten landscape.

They have a historical interest for another reason as well. Like the *Natural History of Selborne,* but unlike almost all the other really popular writing on nature during the intervening years, they are devoted especially to birds.

From as far back as the Sixties Hudson had been obsessed by birds. Even his dreams by night 'were often of some . . . bird . . . which had never been named and never even seen by an appreciative human eye'.

Clearly, they held for him a deep and special meaning, as if they embodied those daemons that drove him to produce his art. None other of his contemporaries seems to have felt their appeal with quite such compelling force, and none of them, either, combined this with literary powers capable of winning and holding a very large audience. As a result his role at this period in awakening an interest in birds—and, even more, in simply watching them—was unique.

All the same, it is hard to claim that it was indispensable. Hudson was probably not so much the author of the taste as the agent who brought about its spread. There is good reason to believe that the surge forward of ornithology that so markedly revealed itself around the turn of the century had originated previous to his essays—and originated, what is more, overseas: in North America. Many of the central innovations of those years, clustered around the wilderness concept—camping, the animal biography, the nature essay, national parks—were American in their birth or in their adoptive parentage. A passion for ornithology was altogether consonant with these and was liable to join them inextricably in their travels. In the grander setting of America birds offered themselves more obtrusively as the epitome of untamed, unfettered wildness. They had an extra dimension there, the means to express more than just the Vitalistic emphasis on a non-static view of nature or to serve as reflectors of the new human mobility. Enveloped in the myth of The West, they also carried the hint of a strong and self-sufficient manliness.

It was this added ingredient that was to be crucial. A more hidebound European manhood needed a substitute prop to its esteem if a switch from the age-old fixation on prowess with the gun was ever to be accomplished. Offered now an acceptable alternative valuation, shooting men felt able to lay down their weapons without any sense of effeteness or loss of social face. As a result the cause of non-violence towards birds enjoyed an unexpectedly rapid triumph and the ingrained stance of aggressiveness with which it had fundamentally had to contend increasingly became converted into a vigorous self-restraint.

Other tendencies of the time helped to bolster this radical about-turn in ethics. The forsaking of roomy country houses for the relative congestion of London flats, as the 'servant problem' grew more acute and the arrival of private cars stimulated 'week-ending', meant that the old collections of stuffed birds began to seem impracticable. Feminine Emancipation brought women into the field by the thousand—and most of them had little liking for weaponry. Field-glasses, too, became more serviceable and efficient.

But these other factors were subordinate, it must be stressed. The simplistic equation of the rise of binoculars with the decline of the gun cannot be allowed to pass: the shift in attitudes was too deep-seated and too broadly based to be attributable to a mere improvement in technology. This improvement, in any case, was much less drastic than has generally been supposed. The small pocket telescopes that the immediate pre-Victorian generation had begun to take to were not an obstacle to satisfactory watching. Only recently, the very one that Bewick owned, bearing the date 1794, has been put to tolerably effective use—for watching, most appropriately, a party of Bewick's Swans. The model typically favoured at that period had a magnification of some thirty times; alternatively, for watching from the house, there was the much more powerful kind regularly resorted to by Waterton, which could be mounted on a trolley and moved about from place to place.

Odd instances of glasses being used can be found even in the 'dark ages' of the mid-nineteenth century, after the torrent of much deadlier fowling-pieces had descended and temporarily arrested such progress as had been made. The last Great Auk to be seen alive by an ornithologist was actually viewed through glasses—by Colonel H. M. Drummond, the first president of the B.O.U., in December 1852. And twice during the 1860s, in successive series of his best-selling *Curiosities of Natural History,* Frank Buckland recommended 'a good pair of double race or opera glasses', urging the sportsman to put down his rifle and take up these instead. The first prismatic binoculars, producing a stereoscopic effect, were patented (in France) in 1859, so there is a good chance that Buckland's own model was of this type. *Birds Through an Opera-glass* was even the title of a book published at the close of the eighties, written by the Audubon veteran, Florence A. Merriam. The schoolchildren for whom this was intended might well find the rapid adjustment troublesome at first, she conceded, but 'an opera or field glass' ought to be the inseparable companion of every careful observer.

It is only in the eighties, in fact, that the first, unmistakable signs begin to reappear of a widely shared interest in watching birds without any attempt to shoot them. And yet, well before this, as we have seen, efficient binoculars were available and could easily have been used. By 1874, even, they were being prescribed as part of the regulation dress for officers in the Army. Ornithologists who did not adopt them clearly had no excuse. The conclusion is inescapable: it was the mood that found the tool, not the tool that caused the mood.

Charles Dixon, whose writings were to prove particularly influential, must have been one of the earliest to voice the fundamentally new outlook, in his *Rural Bird Life,* published in 1880. In this, the words 'observer' and 'observing' crop up with conspicuous frequency. A notebook and a first-class telescope or field-glass are seen as the basic indispensables, while watching is recommended 'from the branches of trees well concealed by the foliage'. Soon afterwards Lord Lilford was advising his nephew, newly up at Cambridge: 'Keep notes of what you see and hear, and consider nothing too trivial to jot down'—sage words from a man who, crippled for much of his life, was famous for sitting still for hours watching birds from a bath-chair. W. Warde Fowler's *Year with the Birds* (1885) was probably even more successful in putting over the new approach.

In these same years Edmund Selous, the quirky, reclusive younger brother of the world-famous big-game hunter, was starting to lay the foundations, in the deepest possible obscurity, of the modern intensive study of bird behaviour, spending up to weeks at a time in the field and jotting down in his 'observational diaries' (subsequently published in part in the *Zoologist* and all now preserved) voluminous, well-nigh illegible notes of a quite extraordinary meticulousness and acumen. Selous was not, in the hackneyed phrase, 'before his time'—like Dovaston, say, in his discovery of bird territory—but he chose to work in such isolation that for many years the influence of his example was minimal. Indeed, in a study of the social development of the subject he deserves to be remembered more for the outstanding bitterness he nursed for all users of the gun than for the truly path-finding character of his field methods.

Around the turn of the century two further important new practices came in which had the immense incidental advantage of bringing the watcher close up to the living bird. These, in turn, provided yet further pretexts for the discarding of the gun.

The first, and by far the most widespread, was the discovery of the simple pleasure of putting food out for wild birds. Extraordinarily, hardly anyone before then had thought of doing such a thing. Bewick, as we have seen, had been one marked exception; Dovaston, to some unknown extent, had popularized his ingenious 'ornithotrophe' (the earliest-known special gadget for the purpose); Loudon fed ivy-berries to blackbirds; Gosse used to encourage a robin to come indoors and peck the crumbs off his breakfast-table; and Morris once fired off a strong letter to *The Times,* advocating the habit. But such concern was rare enough to be dismissed as crankish. Worse, it infringed the Victorian domestic code. In that golden age of Home Economy waste was anathema. Stale bread was either saved for puddings or put into the oven, baked hard and converted into breadcrumbs. The place for other scraps was in the stock-pot, for making into soup. It was the long frost of 1890–91 that finally seems to have broken down resistance. All the leading newspapers that winter joined in urging the public to assist the birds in their plight; and, as a measure of their success, one dealer in bird-seed reported that he had never before sold so much in small quantities, which he reasonably deduced was being bought for putting out for species in the wild. One kindly old lady even went so far as to heat up their food for them. From that point the habit caught on. Two winters later, when another severe frost occurred, 'every day for a period of three to four weeks', according to Hudson (who stood and watched the phenomenon in wonder), 'hundreds of working men and boys would take advantage of the free hour at dinner time to visit the bridges and embankments (of the Thames), and give the scraps left from their meal to the birds.' For some years it remained a sophisticated practice largely confined to townsmen. When Hudson went down to Cornwall in 1908 and proceeded to engage in this by now standard Metropolitan routine, the locals were quite astonished: 'the passer-by would stop and examine the scraps or crusts, then stare at me, and finally depart with a puzzled expression on his countenance, or perhaps smiling at the ridiculous thing he had witnessed'.

By 1910, if *Punch* is to be believed, 'feeding the birds' had become a national pastime. A wide variety of associated furniture resulted: bird-tables, seed-hoppers, bird-baths, nestboxes, even a table and box combined and sold as a kind of imitation dovecote. Nestboxes, it is true, had been around for centuries, but always till now their function had been strictly utilitarian. The new vogue for them originated in Germany; and it was from there that most of the earlier British examples had to be imported. By 1897 their popularity was sufficient to call forth a specialist handbook, *Wild Bird Protection and Nesting Boxes*—a title coupling them with that other newly fashionable concern. Appropriately, one of the many ways of making a nestbox recommended in its pages was boring a hole in a gunmaker's cartridge-box. The 100-cartridge size, we are assured, made a perfect home for tits and the double version of this was spacious enough even for jackdaws.

The other major new practice was taking photographs of birds. Here, for a change, the stimulus was purely technological. For many years following the original invention, in 1835, of the negative/positive process (from which all modern techniques descend) photography had been limited to subjects that were static; it had required, as well, immediate access to a laboratory. One or two naturalists had made use of it to heighten the informativeness of their collections—for example, a Southampton lepidopterist, J. B. Crawford, who in the fifties took portraits of his larger specimens, 'showing all the markings, etc., with the greatest exactness'. By then the first picture of a living creature (a fish, at the London Zoo) had been secured; but the expertise required for this was so daunting that for thirty years there were hardly any imitators.

The breakthrough came with the perfection of a type of 'dry plate' that was comparatively rapid. This revolutionized photography by allowing the laboratory to be left behind: work in the field thus at last became practicable. Very soon after the new 'dry plates' arrived on the market, action pictures of birds began to be achieved. The earliest satisfactory ones known were of Gannets in the Gulf of St Lawrence in the summer of 1881. In the following spring a French professor conceived the idea of a 'photographic gun', with which he succeeded in taking 'shots', in series, of seagulls in flight (a nice illustration of how photography was thought of as merely a new type of markmanship). In Britain two professional portrait photographers compete for the honour: Benjamin Wyles, of Southport, had successfully taken birds in flight by 1888, but R. B. Lodge, of Enfield, may conceivably have anticipated him. To Lodge, more certainly, belongs the credit for the first close-up in this country of an individual wild bird on its nest—in 1895.

By the mid eighties hand-cameras were available for those who merely wanted a rough pictorial record of where they had been. One by-product of this was an increase in the frequency with which naturalists themselves had to submit to being photographed. Group poses were then still *de rigueur,* and at least one writer was moved to complain of the enormous waste of time this caused on field club excursions.

At this point the pace of technical advance quickened markedly. The first film, flashlight photography, the telephoto lens, even (though its hour was yet to come) colour—all these were invented within the ten years ending in 1895. At the same time there was great improvement in the sensitivity of plates. With the promise of better-quality results to show for their efforts, more naturalists were consequently attracted to the study. One or two of these in particular were noted 'characters' and, besides producing first-class work, did a lot to publicize this new approach to natural history, especially by illustrated lectures. The Kearton brothers are deservedly the best remembered in this connection. Their *British Birds' Nests,* published in 1895, was the first bird book illustrated throughout with photographs all taken in the wild. In it can be found this feeling comment by one of them:

> No one who has yet to try this particular branch of photography can possibly appreciate its troubles and disappointments. As an instance of the latter, my brother on one occasion travelled upwards of five hundred miles by rail, and dragged his camera at least twelve miles up and down a mountain side, in order to take a view of one bird's nest, and was defeated by the oncoming of a thick mist at the very moment he was fixing up his apparatus.

Perhaps best of all the Keartons are known for their stylish experiments with camouflage. Their 'hide' built in the likeness of a hollow tree-trunk proved an enduring gift to cartoonists; they also made use of the skin of an ox, after the manner of Red Indians when stalking buffalo. Just in case these failed, they wore reversible coats, brown on one side and green on the other. The irony of all this, it later turned out, was that most birds will happily tolerate any contraption at the nest, whether disguised or not, provided only they are first given a chance to become used to it.

It was during the Edwardian era that nature photography really caught on. By then, it had lost much of the initial, off-putting aura of an almost infuriatingly complicated technique and begun to be accepted as a workaday tool. Concurrently, the profuse appearance of its results in books and magazines attracted more people to try their hand, even as it heightened the appeal of an ornithology that was already of itself attracting a fast-growing public.

The arrival of film heightened this appeal still further. By 1903 F. Martin Duncan, in conjunction with the company run by the film pioneer Charles Urban, was utilizing cine-photography to record the movement of animals, and two years later some of the results of this were put on exhibition in London at a special series of matinées at the Alhambra Theatre. In August 1907 a 'movie' with a natural-history theme ran for a whole month at another, neighbouring establishment. As this was before even the first permanent commercial cinema had opened in the Capital, it is clear that naturalists were quick to grasp the special value for their subject of this further medium. For the arrival of animation ensured, in yet another way, a bracing infusion of mobility.

With much larger numbers engaged in the study, ornithology was now in a position for one further stride towards the goal of permanent cooperative inquiry. The migration work of the eighties had been a heroic and profitable undertaking; but the percentage of people involved had nevertheless been tiny. Now, with collecting firmly on the wane, potential recruits to such a way of working were likely to have increased much more than proportionately. All that was required was for the necessary leaders to come forward, to present the blueprints for schemes and, more crucially, to institute the new high standards of field identification on which a now gunless study had become dependent.

These leaders soon materialized. The most influential by far was Harry Forbes Witherby—more particularly through his editorship of the new and forward-looking monthly that he brought into being in 1907 (the year of Newton's death), *British Birds*. A publisher also by profession, Witherby was to hold this position for over thirty-six years, coming to personify British ornithology in the process. From now on this journal was the primary medium for publication of the results of the studies especially identified with the new outlook. Of more immediate moment, it also provided a perfect vehicle for the long-term coordination of a major collective scheme. As a dress-rehearsal for this, and in order to lose no time in attuning his readers to the new way of thinking, Witherby conducted through its pages in only the second year of the journal's existence a nation-wide inquiry on the Wood-pigeon. Over a hundred people volunteered their help and, at least as a beginning, it was adjudged a success.

The obvious next choice was systematic ringing. For many centuries people had been marking birds, either as a brand of ownership or simply in curiosity about where they disappeared to. Nothing scientifically worthwhile had ever come of any of this. But two factors which had chanced to coincide had now led to the resurrection of the device for the purpose of serious research. These were the widespread awakening of interest in migration and a steep fall in the price of the most suitable raw material, aluminium. Around 1890 a Danish schoolmaster, H. C. C. Mortensen, had started experimenting with strips of zinc. By 1899 he had progressed to leg-rings of pliable aluminium, on which was stamped a serial number keyed to a register recording the place and date. The ringings he made were publicized in appropriate periodicals and even in the local press. This was done to such good effect that a large number of recoveries were notified back, some of them even from distant countries. So impressed was the scientific world with these results that Mortensen's example was soon being copied in many other areas; In 1909 the American Bird Banding Association was formed and ringing schemes were launched both in France and in Britain. So great was the enthusiasm over here indeed that two started up almost simultaneously: one run by A. (later Sir) Landsborough Thomson and based on Aberdeen University; and another, considerably more ambitious, conducted by Witherby through the pages of *British Birds*. This second scheme has continued, in varying guises, down to the present.

From the first, ringing proved an appealing yet useful task for compulsive accumulators to devote themselves to with Stakhanovite fervour. The unexcelled champion of this fraternity, Dr H. J. Moon, ringed over the next thirty years some 78,000 birds—a figure rendered the more amazing by his firm principle of never ringing where nesting was in colonies. When this is compared with the 15,000 specimens of British flowering plants and ferns (many of them rare, most of them in some way or other 'critical') that a leading botanical collector, the Rev. Augustin Ley, selflessly contributed to the Botanical Exchange Club up to the time of his death in 1911, we begin to gain some idea of the difference that the shifting of such exertions into new and harmless channels was capable of making to the country's fauna and flora.

In the meantime another important collective undertaking had been launched by an offshoot of the B.O.U., the British Ornithologists' Club. In 1906 this body had appointed a special committee, under the chairmanship of F. G. Penrose and the secretaryship of Norman Ticehurst, to continue the work that Eagle Clarke and his collaborators had embarked upon, by collecting from a network of observers details of the arrival of the summer migrants. Nine annual reports were published, each as a special volume of the *Bulletin* of the Club; but unfortunately no overall summary ever appeared, which deprived this scheme of much of its impact. Even so, it served as a salutary reminder of a major inherited task that was still far short of completion.

Unlike ringing—which was relatively foolproof—this and other types of cooperative work now had to rely on the wholesale acceptability of sight records made by observers of unknown individual standing. Always up till then sight records had conventionally been disregarded, or at best treated as suspect, in the absence of a 'scalp' as a testimony. That this iron line, entirely praiseworthy in the circumstances that had prevailed hitherto, was now at last able to be abandoned was due to two individuals in particular: to Witherby himself, and to yet another of those seemingly inexhaustible naturalist clerics, the Rev. F. C. R. Jourdain, a noted egg-collector and a notorious *'pastor pugnax'*.

Witherby's contribution was to submit the records sent in to him with a view to publication in *British Birds* to the most rigorous and relentless screening. In this way he ensured that any that found their way into print carried the guarantee of well-above-average reliability—and could thus be drawn on for secondary purposes with a minimum of qualms. Jourdain, meanwhile, set about inculcating what amounted to a drill, designed to ensure that in the field all points conceivably helpful for identification were noted down systematically and in the necessary detail. If the record then came to be queried, the evidence contained in the notebook would at least have a verisimilitude that assertions based solely on memory could not hope to match.

The general switch to exclusive reliance on field-characters that consequently took place brought into being an entire new breed of handbooks. All of these hitherto had been conceived on the assumption that descriptions would be minutely compared against skins and the characters used had been selected accordingly. With the bird no longer in the hand, a totally novel set of criteria had to be adopted, with emphasis laid on features, like call-notes, that had previously been undervalued. Most observers, too, now wanted a guide that could be taken out into the field and referred to in hurried, alternate glances, as they held their binoculars on something problematical. For these reasons the new type of handbook tended to be more compact than its predecessors and its descriptions progressively more condensed, in many cases reduced to the barest minimum of key distinguishing features and made as speedily consultable as possible with the aid of a good deal of typographical ingenuity—a trend also found in botany, most notably in the shape of *Hayward's Botanist's Pocket Book* and especially in the later editions of this edited by Druce. In short, the field manual underwent a process of 'streamlining'. In true twentieth century style, it turned into a plain utility article: a knockabout tool, in place of the prized triumph of artistry.

At the same time identification was no longer such an exclusive concern of field ornithologists. Interest was turning to how birds behaved; and this compelled a great narrowing of attention. Self-denial was of the essence of this novel and difficult line of study (soon to be distinguished as 'ethology'). It involved an almost monkish austerity and was utterly unsocial. Successful practitioners of the art were often men of a shy and retiring disposition. Edmund Selous is in this respect the exemplar, at the same time as he is the prototype, of the modern bird behaviourist.

In the chronic absence of Selous, as private in his habits as any of his warblers, the role of popularizing such work fell to a young lecturer in zoology at Oxford, Julian Huxley, and to a wealthy Midlands steelmaster, Henry Eliot Howard. A paper in the Zoological Society's *Proceedings* in 1912 on the courtship of the Redshank was the start of what was to be a long line of brilliant contributions by Huxley on the topic of bird courtship in relation to Darwin's theory of sexual selection. Through them, in no small degree, Huxley (as he himself has put it) 'made field natural history scientifically respectable again'. In a parallel series of equally important volumes, stretching from 1907 to 1929, Eliot Howard elucidated the nature of territory in birds. In admirable prose and with great intellectual penetration, this lone amateur (like Selous) whose only scientific contact was Professor C. Lloyd Morgan—renowned for his then unfashionable work on animal psychology—gradually unfolded before the ornithological world a whole area of behaviour that had been overlooked. We now know that Dovaston, around 1830 (and in a county abutting on Eliot Howard's own Worcestershire), as well as the Irish naturalist C. B. Moffat, in a paper published in 1903, had both substantially anticipated his thesis; neither of them, however, had produced anything like so elaborate and convincing an account backed up by such a wealth of illustrative detail.

On the other hand, Dovaston had one extra achievement to his credit which Eliot Howard, an observer *par excellence,* felt no inclination to repeat: he had trapped birds, marked them and done some tentative mapping of their territories. This gap in an otherwise comprehensive corpus was filled in the early 1920s by another, scarcely less remarkable lone investigator: J. P. Burkitt, the County Surveyor of Fermanagh. In his garden in Enniskillen Burkitt caught Robins and marked them with metal bands of different patterns (different colours would have been simpler still, but it so chanced that he was colour-blind). He was thus able to study—possibly the first zoologist ever to do so—a complete population in terms of its component individuals, as a result proving that the show of pugnacity for which the Robin is well-known is not courtship display, as some had supposed, but threat-display in defence of territory. He was also the first to make use of the recovery of marked birds as a means of estimating average age.

That two of these highly original contributions on behaviour should have emanated from Ireland is a striking tribute to the vigour of Irish natural history in these years. From the time of More and Barrington it had been blessed with a sunburst of talent. Men like Robert Lloyd Praeger—already the acknowledged leader of this group—combining in one frame unparalleled breadth of knowledge, organizing skill, considerable literary gifts, a prolific output and an unwavering intellectual purpose, are rare anywhere at any period; in a community as small as Ireland their impact could hardly help but be torrential. That it was from this quarter that the most ambitious collective undertaking of all up to this time—a kind of inverted piece of network research—should now have come is therefore not surprising.

From start to finish, the initiative was largely Praeger's. In 1903 the Hon. Cecil Baring (of the well-known merchant bank) had celebrated his marriage by purchasing the small island of Lambay, just off the Dublin coast. Entranced with the place, he determined to discover all he possibly could about it. This led him immediately to Praeger—who by then had exchanged a prior vocation as a civil engineer in his native Ulster for a more secure post in the National Library in Dublin. Praeger's prompt suggestion was that the flora and fauna of the islet should be made the subject of a specially intensive survey; and this having been agreed, in 1905–6 a score of specialists in the various branches went over in relays to stay as guests of the owner. The results were startlingly fruitful: of the species collected, no fewer than seventeen were new to the British Isles and five even to science.

Much struck by this, Praeger thereupon decided to launch an even larger 'mass-attack' on one of the islands lying off the western coast. For this he chose Clare Island, in Co. Mayo, by virtue of its manageable size and the not too difficult problems of transport and accommodation. Even so, it was undeniably remote; and the fact that in the three years 1909–11 approximately a hundred workers, many of them of great distinction and quite a number of them from the Continent, journeyed there and spent a week or more in groups of up to a dozen at a time, is a testimony to Praeger's powers of inspiration. Even more remarkable is the fact that, unlike so many similar enterprises, the published results—a series of sixty-seven separate reports, in three large volumes—were brought out with the minimum delay, thanks both to Praeger's tactful chivvying and to the traditionally munificent support of the Royal Irish Academy (on which natural history in that country has for so long been able to rely).

It may not be far-fetched to see behind this superb response on the part of a considerable section of Europe's zoologists and botanists the new awakening to the advantages and pleasures of working side-by-side engendered by Dohrn and his colleagues at Naples. For the Clare Island Survey, in essence, was a marine station deliberately induced to straggle—inland, instead of seawards. It confirmed afresh the predictably spectacular outcome (in this case 109 species of animals new to science) of concentrating on one spot a large number of experts in a large number of branches. It also showed that the promise of taking part, with fellow experts of standing, in a large-scale but finite and well-organized project need be no less a draw than the assurance of first-class working facilities. In a sense, therefore, Clare Island formed the intermediate stepping-stone, both functionally and chronologically, from Naples to the ideal of a modern field centre (but which no field centre, for simple reasons of economics, has ever yet fully been able to live up to).

The awakening of interest in behaviour was not confined to birds. In botany, too, there was the same shift to movement and dynamism so characteristic of these years: from the dead specimen to the living plant, from a static viewpoint to an emphasis on change. But here it was not intensive studies of individual species that came in for most attention, but the disentangling of the broad relationships between vegetation and the environment and a transfer of classificatory instincts to the delineating of plant communities.

Appropriately, it had been an agriculturist who first perceived some of the key principles involved. In 1785, while acting as a land agent on the Warwickshire-Leicestershire border, William Marshall set about discriminating the different types of local grassland by listing their salient species and trying to work out their proportional occurrence. In *The Rural Economy of the Midland Counties* he commended this exercise to farmers generally, at the same time showing how natural was to be distinguished from artificial woodland and stressing that 'soils will ever find, in process of time, their proper produce'. A few years later the great German explorer, Alexander von Humboldt, offered a detailed equation of the zones of vegetation on high mountains with temperature and other factors, picked out different lifeforms and proposed the mapping of plant associations. Two French marine naturalists followed this up by describing the zonation of the shore and pinpointing various 'indicator' species.

But these were isolated insights. Most of those who attended to such aspects went no further than a crude identification of the factors of soil and climate that determined the distribution of individual species. There was scant attempt to come to grips with the physiological details and scarcely any realization that the plants themselves interacted with one another spatially in an ascertainable order.

Even so there were some who sensed that they were at least close to a key frontier for natural history here. In 1871, in a lecture to the Scientific Society of Winchester, Charles Kingsley felt sufficiently convinced of the central importance of this approach to propose a special name for it: 'bio-geology'. About the same time the Rev. E. A. Woodruffe-Peacock embarked on a 'rock-soil Flora' of Lincolnshire, an impossibly ambitious project which ran to the detailed noting of the full range of environmental conditions under which each species of flowering plant and fern occurred, of the dates of first opening, of all insect visitors and of all the influences on dispersal. The quarter of a million observations that resulted still lie unpublished, sadly neglected, in the Botany School at Cambridge.

In the end it was Vitalism that gave birth to a true ecology in Britain rather than any deliberate scientific endeavour. This primarily philosophical impulse meant that the study developed in this country from a distinctive historical root, which merely served to reinforce a prolonged aversion intellectually to the tradition that came to prevail on the Continent, the elaborate classificatory system identified with the Zürich-Montpellier school of plant sociology.

As one of the founding fathers, Sir Edward Salisbury, has pointed out, British vegetation studies essentially had their origin in the nineties, in the inspiration of two brothers, William and Robert Smith, by the teaching of Patrick Geddes and D'Arcy Thompson at University College, Dundee. To both of the latter the static concept of the Continental ecologists was emotionally repugnant: the whole bias of their minds was towards the unfixed and the fluid. They had eyes only for a Vitalistic mobility, and it was inevitable that those should come to fasten on the dynamic character of vegetational succession. As this presupposed that every area of country had its own idiomatic natural covering, perfectly adapted to and reflecting the wider enviromnental features, it also provided welcome justification for that special ideological passion of Geddes, panoramic regional surveys.

An impressive quantity of work along these last lines was quickly achieved by the Smith brothers, including the production of a number of Ordnance Survey sheets on which the major different types of vegetation were printed in colour. The result was that by the time the leading text advocating the more penetrating approach through physiology, Schimper's *Plant Geography*, had been published in an English translation in 1903, the British ecological world was dominated by the regional-survey enthusiasts. Thus, when late in the following year a Central Committee for the Survey and Study of British Vegetation was formed, signalling the real arrival of the subject in scientific circles in this country, exponents of the 'geographical' approach were able to impose their views. The cleavage persisted till a year or two short of the First World War. At that point the founding of the *Journal of Ecology* and, a few months later, of the British Ecological Society served to consolidate the scene and the triumph of the physiological approach was ensured.

Against the confident expectation of people like A. G. (later Sir Arthur) Tansley, whose *Types of British Vegetation* had lately embodied all the work achieved to date and aimed at reconciling the two contrasting standpoints, the keen interest in ecology shown by many amateurs now fell away. The taking over of the subject by the physiologists at once pushed it outside the amateur domain. The 'geographical' approach, with its description of communities, had had a ready appeal to the ordinary, classification-minded field naturalist; a laboratory-based investigation of processes could only deter him. Matters were made worse by the reckless identifications that now found their way into so much of the ecological literature and by the ponderous discovering of facts which the average experienced amateur had long known perfectly well. It was an alien world that had appeared in the field; and the opportunity of re-uniting professionals and amateurs, which ecology had at first seemed to offer, had to be indefinitely deferred.

Nevertheless, the advent of ecology did bring some benefits to natural history, even while it disappointed functionally. In the first place, it conferred a view-in-the-round that had long been felt to be needed. That other great integrating clutch of principles, the theory of evolution, had proved insufficient on its own for comprehending the natural world. It involved too much still that seemed incapable of proof; it operated too elusively; it was too slow-moving to be readily demonstrable. Ecology, by contrast, was instantly accessible, and it more patently linked in an overall logical framework what had previously been atomized and disjointed. Unlike Evolution, it also stressed mutual interrelationship. To this extent it served, if dimly, as the intellectual sanction for a more constructive ethic.

Above all, the concept of the ecosystem started to accustom naturalists as a whole, no longer only geologists, to visualizing nature as in a perpetual state of flux. In this way it introduced them to a mode of thought more familiar to social science. Like sociologists, psychologists and anthropologists in those formative years just prior to the First World War, they began to re-order their mental imagery so as to conceive of living behaviour as a series of patterned structures, in which all things stand in some defined, systematic relation to all others. It was no coincidence, surely, that Tansley, the commanding figure in British ecology all through the first half of this century, journeyed intellectually in one of these contrapuntal fields, giving the world an influential book, *The New Psychology*, and even travelled to Vienna to study under Freud. The very language of ecology is replete with words echoing that parallel creed of the period: 'association', 'balance', 'complex', 'regression'. At long last, without anyone really noticing, man's view of nature was beginning to be transformed into a finally true reflection of the processes that animated his own mind.

CHAPTER THIRTEEN

A Break for Play

THE DECADE after the First World War was not at first sight an encouraging one for natural history. For a start, the swing against collecting had thrown it seriously off balance. While bird-watchers continued to abound, workers in other fields were fast dying off without replacement. Cabinets of insects, drawers of fossils, neatly labelled herbaria: these were no longer passing on from father to son; instead, the sons were taking up cameras or binoculars or, in outright reaction, rejecting such stuffy Victorianism altogether. In all too many areas of the subject the former profusion of experts had catastrophically disappeared.

This break in the normal succession was compounded by the War itself. Of the entire age-group of young men due to arrive at full maturity in the Great Britain of the mid 1920s, no less than a sixth had been killed. Many of these had been naturalists of promise and were likely to have come to the fore. Now, by their absence, they served only to underline how heavily dependent pursuits like this are ever bound to be on the energies and initiative of the few who stand out from the general run.

Heavy falls in the membership of many of the older societies occurred in consequence, in some cases so drastically that their very continuance was called in question. The Ray Society, a typical example, had been able to boast upwards of 600 subscribers in the palmy 1850s; by 1915 these had dwindled to 262. Few realized that the inevitable wartime erosion masked a deeper and more worrying long-term decline. In entomology, as a careful count of the notes and papers published each year in the three leading specialist journals would have shown, the mid-War low in popularity represented merely a steepening of a general downward trend that had been under way since the turn of the century. After the War the expected revival failed to come about, and by 1931, it has been calculated, there was only one active collector where there had been three or more some forty years earlier.

A further substantial loss of members came with the general bound in subscriptions compelled by the post-War inflation. In a mere twelve months, in 1919–20, wholesale prices spiralled by 50 per cent. Printing costs moved up in parallel and the Penny Post, which had reigned undisturbed ever since 1840, suffered the same, ultimate demise as that other cornerstone of nineteenth-century stability, the Gold Standard. This double blow also meant the end for numerous learned journals and a brutal slimming-down for many of the survivors.

More fundamentally, there was something in the atmosphere of the years following the War that was inimical to earnest endeavours in general. As in that other dead period for natural history, the second quarter of the eighteenth century, the climate had turned bleak, shallow, cynical, restless. The national taste was for less demanding activities. 'It becomes increasingly difficult to fill their places,' Dr Druce observed ruefully in 1925, as he wrote the obituary of yet another one-time stalwart of the Botanical Exchange Club:

> . . . the competing attractions of football, cinemas, golf, revues and dances appear to be too powerful rivals, and one has to acknowledge that the interest in our and other branches of natural science seems to lack the presence of devotees such as the last half of the nineteenth century afforded excellent examples in all grades of life.

Even natural history itself was not immune from these new-fangled infections. In 1926, and in the two years following, that always adventurous body, the Geologists' Association, not content with a conversazione followed by a dinner as the features of its annual get-together in Bloomsbury each November, voted to add to these a dance—with extension till as late as 2 a.m. And there was one local society, too, at least, that fell prey to just these same temptations, its members eagerly rolling back the carpet once the evening's formalities were over, winding up the gramophone and stepping out into a fox-trot or the Charleston.

One reason for the restlessness was the new and exhilarating sense of movement conferred by the ownership of cars. A car was too expensive to be allowed to lie around unused; the Country was in fashion; to have failed to apply the one to the other would have pointed to a shameful lack of ingenuity. One consequence was that 'species-spotting', already a bad disease of natural history, now became epidemic. At the very lowest, like 'Beaver' or collecting car numbers or road signs, it was one of those pastimes that added piquancy to motoring. At its best, it carried naturalists into hitherto undervisited, even unlikely areas—and led to many valuable discoveries. Even so, in essence, it was retrograde: it was merely collecting without the taking, a still largely mindless reflex action which represented improvement only in that it now stopped short of conversion into booty. The hands that had formerly itched so dangerously now occupied themselves with fieldglasses or pencils or cameras; but they continued to itch, none the less, and a great deal of effort had to be devoted simply to keeping them busy.

The more earnestly scientific found it difficult not to deplore these parvenu hundreds of wildlife commuters, who shuttled so ceaselessly to and fro across the countryside, who spent their often endless leisure 'dashing from one sanctuary or haunt of rare species to another, bagging fresh experiences'—like people 'moving on to the next night-club' (to use E. M. Nicholson's contemporary simile). To treat natural history like this was to reduce it to a frivolity, to put it on a par with pogo-sticks or Oxford Bags. It seemed a shocking waste of many a good mind that could have been employed on more constructive work.

In their defence, these motorized huntsmen did have certain extensions to knowledge to point to that would hardly have come about but for their activities. In particular, in their constant casting around for every possibility of bumping up their annual scores, they happened upon some unexpectedly rich sources of rarities in the various forms of waste produced by an increasingly luxurious standard of living. Botanists had long since discovered the special joys of rubbish-dumps; now, bird-watchers woke up to the comparable attractiveness of sewage. This was doubly the outcome of an accident: in 1922, while recuperating from a motor-cycle smash and unaccustomedly townbound as a result, Dr Norman Joy found that the sewage-farm at Reading was a regular haunt of waders and other birds previously thought of as rare or unknown so far inland. He at once made this news public, and very soon all the sewage-farms of any size had equally become a regular haunt of watchers. Around the same time the potential of some of the new and extensive reservoirs was similarly realized.

There was something about this wayward sampling of nature that was peculiarly aristocratic: not too much intensity, not too much probing, a certain languor. What was sought after was not scientific understanding, but a connoisseurship of the countryside. And indeed this social nuance was by no means an illusion. Just as in the eighteenth century, a newly arrived and temporarily prestigious mobility was luring the upper classes out of their normal seclusion and inciting them to travel far afield on journeys of discovery. Once again, High Society had become obsessed with 'Country Life', in which an enthusiasm for natural history was a well-marked and respectable ingredient.

Just how respectable can best be gauged from the fact that in one of the best-selling novels of 1924, John Buchan's *The Three Hostages*, it is not the daring hero but the stuffily conventional Sir Archibald Roylance, that English Clubman incarnate, who proves to have fallen victim to the new bird-watching mania and spends his time dashing hither and thither after Greenshanks and Phalaropes. To go in for such pursuits was no longer the mark of the middle class, let alone of the odd or forgivably eccentric; rather, as the political world was quick to perceive, to be able to present oneself as a countryman at heart, with all that this implied by way of a reassuring simplicity and a firm grasp on fundamentals, had suddenly become a public asset. Today we tend to remember only Baldwin and his pigs, or maybe idly turn the pages of *The Charm of Birds* by that eve-of-war Foreign Secretary, Sir Edward Grey. But there were many others like them in that period for whom nature and the country held a conspicuous appeal that was not necessarily synthetic, however modishly acceptable. Understandably, therefore, it was not without some pique—and irony too—that the one leading political figure of those years with a sound claim in his own right to be a competent all-round natural historian (his large and rich collection of lepidoptera, for example, now graces one of our more important museums) found himself irredeemably identified with the unglamorous antithesis. Neville Chamberlain, alas, with that invariable black umbrella, will always appear the least rustic of our premiers. And yet, as he is said once to have grumbled to a colleague: 'I know every flower; S. B. knows none. I shoot and fish; S. B. does neither. Yet he is known as the countryman and I as the townsman.' In politics, that unfair profession, it is not enough to be the genuine article: it is essential to look the part as well—and it was Stanley Baldwin's great good luck to have the face and physique of a farmer.

Even Labour governments, despite their roots in the streets, were not immune from this rural inclination. Fabians, by tradition, were the heartiest of ramblers and in the spirit of agrarian populism had grown accustomed to work themselves into a fury at the blatant damage to the country's beauty increasingly perpetrated by Money. This was a strand of William Morris Socialism with which that inveterate romantic, Ramsay MacDonald, must have found it particularly easy to identify. Along with his Secretary of State for India, Sydney Olivier, he is known to have toyed with ornithology in later life.

So wide a catchment-area produced a bizarre assortment of enthusiasts: fierce retired rear-admirals, sandalled bohemians, drooping curates, exquisite ladies in tubular gowns and cloche hats. Some very unlikely friendships in time resulted. Henry Salt himself, the arch-progressive who had devoted a lifetime to denouncing violence in all its forms, teamed up with a man who, as head of the Bengal Police, had spent *his* lifetime seeing people sentenced to the lash. One day the two came upon a specially fine array of wild violets. Their wish to see these preserved was mutual; we are not told, however, what Salt's response was when his companion, in a fit of passion, suddenly cried: 'Anyone who picks these ought to be flogged!'

It was in botany, indeed, that the most startling social transformation occurred. To a large extent this was the deliberate doing of that beguiling Arnold Bennett character, George Claridge Druce. Having early showed his flair for constructing societies out of distinctly unpromising membership material, by running up a show-piece one for the town and county of Northampton, Druce had moved on to Oxford and there speedily turned a chemist's in The High into a very prosperous business. At the same time he became first sheriff and then mayor of his adoptive city and made himself into the most active and prolific amateur botanist in Britain. In this last capacity, in the year 1903, he had succeeded to the little-valued office of honorary secretary of the Botanical Exchange Club, which hitherto had consisted very largely of organizing the annual parcelling-out of specimens and arranging for a short report to be printed, embodying the comments made on these by the various contributors and referees.

This was no job for someone of Druce's ambition and abilities. Almost at once he had set out to graft a new and different structure a society in the full meaning of the word, no less—on to this largely wilted stem of what had once been the Botanical Society of London. Ever since that had collapsed in the 1850s, field botany in Britain had clearly been flagging for want of a proper coordinating body. Instead of founding one *ab initio*—which would have been seriously divisive—Druce's instinct had been to work for a surreptitious altering in content of the existing B.E.C.

To this end he started off by slipping the word 'Society' into the long-familiar title. Then, in order to justify this with some substance, he proceeded to scour the country for likely-looking members. There he made use of one particularly cunning dodge. This was to delight chosen individuals with the unsought news that the Society had elected them to honorary membership—and then the very next year dun them for a subscription (which hardly anyone had the courage to refuse).

By means of this and other devices the Society grew fast and impressively. So, in step with it, did Druce's prestige. By a combination of charm, audacity, unsurpassable industry, even a certain deviousness, he quickly achieved an almost magical supremacy. Like Smith and Jameson before him, he had formed an indissoluble attachment to the body of which he was—in effect—the begetter. Unlike them, he did not even have to worry about acting constitutionally: to all intents and purposes there was no constitution. It was essentially *his* society—and in return for acceptance of this fact (for he was ever impatient of criticism, acutely sensitive beneath his mask of worldliness) he was happy to play the part of a benevolent philosopher-king, making authoritative pronouncements, raising and handing out largesse, cultivating alliances, giving help to anyone who seemed in need of it ('If the plant is too abstruse', in the words of a contemporary ditty, 'pack it off to Dr Druce'). Blessed with a venerable appearance, he finally found himself lionized and progressively and resplendently belaurelled—not least with two honorary degrees and an F.R.S.: no mean prize for a non-experimentalist, and an amateur, and a largely self-educated amateur at that, even as far back as the later 1920s.

After his death, in 1932, the Society was hurriedly placed on a democratic footing. But it was not for some years even then that the full extent of his feat was realized. For while he had done field botany in this country a tremendous service, by putting together and passing on the necessary substantial basis for what has since become the flourishing Botanical Society of the British Isles, it eventually came to light that much of this had been achieved by a sleight of hand. As a later honorary treasurer quickly found, the membership records—such as they were—bore singularly little relation to the advertised reality. Many whose names had long featured in the printed lists had not paid a subscription in years. Some were not even aware of being members. As Swainson would have said of the Society, there was 'quackery in its composition'. Druce, in short, had been nourishing a phantom: without his constant, secret financial intercession the Society would have amounted to nothing very much.

In part, he was probably no more than a victim of optimism. At the time it must have seemed reasonable to assume that most of the enthusiastic newcomers he was managing to turn up would stay permanently enlisted. In any case, field botany gave every appearance of having come to stay as a fashionable pursuit in high circles: as it inevitably filtered downwards, far greater numbers of recruits could be confidently predicted.

Unfortunately the popularity he witnessed was deceptive. Much of it, we now know, derived from a passing fancy among a group of Edwardian debutantes. Among these a competition had caught on in 'painting one's Bentham' (more accurately, painting one's Fitch and Smith—for Bentham, for all his virtues, was not responsible for the volume of black-and-white figures that was later issued as a supplement to his long-popular *Hand-book*). The rules were that one must hunt down every wild flower illus-trated in that volume, searching them out for oneself in their natural hab-itats and registering each new addition by painting it in straight from life. For most of them it turned into an enduring interest. But just because of its coterie character, all who shared in it tended to be acquainted with one another. It was thus a comparatively easy matter for Druce to sweep them into the net more or less at once. The sudden, strongly blueblooded influx that this meant may well have misled him into supposing that there was a large potential following for the study in such circles still waiting to be won. It was to help shake this loose, one must suppose, that he embarked on his shameless policy of especially enrolling the titled. All through the twenties never less than one member in every eight of that very unusual Society either belonged to the peerage, possessed a knighthood, or was something both grand and exotic—such as a maharajah. No wonder the professionals of the day tended to look at it askance.

In the event, the return to the natural history scene of this long-absent section of society proved to be a transient phenomenon. After the end of the twenties High Society—in so far as its prevalence had at the best of times been more than an optical illusion—receded into inconspicuousness.

Yet without the fashion that had served to bring such people into the field in the first place, natural history would probably never have acquired even the few who remained. And without their presence in its counsels, natural history between the Wars—and, still more, subsequently—would have been a good deal less bold and effective in quarters where it was vital that its voice should not go unheard. Thanks to the accident of this deep infiltration into Clubland, the cause of Conservation, for a start, is unlikely to have triumphed so steadily and surely as it later did. From this time forward it was this true representativeness that was to be for the subject one of its greatest strengths.

CHAPTER FOURTEEN

The Eventual Combining

ON ANOTHER FRONT, meanwhile, natural history had suddenly woken up. In that very same city from which Druce was stage-managing his amateur theatricals, plans were being laid for what was to prove to be the final 'take-off'. Oxford, in those few years of recuperation immediately following the War, also chanced to house an unusually serious and thoughtful crop of undergraduates. Many of these shared the conviction that this was a moment to be designing new and better worlds, gathering up the fragments of what was left from pre-war days and re-fashioning them into something finer and more enduring.

Among the many who inhaled this heady atmosphere were two young men who also happened to be fanatical ornithologists. One of these was B. W. Tucker, then reading zoology under Julian Huxley and shortly to become himself one of the University's teachers of that subject. The other was E. M. Nicholson, by contrast a historian and for long an amateur in the subject, but destined to rival De la Beche in the bountifulness of a career of natural history institution-building. Each in his own way exemplified that always rare being, the practical visionary. Between them they founded modern British field ornithology, to such effect and with so sure a touch that it has continued to thrive basically unchanged and has gone on to influence many of its sister studies.

They were, as we have just seen, fortunate in their time and place. They were also fortunate to find themselves among a sizeable number of similarly inclined contemporaries. These were sufficient to justify the forming, in 1921, of an Oxford Ornithological Society—in its very name proclaiming a conscious break with the broader natural history of the past. Like that other small circle of bright young men who came together as the Botanical Society of Edinburgh almost a century earlier, this was to have an impact out of all proportion to its size or to the youthfulness of its members. For in a field without professionals anyone lucky enough to carry away from this most intense and formative period in life a dearly visualized programme is always bound to be at an advantage. If, as well, those who shared the thinking and the convictions that went into the formulation of this continue to keep in touch and see themselves as the vanguard of something important and new, then their dominance is likely to be total.

Like the Edinburgh botanists again, the Oxford ornithologists put their trust in Method. They saw that voluntary studies were unlikely to be scientifically very productive without careful forethought and disciplined rigour. Planning was in any case the hero of the hour and an irresistible ingredient in the average fledgeling ideology. Had they not chanced to be naturalists, some larger area of life would assuredly have been found to express this insistent trend of their energies. As it was, several of the most prominent advocates of the novel cooperative work on birds did go on to play a similarly catalytic role in the comparable study of human beings: Tom Harrisson, fresh from the experience of censusing the country's grebes, co-founded Mass-Observation; Nicholson and Huxley both helped to launch the new social and economic research institute, P.E.P.

The Oxford Ornithological Society was in the main the contribution of Tucker. From the start he acted as its honorary secretary, and for most of the next thirty years the many new paths it set out on were principally due to him. Though shy and modest, he combined a glittering selection of virtues and talents: infectious enthusiasm, an insatiable appetite for work, an all-round engagement in the subject, a flair for committees. Early on, he was also able to draw on the experience of one of the greatest of the Edwardian veterans, the formidable Jourdain, who by good fortune was then a country rector in the vicinity of Abingdon, conveniently near at hand. With Jourdain as the Society's co-editor, a very high standard was virtually guaranteed; and in the years that followed the two made the annual Oxford bird reports—and, in a wider sense, the Society itself—the model for all the other specialist ornithological societies that presently came into existence, appreciably raising the general level of accuracy in published records.

While Tucker was thus busily engaged in rehearsing the orchestra, Nicholson was giving a masterly solo performance on the trumpet. His contribution, that is to say, was first and foremost as a propagandist. *Birds in England,* published in 1926, when he was still only twenty-two, was the first of a sudden volley of books (to say nothing of articles in numerous periodicals, from the *New Statesman* downwards) in which he sought to capture the attention of a wider public and persuade it of the need for major changes in the approach then prevaling.

Birds in England: An Account of the State of Our Bird-Life and A Criticism of Bird Protection—to give its full title—is a fascinating book, from several aspects and on more than one level. As the subtitle rather hints, with its faint suggestion of a socio-political tract, it is essentially a polemic: the spirited manifesto of someone who has recently seen the light—one who, 'until four years ago', was even a collector of eggs.

Since the War, the book begins by pointing out, a considerable re-crudescence of collecting has been taking place, most of it at the hands of ex-Army men and successful merchants—a new element unexposed to the previously established constraints. Such behaviour, however, while repre-hensible, is only part of a more general tendency with which the subject is presently afflicted: 'a modern selfish lust for quantities and records', so overridingly obsessive that it now almost chokes what is in true reality 'an ancient reasonable hobby'. With or without the gun, it all boils down to much the same. Ornithology is being chronically distorted and stunted by the empty competition of the bag. And while there have grown up the now standard counterblasts to this, 'the foolish one-sided tirades' of the protectionists, these can hardly be regarded as a constructive alternative: they merely amount to an over-reacting emotionalism. Instead, in place of both—and this is the main theme of the book—what is urgently required is the more mature point of view represented by the newly emergent study of the 'balance' of birds (the actual title given to two consecutive chapters) and of their relation to the habitat: 'their ecology, as a botanist would call it'.

With admirable insight, Nicholson had perceived the significance of var-ious apparently unrelated thrusts in knowledge just then becoming evident and at once discerned that what was coming into view was a revitalizing integration. Here was the patently right route out of the current impasse. Unlike those before him who had also sensed an impending deliverance through ecology, he was able to temper his excitement with a cool ap-praisal of the form in which this was likely to come about and identify with some precision those existing elements in the study most responsive to a helping nudge in that direction. Nor was he misled into supposing that the course of ornithology must necessarily resemble that of botany. His grasp of its shape was sufficient to warn him that the study must be allowed to develop in its own way and that the eventual pattern might be very different. For his own part he showed himself prepared to feel his way forward and rely on intuition.

1927, the year which saw the appearance of his next book—*How Birds Live* (with, as before, a sting in the sub-title: *Bird Life in the Light of Modern Observation*)—was also the year of the first major organizational advance. Tucker had then just returned to Oxford after a brief spell at Cambridge. With the benefit now of his entire attention, and with Nicholson only one of many contributing their forceful energies to it, the Oxford Ornithological Society quickly became a kettle on the boil. It was clearly the moment for a move; and, largely on Tucker's initiative, 'The Oxford Bird Census' was launched.

At first this hardly amounted to anything very substantial. It was a convenient label for a long-term programme of a certain distinctive kind of work, which happened also to serve as the proving-ground of the novel method of team-research. One showpiece example of this, the first cooperative trapping station of any size to be established in Britain, was set up in Christ Church Meadow that autumn. Visited four times a day by different people working on a rota, this not only performed its avowed function with efficiency but also served to illustrate how, by simply pooling their efforts, groups of individuals could bring into being new kinds of research facilities which made possible lines of inquiry that they could not hope to embark on on their own.

But it was census work, as its name implied, with which this new organization was more especially identified. Here, the results of the small-scale, exploratory work that it was able to achieve proved so encouraging that in the very next year Nicholson was emboldened to try his hand at the first, true mass-count of a single species, with a view to demonstrating the possibilities to the bird world in general.

For this purpose the Heron, by virtue of being big and more or less unmistakable and building bulky nests in colonies, was an ideal subject. And *British Birds,* because of its uniquely wide coverage and in recognition of the fact that it was already identified in people's minds as a seasoned exponent of this particular type of undertaking, similarly commended itself as the overall sponsor and the main medium of communication. At the same time, it offered a useful means of formally linking the new Oxford outlook with that other older-established but equally progressive tradition in British ornithology specifically associated with Witherby.

British Birds, however, was not relied upon exclusively in raising the necessary large corps of volunteers. In keeping with the much more ambitious scale on which Nicholson now proposed to operate, appeals were published in other leading specialist periodicals, in a great many local newspapers and even in the *Daily Mail* (making this probably the first occasion on which the natural history world had ventured on national advertising). Altogether, just under four hundred people registered to assist as a result—and probably another four hundred took part of whom no actual record was kept. This was a far larger number than had ever combined in a single, very short-term project (all previous record-collecting networks on this scale had, by comparison, been leisurely, long-drawn-out affairs) and, inevitably, the administrative effort required was prodigious. This was considerably eased by two important innovations. The first was a system of delegating responsibility for certain large portions of the country to some of the most reliable among those assisting. The second was the extensive use made of private cars.

The operation proved a huge success. The first reasonably complete national census of a resident bird had been accomplished; a great deal of attention and enthusiasm had been aroused; the machinery had been installed for the future. The final score—roughly eight occupied nests to every one observer—was also testimony that the coverage could be made sufficiently intensive to allay reservations about the general accuracy of the method.

The Great Crested Grebe Inquiry followed three years later, in 1931. The scale this time was much larger still. The bird chosen, moreover, was less familiar and more elusive in its habits. Nevertheless, making use of the lessons already learned, the two organizers, Tom Harrisson and P. A. D. Hollom, set to work to raise a fresh volunteer army. Their press campaign was truly stupendous: apart from notices in daily, evening, local, weekly and even sporting papers, *The Times* carried a special feature, selected learned journals published articles on the project, and the B.B.C. even broadcast an appeal for volunteers, just before the general News. The harvest this time proved to be over 1,300—three times the number that had taken part on the previous occasion. Every piece of fresh water in England and Wales over four acres in extent was visited by at least one observer in the course of the year, and in all about 2,650 adult birds were recorded— an even more startling ratio of two birds to every one observer.

Although some financial support was provided by Witherby and his journal, any project on this scale was bound to leave some of the participants heavily out of pocket. Quite apart from this, Harrisson and Hollom, though spare-time workers only, found themselves having to cope with 5,000 letters from fifteen different countries, while also writing personally to every well-known ornithologist in Britain, to many local naturalists, to taxidermists, town clerks, landowners and such clergymen as they could trace with lakes in their parishes.

Obviously, at this rate, the supply of capable people willing to run a major national inquiry would soon be running out. Some means had to be found of running the machine in lower throttle; and in order to permit this, some established body had to be found to take over the task as a permanent routine and thus make possible the abandonment of this ruinously *ad hoc* way of operating. But the snag was that the projects had now become so daunting in their scope that none of the conceivable candidates was likely to be keen on this. The only alternative, therefore, seemed to be to float an organization that was entirely new and that would have the advantage of being tailor-made.

As it happened, other developments had begun to point in this same direction. Firstly, there had been a quantum jump in the size of the following for the study. Between 1925 and 1930 the number enrolled in the *British Birds* Ringing Scheme suddenly leapt by 150 per cent. Reflecting this, in 1928 the London Natural History Society found it necessary to appoint a special Bird Ringing Secretary. Two years later, when Julian Huxley, in the course of a series of radio talks on bird-watching, requested information on the attacking of crocuses by sparrows, more than a hundred letters resulted.

Secondly, the Oxford Bird Census had become sufficiently firmly established to afford a paid Director. This was in 1930, the appointment going to W. B. Alexander, a veteran of ornithological work in Australia. The funds came from the Ministry of Agriculture and the new Empire Marketing Board, on the strength of a programme of research with a strong applied slant.

With its existence thereby assured for at least three years further, the Census now began to appear as the obvious organizational trellis over which could be trained a broader-based Institute of Field Ornithology such as Nicholson and Tucker had for some years been envisioning. 'Ornithology urgently needs a general staff to direct and make effective its efforts', he had lately written; and as his metaphors turned military, it had become increasingly apparent what he had in mind.

In May 1932 matters came out into the open, with the designation of a 'British Trust for Ornithology'. In this was to be vested the money for just such an institute—assuming the requisite sum could first be raised. A public appeal for the purpose was thereupon launched, with £8,000 as the stated target.

For once things failed to go as planned. While the University was prepared to support the scheme to the extent of providing free accommodation, it was not yet ready to do more. Worse, the appeal itself was savaged by the Slump and turned out extremely disappointing. The one bright feature was the generosity of Witherby, who, as a token of his fervent approval of all that the Oxford scheme stood for sold his extensive collection of bird-skins to the British Museum (Natural History) and donated to the Trust a large part of the proceeds. Even then, the total amount fell far short of what had been envisaged. And although the Trust (with Nicholson, entirely appropriately, as its first honorary secretary) duly went through the various intended motions, what emerged was a sadly truncated entity. At the same time, if it was still in essence the Oxford Bird Census which it had been meant to supersede, the fact that it now had a national status was an important advance. This at least ensured that it became the accepted focus for cooperative research on birds in this country and was able to lay its plans accordingly.

The first signs of succour eventually came in 1938. In that year the University at last saw its way to conferring formal recognition and started contributing a small annual grant. Not long after, a legal initiative enabled £3,000 to be transferred to it from the Viscount Grey Memorial Fund. This finally made it possible to realize the original conception, and in gratitude it was christened the Edward Grey Institute of Field Ornithology.

———

In the meantime, another aspect of the 'take-off' was in the process of being accomplished in quite a different quarter—and with notably fewer problems. This was the establishment of bird observatories in the fullest sense.

Once again, the roots of this lead back to the Oxford Ornithological Society. In this instance, it was W. B. Alexander who provided the continuing inspiration. Very soon after arriving to take up his post with the Oxford Bird Census, he succeeded in infecting a number of others in the Society with enthusiasm for this very special hobby-horse of his, with the result that in 1931–2 a preliminary trial of the idea was carried out on Holy Island, off the Northumberland coast. Although this had precedents in the much earlier, embryonic attempts of Eagle Clarke, Gätke and others, the possibilities had largely become lost to sight in this country. A fresh impulse had now been provided by the Dutch, whose *Vogeltrekstation* on the island of Texel had lately made a name for itself and set off a revival of interest in visible migration. Behind this Dutch work, in turn, lay still more impressive achievements on the part of the Germans and the Swiss, more particularly on Heligoland. Here, an ingenious, funnel-shaped type of trap long in use among the locals for catching the large flocks of thrushes that regularly descend on the island had been converted to scientific ends. The 'Heligoland-Trap' proved so efficient that it came to be regarded as the vital centre-piece of any other ringing-station set up along these lines. A trip to Heligoland, accordingly, was the obvious next step for Alexander and his team.

They were able to make this in 1933—and returned with their enthusiasm redoubled. One of the party, R. M. Lockley, was in the rare and enviable position, it so happened, of actually living on an islet perfect for just such a venture. This was Skokholm, at the mouth of the British Channel, which he had been able to lease for an almost nominal £26 a year. Here, in his vegetable garden, a faithful replica of the *troosel-goard* of the Heligolanders was speedily erected later that year, and in the following summer—on very much the Lambay pattern—he welcomed a relay of visiting ornithologists as paying guests to help him with its operation.

Although Skokholm ranked as the first bird observatory of the modern type to start up in this country, it was for long a private and essentially individual undertaking. The credit for the first to be run and manned throughout on a cooperative basis belongs instead to a group of Edinburgh schoolboys, headed by George Waterston, who about that time had constituted themselves as the Midlothian Ornithological Club. In January 1934, at their instigation, one of the leading scientific societies in that city, the Royal Physical, had enthusiastically adopted a resolution that a bird observatory should be established on the nearby Isle of May (which Miss Baxter and Miss Rintoul had highlighted already as unusually well-favoured for the study of migration). This led to Alexander and Lockley being invited north to contribute their experience; and by September of that year the youthful members of the Midlothian Club had the Heligoland Trap they had dreamed of and were hard at work out in the Firth of Forth. This and Skokholm were to remain the only British observatories until after the Second World War.

Oxford was the source of yet one further breakthrough that came in that brief span of years around the end of the twenties. Once more it was substantially the work of a member of that first post-War wave of undergraduates—and also, like Tucker, a one-time pupil of Julian Huxley's. This was Charles Elton.

Although Huxley's own deep interest in bird behaviour played its part, the advances already made by botanists in comprehending the dynamics of vegetation could hardly fail to turn the attention of some of the younger zoologists in the same direction. Because they lent themselves much less obviously to analysis in terms of communities, being on the whole less static as well as commonly invisible, animals had tended to be ignored as a field for ecology, at least in this country. The early geographical bias of the science doubtless also acted as a deterrent, for on the whole animals were less amenable to mapping. For a considerable time, in so far as there was any animal ecology at all in Britain, it remained pre-eminently marine, the very obtrusiveness of the intertidal zonation leading to a spill-over of botanical activity into the sphere of zoology.

The first notable attempt to interest the ornithological world in work along these lines seems to have been in 1914. In that year, in a lengthy paper in *British Birds*, S. E. Brock pointed out various apparent correlations between bird-distribution and the types of community distinguished by plant ecologists. In 1921 he followed this up with an account of 'Bird Associations in Scotland', published in the *Scottish Naturalist*. His whole approach, unfortunately, was conceived from too dominant a botanical standpoint to capture the imagination of students of birds; and the same could be said of a later, more ambitious paper by W. H. Thorpe in 1925.

By that time other studies were beginning to appear in the more orthodox behaviourist tradition that stemmed from Darwin and Lubbock. In 1922 H. M. Morris produced the results of a census of all the invertebrates located in a small stretch of arable soil at Rothamsted. Shortly after, a stream of papers on the habits of spiders began to come from W. S. Bristowe, and C. B. Williams started out on a long-term programme of work on the migration of insects which was to extend to scrutiny of aerial currents. These were signs that a groundswell of interest was building up at last among non-marine zoologists as well.

We have Tansley's word for it that it was in the mid-1920s that the botanical side of the science also gave the first definite evidence of prospering—due in no small part to his own, enormously popular textbook *Practical Plant Ecology*, which was chiefly instrumental in securing its acceptance in both the universities and schools. The moment was evidently ripe for a parallel zoological initiative; and in 1927 Elton came up with a book that was speedily to become a classic, *Animal Ecology*. Through this, and through subsequent papers and books, Elton introduced into general currency a well-articulated body of theory that stood comparison with anything so far elaborated for plants, popularizing notions such as food-chains, habitat niches and the natural regulation of numbers which instantly rang more true with those familiar with the patterns characteristic of the animal kingdom. Within five years the number of zoologists in the ranks of the British Ecological Society had grown so large and their interests so broadly different that a separate *Journal of Animal Ecology* was having to be hived off for them. The founding in 1930 of the Freshwater Biological Association and in 1932 of an Oxford sister to Nicholson's ornithological institute, Elton's own special Bureau of Animal Population, was also further evidence that they were fast developing institutional muscle.

'Population' was now a key word of the period. Zoologists as well as botanists were learning to view nature as a mosaic of collective entities, each with its own internal dynamics and flux of variation. The work of

Turesson in Sweden, disclosed in a long series of papers starting in 1922, alerted botanists to the use of techniques of experimental cultivation for studying plant species in terms of the genetical make-up of their different spatial portions. Work of this kind in Britain developed in the 1930s and became associated more particularly with the names of W. B. Turrill, a member of the herbarium staff at Kew, and his regular collaborator, E. Marsden-Jones, an amateur and a landowner experimentalist in the best traditions of the past. The zoological counterpart of this 'genecology' was similarly to be unfolded in the 1930s, though somewhat later, at the hands of another fruitful amateur-professional partnership, this time between another Oxford professional, E. B. Ford, and a schoolmaster, W. H. Dowdeswell. Their work on the genetical structure of populations of butterflies and moths also gained from the active interest of R. A. Fisher, who was engaged in these years in the epochmaking task of furnishing conclusive statistical proof of evolution and underpinning Darwinian theory with an updated Mendelism. Unfortunately, the heavily quantitative approach that this involved removed it from the attention of all but a very few.

Such partnerships between amateurs and professionals signalled a growing convergence at last between natural history and biology. More and more, the average field worker was being familiarized with a variety of novel scientific methods and expertise, in part grounded in the laboratory and requiring a more or less professional level of competence for their productive application. The lineaments of the so-called 'New Naturalist' were emerging: the upholder of the great field tradition who was nevertheless ready to make use of these fresh forms of knowledge in order to make his understanding of nature more incisive and at the same time more helpful for scientific purposes. The sense of direction that had been lost with the passing of private collecting was now being recovered in this hopeful re-fusion.

In 1928, as if to celebrate this event, the British Ecological Society announced a major collective undertaking of its own: the *Biological Flora of the British Isles*. This was to consist of the serial publication in its own journal of exhaustive studies of the ecology and behaviour of each of the individual species of flowering plant and fern on the British list, contributed by different authors. The scheme had a magnificent all-inclusiveness that was as optimistic as it was bold. It was clearly going to require very many years to be brought to completion, even though it was fortunately a task that called for relatively little coordination.

The *Biological Flora* showed that the ecological world was surging with confidence. Increasingly, this now began to brim over into every corner of natural history. At the same time ecologists themselves started to become a major force in a wider setting, exercising a valuable binder effect on the many hitherto disparate and semi-isolated branches of the subject, stiffening it throughout with a healthy re-orientation in outlook and contributing to its counsels some exceptionally wide-thinking people, many of whom were to play a leading role in the later campaign for a government initiative on conservation.

The point had now been reached when other branches of natural history could be expected to try to reproduce some of the organizational achievements of the ornithologists. As they could not field such numbers, these attempts were necessarily going to have to be more modest. As latecomers, too, they could scarcely hope to repeat the dash of the original explorers. But even allowing for these handicaps, the response was singularly slow and disappointing.

The inertia of the botanists, in particular, was made more marked by the launching at that very point in time of the immense Land Utilization Survey of England and Wales (a mere two years after the much-publicized Census of Heronries). Organized under the auspices of the Geographical Association, this was just the kind of exercise in thorough spatial coverage that held a natural appeal for the average field botanist and in other circumstances would have prompted a major distribution mapping scheme (such as was eventually to be undertaken in the 1950s). As it was, the chief national body, the Botanical Society and Exchange Club, was in an abnormally dazed condition, trying to recover its balance after the traumatic loss of Druce. The most it was capable of at that juncture was an overdue tightening-up of its record-accepting procedures and, at the instance of its new honorary secretary, W. H. Pearsall, the instituting of a system of decentralization in the form of county Local Secretaries, 'to secure completeness and accuracy in our records of plant distribution and its periodic changes . . . and to whom we can refer botanical inquiries as to their authenticity'. Clearly, it had yet to progress beyond the stage reached by British ornithology back in the days of Jourdain and Witherby.

The entomologists did a great deal better. In 1931 a retired naval officer, Captain T. Dannreuther, working through his local society, the Hastings and St Leonards N.H.S., brought into being an Insect Immigration Committee. The idea behind this was in effect to replicate the system perfected in the eighties for the study of migration in birds. Though it was originally intended to be confined to the South East, Dr C. B. Williams of Rothamsted Experimental Station—for whom this presented an excellent opportunity of securing large quantities of data to further his professional research in this direction—was able to prevail on the Committee to make the scope national. A standard record card was devised and, following a notice inserted in numerous journals, a good flow of volunteers came in and were each equipped with a supply. For over twenty years Captain Dann-reuther was to run the scheme single-handed, making himself responsible for the gathering in of the cards and then passing them on to Rothamsted for detailed analysis and storage. The results appeared annually as special reports in the *Entomologist*.

While less spectacular than some of the survey work on birds, this well-conceived undertaking was successful to the extent of latterly being copied by the Dutch—a high tribute indeed. It was also of great importance his-torically, for it was the first case ever in which amateur volunteers carried out work of this type expressly on behalf of professional scientists who had no direct hand in the administrative operation. In this respect it was a significant advance on the studies associated with Eagle Clarke, signalling that the amateurs now had in their gift a new scientific tool capable of procuring certain types of information which the professional, working on his own, unaided, could not hope to come by. Suddenly the Amateur had become scientifically indispensable.

Even had this been generally realized, however, the situation would scarcely have been welcomed unreservedly. There were many naturalists who were frankly hostile to what they saw as the advent of a bureaucratiza-tion of the subject. Indeed, it cannot be pretended that doubters do not continue to exist. For some, form-filling of any kind is deeply distasteful: it bears the mark of the official and seems out of keeping with a subject that for so many represents a thankful escape from the daily routines of the office. There are others, too, who claim to detect in all this emphasis on drills and discipline, on team-work and training, the nasty smell of over-organization, sufficient to stifle the essential spontaneity. More than one natural history journal bears in its back-issues the bullet-holes of the peri-odic sniping that has broken out over this.

Undeniably, mistakes have been made. Those who shuffled the paper at the end of the lines of communication have sometimes been guilty of re-moteness or have fallen prey to other insidious diseases to which the chair-bound are prone. On occasion, the amassing of records has seemed to become an end in itself or to be undertaken merely in order to satisfy the appetite of the teams of volunteers. Even when the purpose was apparent and important, at times the resulting data have been allowed to lie ne-glected and a mountain of labour misused to bring forth the proverbial mouse. Too often, the groundwork supplied by these means has been left under-exploited.

Yet, despite these imperfections, it was apparent from the first that the new methods had come to stay. Without them, natural history would have found it infinitely harder to progress. Those who found them distasteful just had to bear with them and prosecute their preferred alternatives regardless.

As Nicholson himself was to stress much later, the fear that the subject would somehow suffer injury from this development has in the event proved groundless:

> . . . on the contrary, fuller organization has released more abundant energy and ideas in an unprecedented wave of vitality and creative growth . . . Within this supple and responsive system . . . the influence of the individual is not diminished but intensified and speeded up.

Another, later, secretary of the B.T.O. perhaps put the matter best of all:

> There is a strong case for a purely recreational interest in nature, but this has not necessarily anything to do with field study . . . for scientific ends, which demands submission to a self-imposed discipline and recognition that the commonplace is ultimately more exciting than the unusual, and the abnormal only to be appreciated when the normal, from which it departs, is intimately known.

Appropriately, the thirties closed with the appearance of two majestic works of synthesis. One was Tansley's formidable compendium, *The British Islands and their Vegetation*, published in 1939. The other was the still more massive *Handbook of British Birds*, which began to appear in 1938 and continued over into 1941, under the joint authorship of Witherby, Jourdain, Ticehurst and Tucker. As the title of the latter implied (though not quite truthfully: it was, in fact, a very hefty armful), it was conceived as an updated version of the essential text of the previous generation, Witherby's *Practical Handbook of British Birds*, which had finally passed out of print in 1934. Tansley's work, similarly, was essentially an expansion of his *Types of British Vegetation* of 1911. The fact that both of them now, without undergoing any major change in pattern, had swollen to almost unmanageable dimensions—in the case of the *Handbook* to as many as five separate volumes—was evidence in itself of the sheer size of the progress in knowledge that had been accomplished during the intervening period. There could have been no more fitting monument to the preceding thirty years of extraordinary endeavour than these two great bibles, in which the combined labours of British naturalists up to that time were so triumphantly encapsulated.

Natural history in Britain now entered a veritable golden age. With the machinery perfected, the prosperity of the subject was assured. Year by year the numbers grew; and contrary to what might so easily have happened—as had happened already once before, at the time of that previous spurt, back in the 1850s—there was no noticeable falling-off in the quality of the work. This time the subject expanded without outgrowing its strength.

So great was the momentum that had been developed that not even the coming of war could halt the ever-mounting flow of recruits. By lucky timing, James Fisher's *Watching Birds* came out in 1940—hardly the most auspicious of years—and provided a rescuing boost. A classic of its kind, this set out to expound the new approach, and to communicate the appeal of the study more generally, to a vast lay audience that it had not previously been possible to reach. Partly as a result, between 1939 and 1944 the membership of the British Trust for Ornithology very nearly doubled— and that at a time when many a line of work that had come to depend on unimpeded movement around the countryside had been brought to a sudden stop.

Even this widespread frustration of fieldwork was turned to fruitful ends. The cooped-up enthusiasm spilled out into still more audacious plans for the shape of natural history in the years of peace ahead. That brief, profusely fertile spell of idealism in mid-war that produced for the wider world the Beveridge Report and the 1944 Education Act was productive for naturalists as well. An entirely novel type of institution, a major departure in publishing, and the start of far greater involvement with government were the three most notable outcomes. The first was the residential 'field centre'—an idea born of the wartime evacuation to the countryside of a London schools inspector, F. H. C. Butler. The second was the *New Naturalist* Series, an unprecedented attempt at combining popularized scholarship, enticing production and the propagation of a distinctive outlook while also, in the process, proving the existence of a worthwhile market at this level to an exasperatingly unadventurous book trade. The third was the succession of authoritative pronouncements, commencing with the report of the Scott Committee on Land Utilization in Rural Areas in 1942, advocating the setting up under government auspices of a national system of nature reserves.

All three initiatives were to prove far-reaching, particularly the last; for out of it, in March 1949, after much patient piloting through an archipelago of committees, came the legislation formally bringing into being the Nature Conservancy.

Thus was achieved the culminating head-piece of a dogged programme of building that stretched back by then almost thirty years. And as if to underline this fact, after an initial and crucial three years under Captain Cyril Diver, there appeared in the Director-General's seat none other than that New Naturalist incarnate, the forceful and imaginative Nicholson.

With the establishment of this body the naturalists of Great Britain (though not, alas, of the whole of the British Isles) acquired what amounted to a kind of merchant bank, designed to serve many of their own special needs. Not only were funds now to be made available, on a hitherto unheard-of scale, for investing in a wide range of medium- and long-term undertakings; but there was also to be a large, permanent and highly skilled staff, which above its ordinary managerial functions would be engaging in recondite operations on its own private behalf and constituting a powerful extra source of entrepreneurial energies. From this point on many a worth-while project that formerly might have grounded, or not even started off at all, for want of more than the inescapably fitful attentions of amateur part-timers, could be confidently put under way in the knowledge that, if the worst should come to the worst, there was always the possibility of this ultimate sustainer. Even better, henceforward there would always exist the chance, as well, that if an established project had outrun the means of its initiators to support it any longer, or at least to continue it on the scale it seemed to merit, the burden might then be transferred to those far better-endowed shoulders.

An early and outstanding beneficiary of this was the British Trust for Ornithology—so much so that by the mid 1960s almost half its annual income was made up of grants awarded from public funds. With this substantial underpinning it was able to expand from one solitary full-time employee lodged cheaply in a garret (in the person of Bruce Campbell) to a staff of twenty-three accommodated in its own imposing headquarters— despite a membership of only around 4,000 and a subscription as low as thirty shillings.

For other bodies not yet ready for the luxury of their own researchers-in-residence the arrival of the Conservancy was no less providential. The Botanical Society of the British Isles, when the great distribution mapping scheme it pioneered in 1954–62 officially came to an end, was able to pass straight over to it the bank of over a million records, the specially developed data-processing machinery and even the full-time team with their unique expertise. These now became the nucleus of a national Biological Records Centre, to act as the counterpart for all other branches of natural history of the type of permanent collecting-office-cum-service bureau already long in existence in ornithology. Under the auspices of the Conservancy, and with updated equipment, this has since revolutionized the study of plant and animal distribution in these islands, with a whole volley of national mapping schemes for a wide range of different organisms.

But it was on the conservation scene, as was only to be expected, that the new body had its most bracing impact. A good scatter of National Nature Reserves and Sites of Special Scientific Interest was almost immediately conjured into being, while a large and varied programme of research on problems relevant to the management of these was launched in the universities and within the Conservancy itself. In 1956, with its active prodding, county naturalists' trusts began to multiply and progressively to cover the country. 1958 brought the Council for Nature, 1959 the Conservation Corps, 1963 National Nature Week, 1970 European Conservation Year. Little of all this would have come about without the Conservancy's background presence and perpetual surreptitious nourishment.

It is too early yet to attempt in detail the history of these most recent years. When the time for that comes, however, we can be sure that conservation will stand out as the dominant impulse of the period. But it will not stand alone; and already one can begin to discern some of the subordinate currents that have simultaneously been shaping the subject.

Among these the most important is likely to be growth—growth in numbers, growth in complexity of organization, growth in the sheer scope of knowledge. Growth can be exhilarating, but there is always a price to be paid for it. There are new strains on natural history today which are largely the outcome of its very success.

The problem of numbers came into view all of a sudden in the middle 1950s. It coincided with the end of petrol rationing and the start of the economic boom with its consequent explosion in car ownership. The spread of television no doubt helped—though it was birds that more or less monopolized the natural history screened and the change in character was by no means limited to just this branch of the subject. What happened, in effect, was the acquiring of an extra dimension. Natural history began to take on some of the characteristics of contemporary mass society, betraying an unaccustomed receptiveness to publicity.

The most visible manifestation was the invasion of the field by crowds. In the summer of 1955 not less than 1,000 people turned up to see a pair of Bee-eaters nesting in a sandpit in Sussex—some of them even in specially organized coach-parties. Four years later over 14,000 descended on the remote loch in the north-west of Scotland where the first nesting of Ospreys in this country for fifty years had been announced, queueing up to peer at them through the highpowered binoculars laid on for the purpose and causing such a dense throng of traffic that the A.A. had to erect special road-signs. Already by then, the quip was going the rounds that bird protection in this country had now become largely a matter of protecting the birds from their admirers, by so ludicrous a margin had the watchers come to outnumber the watched.

It was not only the numbers that were novel, but the almost instantaneous way in which so many acted on 'news' and poured into a particular locality. There was something in the mass reaction that people seemed to enjoy almost more than they enjoyed the ostensible objects of their attention: the very act of participating in a widely shared pursuit appeared to be an end in itself. This was a phenomenon commented on at the time in other fields as well—in archaeology, for instance.

In the process, the subject had once again burst through a kind of respectability barrier. People henceforward bought books on it and enrolled in societies devoted to it in the belief that these were conventional—and not, as for so long before, unconventional—things to do. Reflecting this, sales of books on natural history soared, surprising everyone—and not least publishers. Several of the less expensive works of identification achieved the 100,000 mark, and one of them, the Rev. W. Keble Martin's *Concise British Flora in Colour,* even created a national sensation by selling half this number of copies almost immediately on publication.

A breakthrough had occurred on to a qualitatively different plane of popularity. Not merely had natural history now become a significant commercial market, but the ease of recruitment was such that this could be deliberately exploited to secure economic benefits for the subject itself. The outstanding exponent, and beneficiary, of this state of affairs has been the Royal Society for the Protection of Birds. By advertising in the mass media this has had little problem in raising its membership more than tenfold, while also acquiring a country mansion and filling it with a large and varied staff. The resulting administrative burden has been huge, but the benefits in other directions have outweighed this. A new type of mass-organization has thus been created. By no means all natural history bodies will be able, or will wish, to emulate it; but its very existence presents them with a challenge—and a need to re-examine some of their basic assumptions.

Perhaps the most serious problem that growth on this scale potentially brings is an upset in the balance between the sophisticated and unsophisticated and, at a deeper level still, between the professionals and the amateurs. The long and fruitful record of collaboration between these different groups is a justifiable boast of natural history in this country. Yet it is all too easy to take this for granted, to underestimate how delicately it depends on a more or less unconscious tradition of compromise between conflicting interests. Without a minimal leavening of active researchers, be they professional or amateur, a society loses a sense of purpose and turns vapid and banal; with too heavy a weight of professionals it is robbed of a certain volunteer dynamism and is liable to be plagued by imported academic rivalries. Each group needs the other, and societies are the gainers by holding these mixtures in a state of perpetual mild tension. Should too great an inrush of one group occur, however, a society—and, in the course of time, a whole area of interest—may be swamped, chronically and even irreversibly.

This danger threatens from not just the one direction. The professionals, too, have been growing uncomfortably fast in numbers. The huge postwar expansion in higher education and the massive stepping-up of government investment in research and postgraduate training have altered the position quite dramatically. Within the space of only twenty years the number of universities has more than doubled and the number of students at them virtually trebled—a substantial proportion of whom emerge with qualifications in the life or the earth sciences. Their influx has brought to natural history on the one hand a sharp improvement in rigour but on the other a deluge of complex techniques and arcane terminology, with which even the most capable of amateurs have difficulty in coping. It is not true as is sometimes uncritically asserted—that the amateur has 'reached his ceiling', for thankfully there still remain ample ways in which he can make a useful scientific contribution, some of them ways that for a long time to come professionals are likely to find unappealing. But there is a real risk that, under the pressure of such a torrent of esoteric new knowledge, the subject will become fragmented—socially no less than intellectually. And this is an outcome that no one who cares about its health in the long term can contemplate with equanimity.

Yet can we really be certain that this growth, the bringer of all these varied benefits and penalties, is from now on to be a permanent feature of the scene? Do we assume too blithely that because it has so far proved not to be transient, it must necessarily have come to stay? If there is one lesson to be drawn from the study of natural history's past, it is surely this: that so far from progressing in a smooth upward glide, it moves in a series of periodic jerks, shaken in and out of the public focus as though underneath a magnifying-glass held in a palsied hand. Moreover, with the means of influencing the public taste now so powerfully heightened, the possibilities of being deceived in this respect are greater than ever before. The more impressive the inflation, the even more extreme and prolonged now the potential aftermath of revulsion. We do well to greet the newfound respect for natural history in Britain with a continuing degree of wariness.

The detail of citation customary for a learned text scarcely seems appropriate for a general survey of this kind intended for a primarily non-academic audience. As the field is not a generally familiar one, however, and some readers may well want to follow up certain aspects in more detail, the common alternative of a selective bibliography would not have been very helpful. The middle course has therefore been chosen of chapter-by-chapter synopses of the sources principally drawn upon. For reasons of space, these have had to be restricted mainly to published items of a specifically historical character—which most students of the subject are in any case likely to want to refer to at least in the first instance.

One—Organization Begins

For the period leading up to 1700 a recent booklet by F. D. and J. F. M. Hoeniger, *The Growth of Natural History in Stuart England from Gerard to the Royal Society* (Folger Shakespeare Library, 1969), provides a useful general introduction. It inevitably leans heavily on the two major works of scholarship relating to this period: Agnes Arber's *Herbals, their Origin and Evolution . . . 1470–1670* (2nd edn, Cambridge, 1953) and Canon C. E. Raven's *English Naturalists from Neckam to Ray* (Cambridge, 1947). Raven's greatest work, his majestic biography of John Ray (2nd edn, Cambridge, 1950)—without any doubt the finest work of biography in the whole natural history field, at any rate in the English language—also relates mainly to a somewhat earlier period, but does contain material of relevance more generally. It should in any case be read by anyone interested in the history of the subject. Canon Raven had begun work on a companion volume to his *English Naturalists . . .* covering the period from 1700 to the present day, for inclusion in the 'New Naturalist' series; unfortunately, this was still uncompleted at the time of his death. The two other books that we have from his hand suggest that the natural history world is immeasurably the poorer by this loss.

The standard accounts of the Apothecaries and their 'Herbarizings' are those by H. Field and R. H. Semple, *Memoirs of the Botanic Garden at Chelsea belonging to the Society of Apothecaries of London* (2nd edn, London, 1878), and, much more recently, C. Wall, H. C. Cameron and E. Ashworth Underwood, *A History of the Worshipful Society of Apothecaries of London, vol. 1: 1617–1815* (London, 1963). The Temple Coffee House Botanic Club was first portrayed in print by R. P. Stearns ('James Petiver, Promoter of Natural Science, *c*. 1663–1718', *Proc. Amer. Antiq. Soc.*, 1952, n.s. 62: 243–365); the original discovery is contained in an unpublished doctoral thesis on William Sherard by G. Pasti, now in the University of Illinois Library. The Edinburgh section of the story is provided by I. Bayley Balfour, 'A sketch of the Professors of Botany in Edinburgh from 1670 until 1887', in *Makers of British Botany*, ed. F. W. Oliver (Cambridge, 1913); J. M. Cowan, 'The History of the Royal Botanic Garden, Edinburgh', *Notes Roy. Bot. Gard. Ed-*

*inb.,*1933, 19: 1–62; and H. R. Fletcher and W. H. Brown, *The Royal Botanic Garden, Edinburgh, 1670–1970* (London, 1970). The Author's 'Joseph Dandridge and the first Aurelian Society', *Ent. Record,* 1966, 78: 89–94 and 'John Martyn's Botanical Society: A Biographical Analysis of the Membership', *Proc. Bot. Soc. Br. Is.,* 1967, 6: 305–24, are recent, comprehensive accounts of these two societies, while W. S. Bristowe's 'The Life and Work of a Great English Naturalist, Joseph Dandridge (1664–1746)', *Ent. Gazette,* 1967, 18: 73–89, is the most substantial of three recent papers embodying the rediscovery of the original Aurelian. Hooke's geological speculations have lately been written up by G. L. Davies in 'Robert Hooke and His Conception of Earth-History', *Proc. Geol. Assoc.,* 1964, 75: 493–8.

The letters of the various leading figures of the natural history world at this period constitute an exceptionally rich deposit of raw material. By far the largest mass is the still only partly studied Sloane collection in the British Museum, which incorporates, *inter alia,* the entire correspondence of Petiver. *The Sloane Herbarium,* ed. J. E. Dandy (London, 1958) serves as a useful biographical index to those of Sloane's correspondents who were active botanically. The lengthy historical appendix to H. Trimen and W. T. Dyer's *Flora of Middlesex* (London, 1869) contains the fruits of what is still probably the most extensive sampling of the Sloane manuscripts specifically for material on the history of British botany yet to have appeared in print. The papers by Stearns, Bristowe and Wilkinson (qq.v.) incorporate some of the results of recent comparable siftings in connection with entomology.

More of these late seventeenth- and eighteenth-century collections of letters have been published than is commonly assumed. A general index to them is badly needed, for there is an extensive and confusing overlap between the two biggest compilations in print, the eight-volume *Illustrations of the Literary History of the Eighteenth Century,* ed. J. B. Nichols (London, 1817–58) and *Extracts from the Literary and Scientific Correspondence of Richard Richardson, M.D., F.R.S.,* ed. Dawson Turner (Yarmouth, 1835).

Two—The Rise to Fashion

Writings of a more general kind on the various stages in the growth of interest in natural scenery discussed in this and the early part of Chapter Three are extremely numerous. On the more restricted aspects with which this book is primarily concerned two of the best (and least-known) sources are in French: Daniel Mornet's *Le Sentiment de la nature en France de J.-J. Rousseau à Bernardin de Saint-Pierre* (Paris, 1907) and *Les Sciences de la nature en France, au XVIIIᵉ Siècle* (Paris, 1907). Another literary historian, W. P. Jones, has made an isolated attempt to follow in Professor Mornet's footsteps, in 'The Vogue of Natural History in England, 1750–1770', *Ann. Sci.,* 1937, 2: 345–52. But for the subject in this country there is so far nothing to compare with Hans Huth's admirable, more recent, excursions in this genre, 'The American and Nature', *J. Warb. & Court. Inst.,* 1950, 13: 101–49 and *Nature and the American: Three Centuries of Changing Attitudes* (Berkeley and Los Angeles, 1957). The latter, in particular, deserves to be better known in Britain. Phyllis E. Crump's *Nature in the Age of Louis XIV* (London, 1928) is also worth singling out as virtually the only substantial discussion of the attitude to nature during the period leading up to 1700. Another useful 'background' contribution is H. Richardson's 'Fashionable Crazes of the Eighteenth Century: With Special Reference to Their Influence on Art and Commerce', *J. Roy. Soc. Arts*, 1935, 83: 733–52.

Da Costa's sad story can be pieced together from the extensive portions of his correspondence printed in Vol. 4 of Nichols's *Illustrations . . .* (q.v.). He himself has left us valuable notes of some of the principal collectors of the day in his 'Notices and Anecdotes of Literati, Collectors, etc.', *Gentlemen's Mag.*, 1812, 82 (1): 204–7, 513–17. The bird-collecting activities of Martyn and Blair emerge from the unpublished Martyn correspondence in the Department of Botany, British Museum (Natural History). Von Uffenbach's strictures on Petiver feature in *London in 1710: From the Travels of Zacharias Conrad von Uffenbach*, transl. and ed. W. H. Quarrell and Margaret Mare (London, 1934)—one of quite a number of accounts of Britain by foreign travellers which have subsequently been translated and published. Several of these provide useful cross-checks on the general state of natural history in this country at the particular periods concerned.

A comprehensive account of the advent of the Linnaean System is given by W. T. Stearn in his introduction to the Royal Society's facsimile edition of the *Species Plantarum* (London, 1957). A subsequent paper by him, 'The Background of Linnaeus' Contribution to the Nomenclature and Methods of Systematic Biology', *Syst. Zoology*, 1959, 8: 4–22, and one by J. L. Heller, 'The Early History of Binomial Nomenclature', *Huntia*, 1964, 1: 33–70, are also useful in this connection. The full range of Linnaeana is, needless to say, very extensive.

On the late eighteenth-century societies the leading sources are: J. E. Smith, 'Biographical Memoirs of Several Norwich Botanists', *Trans. Linn. Soc. Lond.*, 1804, 7: 295–301; A. T. Gage, *A History of the Linnean Society of London*, (London, 1938); and J. M. Sweet, 'The Wernerian Natural History Society in Edinburgh', *Freiberger Forschungshefte* (Leipzig, 1967).

Among the leading figures of whom extended biographical (or autobiographical) accounts have appeared are: Bradley, Collinson, Curtis, Dale, Ehret, Mrs Glanville, Hill, Hooke, Lee, Pennant, Petiver, Smith, Stillingfleet, Stukeley and Withering—in addition to the numerous ones on Gilbert White. For Curtis, Ellis and Smith there are also published volumes of letters.

Three—Wonders of the Past

Of all the literature relating to the history of natural history in Britain, that on the 'Heroic Age' of geology is easily the largest. This reflects the fact that, of all the branches of the subject, it is geology (as one would expect, in view of its very nature) that regularly has the greatest number of followers who are historically minded. Of the many books and papers that have appeared there is room here for only a selection.

As openers, Sir Archibald Geikie's *Memoir of John Michell* (Cambridge, 1918), S.I. Tomkeieff's 'James Hutton and the Philosophy of Geology', *Trans. Edinb. Geol. Soc.*, 1948, 14: 253–76 (also in *Proc. Roy. Soc. Edinb.*, 1950, 63B: 387–400). and M. MacGregor's 'Life and Times of James Hutton', *Proc. Roy. Soc. Edinb.*, 1950, 63B: 351–6 should be cited. On William Smith there has been published:

T. Sheppard, 'William Smith: His Maps and Memoirs', *Proc. Yorks. Geol. Soc.*, 1917, 19: 75–253; V. A. and J. M. Eyles, 'On the Different Issues of the First Geological Map of England and Wales', *Ann. Sci.*, 1938, 3: 211–16; L. R. Cox, 'New Light on William Smith and His Work', *Proc. Yorks. Geol. Soc.*, 1942, 25: 1–99; and A. G. Davies, 'William Smith's Geological Atlas and the Later History of the Plates', *J. Soc. Bibl. Nat. Hist.*, 1952, 2: 388–95. J. Challinor's 'The Beginnings of Scientific Palaeontology in Britain', *Ann. Sci.*, 1948, 6: 46–53 should be read along with these as a salutary corrective to the traditional overemphasis on Smith.

J. Ritchie's 'Natural History and the Emergence of Geology in the Scottish Universities', *Trans. Edin. Geol. Soc.*, 1952, 15: 297–316 paints in the setting for the thorough study of Jameson's work (by Jessie M. Sweet and C. D. Waterston of the Royal Scottish Museum) currently in progress. The successive doctrinal feuds from Jameson onwards are covered learnedly yet entertainingly in C. C. Gillispie's *Genesis and Geology: A study in the Relations of Scientific Thought, Natural Theology, and Social Opinion in Great Britain, 1790–1850* (Cambridge, Mass., 1951). M. Millhauser's 'The Scriptural Geologists. An Episode in the History of opinion', *Osiris*, 1954, 11: 65–86 and W. F. Cannon's 'The Uniformitarian-Catastrophist Debate', *Isis*, 1960, 51: 38–55 usefully supplement this.

H. B. Woodward's standard *History of the Geological Society of London* (London, 1907) has recently been notably added to (with special reference to the role of Greenough) by M. J. S. Rudwick in 'The Foundation of the Geological Society of London: Its Scheme for Co-operative Research and Its Struggle for Independence', *Brit. J. Hist. Sci.*, 1963, 1: 324–55.

More general works include Sir Archibald Geikie's classic, *The Founders of Geology*, (2nd edn, London, 1905)—worth reading for its mesmeric prose alone; A. C. Ramsay, *Passages in the History of Geology* (London, 1848–9); F. J. North, 'From the Geological Map to the Geological Survey', *Trans. Cardiff Nat. Soc.*, 1932, 65: 41–115; H. Hamshaw Thomas, 'The Rise of Geology and Its Influence on Contemporary Thought', *Ann. Sci.*, 1947, 5: 325–41; S. I. Tomkeieff, 'Geology in Historical Perspective', *Adv. Sci.* 1950, 7: 63–7; W. F. Cannon, 'The Impact of Uniformitarianism', *Proc. Amer. Phil. Soc.*, 1961, 106: 301–14; and—a British Museum (Natural History) handbook—W. N. Edwards, *The Early History of Palaeontology* (London, 1967).

In addition, biographies of most of the major figures have been published.

Four—The Victorian Setting

The numerous published biographies are a prime source here. Those brought out in the last century vary a great deal in informativeness and readability, the best ones being by fellow-naturalists. The ones on Forbes, Loudon, MacGillivray, Morris, Prestwich and Wood have been drawn on for the respective material in question utilized in this chapter. *The Journal of Gideon Mantell, Surgeon and Geologist,* ed. E. C. Curwen (London, 1940), is especially valuable, inasmuch as it is virtually the only early journal of a naturalist at work in Britain that appears to have been published.

The origin and early years of the Geological Survey are well covered in its two standard histories, by J. S. Flett (London, 1937) and Sir Edward Bailey (London,

1952). F. J. North's 'Sir H. T. De la Beche: His Contributions to the Advancement of Science, and the Circumstances in Which They Were Made', *Bull. Brit. Soc. Hist. Sci.*, 1951, 1: 111 helps to complete the picture in an important respect.

W. F. Cannon, in two papers in 1964, 'Scientists and Broad Churchmen: An Early Victorian Intellectual Network', *J. Brit. Studies*, 4: 65–88, and 'The Role of the Cambridge Movement in Early 19th Century Science', in *Proc. Tenth Intern. Congr. Hist. Sci.*, 1962, 317–20 (Paris), first introduced the 'Cambridge Network'. In similar fashion Noel Annan introduced the 'Intellectual Aristocracy' in *Studies in Social History,* ed. J. H. Plumb (London, 1955).

The pattern of natural history entertaining in Victorian times has been best described by H. T. Stainton ('At Home', *Ent. Weekly Intell.*, 1859: 73–4), Sir Arthur Smith Woodward ('Geology, 1846–1926', *Proc. Cotteswold Nat. Field Club* for 1927, 1928, 23: 15–23) and A. S. Kennard ('Fifty and One Years of the Geologists' Association', *Proc. Geol Assoc.*, 1948, 58: 271–93).

Five—The Fruits of Efficiency

The complicated manoeuvrings in the zoological world have been successively unravelled by P. Chalmers Mitchell in his *Centenary History of the Zoological Society of London* (London, 1929), by S. A. Neave and F. J. Griffin in *The History of the Entomological Society of London, 1833–1933* (London, 1933) and, most recently, by J. Bastin in 'The First Prospectus of the Zoological Society of London: New Light on the Society's Origins', *J. Soc. Bibl. Nat. Hist.*, 1970, 5: 369–88. William Swainson's *A Preliminary Discourse on the Study of Natural History* (London, 1884) is easily overlooked as an excellent source of information on this and many other matters at this period.

The key to explaining the rise of field botany was supplied by S. W. F. Holloway's 'The Apothecaries' Act, 1815: A Reinterpretation', *Medic. Hist.*, 1966, 10: 107–29, 221–36. Other sections of this story have been filled in by J. E. Lousley's 'The Contribution of Exchange Clubs to Knowledge of the British Flora', in *Progress in the Study of the British Flora,* ed. Lousley (London, 1957); the Author's 'H. C. Watson and the Origin of Exchange Clubs', *Proc. Bot. Brit. Is.*, 1965, 6: 110–12; Gertrude Foggitt's 'Annals of the B.E.C. I. The Botanical Society of London', *Rep. Bot. Soc. & E.C.* for 1932, 1933, 10: 282–8; and J. E. Lousley's 'Some New Facts about the Early History of the Society', *Proc. Bot. Soc. Brit. Is.*, 1962, 4: 410–12. Of Watson, unfortunately, there is no adequate biographical account.

Progress in the Study of the British Flora also contains two contributions central to the history of natural history mapping: J. E. Dandy's 'The Watsonian Vice-County System' and S. M. Walters's 'Distribution Maps of Plants—An Historical Survey'. Both these authors have subsequently written further on their respective topics— Dandy in his *Watsonian Vice-Counties of Great Britain* (London, 1969) and Walters, jointly with F. H. Perring, in an introductory section of the *Atlas of the British Flora* (London and Edinburgh, 1962).

The origin of the Palaeontographical Society is recounted by F. W. Rudler in 'Fifty Years' Progress in British Geology', *Proc. Geol. Assoc.*, 1888, 10: 234–72, while a recent paper by A. D. Orange in *Science Studies*, 1971, 1: 315–30 clarifies the circumstances attending the founding of the British Association, which are unsatisfactorily covered in the otherwise excellent standard history by O. J. R. Howarth, *The British Association for the Advancement of Science: A Retrospect 1831–1931* (2nd edn, London, 1931).

For fuller details of the various innovations in bird-watching the Author's papers on Dovaston, in *J. Soc. Bibl. Nat. Hist.*, 1967, 4: 277–83 and *Birds*, 1969, 2: 296–7, may be consulted.

Six—Exploring the Fringes

Surprisingly, the Victorian discovery of the sea-side and its natural history has been the subject of little serious historical work. The account in this Chapter of the invention of the aquarium, for example, appears to be the first detailed one of its kind, the only other considerable sources being Shirley Hibberd's *The Book of the Marine Aquarium* (London, 1856) and J. E. Taylor's *The Aquarium: Its Inhabitants, Structure and Management* (London, 1876). Sir William Herdman's *Founders of Oceanography and Their Work* (London, 1928) is also useful on the early history of dredging. The Author's *The Victorian Fern Craze: A History of Pteridomania* (London, 1969) is a first attempt at reconstructing in detail the effects on the subject of a powerful social fashion.

Seven—Deadlier Weapons

The only item of field equipment so far to have been made the subject of a more or less exhaustive study is the botanist's vasculum. This is embodied in two papers by the Author in *Proc. Bot. Soc. Brit. Is.*, 1959, 3: 135–50 and 1965, 6: 105–9. 'English Entomological Methods in the Seventeenth and Eighteenth Centuries', *Ent. Record*, 1966, 78: 143–50, 285–92 and 1968, 80: 193–200 together with 'A Note about Nets', *Michigan Ent.*, 1966, 1: 102–8 constitute the first instalments of a thorough history of entomological equipment on which R. S. Wilkinson is currently engaged.

Two papers by the latter and by the Author, in *Michigan Ent.*, 1966, 1: 3–11 and *Ent. Record*, 1976, 88: 23–5, another by the author in *Ent. Record*, 1965, 77: 117–21, and a section in P. B. M. Allan's *A Moth-Hunter's Gossip* (London, 1937) jointly say probably all that there is to be said on the history of 'sugaring'.

Eight—The Field Club

Quite a large number of local societies now have published histories, many of them produced in celebration of their centenary. Obviously, these are a prime source of information (and, very often, entertainment too). That of the biggest society of all, however, has only been brought out serially in a journal and for that reason needs to be drawn specially to notice: by L. G. Payne and entitled 'The Story of Our Society', it appeared in the *London Naturalist*, 1948, 27: 3–21 and 1949, 28: 10–22.

James Cash's quaintly titled *Where's There's a Will There's a Way: An Account of the Labours of Naturalists in Humble Life* (London, 1878) is still the best source on the early working-men's societies of the Manchester area. A presidential address by

Sir Walter Elliot, printed in *Trans. Bot. Soc. Edinb.*, 1871, 11: 11–33, is likewise the best source on the Berwickshire Club. The Chester breakthrough is described in W. A. Herdman's *Charles Kingsley and the Chester Naturalists* (Chester, 1921), supplemented by 'A Kingsley Note and Reminiscence' by A. A. Dallman, *N.W. Nat.*, 1947, 22: 163–4, while that at Northampton has been handily chronicled by Druce himself: 'Formation of the Northamptonshire Natural History Society', *J. Northants. Nat. Hist. Soc. & F.C.*, 1918, 19: 131–42.

Useful remarks of a more general character are to be found in: G. Brady, 'Naturalists' field clubs; their objects and organization', *Nat. Hist. Trans. Northumb. & Durh.*, 1867, 1: 107–14; two anonymous articles in *Nature* in 1870 (3: 141–2) and 1873 (9: 24–5, 38–40, 97–9); G. Abbott, 'The Organization of Local Science', *Nat. Sci.*, 1896, 9: 266–9; and J. Ramsbottom, 'The Natural History Society', *Adv. Sci.*, 1948, 5: 57–64. Some recondite information on school societies can be found in R. Patterson's *On the Study of Natural History as a Branch of General Education in Schools and Colleges* (Belfast, 1840).

Nine—The Parting of the Ways

Many people have written on the reactions of leading individual figures, or of particular groups of naturalists, to the ideas propounded in *The Origin of Species*. Among the more substantial accounts are: J. W. Judd, *The Coming of Evolution* (Cambridge, 1925); R. M. MacLeod, 'Evolution and Richard Owen, 1830–1868: An Episode in Darwin's Century', *Isis*, 1965, 65: 259–80; A. Newton, 'Early Days of Darwinism', *Macmillan's Mag.*, 1888, 57: 241–9; and F. C. R. Jourdain, 'Progress in Ornithology during the Past Half-Century', *S. E. Nat. & Antiq.*, 1935: 43–51.

The standard work on the New Biology is J. Reynolds Green's rather austere *A History of Botany, 1860–1900* (London, 1909). F. O. Bower's *Sixty Years of Botany in Britain (1875–1935): Impressions of an Eye-Witness* (London, 1938) provides some lighter relief. A recent paper by the sociologist Edward Shils ('The Profession of Science' *Adv. Sci.*, 1968, 24: 469–80) is also worth reading for a broader perspective on the period.

Biographies of both Babington and Newton exist, besides several briefer reminiscences of Newton by various of his former students.

P. B. M. Allan's *Talking of Moths* (Newtown, 1943) contains the most extensive account of commercial fraudulence in Victorian entomology. The two newcomers among the national societies have their respective births and infancies recorded by P. L. Sclater, 'A Short History of the British Ornithologists' Union', *Ibis*, 1908, Ser. 9, 2: Jubilee Suppl. 19–69 and T. Rupert Jones, 'The Geologists' Association: Its Origin and Progress', *Proc. Geol. Assoc.*, 1883, 7: 1–57.

Ten—Dispersed Efforts

There are three general histories of bird protection in Britain: Phyllis Barclay-Smith, 'The British Contribution to Bird Protection', *Ibis*, 1959, 101: 115–22; F. E. Lemon, 'The Story of the R.S.P.B.', *Bird Notes & News*, 1943, 20, 67–8, 84–7, 100–102, 116–18; and E. S. Turner, *All Heaven in a Rage* (London, 1964).

The last extends to animal welfare in the larger sense and thus overlaps with E. G. Fairholme and W. Pain's *A Century of Work for Animals: The History of the RSPCA, 1824–1924* (London, 1924). More narrowly, Phyllis Barclay-Smith has recounted 'The Trade in Bird Plumage' in *UFAW Courier*, Oct. 1951. There are some major American sources which helpfully widen the perspective: W. Dutcher, 'History of the Audubon Movement', *Bird-Lore*, 1905, 7: 45–57; T. G. Pearson, 'Fifty Years of Bird Protection in the United States', in *Fifty Years' Progress of American Ornithology 1883–1933* (Lancaster, Pa., 1933); T. G. Pearson, *Adventures in Bird Protection: An Autobiography* (Appleton, 1937); and R. H. Welker, *Birds and Men: American Birds in Science, Art, Literature, and Conservation, 1800–1900* (Cambridge, Mass., 1955).

There apears to be no general history of Nature Study in Britain. Of obvious relevance, however, is E. L. Palmer's 'Fifty Years of Nature Study and the American Nature Study Society', *Nature Mag.*, 1957, 50: 473–80.

Eleven—Recovery on the Coasts

C. A. Kofoid's *The Biological Stations of Europe*, U.S. Bureau of Education Bull., No. 440 (Washington, D.C., 1910) is the nearest approach to a general history of marine stations. More specifically British sources are: Anon., 'An English Biological Station', *The Times* 31 Mar. 1884: 4; Anon., 'The History of the Foundation of the Marine Biological Association of the United Kingdom', *J. Mar. Biol. Assoc.*, 1887, 1: 17–21; and Sir John Graham Kerr, 'The Scottish Marine Biological Association', *Notes & Rec. Roy. Soc.*, 1950, 7: 81–96. A biography of David Robertson also exists. There are naturally many, more or less contemporary, accounts of the Naples station and its development, among them one by Dohrn himself in *Nature*, 1891, 43: 465–6. A recent stocktaking of the venture is included in J.-J. Salomon's 'Some Aspects of International Scientific Cooperation', in *International Scientific Organizations* (OECD: Paris, 1965). There is a fairly recent biography of Dohrn in German.

Knowledge of More's work comes mainly from one of those invaluable volumes of posthumous 'Life and Letters' for which the Victorians had such a penchant. The Newton correspondence (at Cambridge) and the Harvie-Brown correspondence (with the Nature Conservancy Council, Edinburgh) will doubtless yield much more material relating to this formative period when they have been thoroughly studied.

J. H. Gurney Jnr's pioneer work is disclosed in an editorial in *Nature* in 1880 ('Migratory Birds at Lighthouses', 22: 25–6). The annual reports of the British Association Committee on Migration and W. Eagle Clarke's two-volume *Studies in Bird Migration* (London and Edinburgh, 1912) jointly provide most of the rest of this story. Gätke's *Heligoland as an Ornithological Observatory: The Result of Fifty Years' Experience*, trans. R. Rosenstock (Edinburgh, 1895) is also a historical document in itself.

Twelve—An Infusion of Mobility

The various forms of motorized transport and most of the new pursuits have had their individual histories written, but no overall study of the rediscovery of the countryside in this century appears yet to have been published. Perhaps the nearest is C. E. M. Joad's *The Untutored Townsman's Invasion of the Country* (London, 1946), which includes a useful history of the rise of amenity agitation.

The history of feeding wild birds has been briefly detailed in the Author's papers on Dovaston (q.v. under Chapter Five). Bruce Campbell's recent 'Birds in Boxes', *Countryman*, 1970, 75: 264–72 may safely be regarded as the definitive work on that topic—though, if only for 'colour', J. R. B. Masefield's *Wild Bird Protection and Nesting Boxes* (Leeds, 1897) still deserves to be consulted.

There is an exceptionally profuse literature on early natural history photography. Among the more notable contributions are: Ralph Chislett, 'Nature Photography and Its Pioneers: Some Influences and Developments of Twenty Years', *Field*, 1938, 171: 60–62; O. G. Pike, 'Early Photographs of Bird Life', *Photogr. J.*, 1951, 91: 200–210; Frances Pitt, 'The Rise of Nature Photography', *Country Life*, 1953 114: 1952–3; R. P. Bagnall-Oakeley, 'Recording Nature with the Camera', *Trans. Norf. & Norw. Nat. Soc.*, 1954, 17: 305–15; and—for comparisons—A. O. Gross, 'History and Progress of Bird Photography in America', in *Fifty Years' Progress of American Ornithology 1883–1933* (Lancaster, Pa., 1933). The question of the earliest person to take action pictures in Britain has been discussed by E. Hardy, 'Early Photographs of Birds', *Country Life*, 1952, 111: 1417–18. A. S. D. Pierssené has also covered a neglected aspect in 'Photographs in Victorian Bird Books', *Country Life*, 1964, 136: 197.

At least three histories of bird-ringing have appeared in accessible languages: H. B. Wood's 'The History of Bird Banding,' *Auk*, 1945, 62: 256–65, W. Rydzewski's 'A Historical Review of Bird Marking,' *Dansk Orn. Foren. Tidsskr.*, 1951, 45: 61–95, and a section in M. Boubier's *L'Evolution de l'ornithologie* (2nd edn., Paris, 1932). R. M. Lockley and Rosemary Russell also include a historical introduction in their *Bird-Ringing* (London, 1953).

The Irish initiatives on Lambay and Clare Island are described by Praeger in his autobiography, *The Way that I Went* (Dublin and London, 1937).

For the early development of plant ecology in Britain there are no fewer than three authoritative accounts—by Tansley himself, in *J. Ecol.*, 1947, 34: 130–37, and by W. H. Pearsall and Sir Edward Salisbury, in respective contributions to the British Ecological Society Jubilee Symposium, published in a special supplement to *J. Ecol.* in 1964.

Thirteen—A Break for Play

The decline in entomology has been plotted in numerical terms by B. P. Beirne in 'Fluctuations in Quantity of Work on British Insects', *Ent. Gazette*, 1955, 6: 7–9. The type of approach pioneered in this extremely interesting paper could usefully be repeated for other branches of the subject.

The history of Druce has not yet advanced beyond obituaries. Equally, there is no published account of his reign and of the B.E.C. at this period.

Fourteen—The Eventual Combining

Nicholson's books are central to an understanding of the history of this period. They should be read in conjunction with his papers on 'The Oxford Trapping

Station', *Br. Birds,* 1928, 21: 290–94 (with M. W. Willson) and 'The Next Step in Ornithology', *Discovery* 1930, 11: 330–32, 338. The general 'philosophy' of network research is usefully summed up by him in 'The British Approach to Ornithology', *Ibis,* 1959, 101: 39–45, and by Bruce Campbell in 'Co-operation in Zoological Studies', *Discovery,* 1950, 11: 328–30.

The starting of the chain of bird observatories has been chronicled by W. B. Alexander, 'Bird Observatories and Migration', *The Nat.,* 1949, : 1–8 (the unwary should be warned that some of the dates in this are incorrect), and by Sir Landsborough Thomson, 'The British Contribution to the Study of Bird Migration', *Ibis,* 1959, 101: 82–9.

———

Finally, the following works of a more general value have been drawn on in connection with no one chapter in particular:

J. Anker, *Bird Books and Bird Art: An Outline of the Literary History and Iconography of Descriptive Ornithology* (Copenhagen, 1938).

Malcolm Burr, *The Insect Legion* (London, 1939). Part IV of this book consists of an informal history of British entomology.

Richard Curle, *The Ray Society: a Bibliographical History* (London, 1954).

S. P. Dance, *Shell Collecting: An Illustrated History* (London, 1966).

James Fisher, *Birds as Animals. I. A History of Birds* (London, 1954).
   The Shell Bird Book (London, 1966). Chapter Ten of this is essentially a potted history of modern British ornithology.

James Fisher and Roger Tory Peterson, *The World of Birds: A Comprehensive Guide to General Ornithology* (London, 1964).

John Gilmour, *British Botanists* (London, 1944). 'How Our Flora Was Discovered', in John Gilmour and Max Walters, *Wild Flowers* (London, 1954).

David Lack, 'Some British Pioneers in Ornithological Research, 1859–1939', *Ibis,* 1959, 101: 71–81.

W. Swainson, *Taxidermy: With the Biography of Zoologists, and Notices of their Works* (London, 1840).

G. S. Sweeting (ed.), *The Geologists' Association, 1858–1958: A History of the First Hundred Years* (Colchester, 1958).

Quite deliberately, the various standard histories of botany, zoology, etc., do not feature here. This is because they tend to be confined to the purely scientific development of their subjects and thus have little relevance for the approach adopted in this book.

No list of general sources could possibly be complete, however, without mentioning the *Dictionary of National Biography.* This has a very special value for a historical work of this kind. Thanks to the prominence of natural history at the time it was first embarked upon, naturalists are represented in its pages very much more fully than would doubtless be the case today. Many of these individual accounts, moreover, are small masterpieces of scholarship, most notably the large number from the hand of G. S. Boulger. A by-product of Boulger's work in this connection was the invaluable *Biographical Index of Deceased British and Irish Bota-*

nists (2nd edn, London, 1931) which he produced in collaboration with James Britten. A new and much enlarged edition of the *Biographical Index*, edited by R. G. C. Desmond, is now (1976) in the press. Apart from one rather limited international index of entomologists, it is much to be regretted that nothing of this kind exists for British zoology. Equally, it must be regretted that for the British Isles as a whole there is nothing to compare with R. Lloyd Praeger's extremely useful *Some Irish Naturalists* (Dundalk, 1937).

Index

Page numbers in italics refer to illustrations. For individual tools see the relevant section of the entry under 'equipment'. Groups of plants and animals are dealt with under the relevant subject headings: for example see 'ornithology' for information on birds and 'cryptogamic botany' for references to ferns and fungi.

Abbot, Charles, 42
Abbot, George, 154
Aberdeen University, 53, 68, 213
Ackermann, Rudolph, 87
Adanson, Michel, 35
Agassiz, Louis, 100
Aikin, Arthur, 59
Albert, Prince Consort, 78
Albin, Eleazar, 24, 30–31, 84
Alexander, W. B., 232, 233–34
Allen, Grant, 173
Alloa Natural History Society, 150
amenity movement, 179, 204
American Bird Banding Association, 213
Annals of Botany, 164
Annals of Natural History, 86
Anning, Mary, 62
Annual Register, 30
Antrobus, Robert, 16
anthropology, 195
Apothecaries' Act of 1815, 94–95
aquarium. *See* marine biology
archaeology, 84, 147, 154, 167, 172, 242
Arnold family, 79
Arnott, G. A. Walker, 95
Arthur, William, 9
Ashmolean Natural History Society, 143, 152, *Plate 12*
Atlas of the British Flora, 103
Audubon Society, 178, 179, 208
Augusta, Princess, 38
Aurelian Society, 11, 12
Aurelian Society (second), 39
Aurelian Society (third), 91
Ayrshire Naturalists' Club, 146
Ayrton, Richard, 111

Babington, Charles Cardale, 165, 166; as entomologist, 91, 93; and evolution, 160; field-work, 67, 96; *Manual of British Botany*, 96
Babington, Churchill, 80
Babington family, 79
Bailey, Charles, 170
Baird brothers, 145
Bakewell, Robert, 51
Baldwin, Stanley, 223
Balfour, Frank, 190
Balfour, J. Hutton, 96
Banks, Sir Joseph, 40; as 'highwayman', 20; at Oxford, 13; as patron, 37, 77, 82
Barbellion, W. N. P. (i.e. B. F. Cummings), 173, 183
Barclay family, 79
Baring, Cecil, 216
Barrington, R. M., 198, 216
Bartram, William, 38
Bateman, John, 15
Bath Field Club, 146
Baxter, E. V., 200, 234
Beaufort, Duchess of (Somerset, Mary), 24–25
Bedfordshire Society, 147
Belfast Academy, 152
Bell, Thomas, 41, 160
Bentham, George, 84, 124; *Handbook of the British Flora*, 96, 124, 226
Bentinck, Margaret Cavendish, Duchess of Portland, 25–26, 43, 112
Bergson, Henri, 180
Berkeley, Miles J., 69, 96, 114
Berkenhout, John, 37
Bernardin de Saint-Pierre, J.-H., 46

Berwickshire Naturalists' Club, 96, 104, 145, 146, 151

Bewick, Thomas, *3*, 88, 105, 208, 209

binoculars. *See* equipment: ornithology

biology, 36, 166–67, 173–74, 188, 236; criticism of, 164–65, 183; development, 161–64, 165–66, 167, 217; laboratories, 163, 165, 174, 187, 190–91, 192; professionalism, 163–64, 165–66, 188–89, 219, 236; teaching, 162, 163, 181–82, 189

Birmingham: Dudley Caverns, 57; Literary and Philosophical Society, 143; Natural History and Microscopical Society, 187

Blackwood's Magazine, 88

Blainville, H. M. D. de, 60

Blair, Patrick, 9, 29

Blake, J. F., 203

bluestockings, 43

Blyth, Edward, 105

Bobart, Tilleman, 15, 16

Boerhaave, Herman, 9

Bolton, James, 25

Bonney, T. G., 57, 74

books, xvii–xviii, 70, 123; in English 42–43, 84; identification manuals, 4, 42, 84, 85, 96, 104, 106, 214–15; illustrated, 30–32, 87, 88–89, 123, 124, 168, 211–12; learned, 104; nature essays, 205–6, 207; 'New Naturalist' series, 240; popular, 27, 34, 60, 63, 66, 85, 86–87, 90–91, 116, 120, 123–24, 184–85, 240; price, 70, 84, 85, 96, 104; printing technology, 85, 87, 123; sales, 123–24, 243

Bootham School Natural History Society, 152

Borlase, William, 17

Boscawen, Mrs, 43

Boston (Lincolnshire): botanic club, 9

Botanical Arrangement, 42

Botanical Exchange Club, 101, 213, 221, 224–25, 241

Botanical Gazette, 139

Botanical Society (John Martyn's, Rainbow Coffee House), 9–11, 16

Botanical Society of the British Isles, xvii, 103, 225–26, 241

Botanical Society of Edinburgh, 42, 97, 98, 101, 107, 167, 228

Botanical Society of Lichfield, 40

Botanical Society of London, 93, 100–101, 102, 103, 107, 110, 224; exchange activities, 97–101, 107; provincial members, 98; women members, 152

botany, 37, 84, 94, 103, 120, 165, 166–67, 169, 217, 224, 225, 236, 237; collecting, 97, 102–3, 109, 111–13, 138, 222; collections, 12, 24–25, 38, 89, 112, 120, 165, 169–70, 213, 220; Floras, 15, 37, 97, 102–3, 116, 153, 168–69, 216, 218; and medicine, 94–95, 98, 167; plant distribution studies, 98–99, 100, 101–3, 169, 217–19, 237, 240; popularity, 26, 107, 143–44, 172, 224–25; teaching, 5–7, 8–9, 13, 74, 95–96, 139, 150, 166–67; and women, 24, 42–43, 124, 225–26. *See also* fieldwork

Boué, Ami, 53

Bower, F. O., 165

Bowerbank, J. S., 82, 121

Bowman, J. E., 71, 86, 115

Boyle, Robert, 129

Bradley, Richard, 13, 24, 27, 117–18

Brand, William, 71, 101, 103

Brander, Gustavus: *Fossilia Hantoniensia,*, 37

Brewer, Samuel, 137

Brewster, Sir David, 55, 76, 114

Breydon Wild Birds Protection Society, 179

Bristol Natural History and Archaeological Society, 148

Bristowe, W. S., 235

British Association, 104–5, 154; Committee on Migration, 198–99, 200; Committee on Zoological Stations, 189, 190; Dredging Committee, 116, 195; meetings, 56–57, 76, 101, 120, 131, 165, 195; as sponsor, 104, 105, 111; women members, 152

British Birds, 212–13, 214, 230, 232, 235

British Correlating Committee for the Protection of Nature, 204

British Ecological Society, 218, 235; *Biological Flora of the British Isles,* 236–37

British Field Club, 185

British Museum: collections, 25, 68, 69, 73, 75, 165, 232–3; staff, 69, 75, 80, 82, 93, 199

British Naturalists' Association, 185

British Ornithologists' Club, 213–14
British Ornithologists' Union, 81, 168, 171, 178, 208; *Ibis*, 171, 194, 196
British Pterodological Society, *Plate 9*
British Trust for Ornithology, 232, 239, 240, 241
Brock, S. E., 235
Brown, Lancelot ('Capability'), 46
Brown, Robert, 113
Browne, Sir Thomas, 29
Buchan, John, 223
Buckland, Frank, 208
Buckland, William, 52, 55, 63, 73, 79, 80, 95, *Plate 2;* geological views, 61; as lecturer, 55–57; *Reliquiae Diluvianae*, 61
Buckton, G. Bowdler, 131
Buddle, Adam, 8, 12, 16
Buffon, G. L. Leclerc, Comte de, 34–35, 43, 48, 49
Bugg, George, 61
Bullock, William, 128–29
Burkitt, J. P., 215
Burroughs, John, 206
Bute, 3rd Earl of (Stuart, John), 38
Butler, F. H. C., 240
Buxton family, 79

Cadbury family, 79
Cambrian Archaeological Association, 205
'Cambridge Network', 79
Cambridge University, 13, 190; botany, 13, 14, 38, 57, 74, 95, 96, 162, 165, 166; entomology, 39, 91, 93; geology, 49, 57, 74; zoology, 74, 162, 166; Botanic Garden, 38; Caius College, 13; Cavendish Laboratory, 162; Herbarium, 165; Magdalene College, 13, marine biology, 190
Campbell, Bruce, 241
Carlyle, Thomas, 54
Carr, Ralph, 146
Carroll, Lewis (i.e. Charles Dodgson), 73
Catlin, George, 180
Central Committee for the Survey and Study of British Vegetation, 218
Chamberlain, Neville, 223
Chapman, Abel, 167–68
Chapone, Hester, 43
Chappelow, Leonard, 80
Charlesworth, Edward, 86
Charlotte, Queen, 25, 38

Chelsea Physic Garden, 5, 8, 31; staff, 6, 11, 16, 39, 40
Chester Society of Natural Science, 149–50, 151
Children, J. G., 75
Christy, William, 110
Clare Island Survey, 216–17
Clarke, William Eagle, 233, 238; migration studies, 198–99, 200, 213; *Studies in Bird Migration*, 199, 200
classification. *See* systematics
Claude Lorrain (i.e. Claude Gelée), 46
Cleland, James, 113
Coleman, W. H., 103; *Flora Hertfordiensis*, 66, 103
Coleridge, S. T., 10, 180
collecting, 32–33, 71, 111, 113, 126, 144, 212, 220; excessive, 109, 110, 113, 116, 124–25, 127–28, 139, 140–41, 177, 213, 222, 229, *Plate 3;* instructions, 28, 32–33, 113, 133–4; professional, 124, 167. *For methods see* references under individual branches of natural history
collections, 25, 26, 32–33, 40, 71, 75, 93, 100, 107, 128–29, 143, 165, 170 181, 207, 220. *See also* references under individual branches of natural history
Collingwood, Cuthbert, 195
Collinson, Peter, 31, 37
Commons, Open Spaces and Footpaths Preservation Society, 179
conchology, 26, 116, 195; collecting, 111–12, 116; collections, 12, 25, 27, 28, 41, 89, 170
conservation, 176–80, 181, 204, 226, 229, 240–41; economic motives, 180; legislation, 176, 177–78; reserves, 177, 179–80, 240–41; scientific motives, 110, 180; and women, 177, 178, 234
Conservation Corps, 241
Conybeare, J. J., 55
Conybeare, W. D., 52, 55, 79
Cook, James, 40
Cooper, Daniel, 97, 98, 110
Cordeaux, John, 197–98
Cotteswold Naturalists' Field Club, 146, 151, 156
Coulter, Stanley, 183
Council for British Archaeology, 154
Council for Nature, 154–55, 241

Council for the Preservation of Rural England, 204
Country-Side, 185
countryside: affected by better transport, 109, 110, 111, *202*, 204, *220*, 222–23; damaged, 110, 140–41, 242; in fashion, 204–5, 222–4; idealized, 205; as 'wilderness', 205–6, 207
Crabbe, George, 113
Crawford, J. B., 210
Critical Review, The, 39, 42
Crowther, James, 144
Croydon Natural History Club, 152
cryptogamic botany, 80, 112–13, 114–15; fern craze, 85, 89, 115, 120, 122, 124–25, 170, *Plate 6;* fungi, 69, 129; lichens, 25; seaweeds, 112–13, 116
Curtis, William, 115; at Chelsea Physic Garden, 6; private teaching, 94
Cuvier, Georges, 60–61, 62

Da Costa, Emanuel Mendes, 28–29, 47
Dale, J. C., 135, 140
Dale, Samuel, 18, 28
Dalyell, Sir John, 118
Dancer, J. B., 114
Dandridge, Joseph, 11–12, 15, 24, 29
Dannreuther, Th., 237–38
Darwin, Charles, 44, 158–59, 182, 235; at Cambridge, 53, 56, 79, 96; at Edinburgh, 113; and entomology, 91, 93, 159, 161; *Origin of Species, The*, 44, 48, 63, 160, 161, 167; theory of sexual selection, 215
Darwin, Erasmus, 40
Daubeny, Charles, 53, 80
Davy, Sir Humphrey, 58
De la Beche, William Henry, 52, 53, 77, 162, 227
Delany, Mary, 43
Dennes, G. E., 100
Dick, Robert, 67
Dillenius, J. J., 10, 27
Dillwyn, Lewis Weston, 53; *Botanist's Guide*, 59
dinosauria, 62
Diver, Cyril, 240
Dixon, Charles, 208
Dohrn, Anton, 188–90, 216–17
Don, George, the elder, 67
Donovan, Edward, 130

Doody, Samuel, 8
Doubleday, Edward, 132
Doubleday, Henry, 132, 133
Douglas, Catherine, Duchess of Queensbury, 26
Douglas, David, 95
Dovaston, J. F. M., 86, 114; and ornithology, 105–6, 133, 209, 215
Dowdeswell, W. H., 236
Druce, George Claridge, 70, 149, 214, *Plate 12;* and Botanical Society, 221, 224–25, 226, 227, 237
Drummond, H. M., 208
Drummond, L. J., 113
Drury, Dru, 39
Du Bois, Charles, 15, 16, 112
Duncan, F. Martin, 212
Dundee: University College, 218

Eccles: natural history society, 40
ecology, 180, 184, 218, 229–30, 236–37; books, 235; 'districts', 101; mapping, 101–2, 217, 218, 237, 241; and psychology, 219; records, 241; 'vice-counties', 102, 195–96
—animal, 180, 234–35; bird, 105–6, 133, 193, 194, 195–96, 229–30, 235; insect, 133, 180, 195, 235, 236; marine, 234–35; plant, 98–99, 101–3, 110, 169, 195, 217–19, 234, 235, 237, 239, 240–41
Edinburgh: Royal Botanic Garden, 8–9
Edinburgh Philosophical Journal, 55
Edinburgh Review, 54
Edinburgh University, 40, 41; botany, 8, 53, 95, 96, 101; geology, 48, 53–54; marine laboratory, 191; medicine, 53; Museum, 55; natural history, 55, 164
education, 123, 181–84; 1870 Act, 162, 181; 1944 Act, 240
Edwards, George, 31
Ehret, G. D., 24, 25, 31
Ellis, John, 17, 31, 37, 112
Elton, Charles, 234, 235
Elwes, H. J., 81
Emerson, R. W., 180, 205
Entomological Club, 92–93
Entomological Magazine, 92, 132
Entomological Society of London, 92–93, 94, 98, 107, 161, 173; *Transactions*, 94
Entomologist, The, 170, 238

Entomologist's Monthly Magazine, 136
Entomologist's Record, 103
Entomologist's Weekly Intelligencer, 73, 103, 131, 147
entomology, 37, *83,* 84, 161, 172, 173, 195, 236; collecting, *ii,* 12, 39, 91, 109, *126,* 130–35, 137, 139, 144, *Plate 1;* collections, 12, 24, 25, 91, 103, 133–34, 135–36, 169–70, 210, 220, 223; insect migration, 235, 237–38; popularity, 88, 89–91, 122, 172, 182, 221; Quinarian theory, 90; and women, 24. *See also* field-work
equipment, 126, 134–35, 136–41, 170; assistants, 138–39; as a badge, 4, 136–37; disguised, 137–38; field notebook, 208–9, 214, *227;* glass bottles, 130; microscope, 112, 113–15, 116, *158,* 182; standardization, 139–40; vivarium, 121
—botany: drying-paper, 96, 139; plant-press, 42, vasculum, 4, 42, 96, 103, 138, 139, 140, 203
—entomology, *ii, 126,* 134–35, 136, 137–38, *Plate 1;* killing methods, 130–31; nets, 4, 12, 134, 135, 203; sugaring, 132–34; traps, 132, 136
—geology, *45,* 56, 138–39; hammer, *vi,* 4, 137; thin sections, 114
—marine biology: aquarium *(see* marine biology); clothing, 117; dredge, 115, 187; tow-net, 115
—ornithology, *227;* binoculars, *175,* 177, 207–8, 220, *227;* feeders, 88, 105, 209–10; guns, 127–28, 177; hides, 105, 177, 211; nesting-boxes, 105, 177, 210; telescopes, 105, 208; traps, 106, 233–34.
—*See also* photography, Wardian case
ethology, 215
Evangelicalism, 65, 67, 71, 73, 79
evolution, 158, 161, 172, 180, 219; controversy, 63, 71, 159–61, 162; Darwinism, 180; and phylogeny, 161; statistical evidence, 236; 'struggle for existence', 180

Fair Isle bird observatory, 199, 200
Falconer, Hugh, 53
Faraday, Michael, 120
Farquharson, Mrs Ogilvie, 152
'Feather Fight', 178

field centres, 240
field clubs. *See* societies: field clubs
field glasses. *See* equipment: ornithology
Fielding, Henry, 170
field stations, 188–89, 192, 197, 199, 200, 216–17
field-work, 19–21, 68, 83, 106, 144–46, 165, 166–69, 174, 182, 203, 215; botanical, 4–5, 7, 9, 53, 57, 95–97, 101–3, 168–69, 224, 226; cooperative, 98, 105, 187, 190, 192–93, 194, 195–98, 201, 212–14, 216, 230–33, 234, 237; costume, 117, 137, 138, 151, 203, 205; embarrassments of, 117, 137–38; entomological, 109, 122, 130–35, 137, 237–38; food, 67, 140; geological, *vi,* 48, 53, 56–57, 95, 107, 111; local, 4, 7, 15, 59, 98, 102–3, 168–69, 173; marine, 195; 'network research', 59, 97–98, 100, 101–3, 105, 107, 169, 194–95, 201, 229, 231, 237–38; ornithological, 83, 84, 88, 105, 168, 193, 227–28; records, 21, 71, 103, 106, 109, 129, 136, 167–69, 214, 229, 237–38, 241. *See also* collecting: individual branches of natural history
Fisher, James, 240
Fisher, R. A., 236
fisheries: international exhibitions, 190, 191; research, 187–89, 190, 195
Fishmongers' Company, 190
Fitch, W. H., 226
Fitton, W. H., 53
Flora's League, 204
Folkes, Martin, 13
Folkestone Natural History Society, 203
Forbes, Edward, 76, 78, 97; and marine biology, 115–16; as teacher, 55, 75, 96, 101, 162, 203; *History of British Mollusca,* 116
Ford, E. B., 236
Fordyce, George, 40
Forster, Edward, 71
Forsyth, Alexander, 127
Forsyth, William, 40
fossils. *See* palaeotonology
Foster, Michael, 163
Fowler, W. Warde, 209
Francis, G. W., 85, 120
Freshwater Biological Association, 235
Freud, Sigmund, 219

Frisch, J. L., 30
Fur, Fin and Feather Folk, 178

Galton, Francis, 159
Gamly, Patrick, 111
Gardener's Magazine, 86, 119
Garner, Robert, 146, 147
Gätke, Heinrich, 199, 233
Gatty, Margaret, 117, 138
Geddes, Patrick, 181, 182–83, 218
General Inclosure Act (1845), 179
genetics, 154, 159, 166, 173, 236
Gentleman's Magazine, The, 37
Geographical Association, 237
Geological Society, 52, 58–59, 75, 78, 82, 98; mapping, 50, 59; Wollaston Fund, 100; women members, 151, 152; *Geological Inquiries,* 59; *Transactions,* 85
Geological Survey, *vi,* 52, 140
Geologists' Association, 171, 221–22; excursions, 171, 203; local branches, 103; specimen exchange, 103; women members, 151
geology, 16, 41, 47, 48–49, 50, 114; 'Catastrophism', 60–61, 90; collecting, 138–39; and evolution, 172; exploration, 48, 51, 110–11; maps, 49, 50–51, 59, 77, 82, 111, 172; mineral collections, 28–29, 47; mineralogy, 53, 55; 'Neptunists', 54, 61; petrology, 114; popularity, 52–54, 58, 59, 60, 63, 107, 171, 172; practical uses, 51–52, 77; professional, 51–52, 53, 77, 172; and religion, 61; stratigraphy, 49–51; support, 52–53, 77–78, 105, 111; teaching, 53–54, 55–57, 74–75, 95, 148; 'Uniformitarianism', 48–49, 54; 'Vulcanists', 54, 61. *See also* palaeontology.
George III, 25, 37–38
Gerard, John: *Herball,* 7
Gibson, G. S., 71
Gifford, Isabella, 127
Gilpin, William, 46
Gisborne, Thomas, 80
Glanville, Eleanor, 24
Glasgow: Natural History Society, 151; University, 95
glass: cases, 29–30, 89, 129; taxes, 122, 129–30. *See also* Wardian case
Glover, Townend, 136

Godman family, 81
Goethe, J. W. von, 47, 90
Goodenough, Samuel, 112
Goodyer, John, 7
Gosse, Philip Henry, 70, 78, 114, 121, 209; *Introduction to Zoology, An,* 74; *Naturalist's Rambles, A,* 121; *Ocean, The,* 121; *Omphalos,* 159
Gould, John, 87
Graham, Robert, 95, 96, 98, 101, 140
Grant, Robert, 53, 113
Gray, J. E., 41, 69, 91, 93, 98
Gray, Thomas, 16, 39, 47
Gray family, 82
'Great Chain of Being', 161
Greene, Joseph, 122
Greenough, George Bellas, 50, 52, 58–59, 98, 100, 107; *Geological Inquiries,* 59
Greville, R. K., 113, 114, 139
Grevillea, 114
Grey, Edward, 1st Viscount, 223, 233
Griffith, Richard, 111
Griffiths, Mrs A. W., 113
Grove, W. B., 174
Gunn, John, 80, 109
Gurney, J. H., Jr, 197
Gurney, J. H., Sr, 197
Gurney family, 79, 80

Haeckel, Ernst, 180
Hanley, Sylvanus, 116
Hardy, James, 198
Harmsworth, Alfred, 1st Viscount Northcliffe, 175–76, 184
Harris, Moses, 12, 24, 39, 135; *Aurelian, The,* 12, 31, *Plate 1; English Lepidoptera, The,* 37
Harrisson, Tom, 228, 231
Hartert, Ernst, 167–68
Harting, J. E., 168
Harvey, W. H., 113, 116, 156
Harvie-Brown, J. A., 194, 197–98
Hastings and St Leonards Natural History Society, 237
Haworth, A. H., 84
Hayward's Botanist's Pocket Book, 214
Heligoland: bird observatory, 199, 233–34
Henslow, George, 80
Henslow, John Stevens, 67, 80, 160; at Cambridge, 57, 74, 79, 95, 96

Henslow family, 80
'herbarizing'. *See* Society of Apothecaries
Herdman, W. A., 191–92
Hey, Rebecca, 66
Hibbard, Shirley, 115
Hill, John, 38, 137
Hoare family, 79
Hollam, P. A. D., 231
Holmesdale Field Club, 147
Holy Island: bird observatory, 233
Honourable East India Company: Museum, 73–74
Hooke, Robert, 20, 26; *Micrographia,* 28
Hooker, Sir Joseph Dalton, 76, 80, 160
Hooker, Sir William, 67, 80; *British Flora,* 96; *English Flora* (cryptogams), 114; at Glasgow, 95, 96; and Kew, 76, 80
Hooker family, 79, 80, 81
Hope, John, 37
Horner, Leonard, 52
Horsefield, John, 144
Horticultural Society, 131
horticulture, 11, 23, 26, 46, 167
Howard, Henry Eliot, 106, 215–16
Huddesford, William, 13
Huddleston, Wilfred, 139
Hudson, W. H., 206–7, 210
Hudson, William, 6; *Flora Anglica,* 37
Humboldt, Alexander von, 217
Hunter, John, 40
Hutchins, Ellen, 112
Hutton, James, 16, 48–49, 54
Huxley, Sir Julian, 79, 227, 228, 234; and ornithology, 215, 232, 234
Huxley, Thomas Henry, 74; and biology teaching, 162–63, 181, 182; and evolution, 160; and marine biology, 189–90
Huxley family, 79
Huysum, Jacobus van, 31

Insect Immigration Committee, 237–38
'Intellectual Aristocracy', 79–81
Irvine, Alexander, 102
Isle of Man Field Club, 146
Isle of May: bird observatory, 200, 234

Jacob, Edward, 15
Jameson, Robert, 41, 53–55, 56, 75, 95, 164, 225
Jardine, Sir William, 44, 53, 80, 87

Jefferies, Richard, 206
Jeffreys, J. Gwyn, 116
Jenyns, Leonard (afterwards Blomefield), 44, 80, 91, 146
Johns, C. A., 123, 140
Johnson, Thomas, 7
Johnston, George, 130; and Berwickshire Naturalists' Club, 104, 145, 146; and marine biology, 104, 117, 138; and Ray Society, 104
Jones, Thomas William, 29
Jourdain, F. C. R., 214, 228, 237, 239
Journal of Animal Ecology, 235
Journal of Ecology, 218
Journal of Physiology, 164
journals, 40; learned, 70, 143, 221, 231, 236, 237; popular, 73, 85–87, 184–85; specialist, 4, 164, 171
Joy, Norman, 222–23

Kant, Immanuel, 49
Kearton, Cherry and Richard, 211, *Plate 11*
Kennedy, Alexander Clark, 168
Kermode, Philip, 146, 198
Kew: Royal Botanic Gardens, 38, 76, 80, 165, 168, 236
Kew Observatory, 189
Kidd, John, 55
Kingsley, Charles, 78, 149–50, 151, 180, 218
Kinnear, Sir Norman, 80, 199
Kirby, William, 18, 90; *Introduction to Entomology,* 90–91, 134, 137, 140
Knaggs, H. G., 136, 171
Knapp, J. L., 88
Knowlton, Thomas, 27, 30
Krutch, Joseph Wood, 206

Lambay Island: survey, 216, 234
Landsborough, David, 116, 146
landscape: admiration of, 46; picturesque, 46
land utilization: Scott Committee, 237, 240
Langley, Batty, 23
Lankester, Ray, 163, 190
Latour, Charlotte de, 66
Leach, W. E., 75
Lear, Edward, 73

Le Coq, Mrs, 112
Lee, James, *22,* 37
Leeds: Literary and Philosophical Society, 143; Naturalists Field Club, 147
Leicester, *142;* Literary and Philosophical Society, 147, 148, 152
Lewin, William, 25
Ley, Augustin, 213
Lhwyd, Edward, 19–20, 27, 53, 167
Lightfoot, John, 20, 25, 38; *Flora Scotica,* 25
Lindley, John, 68, 122
Linnaeus, Carl, 27, 31; censorship, 42; classification, 16, *22,* 27, 35–37, 40, 43, 46–47; collections, 40, 41; nomenclature, 35–36, 144; *Hortus Cliffortianus,* 35; *Philosophia Botanica,* 37; *Species Plantarum,* 36; *Systema Naturae,* 36–37
Linnean Society of London, 40–41, 90, 92, 93, 100; meetings, 58, 155–56; *Transactions,* 40, 41; women members, 152, *Plate 8;* Zoological Club, 91–92, 93
Lister, Martin, 28; *Historiae Animalium Angliae,* 4
lithography, 87
Liverpool Marine Biology Committee, 191–92
Liverpool Naturalists' Field Club, 148, 150, 151, *Plate 7*
Liverpool University, 191
Lockhart, John Gibson, 61
Lockley, R. M., 234
Loddiges, Messrs (nurserymen), 119
Lodge, R. B., 211
London: Battersea Fields, 110; College of Physicians, 95; Epping Forest, 179; Freemasons' Tavern, 58; Geological Museum, 77; Great Russell Street naturalists' quarter, 170; Hampstead Heath, 179; Kensington Palace, 38; King's College, 74, 75, 96; 'London Museum of Natural History' (W. Bullock), 128–29; Mining Record Office, 77; Newhall's Coffee House, 11; Rainbow Coffee House, 10; School of Mines, 77, 162, 163; Swan Tavern, 12; Temple Coffee House, 8; Tower, 127; University College, 74; Working Men's College, 171; Zoo, 210
London Catalogue of British Plants, 99

London Natural History Society, 147, 232
Loudon, John Claudius, 18, 69, 119, 209; *Encyclopedia of Gardening,* 143; periodicals, 18, 73, 86
Lowell, James Russell, 44
Lubbock, Sir John (later Lord Avebury), 70, 82, 182, 235
Lubbock family, 79
Lyell, Sir Charles, 48, 52, 53, 55, 78; and evolution, 48, 63, 160, 162; *Principles of Geology,* 63
Lyons, Israel, 13, 38

Macaulay family, 79
Macdonald, Ramsay, 224
MacGillivray, William, 53, 67, 68–69, 71; *History of British Birds,* 89, 105
MacKay, John, 53
Maclaren, Charles, 53, 184
Macleay, Alexander, 90
Macleay, William Sharp, 90
Maconochie, A. A., 119
Magazine of Natural History, 73, 86, 116; quoted, 18–19, 87, 97, 102, 105, 110, 116
Magazine of Zoology and Botany, 86
Malthus, Thomas, 48
Malvern Field Club, 80, 146, 157
Manchester: botanical societies, 143; Field-Naturalists' Society, 148; Literary and Philosophical Society, 143
Manningham, Sir Richard, 15
Mantell, Gideon, 56, 60, 62–63, 70, 78, 109
Marine Biological Association, 190
marine biology, 115–16, 186; aquarium craze, 117–19, 121–22, 124, 186, 187; books, 113, 116–17, 121–22; collecting, 111, 113, 124–25, *Plate 5;* collections, 117–18; dredging, 112, 115–16, 187, 188, 195; government support, 187–88, 190–91, 192; minute animals, 112, 115, 187; popularity, 111–12, 113, 116–17, 187; sea-side holidays, 111, 112, 113, 116, 121; research stations, 187–92; teaching, 189, 191, 192; trawling, 112, 115; and women, 112–13, 117
Marlborough College Natural History Society, 152
Marsden-Jones, E. B., 236

Marsh, G. P., 180
Marshall, William, 217
Marsham, Robert, 23
Martin, W. Keble, 243
Martin, William, 60
Martyn, John, 10, 15; botanical society,
10–11; at Cambridge, 13, 14, 15, 16,
38; and ornithology, 29; *Historia Plan-
tarum Rariorum,* 31
Martyn, Thomas, 10, 34; at Cambridge,
13, 37, 38; translates Rousseau's *Lettres
... sur la botanique,* 42–43
Meade, R. H., 130
Meldola, Raphael, 161
Mendel, Gregor, 154, 159, 236
Merret, Christopher, 167; *Pinax,* 28
Merriam, Florence A., 208
Merrin, Joseph, 66
Michell, John, 49, 51
microscope. *See* equipment
microscopy, 113–15; dissection, 113, 114
Midland Union of Scientific Societies,
153–54
Midlothian Ornithological Club, 234
Miller, Charles, 38–39
Miller, Philip, 11, 39, 40
Millport, Isle of Cumbrae: marine station,
188
Moffatt, C. B., 215
Montagu, George, 41, 83–84, 104, 112
Montagu, Mrs, 43
Moon, H. J., 213
Moore, Thomas, 115
More, Alexander Goodman, 195–96, 198,
216; *Cybele Hibernica,* 194–95
Morgan, C. Lloyd, 215
Morris, F. O., 69, 124, 132, 160, 177,
209
Morris, H. M., 235
Morris, William, 180, 224
Mortensen, H. C. C., 213
Moyle, Walter, 14, 29
Müller, O. F., 115
Murchison, Sir Roderick, 52, 61, 82, 160
Murray, Sir John, 191

National Trust for Scotland, 204
natural history, 106–7, 141, 161, 165,
176, 183–84, 196, 199–200, 201, 205,
215, 217–18, 219, 239–40, 242–44;
and biology, 172–74; *conversazioni,* 43,

74, 82, 144, 156, 161, 221–22; and
government, 75–76, 77, 105, 187–88,
189, 190–91, 232, 240–41; in Ireland,
113, 173, 194–95, 198, 216, 217; organization, 81–82, 171, 172–74, 187,
238–39, 242; popularity, 18–19, 26,
31, 34, 37, 38–39, 42, 43–44, 85–86,
87–88, 106, 122, 140–41, 205, 221–
22, 225–26, 242–44; post-war, 203,
220, 221–23, 226, 227, 229; publicity,
37, 231, 232, 242; and religion, 159,
160; specialization, 92–93, 161, 171,
172, 228, 244; teaching, 13–14, 15–16,
55, 74–75, 152–53, 181–84, 211, *Plate
4;* and Vitalism, 181
Natural History Society of Edinburgh, 40,
41
Naturalist (N. Wood), 128, 132
Natulalist (Yorkshire Naturalists' Union),
153
naturalists, 10, 46–47, 53, 136–37, 140–
41, 155, 159–60, 161–62, 167, 183,
184, 196, 203, 205, 211; amateur, 93,
99, 104, 164, 165–66, 172–74, 182,
192, 219, 228, 236, 238, 243–44; clergymen, 18–19, 69–70, 168; Evangelical, 79–80, 177; 'New Naturalists', 236,
240; post-war, 220–21, 222–24, 226,
234; professional, 10, 71, 73–77, 93,
99, 152, 163–64, 166, 167, 172, 219,
237, 243–44; Quaker, 44, 79, 152,
177; Victorian, 67–71, 73, 78, 83,
122–23; women, 42–43, 150–52, 207,
225–26; working-class, 143–44, 171
—correspondence, 8, 17–18, 31, 169,
194, 196, 231; interrelationship, 78–82,
83; isolation, 7, 17–18, 167, 168, 169,
209, 215; numbers, 85–86, 106, 220–
21, 239, 242; sociability, 43, 74, 82, 92,
155, 187
nature, 219; admiration of, 23–24, 164–
65, 179–80, 205–6; and Evangelical
Revival, 65, 177; moral interpretations
of, 180–81, 183; as recreation, 179,
204–5, 239; and Romantic movement,
46–47, 65–66, 205; in taste and fashion, 87–88, 89, 113, 115, 120, 170,
177, 183, 184, 225–26; as wilderness,
179–80, 205–6, 207
Naturalist's Library, 87
Natural Science, 154

'Natural Theology', 65, 71, 161
Nature Conservancy, 240–42; Biological
  Records Centre, 241
nature study, 181–84, *Plate 13*
Nature Study, 185
Neill, Patrick, 118
Newbould, W. W., 168
Newcastle: Literary and Philosophical Society, 143; Natural History Society, 152
Newman, Edward, 44, 82, 127; and entomology, 92, 138, 140; writing, 70, 91;
  History of British Ferns, A, 120
newspapers, 209, 230–31; increased circulation, 123; 'popular', 176, 184
Newton, Alfred, 212; at Cambridge, 74,
  166, 171; and evolution, 160, 161; and
  ornithology, 171, 177, 194, 196, 198
Nicholoson, E. M., 222, 240; and ornithology, 227, 228, 229, 230–31, 232,
  233, 235, 239; *Birds in England,* 229
nomenclature, 33–34, 106; binomial, 35–
  37; botanical, 99; zoological, 84, 167–
  68, 192
Northampton Field Club, 147, 149, 152,
  224
North London Natural History Society,
  203
North Staffordshire Field Club, 146
Norwich: botanical club, 39, 143; Geological Society, 80

Oliver, F. W., 165
Olivier, Sydney, 224
Ord, Mrs, 43
Ordnance Survey, 77, 218
ornithology, 74, 83–84, 105, 167, 171,
  172, 183, 192, 193, 201, 233, 242; behaviour, 106, 209, 215, 234; bird-
  feeding, 88, 105, 209–10; bird-
  watching, 105, 137, 175, 183, 199,
  206–7, 208–9, 220, 222–23, 224, *227,*
  232, 240, 243; books, 69, 168, 195,
  206–7; census work, 193–94, 196, 199,
  228, 230–33; collecting, 29, 127–28,
  200, 229; collections, 12, 25, 29–30,
  68, 88, 129, 170, 207, 232–33; on the
  Continent, 196–97, 199–200, 233;
  eggs, 12, 25, 29, 55, 88, 170, 214, 229;
  and field sports, 127–28, 171, 177, 192,
  194, 200, 207–8, 209, 229; government

support, 232, 241; identification, 177,
  212, 214–15, 239; local avifaunas, 168,
  194; migration studies, 105, 192, 196–
  200, 212, 213–14, 233–34; observatories, 192, 197–98, 199, 230, 233–34;
  popularity, 88, 89, 172, 192, 207–8,
  212, 227–28, 231–32; protection of
  birds, 177–79, 210, 229, 243; records,
  214, 229, 231, 232; ringing, 199, 213,
  230, 232, 233; territory studies, 105–6,
  209, 215; and women, 200, 207, 234
Oswestry and Welshpool Naturalists' Field
  Club, 156
Owen, Sir Richard, 62, 78, 160
Oxford Bird Census, 230–33
Oxford Ornithological Society, 228–29,
  230, 233
Oxfordshire: natural history society, 152
Oxford University, 13, 190, 227; Ashmolean Museum, 13, 27; biology, 163;
  Botanic Garden, 13; botany, 13, 14,
  164; Bureau of Animal Population, 235;
  Edward Grey Institute of Field Or-
  nithology, 232–33; geology, 53, 55–57;
  Gresham College, 14; marine biology,
  190

painting, 25, 30–31; animals, 24; plants,
  24, 26, 226
Palaeontographical Society, 103
palaeontology, 37, 60, 100, 103, 172;
  books, 60–61; collecting, 28, 29, 51,
  62, 139; collections, 12, 27–28, 47, 55,
  60, 220; guide fossils, 50, 51, 60; 'mon-
  sters', 55, 61–62, 172; popularity, 60;
  theories, 16, 27–28, 60–61
Paley, William, 65
Palgrave, Thomas, 80
Parkinson, James, 60, 62
Parkinson, John, 7
patronage, 14, 25, 30, 38–39, 75–76, 77–
  78
Pearsall, W. H., 237
Peel, Sir Robert, 77
Pennant, Thomas, 20, 46, 59, 193; *British
  Zoology,* 31, 84
Penny Magazine, 123
Penrose, F. G., 213
Petiver, James, 8, 11, 12, 16, 24, 32–33;
  Memoirs for the Curious, 4

Phillips, John, 87
photography, 131, 210–12, 220, *Plates 10–11;* in book illustration, 168, 185, 211–12; cine-photography, 212; micro-photography, 114
Phytologist, The, 103, 110
Pigott, Richard, 128
Pitt-Rivers, A. G. L. F., 84
Playfair, John, 49, 54
Plinian Society of Edinburgh, 96–97, 144–45
Plot, Robert, 4, 28
Pluche, Abbé, 34
Plukenet, Leonard, 16
Plumage League, 178
Plymouth: Marine Laboratory, 190–91
Pope, Alexander, 23
Portland, Duchess of. *See* Bentinck, Margaret Cavendish
postal service, 17–18, 69, 103, 123, 221
Poulton, Edward B., 173
Poussin, Gaspar, 46
Powys, Thomas Littleton, 4th Baron Lilford, 208–9
Praeger, Robert Lloyd, 216
Prestwich, Joseph, 70, 72
protection. *See* conservation
Puffin Island: marine station, 191, 199
Pulteney, Richard, 18, 25, 34, 43; *General View of the Writings of Linnaeus, A,* 37
Punch, 210, *Plate 3*

Quarterly Review, 61, 76
Queenberry, Duchess of (Douglas, Catherine), 26
Quekett, Edwin, 82
Quekett, John, 82
Quinarian theory, 90, 161

Raffles, Sir Stamford, 92
Ramsay, A. C., 54, 160–61
Rand, Isaac, 15, 16
Ray, John, 7, 9, 20, 23, 83, 104; at Cambridge, 38; classification, 16, 27, 35; and entomology, 135; and geology, 28, 60; *Catalogus Plantarum Angliae,* 4; *Synopsis Methodica Stirpium Britannicarum,* 4, 27, 35; translates Willoughby's *Ornithologia,* 4, 31; *Wisdom of God, The,* 34
Ray Club, 166

Ray Society, 78, 93, 103–4, 221
Réaumur, René A. F. de, Comte de, 30
Religious Tract Society: *Insect Lives,* 183
Repton School Natural History Society, 152
Richardson, Richard, 15, 29; correspondence, 15, 17, 19, 20, 27, 31, 112
Richmond and North Riding Field Club, 146–47
Rintoul, L. J., 200, 234
Robertson, David, 187, 188, 195
Robinson, E. Kay, 185
Romanticism', 115; Transcendentalism, 179–80
Romantic Movement, 44, 46, 47, 48, 52, 62, 65–66, 90, 147 204–5
Rosa, Salvator, 46
Rousseau, Jean-Jacques, 35, 42–43, 46, 47, 66
Royal Academy of Science (Brussels), 196
Royal Botanic Society, 82
Royal College of Physicians, 31, 95
Royal Dublin Society, 111
Royal Institution, 120
Royal Irish Academy, 216
Royal Microscopical Society, 82
Royal Physical Society of Edinburgh, 42, 234
Royal Society, 7–8, 14, 29, 93; amateurism, 79; eighteenth-century decline, 12–13, 17; and geology, 49, 58; model for local societies, 142; supports collecting, 167; women members, 152; *Philosophical Transactions,* 4
Royal Society for the Protection of Birds, 178–79, 243
Rugby School Natural History Society, 152
Ruskin, John, 164, 180
Russell, Richard, 111
Rutherford, W., 163

St Andrews University: marine laboratory, 191
Salisbury, Sir Edward, 218
Salisbury, William, 94
Salmon, J. D., 105, 196
Salt, Henry, 181, 224
Salvin, Osbert, 81
Samouelle, George, 88, 92

Sanderson (lapidary), 114
Saunders, Howard, 89
Saussure, Necker de, 53
Schimper, A. F. W., 218
School Nature Study Union, 183
science, 14, 16, 71, 78–79, 162, 172, 221,
239; criticism of, 162, 164–65, 183;
and government support, 76–77, 78,
105, 189; popular, 182, 228, 240; pro-
fessional, 73–76, 77, 188, 213, 228,
232, 236, 237, 238, 241; specialized
language, 73, 164, 173; teaching, 162–
63, 172, 181–82. *See also* biology; natu-
ral history; references under the individ-
ual branches of natural history
Sclater, P. L., 189
Scottish Meteorological Society, 191
Scottish Naturalist, 235
Sedgwick, Adam, 57, 61, 79, 138–39, 160
Selborne League, 178
Selborne Magazine, 203
Selby, P. J., 132–33
Selous, Edmund, 209, 215
Shaw, George, 75
Sherard, James, 10, 12, 15, 20, 27
Sherard, William, 12, 15, 24–25, 31, 112
Sibthorp, Humphrey, 13, 14
Skokholm: bird observatory, 234
Sloane, Sir Hans, 13, 118; collections, 12,
25, 29; as patron, 31, 77
Smith, Sir James Edward, 13, 39, 143; at
Edinburgh, 40–41; and Linnaean
methods, 37; and Linnean Society, 40–
41, 91, 155, 225; *English Botany,* 41;
English Flora, 41, 84, 96, 114
Smith, Robert, 218
Smith, William, 218
Smith, William ('Strata'), 49–51, 60, 109
Smith, Worthington, 226
societies, 4–5, 7, 12–13, 14, 17, 40, 41–
42, 73, 85, 100, 142–43, 155–56, 221,
243; botanical, 4, 143–44, 224–25;
conservation, 177, 178, 204, 240–42;
dining-clubs, 58, 92; entomological, 11,
12, 91, 92–93; field clubs, 96, 142,
144–51, 153–57; geological, 54, 58,
103; local, 143–44, 145, 146–47, 153,
155, 156–57, 185, 200, 222; national,
92, 100, 104, 107, 152, 154, 171, 185,
233; ornithological, 107, 171, 228–29,
233; school, 152–53; zoological, 11,
91–94, 107
—consolidation of, 144, 153–55, 185; excursions, 95–96, 110, 144, 145–46,
148–49, 171, 187, 203, 211; membership, 98, 149–50, 151–52, 153, 221–
22, 224–25; publications, 4, 85, 143,
153, 154, 228–29; sectarian and political leanings, 147, 149–50; women
members 145, 148, 150–52, 178–79.
—*See also* the names of individual societies
Society of Apothecaries: 'herbarizing', 5–7,
9, 10, 12, 94, 95, 145; as medical organization, 5, 94–95. *See also* Chelsea
Physic Garden
Society of Aurelians. *See* Aurelian Society
Society for the Diffusion of Useful Knowl-
edge, 123
Society of Gardeners, 11
Society for the Prevention of Cruelty to
Animals, 176
Society for Promoting Natural History, 40
Society for the Protection of Rural En-
gland, 179
Society for the Protection of Wild Flowers
and Plants, 204
Solander, Daniel, 25, 37, 40, 43
Somerset, Mary, Duchess of Beaufort, 24
Sorby, H. C., 114
South-Eastern Union of Scientific Soci-
eties, 154
Southwell, T., 168
Sowerby, G. B., the First, 113
Sowerby, James, 41, 60
Sowerby family, 81, 82, 87
Spalding Gentleman's Society, 142
specimens: domestic *vs.* foreign, 136; ex-
change of, 28, 29, 97, 98, 99, 100–101,
103, 107, 213, 224; fraudulent, 170–
71; labelling, 71, 97, 98, 99, 129, 136;
living, 214, 217; preservation, 29–30,
71, 89, 113, 119, 128–30, 135–36,
192; sellers of, 91, 113, 116, 124, 134,
167, 169–70, 190. *See also* collections;
references under individual branches of
natural history
Spence, William, 90; *Introduction to Entomology,* 90–91, 134, 137, 140
Stackhouse, John, 112
Stainton, H. T., 70, 73, 83, 93, 94

Stazione Zoologica (Naples), 190, 191, 216–17
Stephens, J. F., 82, 131
Stephens, Lewis, 112
Stevenson, H., 168
Stillingfleet, Benjamin, 37, 43
Stout, George, 199
Strickland, H. E., 80, 104, 111
Stuart, John, 3rd Earl of Bute, 38
Stukeley, William, 9, 23, 28, 138
Sutherland, James, 8–9, 17
Swainson, William, 75, 87, 90; quoted, 35, 75, 89, 93, 94, 128, 129, 135, 139, 225
Symonds, W. S., 80, 146
systematics, 12, 34–37, 90, 163, 165, 169, 172; botanical, *22,* 25, 27, 35, 36–37, 38, 84; Linnaean, 16, 27, 35–37, 39, 43, 144; natural system, 16, 27, 35, 36; splitting and lumping, 169–70; zoological, 36–37, 84, 167–68

Tancred, Sir Thomas, 146
Tansley, A. G., 219, 235, 239
taxidermy, 29–30, 89, 128–29
Temple Coffee House Botanic Club, 8, 12, 15–16
Thiselton-Dyer, Sir William, 80, 163, 168
Thomas, William Beach, 184
Thompson, D'Arcy Wentworth, 137, 218
Thompson, J. V., 115
Thomson, A. Landsborough, 213
Thomson, J. Arthur, 181, 182–83
Thomson, Spencer, 124
Thoreau, Henry, 205–6; *Walden,* 205
'Thoreauists', 206
Thorpe, W. H., 235
Threlkeld, Caleb, 20
Thynne, Anna, 118
Ticehurst, N. F., 213, 239
Tournefort, Joseph Pitton de, 27, 35
Towndrow, R. F., 157
Townley, Richard, 128
Tradescant, John, the elder, 29
Tradescant, John, the younger, 29
transport, 19, 111; air, 203; bicycle, 175, *202,* 202–3; canals, 51; car, 203, 204, *220,* 222, 231, 242; coach, 20, 57, 49, 56, 108–9; horseback, 20, 49, 56, 57; motor coach, 203; motorcycle, 203; rail-

way, 103, 108, 109–11, 123, *142;* road, 20, 108–9; walking, 19, 56, 57, 206
Trevelyan, Sir Walter, 79
Trevelyan family, 79
Trimen, Henry, 168
Tristram, H. B., 81, 160
Tucker, B. W., 227, 228, 229, 230, 232, 234, 239
Turesson, G. V., 236
Turner, Dawson, 59, 71, 80; *Botanist's Guide,* 59; *Fuci,* 112
Turrill, W. B., 236
Twamley, Louisa, 66
Twining, Thomas, 139
Tyndall, John, 67
Tyneside Naturalists' Club, 146

Uffenbach, Zacharias von, 33
Union Jack Field Club, 185
Union Jack Naturalist, 185
Urban, Charles, 212
Utilitarianism, 52, 65

vasculum. *See* equipment: botanical
Velley, Thomas, 112
Vernon, William, 16
Verrall, G. H., 92
'Verrall Suppers', 92
Vesey, Mrs, 43
Victoria, Queen, 78
Victorianism, 56, 64–65, 67, 68–69, 70, 73, 89, 106–7, 115, 135–36, 170, 172, 209, 220
Vigors, N. A., 90, 93
Vines, S. H., 163, 164, 166–67
Vitalism, 180, 181, 206, 207, 218

Walpole, Horace, 19, 43
Walters, Mrs (entomologist), 24
Ward, Marshall, 165
Ward, Nathaniel Bagshaw, 70, 82, 118–19, 120, 122
Wardian case, 50, 89, 119–20
Warington, Robert, 121
Warner, Richard, 50
Waterson, George, 234
Waterton, Charles, 107, 128, 177, 179, 208
Watson, H. C., 95, 97, 98–103, 107, 160, 196; *Cybele Britannica,* 100, 194; and

Watson, H. C. (*cont.*)
  plant distribution, 98–99, 100, 101–2, 103, 193, 194–95; and specimen exchange, 97, 98–100; Topographical Botany, 101–2
Watson, Sir William, 37
Webb, R. B., 66
Wedgwood, Mrs M. L., 139
Weir, T. D., 105
Werner, A. G., 41, 53, 54, 164
Wernerian Society of Edinburgh, 41–42; *Memoirs,* 54
West Riding, Consolidated Naturalists' Society, 153
Westwood, J. O., 160
Wheeler, Thomas, 6–7, 95
White, Gilbert, 18, 20, 23, 43, 45, 47, 83, 193, 203; *Natural History of Selborne, The,* 18, 43–44, 45, 88, 206
Wild Bird Protection Act of 1880, 178
Wild Bird Protection and Nesting Boxes, 210
Wild Plant Conservation Board, 204
Wilkes Benjamin, 15, 24; *English Moths and Butterflies, The,* 11, 134–35
Willcocks, Thomas, 66
Williams, C. B., 235, 237
Williamson, Henry, 184
Willisel, Thomas, 167
Willoughby, Francis, 20, 29, 83; *Ornithologica,* 4, 31
Wilmer, John, 16
Wilson, William, 95
Winchester College Scientific Society, 218
Witherby, Harry Forbes, 212–13, 214, 230, 231, 232, 237; *Handbook of British Birds,* 239

Withering, William, 42
Wollaston family, 80
Wolley, John, 194
Wood, Edward, 146–47
Wood, J. G., 69, 124
Woodruffe-Peacock, E. A., 218
Woodward, T. J., 112
Wordsworth, William, 66
Wyatt, Mary, 113
Wyles, Benjamin, 211

Yarrell, William, 71, 78, 93, 129, 177; *History of British Birds,* 88–89
Yeats, Thomas, 25
Yorkshire Association for the Protection of Sea Birds, 177
Yorkshire Naturalists' Union, 153
Young, William, 38
Younge, William, 155
Young Lady's Introduction to Natural History, The, 42

Zoological Club. *See* Linnean Society
Zoological Journal, 91–92
Zoological Society, 92, 93, 121; *Proceedings,* 215; women members, 152
Zoologist, The, 133, 195, 209
zoology, 11, 105, 107, 120, 171, 215, 235–36; collections, 12, 25, 120–21, 128–29; invertebrate, 115, 120, 235; local faunas, 153, 168–69, 194, 216; teaching, 163. *See also* ecology; entomology; marine biology; ornithology